GUN COUNTRY

.45
LONG COLT
$97.50

SMITH &
WESSON .38
SPECIAL $97.50

.44
SMITH & WESSON
SPECIAL
$125.00

.357
ATOMIC
$125.00

.22 CAL.
$84.50

SHERIFF'S
MODEL
.45 $97.50

GUN CAPITALISM, CULTURE, AND CONTROL IN COLD WAR AMERICA

ORDER
NOW

PRICE SCHEDULE
.22 Caliber (Standard Model) . . $ 91.50
.38 Special (Standard Model) . . 99.50
.44 Special (Standard Model) . . 105.50
.45 Caliber (Standard Model) . . 99.50
.357 Atomic (Standard Model) . . 105.50
.44 Magnum (Standard Model) . . 124.50
CHOICE OF 4¾", 5½" or 7½" barrel
—SPECIAL FINISHES—
Case Hardened Frame . . . . $ 7.50
Nickel Plated Finish 14.95
Chrome Plated Finish 16.50
BUNTLINE SPECIAL 12½" Bbl. $125.00
Available In All Calibers
GREAT WESTERN PARTS AVAILABLE (Send For List)

GUN COUNTRY

ANDREW C. McKEVITT

We can supply
new parts to
convert the
Model 1917
.45 ACP to
other cali-
bers.

$24.95

HOLSTERS FOR MODEL 1917: Bold with gun
only. Special cowhide — a $7.50 value for only
$3.95. Or fancy tooled leather holsters — a $14.00
value for only $9.95. None sold separately at these
special prices.

LIMITED SUPPLY!

WINCHESTER (MC)
AMMO IN STOCK
25-LOADABLE
ONLY $6.00 PER 100

The University of North Carolina Press
CHAPEL HILL

Designed by Lindsay Starr
Set in Warnock Pro
by codeMantra

Manufactured in the United States of America

LIBRARY OF CONGRESS CATALOGING-IN-PUBLICATION DATA
Names: McKevitt, Andrew C., author.
Title: Gun country : gun capitalism, culture, and control in
    Cold War America / Andrew C. McKevitt.
Description: Chapel Hill : The University of North Carolina Press, 2023. |
    Includes bibliographical references and index.
Identifiers: LCCN 2023017164 | ISBN 9781469674964 (cloth ; alk. paper) |
    ISBN 9781469677248 (paperback ; alk. paper) | ISBN 9781469674971 (ebook)
Subjects: LCSH: Gun control—United States—History—20th century. |
    Firearms ownership—United States—History—20th century. | Cold War—Social
    aspects—United States. | United States—Economic conditions—20th century. |
    United States—Social life and customs—20th century. | BISAC: HISTORY / United
    States / 20th Century | POLITICAL SCIENCE / International Relations / General
Classification: LCC HV7436 .M364 2023 | DDC 363.330973—dc23/eng/20230607
LC record available at https://lccn.loc.gov/2023017164

FOR MY GRANDFATHER, CARL E. FAZZI (1928–2002),
WHO WOULD HAVE HATED EVERY WORD OF IT.

ALOOF WITH HERMIT-EYE I SCAN
THE PRESENT WORKS OF PRESENT MAN—
A WILD AND DREAM-LIKE TRADE OF BLOOD AND GUILE,
TOO FOOLISH FOR A TEAR, TOO WICKED FOR A SMILE!

—SAMUEL TAYLOR COLERIDGE, "ODE TO TRANQUILLITY"

CONTENTS

ILLUSTRATIONS

PREFACE

AMERICA IS THE GUN COUNTRY.

It might be the one point on which gun control and gun rights advocates agree, the former condemning it and the latter celebrating it. Not *a* gun country, but *the* gun country—the original, the touchstone, the incomparable paragon. There is simply nothing else like it anywhere on Earth, and there never has been.

When the United States stood at the zenith of its global power in 1945, there were about 45 million guns and 140 million people in the country. Less than a quarter-century later, the number of guns had doubled, while the population had increased only half as much—the era's baby boom was just a blip compared to the boom in guns. Another twenty-five years later the stockpile had once again doubled while population growth had slowed. By 2020, the US population was not quite two and a half times what it was in 1945, whereas there were nearly ten times as many guns. America had become a nation with more guns than people, a condition unprecedented in world history.[1]

You could argue that the United States was always defined by its guns, even before it was an independent country. Historians have tracked guns through colonial North America, the revolutionary era, and the "Wild West," through slavery, attempted indigenous genocide, and nineteenth-century continental expansion.[2] Scholars have recounted and debated endlessly the origins and shifting meaning of the Second Amendment.[3] But none of these histories explain how the country could have accumulated guns after the Second World War at a rate nearly four times faster than population, or how it managed to diverge so exceptionally from global patterns. Not only does the United States hold nearly half of all civilian-owned firearms in the world, but it has more than twice as many guns per person as any other country, three times as many as Canada, six times as many as Germany, and 120 times as many as Japan.[4] No country, wealthy or poor, at war or at peace, anywhere on Earth compares.

And the stockpile continues to grow. The two biggest years on record for gun sales were 2020 and 2021, years fueled by a global pandemic, the Black Lives Matter movement, a contentious presidential contest resulting in the election of a Democrat promising new gun control initiatives, rising crime rates, and the violent attempt by supporters of President Donald Trump on January 6, 2021, to disrupt the peaceful transfer of power. A University of Chicago survey indicated that one in five US households bought a gun during the pandemic, and data suggested the population of new gun owners was growing more diverse.[5] In what felt like a moment of unprecedented crisis, Americans turned to guns. It wasn't the first time, and it won't be the last.

The first years of the 2020s demonstrated that guns are a visceral, material presence in Americans' lives. And yet the way we talk about gun history too often centers abstractions, like the Second Amendment or rights or law or culture, rather than the changing material conditions that produced the gun country and placed nearly a half-billion guns in the hands of 100 million people. Just about all of those guns have been bought and sold since 1945. As important as guns have been to the rich US history of violence and conquest, why and how the country came to be so abundantly well armed after the Second World War remains shrouded in myth. With rare exception, gun histories assume a natural state in which the supply of guns is simply always there, or the consumer demand is unswervingly insatiable, or both. But the gun country is not natural and immutable; it had to be made, and it could be unmade.

To understand how America became the gun country, we need to investigate how and when the guns arrived, why so many people bought them, and how resistance to those developments worked in tandem with historical myths and evolving ideas about gun rights and American identity to shape what we call "gun culture." To tell those stories we must find the guns, and to find the guns in postwar America we need to turn to the Cold War and consumer capitalism, the interconnected forces that produced America the Gun Country in the second half of the twentieth century.

Rather than start at the beginning, I want to tell you first about the story that compelled me to reckon with America the Gun Country over the past decade. It's a story about a boy named Yoshi.

GUN COUNTRY

$24.95

$19.95

$29.95

$38.50

INTRODUCTION

TWO HOURS BEFORE HIS DEATH in Baton Rouge, Louisiana, on October 17, 1992, Yoshihiro Hattori—Yoshi to his friends—donned the white tuxedo jacket, ruffled shirt, and black polyester pants he had rented for a Halloween party that night. The sixteen-year-old exchange student from Nagoya, Japan, slicked back his hair, unbuttoned the shirt's top buttons to reveal his skinny chest, and hung a borrowed silver chain around his neck. Tonight he would be Tony Manero, the disco dancer brought to life by John Travolta in *Saturday Night Fever* (1977), a film almost as old as Yoshi was.[1]

For the past two months Yoshi had attended McKinley High School, just blocks from the campus of Louisiana State University, where his host parents, Holley and Richard Haymaker, worked. In Japan he'd been an accomplished student, but in Baton Rouge Yoshi's nascent English skills made classes challenging. But he was funny, gregarious, and warm, he made friends quickly, and what he lacked in vocabulary he made up for with a disarming physicality. When he walked, he seemed to dance, lean, athletic, and graceful on his feet. He took jazz dance classes in Baton Rouge, and he liked to give impromptu performances for friends at school. This love for dance was responsible for the only time he'd found himself in any trouble—teachers thought Yoshi's after-lunch shows were disruptive and worried he "might have gotten too suggestive." The principal called the Haymakers to ensure that Yoshi got the message: no more dancing at school.

The principal and teachers wouldn't be around tonight, though. Yoshi was headed to a party where he would mingle with other foreign exchange students, including another girl from Japan, and he meant to celebrate with his new friends by dancing like John Travolta. At about 7:00 p.m. he and Webb Haymaker, Richard and Holley's sixteen-year-old son, drove a red 1979 Volvo out of the Haymakers' upper-middle-class neighborhood. Webb too was in costume, dressed like an accident victim, which was not far from the truth: he wore a genuine neck brace, thanks to an errant dive into the family pool in August, which broke vertebrae in his neck and scared his parents half to death.

They were headed to Central, a predominantly white, lower-middle-class enclave about twenty miles away on the northeastern edge of the city. Webb was a smart and responsible kid, equipped with a hand-drawn map from his father, but he got lost anyway. He stopped for gas, then pulled into a post office parking lot to ask for directions. As they drove around town, the pair chatted about teenage boy things. Webb had spent two months now with Yoshi and understood him easily—Yoshi could struggle to find the best phrase to describe what he meant, and often waved his hands around as he talked, as if he were trying to pluck the right word from the air.

Eventually the boys found the street they were looking for. On the right side of East Brookside Drive was a row of small single-family homes; on the left, Central High School. Richard's hand-drawn map included the address for the party, 10311 East Brookside. Webb remembered it as a three and a zero and some ones. He made a pass down the road and turned around, seeing a house decorated for Halloween. The address, 10131, looked right—Webb didn't double-check his father's map, which he had tossed in the backseat. A little after 8:00 p.m. they hopped out of the car.

Was this the place? The carport light was on and the festive decorations matched the occasion; Webb thought they looked appropriately "spooky." But he and Yoshi couldn't see or hear any party-like commotion. Webb knocked on the front door—or maybe he rang the doorbell, if there was one; he couldn't remember later—and nothing happened. Then the boys heard a noise in the carport. They moved to investigate, and saw a small child peeking out the blinds of the carport door. As they approached, the child's mother, Bonnie Peairs, wearing a robe and glasses, opened the door. "Excuse me," said Webb, moving toward the door, shuffling alongside Bonnie's Toyota station wagon, Yoshi behind him. She quickly slammed the door.

Clearly this wasn't the right house. Webb and Yoshi walked back toward the car and stood on the sidewalk by the Peairs's mailbox, looking up and down the street, wondering where the party might be. Then the carport door swung open, loud enough for Webb and Yoshi to hear. They saw the silhouette of a man standing in the doorway, holding a gun made famous by another 1970s Hollywood icon, Clint Eastwood's *Dirty Harry* (1971).

INSIDE 10131 EAST BROOKSIDE DRIVE, Rodney Peairs had just sat down to dinner—eggs and grits, washed down with a whiskey and Coke to take the edge off after a long day on the job at a local Winn-Dixie supermarket, where he worked as a butcher. In contrast to Yoshi Hattori, who had traveled halfway around the world to Peairs's doorstep, thirty-one-year-old Rodney had never lived outside of East Baton Rouge Parish. Rodney described himself as a "country boy," and had grown up in rural Zachary, about twenty miles north of the State Capitol. He claimed he didn't have a racist bone in his body, that he was raised in a family without prejudice. But his own son later said, and a previous wife confirmed, that Rodney and his father "constantly used racial slurs." Investigators would be tipped off that Rodney's father had connections to the Ku Klux Klan. In a deposition the elder Peairs admitted that he had been president of a local chapter of the National Association for the Advancement of White People, the organization founded by infamous white supremacist David Duke in 1979 after his own break with the KKK.

Rodney's father had taught him not only the white southern tradition of race but also the white southern tradition of guns. Rodney kept five of them in the house, none of them locked up, even though three children lived there. One handgun, a .25-caliber pistol, had recently gone missing. It would later turn up in the room from which Rodney emerged into the carport that October night. Like many other southern white men, Rodney had no formal training to handle any of his guns—his was the first generation to come of age in the era of the all-volunteer military and he didn't volunteer—but he was comfortable firing them. He had shot stray animals on his father's farm in Zachary, and one time he killed a dog that had wandered into his backyard in Central.

Rodney also thought of his guns as tools for defending himself, his family, and his home. Baton Rouge was in the midst of a half-decade climb in violent crime, even if it rarely touched predominantly white neighborhoods like Central. The era's crime spike was concentrated instead in working-class Black neighborhoods, where the twin crises of poverty and the crack epidemic pinned in residents, an urban phenomenon replicated throughout the country in the late 1980s and early 1990s. Media in cities like Baton Rouge reproduced images of Black urban violence, which provoked anxiety about street crime among the white residents of neighborhoods like Central.[2] Yet random acts of violence by strangers were statistically rare in Central, as was the case just about everywhere else in the United States. Since the advent of reliable crime data in the mid-twentieth century, the vast majority of gun violence victims have known their shooters personally. And Rodney was especially worried about someone Bonnie knew all too well.

Bonnie always seemed to be on edge. She forbade the children from looking out the windows if she wasn't home; she avoided grocery shopping at night for fear of being abducted; she wouldn't even put the garbage cans out to the curb after dark if she could see anyone walking down the street. It might have been the general panic about rising crime that got to her, though it may also have been her ex-husband. She had married him when she was just sixteen, and she claimed that he had been a drug dealer. Someone had stolen tools from the Peairs's carport recently, leading Rodney to suspect Bonnie's ex and to tell a neighbor, "If I ever catch him under my carport, I'll shoot him." It had all combined to leave Bonnie "skittish," a neighbor said, "afraid of her own shadow."

When she heard a knock at the front door after 8:00 p.m. that Saturday night, Bonnie's internal alarms went off. She decided not to answer, hoping the visitors in the dark would go away. Her young son peeked out the blinds of the carport door and could see two people standing in the driveway. Bonnie opened the door halfway to get a better look, at which point the visitors approached. She could make out two teenagers, one who appeared to be hurt and the other "oriental, Mexican or whatever," she would later say. The injured one said, "Excuse me," as he moved toward her, sidling alongside Bonnie's Toyota station wagon. She slammed the door as adrenaline flooded her nervous system. In that moment "there was no thinking at all," she later recalled. She shouted to Rodney in the kitchen: "Get the gun!"

Rodney rushed from the kitchen to the bedroom closet and found a case holding a Smith & Wesson .44 Magnum six-shot revolver, a massive handgun made famous by Eastwood's eponymous character in *Dirty Harry*; Rodney's was modified with a large scope, purportedly for hunting. Bonnie shoved her three kids into the bedroom and followed Rodney to the carport door. She said nothing to him about what she saw and he didn't ask any questions. A minute hadn't passed from the time Bonnie slammed the door on Webb and Yoshi and the moment Rodney opened it, armed with one of the most powerful handguns ever made.

WHEN HE HEARD THE DOOR SWING OPEN, Yoshi started back toward the carport. Maybe this was the house after all, he might have thought. "We are here for the party," he said, moving quickly up the driveway, light on his feet as always. But Webb could see that something wasn't right. The man was standing, silent, in a "firing position," two arms extended, two hands gripping a large handgun. "Yoshi, no," Webb said, "Yoshi, come back." He followed Yoshi up the driveway at a more cautious pace. "Yoshi, come back."

Bonnie stood behind Rodney. She told him to close the door. He ignored her.

"We are here for the party," Yoshi repeated.

"Freeze!" shouted Rodney.

"We are here for the party," Yoshi said again. Webb sensed Yoshi hadn't understood the command. As for Rodney, he later explained that he had "waited on a lot of orientals [sic] at the supermarket," but he struggled to understand them. He said he heard Yoshi say something that night, "but it wasn't English."

As he moved closer, Yoshi held up his hands, in that way he tended to do when he was trying to make himself understood to English speakers. In his left hand he gripped the camera he had used the last two months to take pictures of the sights of America, of new friends and family; just a week earlier in Baton Rouge, he had snapped some photos of a presidential candidate on the campaign trail named Bill Clinton.

The criminal and civil trials that would follow the events of that evening were notable for how few of the facts of the incident were in dispute. The only one of significance concerned the distance between Yoshi and Rodney when Rodney pulled the trigger. Rodney claimed it was three to five feet. But was that three to five feet from Rodney's face, or from his outstretched arms holding a gun? If the former, then pulling the trigger would have meant a near point-blank shot. The lawyers representing Yoshi's family would say, based on Webb's testimony, that it was between six and eight feet, that Rodney had more time and distance to assess the potential threat.

Walking quickly up the driveway and into the carport, Yoshi had reached the passenger side rear door of Bonnie's Toyota station wagon when Rodney pulled the trigger, sending a .44-caliber bullet crashing through Yoshi's chest and out the other side.

What was Rodney thinking in that moment? At the criminal trial, his lawyer, Lewis Unglesby, a New Orleans character who could have been the invention of John Kennedy Toole, wanted jurors to believe that his client legitimately feared for his life. "This person is not afraid of my gun. He's not respectful of my property. He has no fear," Unglesby said, narrating Rodney's state of mind. "I wanted him to stop," Rodney said after the trial. "He didn't. He kept coming. The next thing I remember, I was scared to death. This person was not going

During a 1994 deposition, Rodney Peairs demonstrates the firing position he assumed when he shot and killed Yoshi Hattori. (Christine Choy and Film News Now Foundation, *The Shot Heard 'Round the World*)

to stop. This person was going to do harm to me." Unglesby encouraged jurors to think that light-on-his-feet Yoshi moved in a way that could be interpreted as "aggressive," "kinetic," and "scary": "He would come right up to you, as fast as he could," Unglesby said.[3]

Yoshi grabbed his chest and fell forward. Rodney slammed the door, locked it, and retreated to the bathroom. He vomited in the toilet, then went to the kitchen, placed the gun on the table and waited for the inevitable arrival of the police. Bonnie stood behind him, grasping his shoulders and speaking in tongues, praying for salvation, or perhaps for forgiveness.

Webb knew immediately what had happened. He ran, crying and screaming "hysterically," to the front door of the Peairs's neighbor, Stan Luckey, and told him to call 911. Luckey's wife called—it was 8:26 p.m.—while Stan rushed outside with Webb. They found Yoshi just a step from the carport door, conscious, moaning and thrashing in agony. Stan elevated Yoshi's legs and told Webb to put pressure on the wound. He shouted for Bonnie's help, pleading with her to bring a towel, but he only heard her yell back, "Go away!"

Webb tried to communicate with Yoshi. "Can you talk to me?" he asked. Yoshi was able to say yes but nothing else made sense. An ambulance arrived at 8:39 p.m., about fifteen minutes after Rodney pulled the trigger. Yoshi remained conscious in the ambulance for ten more minutes, eyes open, struggling to breath, groaning. Then he stopped breathing, his lungs filled with his own vomit. He was dead by the time he reached the hospital.

DEPUTIES FROM THE EAST BATON ROUGE Parish Sherriff's Department arrived and detained Rodney. "Boy I messed up," he told one as he got into the back of a car. "I made a mistake." But the deputies were not so sure. Louisiana's "castle doctrine" law, dating to the 1970s, permitted homeowners to use deadly force to defend themselves or others on their property. Rodney spent the night at the sheriff's office and gave a statement but walked out of the station the next day, having convinced the sheriff that he had acted justifiably in self-defense and with no criminal intent.

By Monday, news of the tragedy had reached Japan. Reporting from Tokyo for the *Washington Post*, T. R. Reid noted that what seemed like "just another accidental killing" for Americans was now a "major national concern" for Japan. Shooting deaths were rare in the country—there were fewer than 100 total annually in the 1990s (a figure that would drop to just nine in 2018) compared to more than 30,000 in the United States.[4] News reports fixated on the colloquial use of the word *freeze*. They displayed dictionary entries of the word that didn't include the definition "stop moving." Nearly every Japanese learned some English in school but few spoke it frequently enough that they might have understood Rodney's command.[5]

Much of the Japanese press took the commentary beyond simple confusion over the mechanics of the incident. "America—what a country!" said Takashi Wada on TV Asahi. "You can't even walk around outside and be safe. Many people live in fear all the time over there." Tokyo Broadcasting System anchor Tetsuya Chikushi saw the shooting as indicative of a deep rot in US society. "The gun lobby says this is a matter of freedom, to have a gun," he said. "This is America's worst disease, I think. Guns everywhere—it's like a cancer."[6]

Eight months later, Rodney Peairs walked free when a Baton Rouge jury acquitted him of manslaughter charges. "You have the absolute legal right in this country to answer your door with a gun," said Unglesby, his lawyer, speaking to the press afterward. "In your house, if you want to do it, you have the legal right to answer everybody that comes to your door with a gun." Unglesby had used his peremptory challenges during jury selection to ensure that each of the jurors supported gun ownership, and juror questionnaires obtained by the Baton Rouge *Advocate* after the trial revealed that those jurors—six men, six women; ten white, two Black—were all "concerned about the current level of crime" in the city; half of them owned guns. Questioned about crime and policing, one said, "Guns get into the hands of criminals too easily," while another wrote, "[I'm] afraid we may have too much gun control, which I don't believe will stop a criminal from getting a gun." In an interview after the trial, one juror said, "Anybody would have done the same thing." Some Baton Rouge residents agreed. "We're just prisoners in our neighborhoods," said a local businessman as he watched the scrum outside the courtroom after the verdict. "It would be to me what a normal person would do under those circumstances."[7]

On the other side of the world, it was nearly unimaginable that such an outcome could be considered "normal." "There is no way you are going to convince Japanese that the reasonable action, even if you are terrified, is to shoot someone in the heart as soon as you open the door," University of Tokyo professor Masako Notoji told the *New York Times*. "We are more civilized," she said. "We rely on words."[8] An American exchange student living in Japan through the same program that arranged Yoshi's stay in Baton Rouge described a "chilling" orientation for Japanese students heading to the United States after the verdict. The students had nervous questions about America and its guns. Daniel Todd Cohen tried "to explain the constitutional roots of the right to bear arms" in his "very limited Japanese," but, as he recalled, he was "usually countered by a Japanese proverb, a piece of Japanese history, or just a statement of common sense."[9]

An elementary school student asked Cohen "why there was a war in America." Confused, Cohen responded that there was no war in the United States. "Is America at peace, then?" the child asked. Yes, of course, Cohen replied. "Why are people always getting shot there," the student countered, "if there is no war?"[10]

WHEN I FIRST ENCOUNTERED YOSHI'S story more than a decade ago, while writing a book about US-Japan relations, I learned that his host family, the Haymakers, along with his heartbroken parents in Japan, Mieko and Masaichi Hattori, had launched an international gun control campaign after Yoshi's death. I found the Haymakers and Hattoris to be compelling characters, inspired by tragedy to coordinate a movement across national borders to address what seemed to be a uniquely American problem. Indeed, that was their pitch to the American people: it doesn't have to be like this—the tragedy and heartbreak of Yoshi's death multiplied tens of thousands of times every year—and Japan, a society of equivalent wealth and development with so few gun deaths, demonstrated it. Americans had bought into the mythology of gun exceptionalism, abetted by the quotidian reality of gun capitalism, their movement argued, and confronting gun violence meant challenging both gun myths and material culture.

Yet by the 1990s attitudes toward the gun country at home and abroad had calcified over the previous two decades, and even with their global perspectives, the Haymakers and Hattoris soon hit a wall. In making their appeal for justice, they joined a gun control movement divided over strategies and tactics after struggling to stem rising rates of gun ownership and violence since the 1960s. They were opposed by a strong gun rights movement, most prominently represented by the National Rifle Association (NRA), that had come to see even the most moderate of reforms as a slippery slope toward tyranny. They criticized a gun industry that had created new mass markets for home and self-defense in the 1970s and 1980s, cultivating fear for profit. As they organized, they befriended countless people in Japan and around the world, but even with global and domestic support, this American riddle remained intractable.

The responses to Yoshi's killing felt so inflexible from the outset because the ideological and material patterns that produced them had ossified a quarter century earlier. As I looked deeper, I learned that the activists inspired by Yoshi were not the first to ask why US gun culture and violence stood in such great relief from the rest of the world. That question emerged in the 1960s, at the center of the first significant postwar gun debate, as rebellions raged in cities across the country and assassins' bullets felled national heroes. As I investigated that history, and combed through archives that scholars have rarely used to write it, I discovered that much of the rhetoric and ideas of the gun politics of the 1990s—and of our gun politics today—emerged in the years leading up to and following the passage of the Gun Control Act of 1968, which, as a result, serves as a crucial turning point in the story that follows. These ideas were forged in the Cold War, draped in patriotism, anticommunism, and antiglobalism through and through. And yet they were inextricably linked to the consumer capitalism that emerged alongside the Cold War, the economic system that deftly transformed a lethal commodity like war surplus guns into collectible curios advertised in young men's magazines, cheap European rifles into tools for self-defense and spectacular homicide, and, later, Armalite Rifles into a whole culture, politics, and identity readily available for purchase.

It was those patterns that I set out to make sense of when I began writing this book. Without an understanding of how the Cold War and consumer capitalism shaped how Americans saw the world and the things they filled it with, Rodney, his guns, his fears, and his community's sanctioning of them all make little sense. The Cold War and consumer capitalism were the structures that made the gun country what it was by the 1990s, opening opportunities for those who would exploit it and limiting the possibilities available to its critics. But historians have yet to produce a history of guns in postwar America that accounts for the influence of Cold War consumerism on the dramatic expansion of mass gun ownership and the concurrent emergence of a contentious gun politics, a politics interwoven with struggles over race and gender in a rapidly changing country.

This book tells that history. It argues that what Americans frequently refer to as "gun culture" today emerged out of the intersections of the Cold War and consumer capitalism in the 1950s and 1960s. I find the term *gun culture* complicated, as many scholars do—sociologist David Yamane, among others, has argued that there are multiple US gun cultures and that criminology and epidemiology only provide distorted glimpses into them.[11] But we nevertheless have an influential historian to credit for its coining. Before his untimely death in 1970, Richard Hofstadter had spent the last years of his life thinking seriously about guns and violence. He coedited a collection of historical sources about violence, the product of his reflections on the 1960s, "a time of unprecedented concern over American violence."[12] In "America as a Gun Culture," published the month of his death, Hofstadter asked why so many "otherwise intelligent Americans cling with pathetic stubbornness to the notion that the people's right to bear arms is the greatest protection of their individual rights and a firm safeguard of democracy." (Four decades later presidential candidate Barack Obama would trigger conservative sensibilities with that same verb when he claimed that disaffected small-town voters "cling to guns or religion.")[13] For Hofstadter the answer lay in a confluence of historical factors, from frontier mythologies and popular culture to misinterpretations of the Second Amendment and the "antimilitaristic traditions of radical English Whiggery," from an outdated federal system that empowered rural politicians to southern pathologies of masculinity and racist brutality. Gun culture was, in short, a vestige of a violent past, and the time had come for the United States to join other modern nations by regulating these uncivilized tools.

But where Hofstadter described gun culture as antimodern so as to shame his fellow Americans into discarding it, I want to suggest that it was very much a modern phenomenon, and specifically a post-1945 one, a product of attitudes shaped by the Second World War and the Cold War and a material world of guns made possible by postwar consumer capitalism and invented by its more imaginative entrepreneurs. Those immediate circumstances help explain why so many guns flooded the market and so many Americans made the decision to arm themselves in the 1960s and after. As they read of rising crime rates, watched urban uprisings on their televisions, and feared that their nation was under assault from without and within, just down the street, at many thousands of commonplace retail establishments across the country, the bounty of postwar gun capitalism offered them solutions to a world on fire.

WAR MADE THE GUN COUNTRY. The Second World War and the Cold War provided the immediate inspiration for the growth and expansion of gun ownership and the justifications for it. Global demobilization after 1945 meant that tens of millions of firearms around the world had little practical use and collected dust in government warehouses. Europe's weapons of war, the production of a half century of continental bloodletting, flooded the US market at rock-bottom prices, imported and sold by little-known figures who nevertheless transformed the gun market as much as their high-profile nineteenth-century counterparts, the Winchesters, Colts, and Brownings of the world, had. The legacy companies of those earlier innovators, with names like Smith & Wesson and Remington, were slow to adapt to the new market opportunities of the mid-twentieth century.[14] The new gun capitalists built a mass gun market to feed a growing armed mass movement.

Once gun capitalism had a ready supply, it proceeded to stoke demand, first in the 1950s for the supply of war surplus weapons from overseas, with new styles of advertising that pitched dirt-cheap rifles as throwaway toys for the weekend warrior eager to escape the stifling confines of the mass-produced suburbs. In the 1960s and 1970s the gun capitalists marketed cheap handguns for self-defense, many of which were also produced overseas, until the 1968 Gun Control Act prohibited it, at which pointed they shifted to assembling these "Saturday Night Specials" in the United States from low-cost imported parts. Congress and successive presidential administrations debated halting this unregulated flow of foreign-born firearms. Pressured by the traditional gun industry, eager to stymie the flow of cheap guns undercutting them on retail price, the Eisenhower-era State Department weighed in on the practice and concluded that it was better for global gun stockpiles to flow into the United States than into the hands of communist insurgents around the world. The Cold War defined the opportunities and limits of postwar gun capitalism.

War helped create the gun country, but it also became a metaphor for understanding it. Journalist Carl Bakal penned the first book to catalog postwar US gun violence, *The Right to Bear Arms* (1966), a scathing indictment of the "gun lobby" and the National Rifle Association—the "vigilante on the Potomac," Bakal dubbed it—that circulated among liberal policymakers in the Lyndon Johnson administration.[15] Bakal initiated what would become, in coming decades, a common rite among advocates of gun control: he invoked the death toll in wars across US history in order to dramatize the scale of the gun violence crisis. Bakal claimed that gun deaths in the twentieth century exceeded war deaths, which in the mid-1960s stood at 530,000.[16] At best it was an act of analytical speculation—there was no effort at rigorous data collection on national gun deaths before the 1950s—but the rhetoric caught on. Richard Hofstadter would replicate Bakal's logic; so too would Attorney General Ramsey Clark, as he urged Congress to pass the Gun Control Act in 1968.[17]

Clark had seen war in Europe as a marine. Bakal had served too. The Senate's stalwart gun control reformer of the 1960s, Thomas Dodd of Connecticut, became the second highest-ranking prosecutor at the Nazi war crimes trials in Nuremberg. Theirs was a generation that knew war and its horrors personally and more intensely than any previous generation back to the 1860s, and any subsequent one since. But instead of peace after the Second World War they got the Cold War and a nuclear arms race, while presiding over a society tearing itself apart over the war in Vietnam. They declared wars on poverty and crime and later drugs; as historian Michael Sherry has written, their generation lived "in the shadow of war," and these reformers watched as the instruments of war flooded society in the 1960s and as American streets increasingly resembled Civil War battlefields—or Southeast Asian ones.[18] They held a liberal faith in the power of the state to control and reform the pathologies of modern societies, and war provided the clearest metaphor for the uncontrollable social changes they witnessed, as well as the last, best means they had of fighting back.

War also shaped the nascent gun rights movement. The Second Amendment of popular understanding today—the "2A" as an individual right to armed self-defense and a communal right to resist "tyranny"—was largely an invention of the gun rights extremists of the 1960s, who blended radical populist traditions dating to the eighteenth century with contemporary right-wing anticommunism and the white backlash to the civil rights movement. Their Second Amendment—the Cold War's Second Amendment, as I call it in chapter 8—emerged out of their fears of totalitarianism, international communism, and internal subversives and enemies. The language of an *individual* right to rebel against a tyrannical government explicitly contrasted with the Soviet Union's violent repression of individual rights and identities in the service of the state.

Today, of course, few gun rights advocates connect the Second Amendment to the Cold War or anticommunism. This constitutional provision is instead fetishized to erase decades of interpretive change and link gun owners with a mythical American past. The gun rights movement has imbued guns with a kind of magic that has spilled onto the Second Amendment to create a near-impenetrable mystique. The gun mystique reaches through the past to bind gun owners to the mythologies of the nation's founding; the experience on the frontier and the "Wild West"; the violent suppression of Indians, Mexicans, and enslaved people; and the tragedy of the Civil War and the white supremacist reconciliation that followed. Such magical thinking lay at the heart of Wayne LaPierre's infamous pronouncement in the aftermath of the 2012 massacre of twenty children and six teachers in Newtown, Connecticut: "The only thing that stops a bad guy with a gun is a good guy with a gun." One group of researchers even found that support for pro-gun policies was higher among Americans who believed in supernatural evils like demons and devils.[19] In his bad-guys-and-good-guys statement, LaPierre echoed similar fantastical notions: "The truth is our society is populated by an unknown number of genuine monsters—people so deranged, so evil, so possessed by voices and driven by demons that no sane person can possibly ever comprehend them. They walk among us every day."[20]

Like the manufactured goods of industrial production that Karl Marx had in mind when he described "commodity fetishism," today's Second Amendment is divorced from history and context, stripped of its production and meaning in the late eighteenth century. Instead of relating to the Second Amendment as many of the founding generation understood it, that is, as a "civic duty," in the words of historian Saul Cornell, to own and maintain a firearm for the purposes of communal defense, gun owners today relate to the Second Amendment almost exclusively through the mechanisms of the market.[21]

The Second Amendment is even marketed and sold, independent of firearms. The "True Patriot Supply Company," for example, offers it in T-shirt form, stylized to look like a Jack Daniel's whiskey label, with the text, "Second Amendment, since 1776." No matter that no draft of the Second Amendment existed until 1789, or that the final version wasn't ratified until 1791. Gun capitalism has rendered the historical reality of the Second Amendment invisible and has put in its place a commodified history that reinforces the mystique of guns as magical totems to protect oneself and one's community from various forms of evil, which include, in more radical interpretations, one's own neighbors or government.

THE FAMOUS TWENTY-SEVEN WORDS OF the Second Amendment say nothing about commerce or consumption—the two crucial verbs in the text are "keep" and "bear," neither of which is a synonym for "sell" or "market" or "distribute" or even "manufacture"—and yet that is the ground on which most of the country's battles about the Second Amendment have taken place. Who can buy a gun, what kinds of guns can they buy, and when and where and how can they buy them?

A massive federal infrastructure exists as a result of Congress's attempts to answer these questions since the 1930s. The National Firearms Act (1934) first clarified the kinds of guns buyers could purchase, at the height of concern over "gangsters" wielding machine guns; its tandem New Deal–era law, the Federal Firearms Act (1938), defined who could be a legal gun buyer or seller. Three decades later, the Gun Control Act (1968) tried to answer all of the above questions for a postwar population rapidly growing and arming, and, having answered them incompletely, required the Brady Handgun Violence Prevention Act (1993) to fill some of its loopholes, but not before the Reagan-era Firearm Owners Protection Act (1986) scaled back some of its scope. In all twentieth-century federal efforts to regulate firearms, Congress acted under its constitutional prerogative to regulate interstate commerce. The two significant congressional actions on firearms of the early twenty-first century— allowing the 1994 Assault Weapons Ban to expire in 2004 and passing the 2005 Protection of Lawful Commerce in Arms Act, which provided gun manufacturers with protection against lawsuits demanding they take responsibility for gun violence—were also connected to Congress's power to regulate gun buying and selling, rather than "keeping" and "bearing." So too was the 2022 legislation signed into law by President Joe Biden after the mass murder of children in a school in Uvalde, Texas.

Given the ground on which so many gun politics battles are fought, I want to suggest that US gun politics is in fact consumer politics, that what gun control and gun rights organizations both demand is consumer regulation and protection.[22] Liberal gun control organizations want Congress and state lawmakers to legislate stronger regulations regarding the conditions under which consumers can purchase guns and the kinds of guns they can buy; gun rights organizations want legislators to continue to secure a relatively free and open market for guns—relative because, while many regulations exist at the local, state, and federal levels, nothing like the openness and scale of the US gun market exists anywhere else in the world.

Magical thinking about the Second Amendment's timelessness notwithstanding, changes wrought on consumer markets by gun capitalism, especially in the formative 1970s, set the consumerist terms upon which Americans continue to battle over guns today. In 1974, for example, the Chicago-area

Committee for Handgun Control Inc. (CHC), petitioned the new Consumer Products Safety Commission (CPSC) to regulate handgun ammunition as a dangerous consumer product. In a story I recount in chapter 7, the CPSC rejected the petition on the grounds that Congress had not granted the agency the authority to regulate ammunition, but a federal judge ruled that the CPSC did have such authority and had to give the petition full consideration. The CHC's gambit ultimately fell short when Congress intervened, but for months the gun debate hinged on how to understand guns as consumer products. One journalist at the time described the NRA as the "largest and most effective consumer lobby in the United States."[23]

Guns, then, are common consumer goods, not unlike cars, refrigerators, and skateboards.[24] While pathologizing guns has led to better understandings of their impact on public health, it has also made them more difficult to understand as objects of consumer desire. After all, only a tiny fraction of guns in the United States is used in a crime each year. People by and large do not buy guns, especially from licensed dealers, with the intention of using them in crimes. Instead, they often see guns not unlike how they see other consumer goods, as objects of desire that hold out the promise of making buyers into the people they dream they might become. Sociologist Colin Campbell has written about consumers as daydreamers who imagine the products they buy as offering the possibility of personal transformation. Of course, fulfillment is ultimately ephemeral, so we look to the fancier car, the bigger house, or the newest assault rifle accessories to continue chasing that elusive daydream of remaking the self through consumption.[25]

Why have we struggled to see guns in the context of consumer capitalism? For one thing, guns are manly, and consumerism has often been coded as women's activity—"consumer desire" evokes images of advertisements in glossy magazines intended to appeal to housewives at the checkout counter. Men produce, women consume, or at least that was the traditional, socially constructed, historical divide. If a man bought a gun, it was not because he was drawn to it by slick marketing but because it served a utilitarian purpose, whether it be to kill wild game, protect the home, or exercise vigilance against government tyranny. But gun control advocates, from the Committee for Handgun Control in the 1970s to the parents of the child victims of the 2012 Sandy Hook massacre, have long drawn attention to the true nature of gun marketing. In 2022 the Sandy Hook families eventually settled a lawsuit for $73 million with Remington, maker of the Bushmaster AR-15 used in the murders. The group focused on a magazine advertisement for the weapon that read, "Consider your man card reissued." Bushmaster had sought to "tap into anxieties about masculinity," in the words of one of the families' lawyers, to provoke fantasies of consumer desire.[26]

While anxiety and fear drive gun-buying, so too does a feeling of empowerment and fulfilling one's (often manly) duty to defend oneself, one's family, or one's community. Sociologist Jennifer Carlson has written about how people (mostly men) who carry guns in public believe they fulfill a civic duty, imagining themselves at their best as "citizen-protectors."[27] Gun consumerism sells buyers such a vision. Of course, people buy guns for lots of other reasons too. Some hunt, others collect or plink or tinker. But since the 1970s, gun marketing has sold a fantasy of guns as tools for self-defense and individual empowerment, and increasingly in the twenty-first century as instruments of war against domestic enemies and even one's own government. Consumer daydreams can become toxic to a democracy, of course, as when armed protesters occupied the Michigan State Capitol in April 2020, or when far-right groups stockpiled weapons in anticipation of the January 6, 2021, attack on the US Capitol.[28] But understanding how gun capitalism met consumer demand and desire, beyond simply manipulating impressionable consumers, leads to a richer understanding of the growth of the gun country since the middle of the twentieth century.

THIS BOOK'S FIRST FOUR CHAPTERS explore the origins of the gun country in the quarter century after the Second World War. Beginning in the 1950s, as I describe in chapter 1, young gun entrepreneurs connected American desires and consumer demand with a previously unexploited source of supply: war surplus guns from around the world, but especially from Europe. Importers would stalk defense ministries and scour military warehouses on several continents to scoop up and ship off millions of them, along with a steady stream of low-quality firearms newly manufactured in pop-up factories in Western Europe, to satiate a growing consumer market, driven by Cold War anxieties and the unprecedented middle-class prosperity of postwar America. The cheap imports drove down prices and expanded the mass market for guns in the United States. Pressured by the gun industry, Congress debated what to do with this "foreign trash," most urgently after Lee Harvey Oswald used two imported guns on the day he murdered the president, which I examine in chapter 2. Chapter 3 explores the place of the booming consumer market for firearms in the social upheavals of the late 1960s. Black rebellions in cities like Detroit and armed demonstrations by radical groups like the Black Panthers generated white fears of a coming race war—and cheap guns were there to arm the combatants. After years of deliberation, Congress finally passed the Gun Control Act (GCA) of 1968, in a moment of unusual introspection about violence in American society, the subject of chapter 4. In the story that follows, the GCA serves as a both an end and a beginning, the culmination of an unprecedented half-decade debate about the role of guns in society and the starting point for political and cultural clashes in the decades to follow.

The next four chapters walk through the aftermath of the 1960s and the GCA from the perspectives of gun capitalists and nascent gun control and gun rights groups. Almost as soon as the GCA went into effect, the law's congressional authors discovered its "loophole"—but not before enterprising gun capitalists had already started to exploit it, a development I recount in chapter 5. In chapters 6 and 7 I turn to Chicago, one of the urban locations where the gun boom of the 1950s and 1960s was felt most acutely. In 1970s Chicago we find the origins of the contemporary grassroots gun control movement. The Civic Disarmament Committee, led by a remarkable activist named Laura Fermi, offered a radical vision of gun abolition, inspiring the first major US gun control organization. In translating her vision to contemporary political realities, however, early gun control activists triangulated to accommodate gun capitalism and the political imperatives of expanding ownership in an era of inflated concerns about crime. The aforementioned Committee for Handgun Control, the subject of chapter 7, took a novel tack toward gun control: as a consumer product like any other, guns should be regulated as such. The group gained brief national notoriety for this approach but couldn't overcome the power of the gun mystique.

Chapter 8 offers an "un-NRA" history of early gun rights organizations. These right-wing groups, mostly forgotten today, preceded the NRA's own radical turn in 1977 and, mixing Cold War anxieties with white racial fears of the 1960s, adopted an uncompromising approach that laid the foundations for the emergence of a national conservative gun rights ideology.

In the final two chapters, to reflect upon the gun country that decades of gun buying and selling had created, I return to Yoshi's story. In chapter 9, Yoshi's parents in Japan and host parents in Louisiana coordinate to launch a gun control campaign, one that urged Americans to reject exceptionalist notions of gun culture and learn from the rest of the world's approach to gun capitalism and violence. They too fell short, unable to get the better of the mystique clouding the inexorable machine of gun capitalism. By the twenty-first century, as I describe in chapter 10, the gun country had gone global, for better or worse. The fears of gun reformers in the late 1960s—that their moment of national crisis marked a now-or-never turning point on guns—proved prescient. There was no turning back.

COLLECTOR'S SPECIAL

Special purchase of antique
European military revolvers in rare
and unusual calibers. Each one from
a different country. Fair condition

3 for $28.50 · 6 for $50.00

THE DUMPING GROUND

LIKE ALL MYTHOLOGICAL SUBJECTS, the gun country has many origin stories. Some of them start in seventeenth-century British law or eighteenth-century colonial North America. Others begin with the nineteenth-century founding and expansion of industrial production. They trace a path through such places as the "Gun Valley" of Massachusetts and Connecticut, where much of the traditional gun industry originated, and track the rise and fall of fortunes belonging to the likes of Samuel Colt or Oliver Winchester. Others still look to the gun violence of the twentieth century in places like Chicago, Detroit, or New York, cities decimated by the "urban crisis" of midcentury America. Rarely does an origin story for the gun country begin 4,000 miles away, in Helsinki, Finland. But that's where this one for postwar American gun capitalism takes us, to where the Finnish government, like its counterparts throughout Europe in the years after the Second World War, grappled for a solution to a gun problem of its own.

For many European countries, the war had coughed up tools of violence by the millions, leaving them to rust and rot and warp in warehouses and depots across the continent as devastated societies tried to rebuild. For a host of reasons, European nations had little use for those tools of war any longer. Their populations were exhausted and depleted, and material reminders of the years of trauma were hardly in demand. The continent remained shattered, and the "miracle" economic recovery of the 1950s, which would create or rebuild middle-class consumer societies, lay in the future. And even if Europeans had the inclination or money to buy these millions of guns, most countries had laws, or were passing new ones, that limited or prohibited civilian firearms ownership. As Cold War Europe faced the possibility of future wars, the time for yesterday's weapons had passed.

So what could you do with them? Storage was only a temporary solution—without regular maintenance, the guns would deteriorate in government warehouses, which needed round-the-clock security. You could dispose of them, of course, but that was expensive: the cost of shipping and dumping hundreds of thousands of guns in the middle of the Baltic Sea was enough to bust the budget of a recovering country like Finland. The price of guns, in both lives and national treasure, was already beyond counting. Tens of thousands of Finns died bearing them, fighting off first Soviet invaders and later the Finns' erstwhile allies, the Nazis. And now these guns were quite literally Finland's, and Europe's, trash.

This is where a young American enters the scene. Chubby, boyish, disarming, looking like a scoutmaster or Sunday school teacher, Samuel Cummings—not Uncle Sam but "Arms Dealer Sam"—arrives at the Finnish Ministry of Defense keen to make a deal.[1] He comes bearing not just cash—though he's got that, in his trademark crocodile briefcase—but something even better: a solution to the problem of old guns. In return for cash and new military hardware, he wants 300,000 of them, mostly Mauser bolt-action rifles. Though increasingly obsolete in an era of automatic rifles, these relics would effectively suit the needs of suburban American men looking to escape to the woods for a weekend. For the low price of less than one US dollar per rifle, Cumming is willing to take the lot of them, along with 70 million rounds of ammunition, guns and bullets manufactured not only in Finland but also in Italy, Germany, Russia, and everywhere else in Europe, before and during the Second World War.[2] Packing and shipping included, of course. What did a war-weary country have to lose?

Sam Cummings had seen firsthand how Europeans treated the refuse from the Nazis' continental war when he toured France and Germany as a college student in 1948. Small arms and large littered the landscape. "The tanks had that new car smell," he later said, flashing his characteristically dark humor. "All they needed was a battery recharge to start 'em up and reconquer France." But the secondhand market for lightly used tanks was tricky, and he opted to start more modestly. Fresh out of the George Washington University and an eighteen-month stint with the Central Intelligence Agency as a Korean War weapons analyst, he set about acquiring small arms for pennies on the dollar—"arsenal-fresh" rifles and sidearms, as he described the guns, "with Hitler's fingerprints still on them."[3]

German rifles sit in a warehouse in Stavanger, Norway, after Germany's surrender, 1945. Stockpiles of war surplus firearms like these made Samuel Cummings millions in the decades before the 1968 Gun Control Act. (No. 5 Army Film and Photo Section, Army Film and Photographic Unit, Sgt. A. H. Jones. © Imperial War Museum, BU 9763.)

Along with an eye for a bargain, Cummings had an abiding faith in his countrymen's appetite for firearms. Having grown up fascinated with guns, he knew that there were millions of American men, especially war veterans, who shared his passion—they just needed something a bit more affordable than the pricy hunting rifles then on offer. By the mid-1960s, Cummings would become the world's most prolific private arms dealer, selling not only artillery and fighter jets to anticommunist dictators and insurgencies but also a quarter million war surplus guns each year to civilians in the United States. Sam Cummings had succeeded in turning Europe's trash into America's treasure.

Cummings was the most prominent of a cohort of unorthodox gun capitalists who bucked the traditional industry and remade gun culture. When the Gun Control Act of 1968 arrived belatedly to curtail their importation business—"They passed the law too late!" he would boast—Cummings's consumer revolution was already a fait accompli.[4] Gun consumers had come to expect easy access to cheap and plentiful firearms, and in the 1960s they began to coalesce around an emerging gun rights ideology to justify it. The entrepreneurs' records are mostly lost to history, but we can see their handiwork forging gun capitalism through congressional efforts to control or eliminate their commercial activities and in the distinctive advertising they used to train consumers to expect a bounty of guns in postwar America.

As the United States reached the height of its postwar economic boom, and as its consumer society flourished as the most robust and vibrant on earth, the country also experienced a boom of gun consumption. For years the Second World War had absorbed all domestic production and its end unleashed pent-up demand.[5] Men who had guns before the war bought more. Men who only aspired to gun ownership could now afford them. Men who had served in the world wars sought mementos to commemorate those experiences. The gun-curious and mostly white men—and they were overwhelmingly men, with all the gendered expectations this implied—who were taking advantage of the growing highway system to move out to suburbs and nearer to rural hunting spaces bought cheap surplus rifles to test their interest in the hobby. Young men especially saw opportunity in the bounty of limitless cheap guns. Cummings and the new gun capitalists gave them a taste, and they wanted more.

The seemingly limitless availability of guns, and their low cost in a market flooded with them, made guns into another mass-market commodity in a consumer culture in which Americans increasingly felt nothing should be out of their reach. Mixed with decades-old mythologies of the gun in American life, the postwar gun bounty raised a new generation to believe in gun ownership, not just in an abstract constitutional or cultural sense but also in a material one, because unlike for previous generations, the guns were everywhere, affordable, and accessible in America the dumping ground.

THOUGH NO ONE DID MORE to create the first postwar gun "problem" than Sam Cummings, few Americans knew who he was. For most of his career, from the early 1950s to his death in 1998, Cummings avoided public scrutiny while amassing a fortune and living an austere expatriate life in Monte Carlo—he did not smoke, drink, gamble, or swear; he rode the bus to the airport; and he preferred his wife's hamburgers to the city's opulent restaurants. Perhaps his one vice—besides guns—was his dark sense of humor about his life's work: he signed off on memos with names like Strangelove and Rasputin, and once, in the lead up to the passage of the 1968 Gun Control Act, he sent a US associate a tongue-in-cheek postcard urging resistance to new gun legislation so that he might "CONTINUE MY LUXURIOUS LIFE ON THE RIVIERA WITHOUT WORRY." "Levity, in the arms trade, is the soul of commerce," he told *Sports Illustrated* in 1970.[6] That sense of humor had charmed the *New York Daily News* in 1965, when it decided that the bright and articulate arms dealer testifying before the Senate did not meet the profile of the "sinister gunrunner who lurks in waterfront ginmills hunting for a chance to peddle a clandestine cargo of weapons, no questions asked."[7]

When the press found Cummings newsworthy it was because of his singular insight into international arms deals: he knew the players in every country, large and small, who had or who wanted the Cold War world's hardware stockpiles. On the record or on background, he frequently served as a source for journalists investigating the global arms trade. When Neil Sheehan of the *New York Times* wrote a series on the subject in 1967, he turned to Cummings. Cummings bragged about his triumphs, like when he negotiated with the Israeli government, "while Mr. Nasser's tanks were still burning," to purchase Soviet-made firearms captured during the Six-Day War.[8] Sheehan figured no private citizen was better positioned to give him dirt on US global arms dealings. His investigation uncovered more than $11 billion in arms sales to allies in the previous five years (upward of $100 billion in 2020 dollars), along with some $30 billion in arms giveaways since 1949. Cummings may have been the "world's leading private seller of arms," but the United States was the "principal source of arms for the whole world." Cummings convinced Sheehan he was merely "a midget compared with the Government salesman," a fortunate middleman who happened to strike while the iron was hot.[9]

Along with occasional stories of the jet-setting boy-wonder arms dealer came rumors of international intrigue that Cummings never bothered to dispel. According to this lore, he had started as a CIA arms analyst during the Korean War (this was true) and founded his company, Interarms, as a CIA front (this was probably not true); he had posed as a Hollywood producer touring Europe in search of guns for film props, buying $100 million worth of German arms and sending them to Nationalist forces in Taiwan; his first job outside government was with the Western Arms Company, a mysterious private gun seller in Los Angeles that also may or may not have been a CIA front; his nascent private intelligence network keyed the CIA into a massive arms shipment from Czechoslovakia to Guatemala in 1954, setting off a chain of events that resulted in the overthrow of the Jacobo Árbenz government; he sold guns to Cuban dictator Fulgencio Batista, then to the insurrectionist Fidel Castro, then to exiles attempting to overthrow Castro.[10] His infrequent appearance in available CIA documents indicates that while he did work for the agency during the Korean War, his official relationship ended there, and while Interarms was "used by CIA to acquire and dispose of weapons, ammunition, etc.," the agency "had no control of the firm and no proprietary interest," as a 1967 memo put it. The same memo did mention that Cummings worked as an informant for the Federal Bureau of Investigation.[11]

As Interarms generated upward of $100 million a year, Cummings, the company's sole owner, tried to stay grounded, cultivating relationships with journalists who admired his introspection and candor, which won him a reputation as the "undisputed philosopher-king of the arms trade," as his *New York Times* obituary put it.[12] In the era of Vietnam, Watergate, and the Church Committee's investigations of CIA wrongdoing, Cummings's stories titillated journalists. He rewarded their interest with apocryphal references and philosophical musings. He was fond of quoting the last lines of his favorite poem, Samuel Taylor Coleridge's "Ode to Tranquility," which concludes with mention of "a wild and dream-like trade of blood and guile, / Too foolish for a tear, too wicked for a smile!" "In my profession I see boundless human folly," he told *Sports Illustrated*, which dubbed Cummings "The Merchant of Menace" in a 1970 profile. "This 50-year arms race, this constant undeclared war, is the greatest folly in the history of man. . . . The arms business is idiocy, it's lunacy without bottom, but it will last as long as man, however long that may be. The world will never disarm. So what should I do but laugh?"[13]

For all the notoriety he gained for his mastery of the shadowy international arms scene, Sam Cummings's greatest impact on American life in the postwar era was much more prosaic: he sold Americans guns, lots of guns, millions of guns, guns that would reach every corner of the country, helping to create a new mass market for firearms and reshape American gun culture. Beginning in the early 1950s, cheap imports opened the gun market to more Americans than ever before.[14] Their seemingly impossibly low prices forced traditional US gunmakers to adapt to a market for cheap guns that they had not anticipated. By 1968, one of every three guns sold annually was an import. The traditional gunmakers had tried to beat Sam Cummings, and they thought they had when the Gun Control Act passed, but he'd already created a monster: cheapness and plenty would define the gun market in the coming decades.

Among the most remarkable aspects of Cummings's career is that he did all of this work selling Americans guns, or selling guns to people who sold

Samuel Cummings inspects war surplus rifles at Interarms' London warehouse, 1966. (Terence Spencer/Popperfoto via Getty Images)

Americans guns, out in the open, with complete transparency. As the *Saturday Evening Post* noted in 1962, "He dare not buy or sell as much as a blunderbuss" without approval from the US (or UK) government, a point confirmed by the State Department years later.[15] Cummings "scorns the idea that successful arms salesmen spend most of their time smuggling guns to revolutionaries at night in unmarked aircraft," said the *New York Times* in 1967. He made a point of following the letter of the law in each country where Interarms operated. Even the company motto, cribbed from the boys' academy Cummings had attended on Philadelphia's Main Line, *Esse quam videri*—"To be rather than to seem"—perfectly encapsulated the openness with which he made millions selling guns. (After his death, his daughter remembered it as "Be more than you seem.")[16]

By the early 1960s Cummings's Interarms had a couple hundred employees, including dozens of overseas agents. They were embedded in Europe's and Asia's capitals, sometimes literally across the street from defense ministries, and their task was to identify and snatch up surplus government arms the moment they came on the market. For bigger catches, Cummings himself would swoop in to charm government officials or even heads of state, occasionally gifting gold-plated pistols. Cummings traveled with an array of tools in his crocodile briefcase that enabled him to inspect large caches of surplus weapons quickly. If he liked what he saw, he would negotiate a deal that could net hundreds of thousands of firearms for a dollar or two each.

Sealing the deal was only the beginning. Though other importers tried to do what Cummings did, Interarms could call upon an unmatched network of buying agents and an established infrastructure for getting large shipments of guns from one place to another. Cummings owned warehouses that could store hundreds of thousands of weapons in London (and later Manchester), Los Angeles, and Alexandria, Virginia, just a few miles down the Potomac from Washington, DC, and the Pentagon. Interarms eventually occupied nearly a dozen warehouses on the Alexandria waterfront, where ships carrying Cummings's bounty could be unloaded easily. (Next door was a warehouse, owned by the *Washington Post*, which housed newsprint imported from Finland— sometimes on the same ships as Cummings's rifles.) In 1965 he shocked a Senate committee when he explained that he owned "the largest private arsenal in the world—big enough to equip 300,000 troops at a moment's notice—within mortar range of the Capitol." He estimated his warehouses in Alexandria held 400,000 rifles and pistols alone. When a writer for *Guns* magazine toured the facility in 1959, he described it as an "arsenal on the Potomac."[17]

The arsenal on the Potomac was the nerve center for Cummings's national and international operations. Alongside machine guns and artillery systems destined for Caribbean dictators sat war surplus Mauser and Carcano rifles bound for weekend hunters in the American suburbs. Cummings sold some of the latter through his own retail business, Hunter's Lodge, which operated a storefront in Alexandria while doing a brisk mail-order business through ads placed in magazines. But it was far more lucrative to serve as a distributor to more than 6,000 retail outlets, department and chain stores across the country, distribution that brought Cummings's cheap guns to a truly mass market. "Rifle sales through these channels," marveled *Guns* in 1959, "have cultivated a completely new and enthusiastic market for firearms, and made our country more a 'nation of riflemen' than ever."[18]

Cummings and other importers brought millions of foreign-made guns into the United States beginning in the early 1950s. This tidal wave would continue to wash over American shores until the Gun Control Act of 1968 slowed it to a trickle. Most of the guns they imported were war surplus, the bounty of Europe's half-century bacchanal of nation-state violence. Others were cheap handguns, manufactured in Western Europe after the war, produced by indus-trial startups taking advantage of the economic devastation and plentiful cheap scrap and labor. In 1966, journalist Carl Bakal estimated that the United States had absorbed anywhere from 75 to 90 percent of Europe's war surplus firearms. The country had become, in his words and those of so many other critics, the world's "dumping ground."[19]

Importers like Cummings helped to produce America's postwar gun crisis. Yet it would be simplistic and inaccurate to say that the guns they imported were, across the board, a "problem." The guns did many things—they aided in crime, to be sure, and policymakers would endlessly debate the meaning of spiking crime rates in the 1960s, but these firearms also remade the consumer market for guns and in the process helped produce a new iteration of Ameri-can gun culture, one intensely more consumer-oriented than its predecessors.

CUMMINGS'S HUNTER'S LODGE magazine advertisements were audacious in their celebration of the bounty the postwar world offered the American small arms collector, or just the gun-curious. A typical ad crammed images of a couple dozen firearms onto a page or two. The sheer variety of weapons jumped off the page. Take the Mauser, for instance, a rifle designed in Ger-many in the late nineteenth century and eventually licensed to manufactur-ers around the world. The consumer imagination dizzied at the international smorgasbord: a single ad offered any number of German, Chilean, Persian, Mexican, Swedish, Irish, Guatemalan, or Argentine varieties. Cummings's ad writers generated a paragraph description for each gun. (A typical two-page ad contained several thousand tiny words of copy.) Those descriptions often nar-rated the international origins of the firearm, connecting it and the potential buyer to the twentieth century's infamous conflicts. "Pride of the Wehrmacht from Narvik to Tobruk—from Calais to Stalingrad," one boasted of German Mausers.[20] A 1962 shipment of Japanese Arisaka rifles reveled in unapologetic racism:

> From the land of the Rising Sun, the great Arisaka family of rifles.
> Heretofore only a closely guarded and highly prized World War II
> souvenir, enviously hoarded by those victorious GI's who survived its
> deathly sting. Three renowned models from Nippon's Imperial Arse-
> nals. The weapons that were the terror of the East from Tsushima to
> Singapore. The weapons that coined for the Japanese the affectionate
> expression 'The Prussians of the Far East.' Only available through
> the honorable practices of Ye Olde Hunter—who else would have

proffered honorable competitors the *Samurai* Sword for final chance to save face by noble '*Seppuku*' as they, in desperation, attempted a disorganized banzai charge in reverse? The final face-saving is now yours to enjoy at *Hara-Kiri* prices [*sic*, throughout].[21]

The ads never mentioned Cummings but they carried his trademark swagger. Despite mimicking a pulp magazine ad's tongue-in-cheek humor, truth lay buried in the copy. Hunter's Lodge's first magazine ads in 1956 joked about the bounties of imports available. A character named "the Old Hunter" (later renamed "Ye Old(e) Hunter") scoured storehouses and stockpiles around the world for deals. The first ad noted "$20,000,000 Worth of Surplus Going for a Song!" and "Over 30,000,000 Items in Stock Assure Perpetual Availability!" (These numbers inexplicably shot up to $25,569,69.69 and 35,999,999 a month later.)[22] Cummings offered the world's stock of surplus arms. If a soldier somewhere on earth had carried it—"From the Land of the Maharajas!"; "The Far East cracked at last!"; "A Middle East mystery solved!"—Hunter's Lodge would eventually sell it.[23]

The imported guns appealed to consumers in part because they were inexpensive, as much as ten times cheaper than equivalent US-made hunting rifles. But advertisements also evoked war and military service as attractive characteristics. After all, these were firearms produced with the nearly unlimited resources of nation-states, designed to injure and kill human beings in less-than-ideal battlefield conditions. Cummings would later make this observation to a Senate committee: "The fact is that men who know guns recognize that these weapons, imported military weapons, have been manufactured to specifications far more stringent than most of the sporting firearms on the market today."[24] Hunter's Lodge and other import retailers would use these characteristics of war surplus imports to their advantage. "Designed for the fast, deadly action of jungle fighting, this arm was used with outstanding success by British and US special troops in New Guinea, India, the jungle of Malaya, and by special commando units in the Middle East," Hunter's Lodge boasted of the .303 Enfield carbine in a 1957 advertisement. "For the man who wants a superlative, light weight hunting rifle, this is it!"[25]

For a while, at least, even the National Rifle Association agreed. The time would come when NRA leaders would join the traditional manufacturers in condemning war surplus imports. Executive Vice President Franklin Orth would tell Congress in 1965 that the NRA supported "properly drawn legislation to curb the flood of castoff military firearms that have been dumped in America."[26] But the largest and most influential US gun rights organization still

Excerpt of Hunter's Lodge advertisement from *American Rifleman*, 1967.
Importers packed their ads with guns to show off the bounty of the postwar
gun market, and they played up the guns' foreign origins. (Hunter's Lodge)

accepted advertising from Cummings and other importers. Much as the NRA
needed the advertising dollars of the traditional industry, as well as direct and
indirect support through other means, it was keenly attentive to the trends
among its membership, and NRA members couldn't get enough war surplus
rifles in the late 1950s.

So popular were surplus military rifles that the NRA's magazine, *American
Rifleman*, ran a four-part series in 1960 and 1961 evaluating the merits of each
country's offerings. The series began by assessing the suitability of military
rifles for the needs of *Rifleman* readers, who by and large identified as sportsmen, not soldiers. Could firearms designed for war be valuable pieces in the
American gunowner's collection?

The answer was an enthusiastic, if qualified, yes. In fact, many qualities of
the surplus military rifle, the NRA explained, made it superior to its sporting

counterparts. Because the resources of major nation-states were invested in the design and production of these rifles, they "have the properties of strength and safety to the highest degree," and thanks to extensive testing their reliability had "reached a level that can be attained in no other way." The rigorous demands for interchangeability in the field meant that these guns could use replacement parts without costly customization. All of that said, the buyer in the market for a surplus rifle needed to know that many of these rifles exhibited extensive wear and tear. They were, after all, weapons of war used in history's most devastating conflicts, and if the buyer couldn't physically review the gun before the sale (i.e., if he were buying it through the mail, as so many did), he might end up with a rifle with a roughly finished stock or a rusted bore. Even so, the NRA concluded, these guns were cheap enough that with a little extra cash and some elbow grease, the ambitious buyer could have a high-quality "sporterized" rifle at a low entry point. Even if an owner went so far as to remove the rifle's action (the mechanism that accepts and handles ammunition) and discard and replace all of the other parts, it was worth the investment.[27]

To find the kind of import rifles the NRA recommended for "sporterization," a buyer needed to look no further than the pages of the very magazine doing the recommending. That same January 1961 issue of *American Rifleman*, for instance, contained a bounty of ads, large and small, from dealers looking to unload stockpiles of imports. Klein's Sporting Goods of Chicago, a major mail-order dealer selling a variety of goods for the active outdoorsman, had a full-page advertisement offering, among other weapons, a "Rare .303 Jungle Carbine," a variant of the popular British-made Enfield rifle, in this case "developed specifically for rough usage and bitter fighting in the jungles of Burma, Borneo and Malaya" ($22.88). The most impressive ad in the magazine came from Cummings's Hunter's Lodge. On a two-page spread packed with thousands of words and dozens of images, Hunter's Lodge offered twenty-three different firearms, twenty of which were imports, ranging in price from $9.95 (for various British, Russian, French, or Italian rifles) to $29.95 (an M94 Swedish Mauser carbine, "the rifle that set that surplus quality pattern for years to come").[28]

Indeed, advertising in gun magazines had looked like this for years by the early 1960s. Europe's stockpiles of surplus weapons were part of the great bounty Americans claimed in their wartime victory and as a postwar "people of plenty." The peace dividend meant unrestricted access to the world's guns. The boom of consumerism in the 1950s included the dramatic expansion of the consumer market for guns—even the creation of a new mass market, as

Guns noted in 1959, one driven by a seemingly endless flow of cheap imports. If prewar American gun culture was one in which the ordinary white man aspired to a gun collection, postwar American gun culture was one in which global gun surpluses made it possible.

Gun magazines testified to that new experience of mass consumerism. The NRA's *American Rifleman* was a legacy publication dating back to the 1920s, a monthly benefit for members, but new magazines sprouted up in the postwar era, tapping into rapid market expansion. Major publications relying on ad revenue, like *Shotgun News* (1946), *Guns* (1955), and *Guns & Ammo* (1958), all launched in the postwar years. They joined older sporting publications, like *Field & Stream* (1895) and *Outdoor Life* (1898), that increasingly catered to the ballooning consumer gun market. The pages of these magazines overflowed with ads for cheap imported rifles and handguns.

These magazines ran ads from traditional gunmakers too, but far fewer of them, and of a markedly different style than those of their import competitors. Ads from old-line firms like Winchester and Browning typically showed only a single model gun, frequently in the hands of a white man, sometimes accompanied by a child, with ducks or deer in the background, drawing on the imagery of heritage and hunting. A May 1962 Browning ad in *American Rifleman*, for example, showed a boy of ten or twelve smiling and holding a .22-caliber rifle, a typical starter gun. The ad describes the gun, the only one featured, as a "Teacher with Unstinting Characteristics." Because these firms didn't offer mail order sales direct to consumers, they urged readers to visit a dealer to see these beautiful firearms for themselves. Except for updated graphic design and improved photography, the ads' themes wouldn't have been out of place in the 1930s.

The importers' ads, in contrast, spoke to the new postwar era of mass consumption. In the same May 1962 issue of *American Rifleman* a reader would be unable to avoid full-page ads bursting with guns threatening to spill off the page. Just a few pages away from the Browning ad, a two-page Hunter's Lodge spread displayed images of twenty-seven different rifles and handguns, each with a paragraph description stuffed with hyperbole and exclamation points. Every gun was for sale at a rock-bottom price. The Browning ad and other traditional ones like it asked readers to appreciate the gunmakers' craft; the importers' ads encouraged readers to buy, buy, buy.

THE IRONY OF THE EARLIEST significant legislative push for gun control in the postwar era, which would focus on importers like Cummings and their trade in war surplus weapons, was that it was powered by gunmakers themselves, a dozen or so traditional manufacturers located primarily in New England's "Gun Valley."[29] Gun critics have called the National Rifle Association the "gun lobby," implying that the organization speaks for US gun manufacturers, but in truth the gunmakers already had their own industry lobby in the 1950s: the Sporting Arms and Ammunition Manufacturers Institute (SAAMI). In the postwar years SAAMI represented nearly 100 businesses connected to the manufacture and sale of guns, including not just the iconic gunmakers but also parts manufacturers, distributors, and trade publishers. And one thing these businesses all had in common was an interest in stymying the flow of cheap war surplus guns.

The traditional industry raised the alarm about Cummings for self-interested reasons—he was an innovative competitor, threatening to remake the market as they knew it—but they couched their concerns in the language of national security and patriotism. In 1958, through SAAMI, the industry brought the import problem to the attention of Albert P. Morano, representative for Connecticut's fourth congressional district. SAAMI had first sought relief from officials in the Eisenhower administration, petitioning for action from the Department of State, which regulated imports, and the Department of Defense, which relied on small arms producers in wartime, but both agencies demurred. The gun industry sensed, however, that pure economic arguments would not win the day.

The gunmakers instead opted for a national security argument, insisting that their own prosperity was linked with Cold War imperatives. The State Department's Office of Munitions Control (OMC), which granted gun import licenses to importers, had brushed off SAAMI's concerns in May 1957, contending that "it did not appear appropriate for the Department to include in its consideration of import cases the factor of possible domestic competition." To that claim SAAMI responded that the OMC "was not properly applying statutory tests for arms control in the interests of world peace and the security and foreign policy of the United States, since national security would be adversely affected by any action which impairs the welfare of the small arms and ammunition industry of this country."[30] In other words, the economic stability of the small arms industry was in the best interest of US national security. OMC officials didn't bite. If the industry wanted action, it would have to get Congress to legislate.

To that end, Morano raised SAAMI's concerns with the House Committee on Foreign Affairs, of which he was a member, in anticipation of submitting a bill to amend the section on munitions control in the 1954 Mutual Security Act. He made no effort to hide his protectionist intentions: the gunmakers of his state, iconic names like Remington and Winchester, wanted Congress to do something about the impact of imports on their industry. He cited precipitous drops in industry employment just over the course of the previous year; Remington, for instance, had let go of about one-sixth of its total workforce.[31] It fell upon the Foreign Affairs Committee to decide the extent to which this industry problem merited government intervention in the free flow of goods across international borders.

Free trade rhetoric notwithstanding, the United States did not shy away from protectionism in the postwar years.[32] Amenable to the interests of national security and economic recovery, the Eisenhower administration and Congress were receptive to the gun industry's argument that imports threatened a venerable US industry and, in turn, national security preparedness. But members of the House Foreign Affairs Committee knew almost nothing of figures like Sam Cummings and the United Nations of guns he had brought to the United States over the last several years. Instead, reports of tens of thousands of US-made rifles shipped from Europe and dumped onto the US market at rock-bottom prices had left the congressmen decidedly uneasy.[33]

The committee had reasons to fear that US wartime and Cold War firearms largesse was returning to American shores. Over the previous two decades, the country had sent many millions of guns overseas, first as the wartime "Arsenal of Democracy," and then through an escalating commitment to the global containment of communism. Before the United States entered the Second World War, Franklin Roosevelt pushed the lend-lease program through Congress to prepare the country for inevitable conflict by scaling up military production and strengthening allies. During the program's five years of operation, the United States shipped 4.4 million "small arms and infantry weapons" overseas—most of them (3.2 million) to Great Britain and its empire, but some 631,000 to China, 204,000 to France, and 154,000 to the Soviet Union. Accompanying those firearms were nearly 9 billion rounds of ammunition.[34] It's impossible to know exactly how many guns there were in the United States in 1945—45 million would be a conservative estimate[35]—but it's not unreasonable to assume that those 4.4 million were the equivalent of at least 10 percent of privately owned firearms in the country, most of which were not rifles designed and manufactured to demanding military specifications. With Europe at peace and rebuilding, and few viable civilian markets for guns anywhere in the world in the mid-1950s, some in Congress sensibly believed its wartime generosity had come back with a bite.

Congress also considered the possibility that the gun shipments were of a more recent vintage. The committee met under the pretext of amending the

Mutual Security Act, a measure first passed under the Truman administration in 1951 and revised in 1954 that had appropriated billions of dollars in military and economic aid to meet the global communist threat as Truman had defined it—it was "world-wide," "total," and "of indefinite duration," the president said when he announced the program. Truman envisioned the Mutual Security Program as the next stage of the Marshall Plan, and one that specifically linked domestic and global security and prosperity. "The one builds upon the other," he said. Foreign aid, whether for development projects in the Third World or guns for a Cold War ally resisting a communist insurgency, "will build more strength in support of our security than we could build at home with the same expenditure of funds."[36] The Mutual Security Act, like the Cold War more generally, explicitly blurred the lines between domestic and foreign policy.

When Morano brought a bill forward in the Foreign Relations Committee, he and his cosponsor, Senator John F. Kennedy of the gun-manufacturing state of Massachusetts, had in mind the unintended consequences of foreign policy on domestic life. The Mutual Security Program sent guns abroad to military allies. But what did those allies do with those guns when they didn't want or need them any longer? They tried to sell them off on the world market as surplus, Morano assumed. And where was the world's largest consumer market, and the one wealthy market in the world that could legally absorb untold numbers of surplus guns? The dumping ground, of course—the United States. And it wasn't just that Americans would buy back guns that they had sent abroad in aid programs. They would buy any surplus guns, even those manufactured abroad, that friendly governments might be looking to unload. In 1958 Congress would discover that many of those guns were going to the United States, courtesy of entrepreneurial importers, like Cummings, who saw a profit to be made in the insatiable American appetite for guns, abetted now by postwar prosperity and expendable incomes. And US foreign policy imperatives—namely, arming Cold War allies with the latest in military hardware—made stockpiles in Europe and around the world obsolete.

When Morano stood to address the House on the bill in April 1958, he had one specific gun in mind: the Italian-made Carcano, an analog to the ubiquitous Mauser. Carcanos coming into the United States, Morano explained, were a 1938 model adapted from the 1891 original. They were plentiful, having been manufactured for decades, and thus easy for importers to scoop up and pass on to American gun enthusiasts at cut-rate prices. But they were also dangerous. The Italian government had said as much, and so did the State Department officials and an NRA expert that Morano consulted. They all pointed to a malfunctioning unsecured bolt that could eject backward when the rifle was fired. These weapons were hardly safe for the regular use of American sportsmen, Morano concluded, given their "tendency to blow up in the shooter's face." His and Kennedy's bill would prohibit the importation of not just the Carcano but all war surplus firearms, a measure both admitted was intended to protect not only the physical bodies of American shooters but also the bottom lines of the arms manufacturing industry in their states.[37]

To import a Carcano, or any war surplus firearm with a barrel larger than .22 caliber (a size generally considered, before the 1960s, too small for battlefield use), Cummings and other importers had to get permission from the US government through the State Department's Office of Munitions Control. Every shipment of guns to the United States required an OMC license indicating the quantity of guns, their type and origin, and the importer's intentions for them. The OMC had fielded SAAMI's May 1957 request to restrict war surplus imports, but State officials decided that to take any action absent a directive from President Dwight Eisenhower would reach beyond their statutory mandate, especially in light of the fact that State's mission was one of national security, not to adjudicate questions of economic competition.[38] The office simply wasn't equipped, let alone authorized, to determine whether gun imports really did hurt US industries.

The State Department did not remain neutral in the conversation, however. While the OMC didn't think it had standing to assess economic competition, officials did see national security and Cold War imperatives at work in the issuing of licenses. State Department officials testified before Congress on the import question and ultimately sided with the importers and against the industry in the name of national security. "I am frank to say that when there are questions of surplus arms cropping up abroad," said Roderic L. O'Connor, whose office supervised the OMC, "it may very often be the better part of valor and indeed the best part of our foreign relations to have them imported into this country rather than float around."[39] He went further to explain that State, in fact, knew of 18,000 Springfield rifles sitting in Italy. State officials had evidence, which remained classified, that those rifles were destined for "a part of the world which quite clearly would have been very troublesome to us from a point of view of foreign policy," and thus expediting their delivery to the United States instead "was highly beneficial," from a national security perspective.[40] He understood the industry's concern, he said, but he couldn't support any legislation preventing the OMC from authorizing imports like these Springfields from Italy, because "you can see that in a particular situation it may be darned important that we have some ability to have those arms come here, rather than go somewhere else."[41] In State's view, letting America remain the world's dumping ground made for sound foreign policy.

Congress was, to say the least, taken aback to hear this. But in the context of a Cold War consensus on fighting communism, State faced little pushback to the idea that guns were better off in the hands of Americans, even private citizens, than in the hands of communist governments or insurgents. Committee members recognized that such a policy unfairly burdened a single industry with the full costs of US foreign policy. Walter Judd of Minnesota noted that to "ask one industry, the arms industry, to pay the cost of a policy from which our whole country will benefit, is a little tough on that industry, to say the least," and Morano agreed that that it was unjust to make "the arms industry pay for a foreign policy to protect the security of all the people." "If it is important enough for our foreign policy that we should buy up surplus rifles at 79 cents apiece," Judd said, "I think we ought to buy them, and the Congress ought to authorize that."[42]

Congress received data from the OMC that clarified the extent, or at least the nature, of the problem. The guns in question were not US-made arms sent overseas as part of Cold War aid packages, as Morano had suspected. State Department officials assured the Foreign Affairs Committee that the OMC hadn't issued any licenses for such firearms to be imported; they had never even received any such request. And their data indicated that only 439 lend-lease guns came into the country in 1957, far less than 1 percent of the total imports. The Department of Defense confirmed the OMC's data. In fact, Defense had established protocols in 1956 for allied countries to dispose of excess arms granted through mutual security programs, but because the department had yet to see a single weapon "declared excess by any recipient country," it was "patently impossible for any such rifles to have legally reentered the United States for commercial resale." To the Pentagon's knowledge, the 18,000 Springfields in question had been recovered on Italian battlefields during the Second World War.[43] Europe's trash, in this case, had been America's leftovers.

BY THE TIME SAAMI APPEALED to Congress, its nightmare was already coming true: imports were remaking the consumer gun market and threatening to leave domestic manufacturers behind. A 1959 report from the Department of Commerce revealed that the gunmakers as a whole had suffered a decline of one-third of their business since the middle of the decade because of the onslaught of imports.[44] Manufacturers reported total production highs in 1956 of more than 2.3 million units, which included shotguns, handguns, and both rimfire and centerfire rifles. (Rimfire rifles typically use cheap .22 caliber ammunition, and thus tend to be inexpensive; centerfire rifles use larger caliber ammunition and thus tend to be larger, sturdier, costlier, and better suited to hunting large animals.) Just two years later, that total had dropped about 30 percent. Few industries could absorb such a sharp decline in production in a two-year period without significant labor force reductions and cost cutting. In total revenues, the decrease was similarly striking, from a high of almost $85 million in 1956 to just over $57 million in 1958.[45]

Parsing the numbers revealed even worse news for SAAMI's constituency. Handguns showed promise—unit sales were up 30 percent from five years earlier, and revenues up nearly 48 percent—but they were relatively inexpensive, and every other category had declined. The most dramatic drop was in centerfire rifles, those expensive, large-caliber hunting rifles that typically earned manufacturers the highest margins, the features-loaded sport utility vehicles of the gun market. From 1955 to 1958 production dropped from 502,000 to 205,000, with revenues plunging 65 percent.[46]

In the face of the onslaught of imports, the industry was already showing signs of contraction. Among the manufacturers the Commerce Department surveyed, total employment had plummeted nearly 40 percent in just two years.[47] Commerce cautioned, however, that the numbers could be deceiving. The decline in shipments of centerfire rifles, for instance, was attributable to a single company's delivery of hundreds of thousands of rifles to the US military in 1954; once that contract was fulfilled, military shipments virtually vanished.[48] Surely this accounted for a significant percentage of total declines in production employment.

Further, while the report seemed to confirm some of the industry's claims, it also supported a counterargument: The gun market, like the market for everything else in the United States—like the country's population itself—was booming. Total centerfire rifles sold jumped 47 percent from 1954 to 1958. Imports accounted for the difference: in 1954 they made up only 2.5 percent of total sales, but they were just about half by 1958.[49]

Commerce was, in a sense, counting apples and oranges, and the importers knew it. Superficially, a war surplus rifle "sporterized" for sale to a shooting-sports enthusiast and a brand-new hunting rifle manufactured by, say, Remington, were the same sort of product. But the latter could cost at retail more than ten times as much as the former. The two didn't compete for the same dollar, at least not in the simplistic zero-sum sense. A buyer in the market for a shiny new US-made hunting rifle would not look at a beat-up Mauser that had seen action in the Winter War between Finland and the Soviet Union twenty years earlier and suddenly change his mind. Further to the point, guns are not washing machines, that is, once you have a washing machine, you don't need another one. Evidence shows, in fact, that gun buyers tend to be serial gun buyers: if you own one gun, you're likely to buy another, and another, and another.[50] Rather than trade up for a better model, as one might do with a dishwasher or a car, gun enthusiasts tend to be collectors like collectors of comic books, stamps, or sports memorabilia. The import explosion fueled the collecting trend.

Sam Cummings and other importers understood this consumer dynamic in ways that SAAMI's clients either failed or refused to. Cummings had caught wind of the industry's protectionist impulses in 1957 and wrote SAAMI officials to inquire "what mutual steps might be taken in order to further benefit the producers of new sporting firearms and ammunition in the United States." It's worth quoting at length how he conceived of the market at that moment:

> Our business greatly enhances the shooting potential of the American public and results directly thereby in increasing to a substantial degree the firearms and ammunition business of the manufacturers in the United States. We feel that the large scale revival in shooting interests which has accompanied the availability of inexpensive used obsolete small arms in the United States through the various importers of these items, can be developed to a point of even greater market activities for the producers of new materiel in this category here in the United States through, for instance, the increased domestic production of certain types of standard ammunition and the possible commencement of production of certain other types of ammunition which, while standard abroad, have never been manufactured here.[51]

In other words, Cummings saw his work as expanding the commercial potential of the traditional US gun industry. He and other importers sought to capitalize on that market expansion by working in tandem with the traditional manufacturers. It was, at the very least, an olive branch offered from the importers to the gunmakers trying to kill their business.

To this, the industry responded, *Thanks, but no thanks.*

Cummings shared this correspondence with Congress as evidence of the industry's intransigence in the face of basic shifts in the nature of the market. The industry didn't want to change, Cummings said; it wanted Congress to sanction an oligopoly. Cummings and a handful of other importers, including big advertisers like Golden State Arms, Pasadena Fire Arms, and Winfield Arms, hired an attorney, Fred Rhodes, to represent their burgeoning industry against SAAMI's claims before the House Foreign Affairs Committee in

March 1958. Rhodes countered SAAMI on a number of points. He noted that reports of the industry's demise were greatly exaggerated. Look at *American Rifleman*, for instance: 54 of 100 pages of the most recent edition of the NRA's monthly magazine burst with advertising, and yet SAAMI members' ads accounted for fewer than five of those pages. No wonder they were hostile to competition. Rhodes and the importers believed the traditional gun industry snubbed its nose at the new age of mass advertising, aiming for an upper-middle-class market while the dealers of imported guns "appeal to all classes of people regardless of the income group in which they fall." Further, some retailers turned to imports because the traditional manufacturers were many months behind on filling orders. In short, the old-timers in the industry refused to hustle for all those new dollars in the marketplace, to "go out and in the good old American way, try to sell."[52]

The traditional manufacturers, Rhodes said, mistakenly interpreted competition as a zero-sum game in which an increasing number of sellers competed for a static pot of buyers' money. None of the millions of newly gun-curious American men with expendable income would walk into their local gun shop and drop $150 on a new Winchester hunting rifle. Instead, like a first-time car buyer purchasing a used car, or a potential camera hobbyist buying a Kodak Brownie, he would dip his toe in first with a $30 surplus rifle. "But if you get bitten by the deer-hunting bug, as undoubtedly you will," Rhodes said, "you will soon be in the market for a $150 gun." The used car becomes a new Cadillac, the Brownie an expensive Leica. And the customer base was ballooning rapidly. Rhodes pointed to the "unprecedented interest in shooting" demonstrated not only by the booming sales of his clients' imported firearms but also by the "staggering" list of new gun clubs formed every month that the NRA sent out to dealers. "These things are growing week by week and month by month."[53]

The importers presented a strong case, then, that the traditional gun industry neglected the mass marketing opportunities of the postwar era, misread the nature of the competition, and failed to appreciate the emergence of a truly expansive consumer gun culture. But here before the House Foreign Affairs Committee they knew that national security concerns proved paramount. The importers spoke of rebuffing the entreaties of Castro's rebels in Cuba. They boasted of buying up a shipment of 32,000 surplus Springfield rifles from Italy that otherwise were destined for Tunisia. Rhodes followed the OMC's lead, representing his clients' activities as in the best interest of national security: "It is better for the material to be brought back into the United States than it is to have it sift into the trouble areas of the world."[54] The importers echoed the State Department's argument that the dumping ground approach made for good foreign policy. Congress soon rejected the Morano-Kennedy bill.[55]

Cummings would repeatedly fall back on the Cold War argument in the years to come, as Congress annually debated new restrictions on firearms. In 1965 he would boast to a Senate committee that his work was responsible for "an almost total recession of any clandestine privately supported arms movements." "The reason for that is very simple," he continued. Guns that might have floated around the world and fallen into the hands of communist insurgencies had been "eliminated from the market . . . by ourselves and other leading importers," who instead brought them to the United States for the civilian consumer market.[56] Gun capitalist Sam Cummings pitched himself as nothing short of a Cold War patriot.

WHEN MORANO AND the House Foreign Affairs Committee asked Sam Cummings about Carcano rifles, he claimed to be the only importer of these surplus Italian guns.[57] He sold them through the mail for as low as $9.95, joking that they were a "throwaway gun," one you could simply leave out in the woods after you bagged your first deer. His tongue-in-cheek ads described the Carcano in his characteristic foreign-language gibberish as a "supre, supremi, Italio supremo if there ever was one."[58] But he started to see the market shift after 1958. Plenty of them, perhaps millions, still sat in warehouses and depots, but in the last half decade Cummings had done the legwork of crisscrossing the continent to inspect personally and buy up every rifle he thought he could sell on the American market. He had no interested in getting stuck in a bubble.

His competitors didn't know that, though. Seeing the profits Cummings and other importers made in the domestic market, the Vanderbilt Tire and Rubber Corporation decided to get in on the action. In 1960 the company established Crescent Firearms in New York City as a subsidiary to import war surplus guns. In its eagerness and naivete, as Cummings told it, Crescent bought up more than a half million Carcanos still sitting in Italy for $1.12 each, guns Cummings had inspected and rejected; if they were worth buying, they would already be sitting in one of his warehouses. Because Crescent lacked Cummings's well-established logistics network, it paid too much (one estimate put it at a total of $3.11 per rifle) to get the Carcanos to New York. Ever the strategist, Cummings saw what was coming and slashed prices on his stock of Carcanos both to undercut Crescent and to get out of the Carcano market before the new shipment of junk saturated it.[59]

Crescent would end up spending years trying to unload its overpriced Carcanos. Eventually, in February 1963, the company shipped an order to

LATE ISSUE!   6.5 ITALIAN
                                                               CARBINE

Only 36″ overall, weighs only 5½-lbs. Shows
only slight use, lightly oiled, test fired and head spaced, ready for
shooting. Turned down bolt, thumb safety, 6-shot, clip fed. Rear open
sight. Fast loading and fast firing.
C20-T1196. Specially Priced............................... $12.88
C20-T750. Carbine with Brand New Good Quality 4X Scope—¾″
diameter, as illustrated.................................. $19.95
E20-T751. 6.5 mm Italian military ammo with free 6-shot clip. 108 rds. $7.50

Excerpt of Klein's Sporting Goods advertisement from *American
Rifleman*, 1963. Lee Harvey Oswald responded to this ad in purchasing his
Mannlicher-Carcano rifle. (Klein's Sporting Goods)

Chicago's Klein's Sporting Goods, which offered a cornucopia of global guns in
its magazine ads. On March 13, 1963, Klein's received a coupon clipped from
one of those ads. This one had run in the February 1963 edition of *American
Rifleman*. Included with the coupon was a money order for $21.45, intended
to cover the $19.95 cost of a Mannlicher-Carcano, specially outfitted by Klein's
with a 4x telescopic sight, and shipping and handling. One week later Klein's
shipped the Carcano to A. Hidell, P.O. Box 2915, Dallas, Texas. And just eight
months after that, that very Mannlicher-Carcano, one of millions of war surplus guns unloaded on the American dumping ground, would be used to murder the president.[60]

CHAPTER **2**

SMITH &
WESSON
.38 CALIBER
38 cal. M & P revolvers. Excellent select grade condition —
Military finish $26.95
Ammo $4.20 50 rds. Holster WW II $2.50

OSWALD'S OTHER GUN

WHEN DEPUTY SHERIFF Eugene Boone and Deputy Constable Seymour Weitzman inspected the sixth floor of the Texas School Book Depository from which Lee Harvey Oswald fired three shots at the president on November 22, 1963, they saw a rifle haphazardly tucked into a corner between some boxes. Neither man touched the gun or got close enough to scrutinize it carefully before the scene teemed with investigators, but Weitzman was pretty sure he recognized it on sight: it was a 7.65mm Mauser. It could have come from Germany, or possibly Argentina, where many imported Mausers originated, or maybe Sweden or Finland. A dozen other countries had manufactured this weapon of war in the first half of the twentieth century, and importers like Sam Cummings had brought them into the United States by the boatloads in the past decade. By 1963, an imported Mauser had become the AR-15 of its day, common enough that a veteran law enforcement officer like Weitzman, or even a recreational hunter, could identify it from across the room.[1]

Weitzman was wrong, of course. Oswald had fired not a Mauser but a Mannlicher-Carcano, serial number C2766, which he had purchased from Klein's Sporting Goods, the prominent Chicago mail-order house, in March 1963. In Weitzman's defense, he had only gotten a quick look at the rifle, and Mausers and Carcanos bore some similarities. Both were bolt-action rifles that originated in the late nineteenth century for military use. As for the C2766 Carcano—the Warren Report referred to the serial number no less than fifty-two times—it wore its international origins on its sleeve, or in this case, on its stock and barrel, which bore the inscriptions "MADE IN ITALY" and "TERNI," for the central Italian town where many Carcanos were

Lee Harvey Oswald's Mannlicher-Carcano rifle, photographed for the
Warren Report, 1964.

manufactured. (Many advertisements from the era offered a good deal on a
"Terni" rifle, which was just another name for a Carcano.) Also engraved on
the gun was "1940," the year of its manufacture, a curious date of production
given the Office of Munitions Control's 1958 denial that the Carcanos flooding
the United States were of wartime vintage.[2]

Oswald's Italian rifle was not the only imported tool of violence used in the
assassination that day. Affixed atop the weapon was a telescopic sight, which
enabled the assassin to magnify his target at a distance of nearly a football
field. When Klein's received C2766 from Crescent Firearms in early 1963, it did
not have a sight attached; Klein's own gunsmith added the accessory, and the
firm used it to justify a price increase from $12.88 to $19.95. Stamped on the
scope were the words "Made in Japan," along with the name of the importer,
Ordnance Optics of Hollywood, California. Like much of the industrial output
of Japan in the early 1960s, it was a cheap but efficient tool—and certainly an
effective one for carrying out the murder of a president, as the Warren Commission's marksmanship expert concluded.[3]

Even the bullets that killed Kennedy were a product of US postwar global
entanglements. Bullet size corresponds with barrel width, and Oswald's C2766
was just over a quarter inch, or .257 caliber. Using European measurements
for a European rifle meant that the Carcano used 6.5-millimeter rounds.

No US manufacturer produced 6.5-millimeter cartridges at the end of the Second World War because no US gunmaker produced a weapon that fired 6.5-millimeter, or .257-caliber, rounds, which were a bit smaller than cartridges typically used for hunting. With the supply and popularity of Carcano rifles in the 1950s surging, however, and existing imported ammunition undependable and poorly made, the National Rifle Association collaborated with the US Army at Aberdeen Proving Ground in Maryland to develop a reliable cartridge for these hundreds of thousands of imported weapons.[4] ("Please don't tell anybody," NRA executive vice president Franklin Orth allegedly pleaded with a Senate committee investigating gun sales, "because we don't want to be hung with having been involved in producing the ammunition that killed the President.")[5] The US government had its own interest in dependable ammunition for this cheap, plentiful, and difficult-to-trace rifle that could be sent overseas to anticommunist allies, particularly of the nonstate variety. The Western Cartridge Company of East Alton, Illinois, stepped in to meet that demand. Sam Cummings speculated that Oswald had purchased 6.5-millimeter Western Cartridge ammunition that had been illegally reimported after the US government had sent it to Greece to help fight off a communist insurgency.[6] The company's decision to produce 6.5-millimeter rounds was just the sort of market-driven move Cummings had in mind in 1957 when he urged the traditional manufacturers to take advantage of the expanding consumer base for guns. Gun capitalism ensured Oswald wouldn't struggle to find ammunition.

And then there was Oswald's other gun. Less than an hour after the shooting downtown, Dallas police officer J. D. Tippit spotted a man matching the suspect's description and attempted to detain him. Oswald drew a Smith & Wesson .38 Special revolver and fired four times, killing Tippit on the spot. This gun too was an import, despite its birth in a US manufacturing plant. On the same day he placed the order for the rifle, Oswald sent away for the S&W revolver using a magazine order form for Seaport Traders, a mail-order distributor based in Los Angeles. Oswald sought the easy concealability of a handgun with a two-and-a-half-inch barrel, which Seaport had sawed down from its original five inches, dubbing it a "Commando" model. In January of that year Seaport Traders had received the Smith & Wesson, serial number V510210, along with ninety-eight other guns, from Empire Wholesale Sporting Goods of Montreal.[7] There was in 1963 no requirement for import licensing through the State Department's Office of Munitions Control for guns imported from Canada, so the Canadian pipeline—shipping war surplus from Europe to Canada and then into the United States, obscuring the guns' foreign origins—proved popular with importers who wanted to stay off the US

Oswald's other gun, a modified Smith & Wesson .38, photographed for
the Warren Report, 1964. Oswald purchased this gun from Seaport Traders and used it to murder Officer J. D. Tippit hours after the Kennedy
assassination.

government's radar.[8] The pipeline was also one of many reasons why it was,
and remains, so hard to count guns in the postwar era.

Smith & Wesson officials had to be shocked when they heard Oswald had
bought a used S&W revolver for $29.95, but they could not have been sur-
prised. They knew that millions of their firearms floated around the country
and the world on the secondhand market. Nearly two years before Kennedy's assassination, S&W president Carl Hellstrom had said as much to the
Los Angeles Police Department, which at the time was investigating Seaport
Traders and other local gun importers and dealers for their contributions to
rising crime rates in the city. Hellstrom explained that, under order of the federal government, the company had produced more than 2 million firearms
for the US military for both world wars and had sold some 750,000 to the
United Kingdom alone. But now "through devious channels they have found
their way into the United States," where, like Oswald's would be, they were
customized for the consumer market and "sold at cutrate prices." Hellstrom

wanted to assure the LAPD that his company did not support commercial activities that put surplus guns in the hands of criminals, as such imports were "a threat to the legitimate arms industry so necessary as a standby for national defense."[9] As guns came under greater scrutiny in the 1960s, gunmakers would attempt to distinguish their legitimate, healthy, traditional industry from the seedy importers of cheap new and war surplus handguns.

Though guns like Oswald's Carcano came to Congress's attention as early as 1957, thanks to the gun industry's protectionist impulses, it was handguns like his Smith & Wesson that drew scrutiny in the years and months before the assassination of John F. Kennedy. In August 1963, Connecticut senator Thomas J. Dodd submitted a bill that aimed to address not an economic threat but the one such handguns presented to the social order as tools of crime and violence. Through two years of investigation via his chairmanship of the Senate Subcommittee on Juvenile Delinquency, Dodd had identified such guns as especially dangerous to young people. By 1964 he and his influential committee had traced the problem to "the mother lode of firearms, cached in foreign countries throughout the world, that fast-buck artists are exploiting to arm the delinquent teenagers, hoodlums, and psychopaths who walk the streets of America."[10] Dodd would spend seven years trying to figure out how best to control such guns, efforts that would lead to the most significant federal gun control legislation in thirty years.

The gun consumer market underwent dramatic changes during the years of Dodd's crusade. Cheap imports made the 1960s the decade of the handgun. In just a six-year span, from 1962 to 1968, US handgun sales quadrupled, and half of all handgun sales by 1968 were imports, which were across the board cheaper than their domestically produced counterparts.[11] And they seemed to pop up in all the wrong places: police departments reported that anywhere from 50 to 80 percent of guns seized in crimes were imports.[12] In 1958, the United States imported about 79,000 handguns; in the summer of 1968, when Congress passed a law intended to limit imports, they were on pace to exceed 1.2 million annually. Domestic producers manufactured roughly the same number of handguns that year, having increased their production threefold in the previous decade, attempting to keep pace with the cheap imports and meet growing consumer demand. And while rifles and shotguns remained popular consumer goods, the share of handguns out of total firearms produced and imported grew from about 15 percent in 1953 to nearly 40 percent fifteen years later.[13] If Oswald's Carcano told a story about the consumer gun market in the 1950s, his other imported gun narrated that market's changes in the tumultuous 1960s.

Dodd never identified gun capitalism as the problem—it's not something he could or would have done as a liberal trying to hold together the country's "vital center" as various radicalisms pulled it apart in the 1960s. But his dogged focus on unrestricted competition from imports and his efforts to identify gun importers as illegitimate practitioners of gun commerce revealed that at root he understood the problem as one of market regulation.[14] He would have to prevent gun capitalism from arming the population, one increasingly suspicious and fearful of not only communists but also neighbors, strangers, and millions of Black Americans marching for political and economic justice and against state violence. But ultimately Dodd, a gun-state senator, would accept the fundamental validity of gun commerce, attempting to navigate between the virtuous and unvirtuous user, buying into the mythology of the "law-abiding citizen." The guardrails Dodd would construct, as they were implemented in the 1968 Gun Control Act, merely gave gun capitalists official endorsement to find markets and buyers with the confidence that what they were doing was protected by law and sanctioned by the liberal state.

THE COLD WAR DREW TOM DODD TO POLITICS, and he made it part of his brand. "I'm just a typical American boy from a typical American town, I believe in God and Senator Dodd and keeping old Castro down," sang Phil Ochs in "Draft Dodger Rag" (1965). "Better dead than red," Ochs had mocked, but Dodd was a true believer. The atmosphere of McCarthyism pulled him into a run for a US House seat representing his native Connecticut in 1952, as Dodd worried that Senator Joseph McCarthy's brand of extremist demagoguery was as much a threat to the American way of life as left-wing extremism. He had seen political extremism up close, first prosecuting Klan members in the South in the late 1930s as part of the Justice Department's earliest iteration of the Civil Rights Division, and then for eighteen months in Nuremberg as a top prosecutor in the trials of Nazi war criminals. "It was a long time before he could sleep soundly again," a 1960s profile noted; so much time gathering evidence of some of history's worst crimes left him "weary and soul-sick." He later recalled how the trials shaped him into the kind of anti-McCarthyite cold warrior he became: "I was conducting a postmortem of the Nazi terror machine, but I saw communism's similarities in a thousand details," he said. "Neither tyranny tolerates opposition; both menace the world with their hate ideologies—the Nazis in the name of race hate, the communists in the name of class hate."[15]

Dodd's public service career was virtually coterminous with New Deal liberalism, beginning right out of Yale Law School in 1933 with the FBI—he was there for a shootout between agents and John Dillinger's gang in Wisconsin, which left two dead—and ending with his failed 1970 Senate campaign.[16] The New Deal faith in an American way between fascism and communism defined Dodd's liberal optimism: the slogan for that 1970 campaign, "Nothing is wrong with America that what's right won't heal," was awkward, to be sure, but it succinctly expressed his belief that New Deal liberalism was the moderate, middle path between the two extremes that tore the twentieth century apart.[17]

In the intense heat of the 1960s American crucible Dodd worried that those extremes could arm themselves too easily. His Senate subcommittee operated under the auspices of investigating "juvenile delinquency," but Dodd interpreted that charge liberally. In 1965, for instance, one of his committee staffers went undercover to gather evidence of the gun-running activities of the Minutemen, a right-wing extremist group preparing its members to resist an imminent communist takeover of the United States. He found the Minutemen encouraging their members to partake in the limitless postwar bounty of cheap guns, especially war surplus—in publications, the Minutemen encouraged members shopping for weapons to choose high-quality authentic military guns and "avoid civilian-made copies of military-made firearms."[18] Later, in the aftermath of urban uprisings in Watts, Detroit, Newark, and dozens of other locations, Dodd would argue that easy access to guns served as kindling for the fires lit by extremists using war surplus rifles to target law enforcement. Dodd's center would not hold if extremists on the right and left could arm themselves for protracted conflict.

Dodd's first foray into gun politics was subtle. Even before becoming chair of the Juvenile Delinquency Subcommittee, he had made entreaties on behalf of the powerful gun industry in his state. In the spring of 1960, his staff had contacted CIA officials to ask if the agency would have any objection if the Senate imposed a "heavy duty on the import of foreign arms"—Dodd's chief concern was Sam Cummings's Interarms, and he wanted to confirm that the company was not operating on behalf of the agency to advance US national security and interest. (As it turned out, Interarms was not, in the words of one CIA official in 1960, "our baby.")[19] In August 1961 Dodd submitted a resolution to the Senate that would have advised the State Department to "clamp down on the importation of foreign surplus military rifles" that were "endangering the survival of our domestic arms industry." His concerns were mostly economic, with a nod to national security; he said nothing of the social impact of firearms or of violence, which would occupy his committee in years to come. He labeled Cummings's trade "competition which cannot be called legitimate." The importers were flooding the market with "goods which were never produced for commercial use, which were never intended for civilian use, and which were produced for the armed forces of foreign nations." He singled out England, Italy, Sweden, and Germany, and accused the importers of bringing in from behind the Iron Curtain firearms that "go on the market in competition with our own sporting rifles made by free American workmen earning decent wages in an industry which is absolutely essential to our national defense." Three months later he pressed his case in a letter to President Kennedy.[20]

The Senate resolution and the petition to Kennedy got no traction, but they demonstrated how the Senate's most stalwart 1960s gun control champion could be vulnerable to criticism about his motivations. Dodd resolved the irony of a gun state legislator fighting for gun control by focusing his efforts on the singular danger of cheap imports, a point he regularly emphasized for voters back home. The week before the 1964 election he sent a letter to the thousands of Nutmeggers who worked in the industry to assure them that rumors that a new federal gun law would mean job losses were "entirely without foundation." Any bill would target mail-order sales, and he claimed that a majority of such sales were for "these cut-rate foreign surplus weapons." Indeed, Dodd emphasized, he was championing their industry: destroying the commerce of "fly-by-night mail order firms which exist by selling cheap foreign surplus weapons" would protect American jobs. Most of the big Connecticut manufacturers had helped him prepare the legislation. "The best thing that can happen to your company," he concluded, "would be to have this foreign gun racket broken up and to have the gun business returned to responsible domestic firms."[21]

Critics were thus able to claim that Dodd was simply toeing the line for the traditional US gun manufacturers. Even his longtime aide on the Juvenile Delinquency Subcommittee recalled a gun industry executive saying, "We've got Dodd in our pocket." Another aide claimed that "often the staff's best efforts were canceled by Dodd's behind-the-scenes deals" with the gun industry. Smelling hypocrisy, longtime Washington political gossip Drew Pearson hounded Dodd over his connections to gunmakers.[22] Writing a decade later, journalist Robert Sherrill said that Dodd's new focus on crime in 1963 was a matter of adjusting course when the national security argument no longer worked. The kinds of restrictions Dodd promoted over the years would do little damage to the traditional manufacturers but were instead intended to crush the importers.[23] As he learned of these undercurrents of gun capitalism and then sought to contain them, Dodd would serve as the bridge between guns as a minor foreign relations problem in the 1950s and guns as a significant social problem in the 1960s.

IT'S IMPOSSIBLE TO TALK ABOUT GUNS in the 1960s without talking about crime, and it's impossible to talk about crime in the 1960s without talking about broader demographic and social change. By the middle of the decade it was an axiom of American life that "crime rates are rising," which only meant in a very specific empirical sense that the numbers Americans relied on to tell them about crime, derived from the FBI's recently implemented Uniform Crime Reporting (UCR) program, demonstrated that "crime rates are rising." The numbers went up each year, no doubt. And politicians concerned with crime, like Dodd, knew how to wield those numbers effectively to push for legislative responses, or, more cynically, to inflame white racial anxieties. But careful observers knew from the outset of the UCR program that the numbers painted an incomplete picture, even if they were persuasive in an era when scientific and bureaucratic authority commanded greater public trust. For one thing, crime rates went up when municipal, state, and federal agencies got better at reporting crimes—which is exactly what happened during this era. You were not necessarily more likely to be robbed in New York City in 1960 compared to 1950, but if you were robbed, it was more likely that your data point would be reported to the FBI as part of its national initiative to gather crime data. The FBI wouldn't even accept crime reporting from New York City until 1952 because the bureau believed it too unreliable, corrupted by local officials who regularly manipulated it with the goal of making city law enforcement look more effective than it was. As standards improved, the new data swelled the crime rate.[24]

These reported rates also generally did not account for the most salient demographic fact of the era: the baby boom. Throughout the decade the percentage of the population represented by the prime age range for committing crimes, fifteen to twenty-four, steadily rose. More young people meant more crime because young people, young men especially, were most likely to be perpetrators of crimes. The percentage of the population in the fifteen-to-twenty-four category grew each year of the 1960s, so it only made sense that crime rates would grow in tandem. There were about 27 million people in that age group in 1960; by 1970 the figure had climbed 50 percent to 40 million.[25] Crime rates also failed to account for rates of urbanization; more Americans were moving to cities or densely populated suburbs, and crime rates go up as population density increases. "What appears to be a crime explosion," wrote prominent political scientist James Q. Wilson in 1966, "may in fact be a population explosion."[26] Critics knew all of this—in fact, Johnson's own crime commission in 1967 said that Americans ought to be skeptical of reported crime figures—but it did not stop politicians from wielding simple numbers without care, or journalists from reporting them without qualification.[27]

Dodd would use the specter of crime to justify spending more than seven years working on gun control in the 1960s. In 1961 he assumed chairmanship of the Senate Judiciary Committee's Subcommittee on Juvenile Delinquency, a body that had attained a small degree of infamy in the 1950s for its investigations into comic book publishing, which led to the establishment of industry self-censorship through the Comics Code Authority.[28] The influence of popular culture on young people remained a theme throughout Dodd's tenure as chair, with representations of violence, sex, and drug use all coming under fire, but Dodd would use his position to attack the seemingly more adult and serious issue of gun violence and the politicians, industry leaders, and national organizations that he believed stood in the way of addressing it.[29]

From the perspective of the twenty-first century, a committee tasked with investigating "juvenile delinquency" might seem an unlikely instrument for tackling an issue as vexing as gun violence, but in the context of the early 1960s it seemed perfectly sensible. Dodd assumed chairmanship of the committee just as the baby boomers entered social life in vast, and, to many people, terrifying numbers. Older generations in the modern era always seem to find something to fear in the young, and this was never more so the case than during the 1960s, when it appeared to members of Dodd's older generation that, left to its own devices, the baby boomers would bring America to its knees. Dodd's generation had inherited ideas about adolescence as a period during which young people are susceptible to the very worst influences.[30] Without proper rearing, rebellious adolescents became irredeemable criminals, and Dodd and the rest of his generation were staring down the barrel of the century's largest-ever cohort of young people emerging into adolescence and young adulthood.

There was a logic, then, to Dodd's Juvenile Delinquency Subcommittee taking on a problem as widespread and challenging as gun violence. More young men meant more crime, and more guns meant greater access to the most lethal weapons used in the commission of crimes, now widely available to a postwar generation raised on consumerism. More cheap accessible guns and more impressionable adolescents meant more terror in the streets, uncontrollable delinquents equipped with a newly infamous variety of gun: the "Saturday Night Special."

THROUGH MUCH OF THE 1950S, if the phrase "Saturday Night Special" appeared in a local newspaper, it was likely an advertisement for a fried-chicken or roast-turkey dinner at a nearby restaurant. At some point in the decade, however, it became a law enforcement term of art. The Marshall, Texas,

"Listen—for just a little bit more we can get a real one," 1964 (republished in 1971). Cartoonist Herblock demonstrates the pervasive belief that the largely unregulated gun market made it easy for children to access firearms. (© The Herb Block Foundation via Library of Congress)

newspaper, for example, reported in 1955 on an FBI firearms expert's visit to the city police department, where he explained that police officers "must know their guns," which they furnished themselves in a small city like Marshall, and that these firearms had to be of a high quality. He warned against "Saturday Night Specials, suicide specials"—whether these guns evoked suicide because they were easily accessible for someone intent on the act or because their infamous unreliability made them dangerous, it was unclear. The mark of a good weapon to this FBI instructor was its higher caliber: .38-caliber at a minimum, .44 or .45 preferably. Saturday Night Specials, being small and easily concealed, tended toward .22-caliber, smaller bullets with less "stopping power," even if deadly enough at close range.[31]

"Saturday Night Special" was still an obscure term in March 1963 when thirteen-year-old Gary Turner found himself photographed on the cover of the *El Paso Herald Post* holding just such a weapon. Gary's mom, Virginia, the city editor for the *Herald Post*, had asked him if he'd like to buy a gun. "It sounds neat," Gary said. "But won't I go to jail? How can a kid get a real gun?" She explained that laws regulating the mail-order shipment of guns were so loose that it was easy for a child to send away for a cheap one. With her nose on a story, Virginia encouraged Gary to scan through some "western magazines" with ads for all sorts of guns and to choose one he liked—she described his selection as an "ugly, deadly snub nose .38 caliber revolver"—and to send a ten-dollar deposit by money order. The California firm wrote back with a statement for Gary to sign, which would affirm that he was a US citizen of "legal age" (which varied by state) and not a fugitive, drug addict, or convicted felon, all categories of people barred from purchasing firearms by the 1938 Federal Firearms Act. The signature form was a common way for mail-order dealers to adhere to the letter of the FFA, even if the loopholes were obvious. Gary and his mom didn't really want to violate federal law, so she initialed for him. Several weeks later the gun arrived at the local office of Railway Express, the country's largest "common carrier" (i.e., privately owned) shipper of firearms, which could not otherwise be mailed to consumers through the US Postal Service, per federal regulation. Virginia and Gary went down to the Railway office, where the agent asked her to sign for the shipment, knowing, based on the company's own serial number identifications, that it contained a gun. If Gary were alone, the agent said, he'd still have to hand over the goods, "if the child has proper identification . . . and if he raises cain [*sic*] about getting the package." Railway Express had no legal authority to deny it. Gary paid the remaining balance of $13.48 and walked out armed.[32]

Virginia wasn't going to let the story end there. The next day she and Gary brought it for examination to El Paso chief of police C. J. Horak. "I sure wouldn't want to trust this thing to shoot," Horak said. The handgun was "obviously a used .38 caliber Webley or Enfield," referring to the handguns issued to British soldiers in the Second World War. A California firearms dealer had mailed thirteen-year-old Gary Turner an imported war surplus weapon, a handgun that, as evidenced by the wear Horak detected, likely saw military action. "There should be some control of this kind of thing," Horak mused, "these 'Saturday Night Specials.'"[33]

It wouldn't be until the urban uprisings of 1967 and 1968 that "Saturday Night Special" fully entered everyday parlance to describe a cheap, unreliable, and easily concealable handgun, which often carried a racial connotation linked to fears of Black rebellion and street crime.[34] According to politicians like Dodd, law enforcement officials, and even the NRA, these guns served no good lawful purpose. In 1967, Dodd asked William L. Cahalan, a prosecutor from Wayne County, Michigan, to clarify what he meant when used the phrase "Saturday Night Special": "That's the jargon of our locality, a colloquialism," Cahalan explained. "That is a cheap gun purchased in Toledo. . . . The Saturday Night Specials are for someone who wants to do a little job on a Saturday night. He goes down to Toledo and buys the pistol. And as you know, of course, most holdups take place on a Saturday night, so we have referred to them as Saturday Night Specials."[35] By the early 1970s, it was a household phrase conjuring up the worst of widespread random urban violence, and a new generation of political leaders would push for stringent control of these easily concealable weapons. Even southern rock icons Lynyrd Skynyrd, in a 1975 song, denounced these handguns, with a "barrel that's blue and cold / It ain't good for nothing but puttin' men in a six feet hole." (The band's solution for handguns? "Why don't we dump 'em, people, to the bottom of the sea?")[36]

Dodd got there before Skynyrd, though he was most likely to call them "mail-order-type" guns, since his committee had been made aware that there were virtually no restrictions on the mail-order trade in these guns. Even where there were restrictions—in Chicago, for example, where a resident who wished to purchase a handgun needed a police permit to do so—thousands of people still bought guns easily through the mail and bypassed local control efforts.[37] Investigators also found that many of these guns went to teenagers. "Mentally ill, rebellious, fascinated by handguns and other weapons of violence, they need protection for their own sake and for the sake of society," Dodd said as he introduced his first gun control bill in August 1963. "We cannot go on tolerating the unrestrained sale of handguns to these juveniles."[38]

The Dodd Committee's first target, then, became the handgun, the cheap kind easily available to anyone with a few dollars and, if one were ineligible to purchase a gun under local or state law, the willingness to lie on a mail-in form like the one Gary's mom signed. Dodd believed as early as 1963 that imported handguns posed a special problem. In that same speech on the Senate floor he criticized the low quality and poor design of imported weapons, which made them "dangerous to the user." He noted that the NRA's official mouthpiece, *American Rifleman*, which accepted ad revenue from dealers selling all varieties of surplus imported rifles, refused to carry ads for cheap imported handguns. Dodd cited an extraordinary number of gun imports over the previous five years, anywhere from 5 to 7 million, which conveniently lumped handguns with rifles and shotguns. Concluding on a point that would become a mantra for the gun control movement in the decades to come, Dodd said that "this situation exists nowhere else in the world. The United States is the only nation that has virtually no control over lethal concealable weapons." He blamed this "scandalous situation" on the "millions of cheap foreign weapons [that] were dumped into our country."[39]

Dodd's 1963 bill proposed modest regulations on mail-order handgun sales. Any buyer would have to sign an affidavit attesting to eligibility to purchase a handgun according to state and federal law. It was as considerate an accommodation to gun capitalism as Dodd could have crafted. But such a limited measure, Dodd believed, would nevertheless keep guns out of the hands of the Gary Turners of the world as well as buyers with criminal records or any other disqualifying "disability," in the language of the time. Less than a week after the killings in Dallas, Dodd revised the bill to include long guns, that is, rifles like Oswald's but also shotguns. "The secrecy which shrouds the mail order gun business," Dodd said days after his president's—his friend's—murder, "has allowed those with the capabilities of committing monstrous crimes against society to clandestinely avail themselves of the means to do so."[40]

The first two years of committee investigations had focused on the process of buying a gun—who bought them, how they bought them, and what kinds of limited measures Congress could pass to help law enforcement control them. In the years following the assassination, the committee would attempt to address the supply side of the gun problem as much as the demand. Dodd turned his attention to stemming the tide of imports.

SAM CUMMINGS HARDLY made a leap of faith when he committed to importing guns to sell on the US market, where supply and demand surged in tandem in the postwar era. Between frontier mythologies and notions of American masculinity connected to gun ownership, the increase in leisure time and disposable income, and a mass media encouraging consumerism as a way to secure the American way of life in a hostile world, selling guns was a good bet in the 1950s. But gun-selling took place in different registers.

Magazines like *American Rifleman* carried ads from iconic gunmakers like Winchester and Remington as well as dealers, like Cummings, who straddled the line between respectable and unscrupulous business. But with the surging availability of cheap guns, most of them imports from Europe, distributors and dealers now had a surplus of firearms to unload, and the traditional means for doing that—local gun stores, pawnshops—wouldn't cut it.

Out there was a national market and a wider audience than what they saw as the traditional gun-buying crowd—men looking for hunting rifles—and they needed a better way to reach it. When they considered the kind of buyers who were fascinated by guns but couldn't afford a name-brand US-made gun with a price tag of $100 or more, they thought of young men, or even teenage boys, who didn't yet have steady incomes, or of war veterans fascinated with Europe's and Asia's wartime weapons, confident in their ability to handle firearms. (Researchers in 1968 discovered that a military veteran was more than twice as likely as a nonveteran to own a handgun.)[41] Importers' ubiquitous advertisements, and the publications in which they ran them—pulp magazines—speak to their efforts to create this new kind of market.

Dodd and his committee zeroed in on the influence of the pulps, publications that were seen, like the guns Dodd sought to regulate, as cheap, seedy, and dangerous. In both their stories and their advertisements, the pulps sold sex and violence to audiences of young men. Americans mourning the assassination of President Kennedy, for instance, might have seen displayed in bookstores and comic shops the latest issue of *Adventure* ("The Man's Magazine of Exciting Fiction"), featuring stories like "He Rides with Death" and "Trapped in a Rattlesnake Pit" alongside a photo display of scantily clad British starlet Margaret Lee.[42] Ads for books purporting to teach men sex techniques to please unsatisfied women were common, and disconcertingly juxtaposed with pitches for training in hypnosis. (A Los Angeles police official described one local gun dealer as "mixed up in several other fly-by-night type businesses dealing in rather nebulous products . . . [including] a breast developer, a lotion to remove facial lines, a book entitled, 'The Sexual Criminal,' and a hair grower.")[43]

Gun ads were commonplace. The December 1963 issue of *Adventure* had several for small handguns, including a "Black Vendetta"—"Imported from Italy"—a small revolver with a white pearl handle promising to fire six .22-caliber blank cartridges and suited for "stage, sporting events, boating, protection." The characteristically seedy seller, who also advertised replica police badges, handcuffs, an "imported wolf killer stiletto" knife, and a deck of cards featuring photos of nude women, received orders at an office on Sixth Avenue in New York City.[44]

Like the "Black Vendetta," most of the guns advertised in these pulps identified their foreign origins. Indeed, the implied or explicit claims about European craftsmanship or exoticism were part of the sales pitch. For just $6.95,
the Best Values Company of Newark, New Jersey, offered a .22-caliber "German automatic 6-shot repeater" that was "Precision made by the Finest West
German Gunsmiths." Advertised just three pages later was an identical looking
gun from Big Three Inc. of New York City that was "machined with all the care
and precision of West Germany's finest gunsmiths"—the New York firm was
asking $7.95. Dealers saw the weapon's Germanness, or general foreignness,
as part of its appeal, surely linked to the sense of conquest over the German
foe during the Second World War. "German precision" was a common theme
in ads, and replicas of the Luger, the famous German pistol that saw service
in both world wars, were popular, like the .12-caliber "Kruger pistol" offered
for $3.00 by the Kruger Corporation of Alhambra, California.[45] Foreign guns
were all over these pulp advertisements to the near exclusion of iconic US
handgun makers like Colt and Smith & Wesson, whose guns could retail for
twenty times the price of a cheap import. A 1957 ad from the Lytle Novelty Co.
of Long Beach, California, promised "authentic replicas" of various German,
Spanish, Russian, Italian, Japanese, Belgian, and Czechoslovakian handguns
for $3.00 each, or two for $5.00.[46] Given the seemingly limitless availability of
cheap firearms in Europe, these "replicas" likely were made overseas, and may
have actually been the genuine article, perhaps broken down at some point
into scrap and reassembled.

Gary Turner's mother Virginia Turner was not the only member of the
press to take notice of this advertising to young people. Investigative journalist
Jack Anderson was on the case too, warning, in an article titled, "It's Easy for
Your Child to Get a Gun," that "comic books and girlie magazines are packed
with advertisements that would make any sane adult shudder." He recounted a
father discovering his fifteen-year-old son had purchased, for $12.88, a ".38 six-
shot, double-action revolver made for British Commandos during World War
II." "Aww gee, Dad, most of the guys have them," the kid reportedly whined.
Anderson cautioned all parents to be on the alert: "Are you sure *your* child
hasn't a weapon hidden around somewhere? For the tools of death are turning
up in the most respectable homes." Anderson explained how these guns ended
up advertised in comic books and tucked away in kids' closets. European manufacturers made small, cheap handguns for less than one dollar each and were
unloading them on the US market by the thousands. They came disassembled
as scrap to bypass higher customs rates, then they were reassembled for sale
to America's eager teens.[47]

Postwar fears of youth rebellion may have been largely imaginary, or least overblown, but the materiality of guns in America was real. Advertisements at once romanticized and demystified guns. They promised to make you instantly powerful and attractive, and they weren't any longer taboo objects hidden away in fathers' and grandfathers' closets and basements. Indeed, guns were part of the bounty America claimed for its victory in the war and for keeping the world safe from totalitarianism. Cheap imports built a market, one that would balloon dramatically in the 1960s. Mixed with white anxieties about urban uprisings and possible restrictions on access to guns, they would help to make the country an armed camp by 1968, and one ever ready and eager to acquire more firepower.

WHEN THE DODD COMMITTEE returned to action in the spring of 1964, its chairman had decided on a new strategy: "We are now concerned," he said at the opening of a new round of hearings, "with those dealers whose firms typically advertise in cheap pulp publications or erotic magazines; whose principle business is in so-called junk guns that foreign governments have found obsolete."[48] Dodd didn't hesitate to make political hay out of the confusing distinction between cheap new handguns manufactured in postwar Europe and war surplus guns made before and during the war, many of which were by necessity of high quality, at least in original design. For the senator, lumping the Carcanos and Mausers in with the "Black Vendetta" and its ilk could kill two proverbial birds with one stone: it would help rescue the traditional New England gun manufacturers while also addressing a perceived source of street crime.

Dodd started by going after high-volume sellers of "junk guns," dealers whom law enforcement believed were responsible for a flood of cheap foreign-made firearms that found their way into the hands of people committing crimes. Dodd wanted to know just what these dealers were thinking when they shipped thousands of guns across the country to strangers who had done nothing more than fill out a cursory form and submit a money order in exchange for a deadly weapon. In addition to subpoenaing their records (or at least trying to), the committee interviewed two prominent "fast-buck artists" who sold tens of thousands of guns by mail, Haywood "Hy" Hunter and George Rose, both of Los Angeles.[49] The investigations into these two characters demonstrated not only the suspect business practices that sent guns into the hands of plenty of people who shouldn't have had them but also the extent to which those practices were built on American access to the world's surplus of firearms.

Dodd first dragged Hy Hunter before his committee. Not yet thirty years old, Hunter was a veteran of the Pacific War and an ambitious businessman with "Hollywood flair," according to a 1955 *Guns* magazine profile. He was photographed examining a revolver alongside war hero and movie star Audie Murphy. Hunter may not have had Murphy's looks, but he had the celebrity swagger. He boasted of operating the "largest gunshop in the world," which included exotic collections like a "stable full of guns from Scotland Yard." Hunter's Los Angeles storefront, opened as a pawnshop on La Brea Avenue in 1949, quickly transitioned to selling guns and recorded $3.5 million in sales by 1958.[50] The *Guns* profile placed Hunter in the context of the postwar gun boom. "The secret of Hunter's success is simple but it is no miracle," it noted. "He cashed in on the hottest hobby in the land—guns." A reader would not be surprised to see a new magazine dedicated to guns proclaim, "America is going gun-happy!" but *Guns* backed up the claim: television romanticized firearms, GIs were comfortable with them, and economic growth meant "increased prosperity for John Q. Public." Keen investors like Hunter saw the demand before the traditional manufacturers and dealers, and he recognized that cheap supply was available in Europe. "The sudden flood of weapons [from Europe] set off a buying spree in the States and sowed the seeds for the postwar boom of the gun hobby," *Guns* concluded.[51]

Hunter's swagger, along with his suspect business practices, also made him well known to law enforcement officials in California and elsewhere. In fact, days before his 1964 testimony he had been arrested in Los Angeles on a warrant issued in Oregon. Hunter had recently contracted with a dealer in Portland to sell 500 guns that Hunter would acquire as surplus from police forces in Singapore. Hunter claimed he had bought these guns sight unseen, bidding $1,250 for the lot of them with the intention of netting several thousand dollars of profit while serving as a middleman in the transaction. When they arrived at customs in Oregon—shipped under a false name, "Krone Internationale Waffenhandelsgesellschaft MBH," because Hunter's name was infamous among customs officials—inspectors assessed the value of the total lot at $69,000 and also discovered a couple dozen machine guns in the shipment. They noticed that Hunter had only listed the value at $481, and he had not declared his intent to import machine guns, putting him on the wrong side of the 1934 National Firearms Act.[52]

Such a violation of federal law was of some interest to the committee, but members recognized that laws already existed to prohibit someone like Hunter from distributing these especially dangerous weapons on American streets. Even Dodd the crusader frequently echoed conservative criticisms that Congress should not be in the business of creating new gun laws to regulate activities old laws already covered. What interested the committee instead was Hunter's legal method for circumventing firearms customs duties. Investigators discovered that Hunter managed to import and sell guns so cheaply by declaring used guns as "scrap" rather than as guns. Import duties on guns in the early 1960s were about 42 percent, while duties on scrap metal were just 12 percent, and the declared value of scrap could be much lower than guns, further cutting costs. Importers like Hunter could claim they followed the letter of the law in the sense that guns like those from Singapore were not new manufactured products but were metal goods that had been "scrapped," but nobody believed importers brought such guns into the country with any intention other than to sell them as guns. They were not hunks of metal to be melted down and reprocessed into some other object; they were good firearms in fine working condition that until recently had been used by a national police force. Hunter told the committee that this was the common method for importing "old guns"—essentially any firearm that was not newly manufactured.[53]

Hunter was not alone in this practice. Just in Los Angeles, many hundreds of people enrolled each year in a correspondence course on importing and selling these sorts of guns through the mail, officials from the city's police department told Congress.[54] Investigators couldn't pin down exactly how many guns came into the country this way, but the number was likely in the tens of thousands annually, and perhaps in the six figures by the time the Gun Control Act passed in 1968. Disassembled gun parts also entered the country at the lower duty rate, only to be reassembled on arrival. Gun capitalism had proven itself adept at navigating whatever mild restrictions were implemented to regulate it.

Los Angeles dealer George Rose admitted as much to Dodd's committee. His firm purchased cheap .22-caliber handguns in Germany. At production both the gun barrel and frame would be stamped with a serial number; the barrel would be removed and a "blank" barrel attached, essentially making the gun a "starter pistol" (one fired to start races but not appropriate for live ammunition). Both the starter pistol and the original barrel would be shipped to the United States, where a 12 percent customs rate would be applied. When they reached Rose's shop in Los Angeles, his employees would reattach the original barrel and have a brand-new handgun to sell by mail-order. Dodd and investigators made much of this "conversion" process, believing that Rose bought starter pistols, which ostensibly were not weapons, and then through some metalworking process "converted" them to guns that could fire live ammunition. Committee members often found themselves discussing the intricacies of various processes for the reboring of gun barrels and other metalworking techniques. Rose made clear that his approach entailed nothing so complicated: "The guns that we import as guns were sold as guns, and the fact that we imported them as starter pistols was just a matter of customs. . . . We do not convert. As a matter of fact, we are not equipped to convert. All we do is assemble."[55]

Such practices made it difficult for the committee and federal officials to know exactly how many guns had come into the country by the mid-1960s. They could use State's Office of Munitions Control data, but such figures could be undependable for several reasons: among other things, an OMC license only indicated the number of guns an importer intended to import, not whether or not they were actually sold on the US market, and licenses expired after six months, at which point an importer could reapply to import the same guns, and individual guns could be double-counted. Also, the OMC only required import licenses for guns with barrels larger than .22-caliber, which meant it did not count the hundreds of thousands of the smallest, cheapest handguns giving law enforcement so many headaches. There was the unregulated Canada pipeline as well. Finally, the OMC essentially eliminated its data collection and processing unit in 1961, a consequence of State Department budget cuts, and the office only resumed data processing in 1967, more than a decade into the import flood. In fact it was precisely because the office fielded so many license requests by 1961 that it had to shift personnel to fulfilling those requests, at which point officials decided to close the statistical unit and just fulfill data requests on an ad hoc basis.[56] So for most of the peak era of imports, the decade after 1958, State officials had neglected data collection and processing, and thus there was no one in the international affairs bureaucracy who might notice the incredible accumulation of foreign weapons and its potential domestic economic and social effects.

Another means of gathering data on gun imports was the Census Bureau, which in turn collected data from the Customs Services. But Hunter and Rose demonstrated how unreliable that data could be: by 1967, the bureau reported a million guns coming into the country annually, but those were only *declared* guns; it also tracked tens of millions of dollars in gun "parts" entering, and that didn't account for the guns that entered the country as "scrap," even if they were, like Hunter's Singapore shipment, fully assembled and operational guns. When Hunter had told Singapore police officials to ship the guns as scrap, they were baffled; they wrote back to indicate that it was "not advisable to transport the arms as scrap material as most of them are still in fairly good condition."[57] They just didn't understand Hunter's con, as so many other overseas sellers surely did. And law enforcement hadn't caught Hunter because of the con; rather they caught him because he mistakenly imported guns he couldn't legally sell in the country.

It was not just their various shady business practices that brought Dodd's committee down on Hunter and Rose. It was also their hostile disposition toward investigation. Sam Cummings wanted legislators to see importers as upstanding operators of legitimate businesses; he was a man, after all, who dined with heads of state and defense ministers. Hunter and Rose did incalculable damage to their colleagues in that regard. Hunter complied with Dodd's 1964 subpoena by supplying the committee a single box of "records"—in reality he gave them a box full of gun magazines—despite the fact that he had been in the gun business for fifteen years, and despite the 1938 Federal Firearms Act's requirements for record-keeping. Dodd was livid: "Do you seriously represent to this committee that this trash that you sent here are your records, as you are required to keep them under the Federal law?" Hunter tried to explain that he had recently relocated his business, and the rest of his life, to West Germany, to be closer to the manufacturing operations that fueled his US trade. He had shipped all of his records to his new offices in Germany, and he invited the committee to fly to Europe to examine them. At one point Hunter tried to evade questioning by claiming that there were some subjects about which he could not speak because they involved an alleged CIA front company called American Weapons Corporation, which had been affiliated with Sam Cummings. Subcommittee investigators contacted CIA officials, and an internal CIA document later released noted that the agency had "no dealings with Hunter or his American Weapons Company [sic]" (though the rest of the sentence was redacted).[58]

When the committee subpoenaed George Rose of Seaport Traders to testify in April 1964, they did not yet know that his company had sold Oswald the handgun used to murder J. D. Tippit.[59] Rose arrived prepared to stonewall the investigation, and his intransigence bordered on the comical. He responded to most queries as if he hadn't heard the question or he misunderstood it. He pretended not to know things someone in his position—a mail-order gun dealer who had shipped tens of thousands of guns nationwide since he started his business in 1956—would know. He pretended not to know that many "deactivated war trophies," or "dewats," could easily be made fully operational with some basic metalworking. He pretended not to know that his firm had sold a dewat machine gun to a student at the University of Mississippi at the height of that campus's recent upheaval over the arrival of African American students. He pretended not to know that Chicago, where his business had sold more than 2,500 guns, had a local ordinance requiring a permit for handgun purchases.[60]

One thing that Rose did know was that admitting to knowing these things would put him in legal jeopardy. The subcommittee found, for instance, that 22 percent of those guns he had sold in Chicago went to people legally prohibited from owning them, and 90 percent went to addresses in neighborhoods plagued by crime. Rose pleaded innocence and said he would no longer ship guns to Chicago. But he also defended cheap imports, arguing that prohibitions against them "would take away the pleasure of shooting from people in the low-income groups."[61] It was the very argument Sam Cummings had made, but if Cummings wanted import defenders of a certain caliber, Hunter and Rose likely weren't what he had in mind. Ultimately, however, the two were small fish in a big pond. When Dodd accused Hunter of conducting "a very substantial business" in mail-order guns, Hunter retorted, "Not compared with men like Sam Cummings, not even one-half of 1 percent."[62]

MEN LIKE HY HUNTER, GEORGE ROSE, AND SAM CUMMINGS found very few friends in politics. Even the National Rifle Association, which had steadfastly opposed new federal gun controls in the 1930s and worked with Congress and the Roosevelt administration to limit their reach, was not willing to go to bat for the importers. From the outset of Dodd's investigations, the NRA was once again a constant presence in negotiations over potential new federal regulations. The organization worked behind closed doors with committee staff to craft legislation that would be acceptable to its surging membership, which had grown by leaps and bounds in the postwar years, swelling with veterans interested in hunting and shooting sports.[63] NRA executive vice president Franklin Orth, responsible for the organization's day-to-day activities, testified before Dodd's committee several times over the years. He stated in 1963 that the NRA was "on the record as being ready and eager to continue to offer to the committee the benefit of our vast experience in the field of firearms legislation," and Dodd repeatedly and publicly thanked the organization for such support. Orth cautioned that the NRA's position was that the "crime problem will not be solved by denying to reputable people the right to keep and bear arms." But he did acknowledge that the federal government had a role to play in restricting certain kinds of arms. Orth observed that Dodd's bill would limit "the relatively inexpensive imported pistols and revolvers that are advertised in many cheap pulp magazines throughout the country." The NRA, he continued, "has conducted product-evaluation studies of many of these handguns and has found them to be largely worthless for sporting purposes." In fact, *American Rifleman* would not even accept advertising dollars from the retailers of these firearms. "We do not want these improper types of weapons to be floating around the United States," Orth concluded. "Somehow we have to find a way to bar them."[64] Even as the NRA became more obstinate later in the decade—Dodd would shift from thanking the organization for its cooperation in 1964 to condemning it for its intransigence by 1968—it remained opposed to the import of cheap handguns.

The committee interviewed a parade of witnesses who testified to the flaws of most gun control proposals. But these same witnesses changed their tunes when it came to the problem of cheap imports. Arizona governor Paul Fannin, for instance, argued that in looking to control guns, Dodd and his Senate colleagues were looking to control a problem that didn't exist. If there was a problem, it was one Congress had yet to address: "Our state, indeed no State, and very few communities, west of the Mississippi has a problem relating to mail-order firearms, unless it be one created by failure of the Congress to restrict the importation of worthless, cheap foreign pistols, and castoff foreign military rifles into this country. This is the real problem, but only Congress can solve it."[65]

Fannin's testimony was joined by fellow Arizonan Ben Avery, a journalist and leader in state gun organizations. He came to speak, he said, "to help stem the tide of unreasoning emotionalism aimed, apparently, at disarming the American people because of a tragedy that all of the laws in the world could not prevent." Like the NRA and Fannin, Avery urged Congress not to punish "law-abiding citizens" for the crimes of a few. But he too had nothing good to say about the "dumping of literally millions of castoff military guns of foreign countries along with a staggering array of cheap pistols made with cheap labor overseas."[66] Avery blamed popular culture like Westerns, which "make killing an act of heroism," for the rapid expansion of this new consumer market—Hollywood glorified a cheap death at the end of the barrel of a cheap gun. These imports threatened the traditional gun culture that Avery and his fellow sportsmen venerated.

Seemingly everyone who came before Congress to talk about the nation's gun problem bashed cheap imports. Even the importers reluctantly acknowledged that their own products could have deleterious social effects. We know that what we do is not in the best interest of the public, importers like Hunter and Rose seemed to say, but we're going to keep making money from it as long as we can do it legally.

Frank Foote of the Nebraska Game, Forestation, and Parks Commission was having none of this. "Perhaps it is time that someone had a good word to say for the firearms importer and for surplus military weapons," he said in a testy exchange before Dodd's committee in 1965. Hunting was an expensive sport, he said. He had brought with him to the hearings one of his own guns, a high-end hunting rifle manufactured by Remington, one of the iconic

US gunmakers with production facilities in Dodd's Connecticut, among other places. ("I hope it is not loaded," Dodd smirked.) Foote contrasted it with a cheap foreign import, like the one Oswald used to kill Kennedy—a gun made in Italy, a scope from Japan, bullets from who-knows-where; Foote's Remington used parts and accessories made in Iowa, Colorado, Minnesota, and Dodd's state. But his rifle, retailing for some $200 (nearly $1,900 in 2022 dollars), was not an "entry-level" weapon for the gun-curious. Sure enough, what had originally drawn Foote into hunting in the first place was instead a cheap war surplus firearm, purchased in 1953 for $35. "This led to a great deal of interest on my part" in hunting culture, and here he was, a dozen years later, testifying before Congress, offering a class-based analysis against a gun control bill that specifically tried to steer clear of rifles and shotguns used for sport but that nevertheless had provoked the ire of sportsmen across the country.[67]

Foote's analysis traded the invented tradition of gun mythology for the invented tradition of consumerism. He connected his experience to a broader consumer culture, one in which shoppers always have their eyes on the next best thing, positioning guns alongside the bounty of manufactured products that transformed the social landscape of postwar America. "It is in our American tradition to trade up—cars, air conditioners, refrigerators, houses," he argued.[68] For Foote guns were another consumer product in that postwar landscape, part of the "tradition" of twentieth-century consumerism as much as they were a part of older mythologies of self-defense against tyranny or rugged frontier individualism.

Sam Cummings couldn't have said it better himself. Foote's testimony reaffirmed the argument Cummings had made eight years earlier in favor of cheap imports: they served as gateways to gun culture for many men in postwar America. Even to this day, many Americans disconnected from hunting culture tend to scoff at it as the pastime of lower-class "rednecks" without realizing that an individual can easily invest tens of thousands of dollars in not just hunting rifles but also the accoutrements of a hunting consumer lifestyle—the camouflage gear, the accessories, even the off-road vehicles that take hunters where standard automobiles can't go. Gun culture is, in short, a robust *consumer* culture, one in which millions of Americans, mostly men (and most of them white) participate enthusiastically, helping national retailers like Cabela's and Bass Pro Shops rake in billions of dollars annually. Importers like Cummings laid the foundations of that robust popular consumer culture in the 1950s and 1960s with cheap foreign guns.

Still, Foote would not defend cheap *hand*guns, and even Sam Cummings joined the traditional gun industry in pushing for restrictions on those sorts of firearms. By 1967, as the likelihood of some kind of gun legislation loomed on the horizon, Cummings's Interarms urged the administration, in a meeting with Treasury officials, to focus its attention on the cheaply manufactured imports and to exclude war surplus firearms, which were in many cases identical to guns manufactured by US companies. They were not "junk," Cummings argued, telling Congress that millions of Americans "would not be likely to spend this much money on junk."[69] Why prohibit a Colt 1911 pistol from being imported when Colt 1911 pistols manufactured in the United States were sold legally every day? Interarms wanted any forthcoming legislation to be sensitive to the differences between cheap newly manufactured handguns and the high-quality surplus firearms that had made the company so much money in the US market. And when Interarms spoke, it claimed to speak confidentially for some 1,400 small dealers across the country who worried the traditional manufacturers' and Dodd's crusade against imports without distinction would slash their bottom lines.[70]

By that time representatives of the traditional manufacturers had come around to Cummings's position too. Behind closed doors, meeting with administration officials, they questioned "the justification for banning military surplus handguns," and instead urged that the "import provisions should be aimed primarily at inexpensive handguns and concealable weapons and that otherwise imported conventional firearms should be treated on the same basis as domestic conventional firearms."[71] By 1967 they had made peace with the likelihood of forthcoming legislation and had come to recognize that a public stance opposing gun control could backfire. In an era of increasing racial violence and urban unrest, gunmakers did not want to be blamed in the event that the public attributed increasing gun violence to legislative failures.[72] Their fears would be tested in 1967 and 1968.

CHAPTER 3

GERMAN 9MM P-38
$42.50
Fine High quality German
Walther, World War II German
automatic. Fires 9mm Luger cartridge. Original condition. Extra clips
$7.50. Ammo 9mm, $9.50 for 100
rounds.
European Army Holster $5.50

THIS MEANS WAR

TO ANYONE WHO had been following the news about the US war in Vietnam, the headlines in late July 1967 would have been nothing new: "Troops Fight Pitched Battle with Snipers"; "Troopers Seal Off Nest of Snipers; Death Toll Grows; Copters Called In"; "New Tactics Flush Out Snipers; Army Chief Feels Battle Is Won."[1] But rather than describing familiar developments in Southeast Asia, these stories were about Detroit, where a July 23 police raid on a "blind pig" after-hours bar had erupted into several days of rebellion, rioting, and pitched battles against law enforcement, National Guardsmen, and thousands of US Army paratroopers.[2] The forces of law and order appeared to be squaring off against an insurgency at home.

Story after story zeroed in on the snipers, perched on rooftops across the city, firing randomly on unsuspecting civilians, police, and troops. In the uprising's first days the *Detroit Free Press* gave readers the impression that a faceless army of Black radical sharpshooters held the city paralyzed. "The Sniper's Sneak Attack Is the Worst Thing," a headline on July 25 read. A photo showed a young, white, nervous National Guardsman, later identified as Gary Ciko of Hamtramck, armed with a bayonetted rifle, looking anxiously to the sky while a building burned behind him. Reporter William Serrin observed that those patrolling the city, like Ciko, most feared "the ugly whine of a bullet fired from darkness." Snipers were "almost impossible to anticipate, difficult to apprehend." "If some s.o.b. shoots at me, he's going to get it right back," boasted one guardsman, surely summoning bravado as a mask for fear. "It is all very military," Serrin observed, drawing on language journalists had learned covering the US war in Vietnam, "fields of fire, position, easy avenues of retreat, familiar terrain." Serrin noted that pawnshops and hardware stores had been looted of their firearms. "If they get their hands on a lot of ammunition, this place is going to look like Bastogne," one police officer said, conjuring memories of Second World War battlefields. Given the probability that those shops carried stocks of cheap war surplus rifles from Europe, his quip was more on the mark than he likely knew. "This is more than a riot," an officer told Serrin. "This is war."[3]

The image of urban snipers fed nightmares nationwide. It also carried a loaded connotation in the 1960s. Both Lee Harvey Oswald and Charles Whitman—the man who killed sixteen people from the clock tower at the University of Texas in August 1966—had received training in marksmanship courtesy of the US Marines and were regularly identified in the press as "snipers." On the second day of the uprising, the *Detroit Free Press* used military-style language to explain that "Negro snipers launched an offensive" against Army paratroopers. But it didn't take long for the stories of coordinated sniper attacks to face scrutiny.[4]

A week after the worst of the street battles, the claims began to fall apart. Journalists were already reporting that "police now believe that there was no tightly organized pattern to the sniping." Of 300 calls received about sniping, the Detroit Police Department claimed to have confirmed only 56, a number that would continue to fall with further investigation. Of the four deaths the Detroit PD attributed to snipers, evidence challenged that conclusion for three—the first alleged sniper victim, for instance, Sharon George, a white woman killed in the passenger seat of her husband's car, had been struck, medical examiners noted, by a bullet that traveled horizontally into the vehicle. (When they heard this, police officials speculated, with no evidence, that a sniper bullet may have ricocheted into George's vehicle.)[5]

The police and guardsmen mounted a zealous response to rumors of snipers plotting a campaign of terror. But there was never evidence of any such thing. Police found no specialized sniper hardware: "most of the shooting from rooftops and windows appears to have been random and undisciplined," and "most of the shots were from low-caliber pistols and rifles." On July 25 the *Detroit Free Press* reported that a guardsman had shot and killed Clifton Pryor, a twenty-three-year-old white construction worker who had allegedly been "sniping" from the roof of his apartment building and refused to drop his weapon, a .410 shotgun—not a sniper rifle. A week later the Associated Press interviewed residents of the building, who said they had all gone to the roof to keep watch for fires, and that Pryor had been unarmed and shot for no reason.

"I know if I were paying a professional sniper I would want him to be a hell of a lot more accurate," Inspector James Bannon quipped. "It was a damn poor performance for a professional ring, if there is such a thing."[6]

A year after rumors of snipers coursed through headlines, Congress passed the Gun Control Act of 1968, the first serious federal firearms law in a generation. Though the most common explanation for this law is that it was prompted by the spring 1968 assassinations of Martin Luther King Jr. and Bobby Kennedy, in truth it was a convergence of multiple overlapping forces and fears. The atmospherics of the previous three years of urban conflict, of millions of guns flooding into cities, of the real handguns and the imagined sniper rifles, had generated profound anxiety among both liberals and conservatives. It would be a mistake to underestimate the extent to which a "silent majority" of Americans opposed to extremism of all stripes wanted militant extremists on the right disarmed as much as those on the left. With the outbreak of Black urban rebellions in the mid-1960s, worries of armed teenagers and lone assassins turned into fears of angry urban populations, understood most often as armed Black populations partaking in the limitless bounty of the American gunscape.[7] To many Americans it felt like a shooting war had broken out, and they drew upon what they knew about US conflicts past and present to make sense of their evolving gun culture. As much as high-profile assassinations would prompt Americans to support gun control, so too would these on-the-ground realities.

WHAT ROLE DID GUNS PLAY IN INSTIGATING and perpetuating the violence? The gunmakers, among others, wanted to know. Several months after events in Detroit and Newark, where another major uprising had played out over a week in July 1967, the two largest US rifle manufacturers, Remington and Winchester, commissioned a study by the Stanford Research Institute (SRI) on the role of firearms in recent urban uprisings. The study painted a complicated picture: misinformation, confusion, and fear, all tempered with spiking demand and a plentiful supply of firearms.

The gunmakers and SRI hoped to put dubious claims to the test. The recent report of the National Advisory Commission on Civil Disorders (better known as the Kerner Commission) had relayed at face value claims about widespread sniping activities in at least half of the uprisings it studied, mentioning snipers more than sixty times.[8] The SRI study countered that of the more than 7,000 people who had been arrested in Detroit during the riots, only 26 were suspected of sniper activities. And of that group, only one was convicted of a crime, a misdemeanor for carrying an unregistered handgun; all of the other cases were dismissed. "Neither Detroit nor Newark experienced the widespread sniping activities described by the media and public officials," the SRI report concluded.[9]

In fact, many people shot in the chaos in July 1967 were likely struck by police or National Guardsmen. Unprepared for what were essentially urban battlefield conditions, they fired indiscriminately toward perceived threats, sometimes even each other. The Michigan National Guard alone fired some 155,000 rounds in just five days.[10] Army paratroopers called into Detroit, however, displayed greater discipline, because, according to their commander, "most had fought in Vietnam before their Detroit duty."[11] In other words, this was war, and they were experienced. In the aftermath, military officials offered their candid assessment of the exaggeration of sniper reports. Major General Charles P. Stone described the military perspective:

> The term "sniper" is used advisedly for it is not considered that there were snipers used in Detroit. A sniper is an individual who is armed with a weapon, often with a telescopic mount, who is highly trained in marksmanship and who hits what he aims at or accomplishes a definite purpose. In Detroit there was little evidence of real organization of a sniper force. What we had were individuals armed with rifles, sometimes under the influence of liquor, firing often without purpose. Had there, in fact, been organized sniping a considerable number of military and law enforcement officers could have been killed because of the manner in which they were exposed at critical locations.[12]

The SRI report placed much of the blame on the media's use of language that inflated fears and spread rumors. One newspaper editor told the Kerner Commission, "We used things in our leads and headlines during the riot I wish we could have back now because they were wrong and they were bad mistakes." "We used the words 'sniper kings' and 'nests of snipers,'" he admitted. "We found out when we were able to get our people into those areas and get them out from under the cars that these sniper kings and these nests of snipers were the constituted authorities shooting at each other."[13] As a subsequent presidential commission observed, "In many cases reports of sniping activity have subsequently proved to be false or exaggerated and most of the gunfire casualties were shot by police or troops."[14] Many of Detroit's forty-three deaths, it appeared, came at the hands of the forces of law and order, anxious over rumors of untold terrors lurking in a city they had come to treat as a war zone. The same could be said for Newark, where only one death among 23 people killed by gunfire in July 1967 was attributed to snipers.[15]

But the rumors did lasting damage. Even if the inaccuracies were identifiable within a week, and fully put to rest by the SRI report and others within months, the myth had already been inscribed on the national consciousness. And the urban uprisings only proved to Senate gun control crusader Tom Dodd that he had been right all along. He was confident that imports contributed to the civil disorder and produced, "as if uncorked by some mischievous genie, a product of 20th Century America, the *civilian sniper.*" Shortly after events in Newark and Detroit, he blamed the limitless availability of firearms, especially rifles, on "turning what might have been minor skirmishes into massive bloodletting." "From the comparative safety of rooftops," he wrote, "snipers picked off firemen and policemen as they tried to control the looting and carnage that ruled the streets." "I do not exaggerate the awesome nature of the civilian sniper," he told his Senate colleagues, exaggerating. "Law enforcement officers are concerned that a few dozen strategically placed snipers can immobilize an entire city and reduce the population to helplessness." Europe's wartime arsenal had brought the war to America's streets: "The death rate on several of the riot days was higher than that announced for the same days in Vietnam," Dodd noted somberly.[16]

Even before the Los Angeles neighborhood of Watts erupted in August 1965, ushering in a new age of urban rebellions, Dodd had argued that the alarming frequency of "sniper attacks" justified an effort to limit the flow of former weapons of war from Europe. In introducing a bill five months earlier, he noted a half-dozen reports of teenagers purchasing war surplus rifles to carry out individual acts of violence. He bemoaned the "heedless and complacent years gone by when ten million weapons were placed in unknown hands, foreshadowing a toll in death and in tragedy that has yet to be reckoned."[17] If Oswald could shop the bounty of postwar Europe's high-powered military rifles, so too could teenagers, rioters, looters, and revolutionaries. But by 1967, with Detroit and Newark in flames, there was no ambiguity as to the racial subtext of such fears.

Despite his own liberal commitments, his support of civil rights and Great Society legislation—indeed, his service in the earliest iteration of the Justice Department's Civil Rights Division in the 1930s—Dodd did not hesitate to connect the threat of racial violence in cities with his gun control agenda. Increasingly after 1965, he attempted to demonstrate that the unregulated flow of war surplus weapons, like the military rifle that killed John F. Kennedy, allowed urban radicals to stockpile firearms in anticipation of a war with the forces of law and order. Imported mail-order rifles became, in Dodd's words, the "favorite weapons of the riot snipers," the "new breed of killer from the rooftop."[18] Increasingly his rhetoric mixed fears of Black urban uprisings with diagnoses of America as a landscape of war.

Dodd was not alone in playing up the threat of urban snipers. The influential head of the International Association of Police Chiefs, a former longtime FBI agent named Quinn Tamm, testified repeatedly over the years on behalf of his organization and in support of gun control legislation. He warned in July 1967, as both Newark and Detroit burned, that law enforcement officials had to adjust to the new "age of snipers." "We are truly living in strange circumstances," he observed, "when the so-called disadvantaged feel compelled to arm themselves and snipe at police in order to demonstrate their discontent with real and imagined social inequities." He too connected social violence to war imports, asserting that the United States had become "the dumping ground of the castoff surplus military weapons of other nations, and that such weapons . . . in recent years have contributed greatly to lawlessness and to the Nation's law enforcement problems."[19] Europe's war trash, in Dodd's and Tamm's framings, had become treasure for the forces of disorder and rebellion in the postwar United States.

Though Dodd hoped to use this sensationalist imagery in the service of gun control, the rumors of snipers that exacerbated white anxieties in northern cities led to a different outcome. In the aftermath of the 1967 riots, Detroit witnessed incredible growth in handgun ownership. Michigan required residents to apply for a permit with a local police department in order to own a handgun and to register the gun's information. In 1965, Detroit PD issued 4,876 permits; that number skyrocketed to 17,760 by 1968.[20] Yet, by the end of the decade, for every legally registered handgun in Detroit, there may have been as many as twenty unregistered, illegally owned ones. Many of these guns came from out of state, from across state lines, from places like Toledo, Ohio, just an hour's drive from Detroit. Toledo police estimated that just a single gun store in the city had supplied more than 7,000 handguns to Michigan residents in the year after the riot.[21] It's no wonder that the chief prosecutor of Wayne County was the first to explain the term *Saturday Night Special* to Dodd in 1967.

Detroit was emblematic of anxious populations arming themselves with the world's cheap guns. The Detroit PD conducted an inventory of handguns seized during the 1967 uprising. They found 75 percent hadn't been registered, and they recorded (when possible) the makes, models, and calibers of the unregistered guns. By my count, at least 62 percent of the unregistered guns on one list were identifiable as imports, the most common made by the West German manufacturer Rohm, which produced the "Roscoe" pistol, infamous among urban police departments for its ubiquitous presence at crime scenes. Some of the guns' makes were unrecognizable and simply listed as .22-caliber—a majority of these were almost certainly cheap imports, given that domestic gunmakers did not produce such guns in quantities that could match the imports. It's also likely that some of the guns manufactured by US firms had been imported as war surplus.[22]

Though the director of the Kerner Commission dismissed the suggestion that the easy availability of cheap guns was to blame for urban disorder, once people decided to arm themselves during and after the uprising, there appeared to be no limit to their ability to do so.[23] "We were faced in the fall of 1967 and the spring of 1968 with literally an arms race there inside the city," was how Jerome P. Cavanagh, the Detroit mayor whose career crashed after the rebellion, remembered it several years later.[24]

THE TERM *ARMS RACE* IMPLIED that two sides were each ramping up preparations for a war. In Detroit in the wake of the riots, it was the white population of the city and its surrounding suburbs that armed in response to the perceived threat of uprisings in Black neighborhoods. And much of it happened out in the open, often gleefully. Local television news showed quirky stories of white women in nearby Dearborn taking target practice with the assistance of local police. A suburban Farmington supermarket advertised rifles with a grocery purchase.[25] While 1967 accelerated the process of "white flight" from the city, and back to the 1940s white neighborhood organizations had practiced an anti-Black "politics of defensive localism," as historian Thomas Sugrue has described it, some white Detroiters established what were essentially paramilitary groups in the aftermath of the uprising in preparation for "the next one."[26] If there was an arms race, it leaned heavily to their side.

One of the city's most notorious white organizers was Donald Lobsinger, a city employee who dedicated his life to anticommunism and founded an organization called Breakthrough in 1963 for that purpose. He grew up Catholic in northeast Detroit, earned a sociology degree at the city's Jesuit institution, the University of Detroit, and attributed his strident anticommunism to his faith. (He also cofounded the anticommunist Catholic Layman's League of Detroit, an organization he used to attack local left-leaning clergy—quite literally, having once assaulted a priest at a rally.)[27] He graduated in 1957 and was drafted into the US Army, which sent him to West Germany for eighteen months. There he decided that fighting communism would be his life's work. He recalled visiting a communist youth festival in Vienna and found himself stunned at the effectiveness of communist propaganda. "It was similar to the Nazi rallies. It has a psychological effect on you," he recounted many decades later. He feared that, in contrast to the young people of Central Europe, who had seen totalitarianism firsthand, young Americans would be unprepared to resist communism's appeal.[28]

Lobsinger returned to Detroit and became a career civil servant, working for the city recreation department until his retirement in the 1990s. His free time, however, went to the cause. The arch-conservative John Birch Society, established in the 1950s by Massachusetts industrialist Robert Welch to be a vanguard against global communism, had inspired Lobsinger, but he was only a member for several months before quitting to launch his own organization, believing the Birchers' "policy of education ought to be combined with action."[29] Lobsinger's new organization aimed to "break through the curtain of silence which has surrounded the Communist conspiracy." To emphasize this goal, he created a logo of a fist smashing through a Soviet flag and adopted the motto "America Forever, Communism Never."[30] He denounced the Kennedy and Johnson administrations' efforts at "co-existence" with the Soviet Union: "Co-existence with Communism is no-existence," went one Breakthrough slogan, as "co-existence" was merely a communist conspiracy "to lull their intended victim to sleep while they prepare for the kill."[31]

By 1965 Breakthrough was clashing with protesters against the war in Vietnam on the Wayne State University campus and picketing events like the Moscow Philharmonic's visit to the city. Lobsinger targeted antiwar protests because, in his words, the "Communist so-called 'Peace' offensive . . . means the removal of all resistance to the Communist Dictatorship and the final establishment of Communist totalitarian rule."[32] Though Breakthrough's membership never exceeded 100 members before 1967, Lobsinger was a recognizable figure, if a fringe one, in city politics, notorious for his confrontational antics. When he challenged an adversary, "he acted as if in a trance, with neck muscles bulging, eyes flaring, a finger slashing through the air and his language ferocious."[33] A 1966 *Detroit Free Press* editorial dismissed him as someone who had "joined or organized more silly societies than an intelligent man would dream of in a lifetime." "What frightens Lobsinger," the *Free Press* explained, "is that people think thoughts that he disagrees with."[34]

Lobsinger had established a reputation as a local right-wing provocateur by the summer of 1967. When violence erupted in July, he holed himself up in his house (through all his organizing, he lived with his parents and never married), armed alongside several other Breakthrough members, and prepared for his "enemies" to come for him. They didn't. But he recalled attending a city council meeting soon after where Detroit's Black leadership "flexed their muscles" and warned him personally that they were "running things now." That incident, he said, inspired a new mission for Breakthrough: "We're changing direction right now from the Vietnam War to opposing the black power movement in the city of Detroit," he told Breakthrough's small but committed membership, an explicit articulation of what historian Elaine Tyler May describes as "the danger of red shading into the danger of black" during the 1960s.[35] The front in the war against global communism had reached Lobsinger's backyard.

Lobsinger believed the riots were not spontaneous reactions to perceived injustices but a coordinated "rebellion"—after all, he said, that was the word radical Black leaders used to describe it, so he would use it too. "Rebellion" best described what he understood to be "an organized training exercise in a plot for the communist takeover of the world," as he told the audiences he addressed in the months after July. And, remarkably, the crowds started to turn out to see this young man who had been dismissed as a crank just a year earlier. By September 1967 hundreds of white residents of Detroit and nearby suburbs were showing up to Breakthrough rallies, drawn there by members who distributed leaflets in neighborhoods earlier in the day. "They say, 'It can't happen here.' But now it HAS HAPPENED HERE!" leaflets proclaimed. He asked his neighbors if they were prepared for "the next one," or if instead they would be "forced to stand helplessly by because you were unprepared to defend your home and neighborhood against bands of armed terrorists."[36]

The crowds at Breakthrough events got larger and larger. Lobsinger hesitated to reveal to journalists how many people joined the organization after July 1967 but the SRI study claimed Breakthrough membership increased "tenfold," which may have put it at around 1,000 contributing members. The personal intensity that made Lobsinger a fringe figure in 1965 gave him a kind of charisma that drew audiences still reeling from that summer's traumas. He became the city's most prominent "white backlash" personality. Journalists observed that he would have made an effective preacher, senator, or used car salesman, a leader in "any field where a talent for persuasion is important."[37]

Anticommunism was Lobsinger's passion, and in that sense Breakthrough's shift in focus from harassing antiwar protesters to working explicitly against Black power politics represented an evolution in anticommunist attention from the international to the local.[38] Like other right-wing figures of the era, he saw a direct line of inspiration, if not material support, from the Kremlin to civil rights organizations like the Congress of Racial Equality. The rebellion was "communist-inspired," Lobsinger was certain of it, and simply a "dry run" for a forthcoming "big push that would result in the takeover of the United States by the communists."[39] As a Breakthrough flyer put it, the "Black National Movement . . . is nothing less than the terrorist arm of the International Communist Conspiracy operating within the shores of our nation."[40]

What could white Detroiters do in the face of the international communist conspiracy on their doorsteps? Lobsinger offered a strategy: SASO, "Study, Arm, Store provisions, and Organize." "Within two years we will have

THIS MEANS WAR   75

a block-to-block home defense system over vast areas of Detroit," he explained to a journalist, which "would make it impossible for terrorists to come in to murder the men and rape the women. They'd never get out alive."[41] Such drastic steps for self-defense were necessary because liberal politicians like Mayor Cavanagh, Governor George Romney, and President Johnson had abandoned the white population of Detroit, allowing Black populations to burn neighborhoods and terrorize the city. (Breakthrough distributed a "Wanted" poster offering $1,000 for George Romney's arrest for "criminal negligence" during the rioting.)[42] Lobsinger intended to see the "entire white population of Detroit" armed, though he admitted the challenge of such a task, given Michigan's already-strict gun control provisions and increasing talk of federal restrictions. But white Americans had to be armed for war, ready for, as Lobsinger put it, the imminent "guerilla-type warfare such as is being waged in Vietnam and was being waged in Algeria."[43]

The 1960s world of cheap guns promised an arsenal for Breakthrough and its followers. They could of course buy cheap war surplus rifles or handguns through the mail. They could also hop in the car and drive an hour down the highway to Toledo to stock up, circumventing Michigan and local Detroit laws. The group reminded members that the Constitution, a "sacred document," guaranteed their right to keep and bear arms. Lobsinger encouraged them to join the NRA and a local affiliate, the General Douglas MacArthur Shooting Club, which would give them access to discounted rifles and free ammunition from the US Army. Through the Civilian Marksmanship Program, the Army had supplied hundreds of thousands of war surplus rifles, along with millions of rounds of ammunition, to NRA members and affiliated clubs since the early twentieth century, a practice criticized in the 1960s for subsidizing extremist groups.[44] A Breakthrough membership form encouraged potential enlistees to join these organizations to get training in "the organization of my block for defense purposes and home survival." A Lobsinger associate named Charles Panos headed the MacArthur Gun Club and encouraged people to join the NRA so that stockpiles of ammunition could flow from the federal government to the NRA to the club and then to individual members. As a result, "the government would not know who had how much ammunition," Panos explained. Panos dismissed concerns that pending congressional legislation might lead to a national registration system for firearms. If that happened, he suggested, members could simply go to a retail outlet like Sears and provide a fake name and address—they never check identification, he said.[45]

In the summer of 1968, Arnold Kotz, author of the SRI report sponsored by Winchester and Remington, drew the attention of the Dodd Committee to the way Breakthrough used the NRA to arm its members. "Should paramilitary groups such as Breakthrough be permitted to arm themselves and use gun club facilities," Kotz asked, "if their announced primary purpose is to prepare for action in the event of future disorders rather than sport-shooting?" It was a question Dodd's committee had confronted in years past, notably with the white anticommunist extremist Minutemen in mind. Kotz clarified that he did not think the NRA condoned this activity, but NRA president Franklin Orth denounced the SRI report anyway.[46]

Lobsinger fought a cold war while arming for a hot war that never came. By late 1967 it appeared that even if many white Detroiters shared his anxieties, they did not agree with his agenda. Breakthrough rallies drew crowds but struggled to maintain an active paid membership to support renting halls large enough to stage those events. An October 1967 newsletter boasted of several thousand attendees showing up for rallies at halls that could only accommodate several hundred people, but it also noted that a "lack of finances" made it difficult to rent larger venues.[47] It seemed that many white Detroiters were vigilante-curious but not ready to make a financial commitment. After the uprising Lobsinger started a newsletter, *Battle-line*, to take advantage of Breakthrough's new relevance, but it fizzled out by 1972. Lobsinger endorsed George Wallace for president in 1968, believing in Wallace's message about the necessary and inevitable separation of the races, and even ran for Detroit mayor himself in 1970. (He explained his failure to gain traction: "The press blocked out my campaign.")[48] He gained more headlines in March 1968 by disrupting an appearance by Martin Luther King Jr. in nearby Grosse Point, leading a crowd of white activists in chants of "King is a traitor" and "Burn traitors not flags," just weeks before King's murder.[49]

White extremists like Lobsinger could attract local press attention in the aftermath of the 1967 uprising. But at a national level, they couldn't compete with the optics of Black radicals armed in the streets.

ON MAY 2, 1967, TWO DOZEN MEMBERS of the Black Panther Party marched into the California State Capitol in Sacramento armed with loaded rifles, shotguns, and handguns.[50] Ten of them pushed their way past state police and into the Assembly Chamber. Legislators took immediate notice of the commotion. The speaker pro tem ordered the Panthers removed. They complied with state police, who disarmed them. After questioning the men, state police acknowledged that the Panthers hadn't violated any laws—they didn't conceal their weapons but rather carried them openly, as allowed by California law—and their firearms were returned, at which point the Panthers drove off in several vehicles. Minutes later they pulled into a gas station, followed by two police vehicles. The police officers drew their revolvers and ordered the men to stay where they were until backup arrived. Only then were they arrested. "They weren't causing any trouble," a station attendant said. "The demonstrators just talked. They didn't put up any resistance."[51]

It was a remarkably brief, albeit tense, moment, given its significance in the historical memory of guns and the 1960s. "The NRA Supported Gun Control When the Black Panthers Had the Weapons," reads a typical internet clickbait headline about the incident.[52] But articles like this only tell part of the story. Undoubtedly, the presence of armed Black militants generated anxiety among white legislators as well as among millions of white Americans who read about it and saw images in the news. In the twenty-first century, though, the story is often simplified to imply that California legislators, and subsequently the US Congress, acted to impose gun control because Black militant groups like the Panthers started to arm and promised self-defense against police brutality in cities like Oakland. The way we tell the story of the Panthers in Sacramento today obscures how that moment was embedded in the decade-long crisis generated by cheap guns and how legislators acted on not just racialized fears of Black radicalism but also the right-wing militancy and vigilantism of the Donald Lobsingers across America when they crafted gun control legislation.

The Black Panthers marched into the State Capitol in May 1967 to protest a bill proposed by Don Mulford, a Republican legislator from Oakland, that would have made it a misdemeanor to carry a loaded firearm in public in California. No doubt Mulford knew of the Panthers and the reputation they had developed so quickly. In October 1966 two Oakland activists, Huey Newton and Bobby Seale, founded the Black Panther Party for Self-Defense, a full title that at once built on that of an Alabama predecessor founded by Stokely Carmichael but which also expressed how central firearms would become to the Bay Area organization's philosophy, at least at first, when guns were an effective way of getting the attention of Black Oakland residents not steeped in revolutionary ideology.[53] The Panthers clashed locally with law enforcement prior to May 1967, following police patrols, carrying guns openly, as they could under California law, intending to demonstrate to police that the Black community would no longer tolerate commonplace abuse. But the mainstream California press only noticed the Panthers in February 1967. On the second anniversary of Malcolm X's murder, the *Los Angeles Times* observed the founding of the new "black nationalist political party." When they crashed the California State Assembly on May 2, newspapers felt the need to explain to readers what the "armed Negro band" was—"a self-proclaimed 'revolutionary' party whose members are best known for their habit of dressing in black clothing and lugging pistols, rifles and shotguns around in public," as the conservative *Oakland Tribune* described them.[54]

It is certainly possible to see the Mulford Act as an attempt by panicked California legislators to impose gun control, backed by the NRA, which supported the law, only when Black people started to take up arms. But such a reading assumes the Panthers were already a household name. And such a reading also misses crucial context, namely, that California legislators had worked for years to take action against the limitless supply of war weapons available to extremists across the political spectrum. Mulford's bill was just one of a range of gun control bills the California State Assembly took up in May 1967. Other bills under consideration echoed many of the concerns gun control legislators like Dodd had worked to address for years. One would have outlawed the private ownership of "heavy military weapons," or firearms above .50 caliber; another would have imposed new requirements on state residents buying handguns from out of state; a third bill would have banned the possession of machine gun parts, while a fourth would define "hand rocket launchers as concealable firearms," and thus subject them to the same regulations as handguns.[55] In other words, when the Panthers marched into the Assembly Chamber, the stunned legislators had already been working, for years in some cases, to confront the growing arsenal of war weapons in private hands.

The concerns embedded in these proposals were not about the Black Panthers. In fact, the committee that wrote these bills had studied the question of what to do with large-caliber weapons for the previous two years.[56] The various bills on offer, with the exception of Mulford's misdemeanor for public carrying of loaded weapons, had been born before the Black Panthers even existed. One Los Angeles assemblyman "blamed gathering of arsenals on laxity of the federal government," a problem that "became evident after World War II when many military-type weapons were allowed in from abroad." These proposals were rooted, then, not in fear of the Panthers but in anxieties about the easy access other extremist groups had to military-style hardware, much of it imported from Europe with virtually no restriction since the early 1950s. California deputy attorney general Charles A. O'Brien testified before the assembly in favor of the bills and was "happy to admit" that he and his office had been engaged in "a crusade against private military groups in California," and that the state saw "no legitimate constitutional reason for tolerating the dangers that exist due to the lack of these laws." Rather than the Black Panthers, such conversations were more likely to mention the Minutemen, the right-wing white extremist group arming itself for a forthcoming apocalypse

against global communism. "Some well-meaning citizens seem bitterly determined to confuse patriotism with armed paranoia," O'Brien said, in an allusion
to the Minutemen.[57] Like Dodd, these legislators struggled to bolster the center in a world pulling between left and right and in a country where it was easy
for each side to arm itself with weapons of war.

The Panthers did succeed in changing the conversation, however, and they
revealed how quickly anxious white legislators could mobilize the gun issue
against Black demands for justice. They became notorious not only for who
they were and what they believed and did but also for their ability to use media
to communicate all of it. After their May 2 stunt, the law that got the most
attention was the law they had marched against: Mulford's bill, which became
the Mulford Act, which did indeed make it a misdemeanor to carry a loaded
firearm in public in California once signed into law by California governor and
future NRA darling Ronald Reagan. Later, Mulford added felony provisions
for carrying a loaded weapon near a school or into the State Capitol or the
governor's residence. New hotlines were installed in the Capitol building and
the governor's residence to connect directly to state police in the event of a
repeat of May 2.[58]

After May 2 the Panthers would be the subject of gun control conversations
in ways they weren't before. While most of the bills proposed for debate that
spring intended to control the kinds of weapons Californians could access,
the Panthers shifted the conversation to the implied control of certain classes
of people built into gun control laws. When war came to Detroit and Newark
two months later, images of Black radicals armed for war were already in white
America's consciousness; increasingly, so too were ideas about gun control.

But returning to the beginning of May 1967—putting the infamous Panther
march into the State Capitol in context—reveals that policymakers and legislators feared a range of extremists across the spectrum having access to the
leftover weapons of war that continued to flow into the United States decades
after the defeat of Nazi Germany and Imperial Japan. In fact, in the days before
May 2, headlines in the Bay Area had been dominated not by armed Black revolutionaries but by the story of William Thoresen III, the white thirty-year-old
heir to a Chicago steel fortune, who, the public came to discover, had amassed
an immense, spectacular arsenal of small arms and light weapons in his San
Francisco mansion.

DESPITE THEIR EXTENSIVE EXPERIENCE in federal firearms investigations, the agents of the Treasury Department's Alcohol and Tobacco Tax
Division (ATTD) who assembled at the Thoresen mansion on San Francisco's

Broadway Street in April 1967 were not prepared for what they were about to find. The imposing structure sat on a corner lot in the expensive Pacific Heights neighborhood, on a small rise overlooking the bay a mile to the north and the offices of the Archdiocese of San Francisco across the street. Thoresen and his wife, Louise, had recently purchased it for $200,000 (more than $1.7 million in 2022 dollars, though an online estimate today puts the current property value at ten times that) and had filed the necessary paperwork with the city for a planned $300,000 expansion, which included an indoor swimming pool. None of the paperwork, it seems, mentioned what was stockpiled inside.

Agents crashed into the mansion on April 21. They had received a tip from a local shipping company that an unusual number of firearms had arrived for recipients at that address. Once inside, they noticed immediately that the unfurnished home was filled with a "fantastic cache of war weapons," crates upon crates of firearms and mortars and enough ammunition to supply a small army. A "realistic toy copy of a sub machine gun lay atop a crate of the real, lethal articles"—the plaything belonged to Thoresen's five-year-old son, who followed agents around the house wearing two holstered plastic pistols, explaining repeatedly, and inexplicably, "I eat flowers." In one room they encountered a mynah bird trained to whistle for attention and shout, "Fuck you!" William Thoresen was nowhere to be found, but agents took Louise into custody. They also called in to the nearby Presidio for assistance from US Army soldiers, who brought several trucks over to cart away the thirty tons of weapons they found on the premises.[59]

Over the coming days, agents tracked down more of Thoresen's cache sitting in shipping company warehouses or stashed in storage units around the city as well as in Oakland and Berkeley. One estimate put the value at $500,000 ($4.4 million in 2022). In total they found more than seventy-seven tons of weapons. Despite initial speculation that Thoresen was simply a rich, eccentric collector of obsolete military oddities—after his arrest, he would tell the press, "I just collect cannons as ornaments. . . . Every lawn ought to have one."—many of the weapons agents discovered were perfectly suited to warfare in the 1960s. US troops in Vietnam at that moment would have known what to do with Thoresen's AR-15 and M-60 rifles as well as his stock of 81-mm mortars. Some of the more outlandish weapons, like the 37-mm antitank gun "complete with a wheel carriage," attested to Thoresen's taste for surpluses from the Second World War.[60]

When Thoresen surrendered to police several days later, it fell to his attorneys to explain just what the son of the president of Chicago's Great Western Steel Corporation had planned to do with an arsenal fit to topple a small country. With Cold War intrigue in the air, the local press couldn't help but speculate about whether Thoresen was some sort of secret operative. An ATTD agent didn't help when he joked aloud for reporters to hear, "I wonder if we torpedoed the CIA again." A deputy US attorney denied any connection between Thoresen's collection and the US government. "This is not really a mystery," one of Thoresen's lawyer's explained. "Nobody is running guns to Cuba and he isn't a member of a society such as the Minutemen." Another attorney suggested Thoresen's eccentricities were to blame: "The young man has gone screwball on collecting guns. . . . He has a childish, frenzied desire to get all these weapons." ("I also collect rocks and stamps," Thoresen added.)[61] He was, it seemed, addicted to gun consumerism. The public, and even the state now charged with prosecuting Thoresen, struggled to understand the scale of what one ATTD agent called the "biggest seizure of this kind in this part of the world." US attorney Cecil Poole quipped, "This guy has so many munitions, I don't know whether the government should prosecute him—or negotiate with him."[62]

The April 1967 raid was not William's or Louise's first encounter with the law. In the late 1950s he ended up in violent scuffles and burglary incidents that occasionally landed him in police stations, including a 1959 theft that resulted in a felony conviction, one that, under the Federal Firearms Act of 1938, would prohibit Thoresen from legally owning any firearm, let alone an arsenal. In 1964 he was arrested for detonating fifty pounds of dynamite near a radio station in Tucson, Arizona, because, Louise later explained, he was bored. In 1966 he was charged with resisting arrest in San Francisco after fleeing from a gun store he appeared to be burglarizing. That same year, Louise was arrested at New York's JFK Airport for trying to bring several machine guns into the country. The couple already had accumulated a rap sheet when the ATTD knocked down their door in April 1967, but they also had money and connections that had allowed them to avoid many of the legal consequences to that point. And their troubles didn't end after the raid. While awaiting trial, William was arrested in Las Vegas for assaulting a woman who refused his sexual advances and for attempting to bribe the two police officers who responded to the scene with $10,000. Six months later he was arrested again, this time for punching an airline ticketing agent who tried to prevent him from boarding a plane that had already fired up its engines.[63]

The California Assembly met just a week after the raid on the Thoresen mansion, leading members to wonder how someone with money and connections could hoard such an arsenal with seemingly no limit. Deputy Attorney General O'Brien focused his testimony on Thoresen, not the Black Panthers.

"You don't even need to limit yourself to a few people," 1964. Cartoonist Herblock satirizes the postwar consumer bounty of weapons of war. The exaggeration became reality in the form of William Thoresen's personal arsenal. (© The Herb Block Foundation via Library of Congress)

He recounted Thoresen's past legal troubles and said, "I believe we should consider the present law which allows such a man to legally own a military arsenal."[64] Anyone who followed the Dodd Committee's investigations over the previous several years knew well the gun bonanza available to buyers, but even they had never seen anything like this. The ease with which Thoresen was able to order so many guns without restriction astounded investigators and legislators. He took advantage of what importers like Sam Cummings offered. In fact, one of the shipments ATTD agents discovered was 174 boxes of guns, ammunition, and gun parts shipped to him from Potomac Arms—a business located on the Alexandria waterfront right next to the Interarms warehouse and shipping complex. It had been founded by an associate of Sam Cummings in 1963. Cummings had moved out of the retail business by 1967 and had shifted much of it to Potomac.[65] Cummings had likely imported most of Thoresen's cache.

The Thoresens' money paid for good attorneys, and those good attorneys managed to place sufficient obstacles in the way of the prosecution to delay trial until March 1969, but they weren't good enough to stop the court from finding the Thoresens guilty on two counts of violating federal firearms law. In the courtroom after the verdict, Louise gestured to two antitank guns the prosecution had staged as evidence. "No more of these," she said. "From now on, it's model trains for us." William was sentenced to six months in jail, while Louise got eighteen months of probation. She filed for divorce eight months later, though they continued to live together in a modest house in Fresno until the morning of June 10, 1970, when Louise ran across the street to tell a neighbor that she had shot William.

Police found William Thoresen's body lying on the bed with several .38-caliber bullet holes in his chest. They also walked into a house full of dozens of crates packed not with model trains but, once again, firearms—"a veritable warehouse of destruction," one officer said. A Fresno jury acquitted Louise five months later, agreeing that she had acted in self-defense, after she testified to William's abusive behaviors and her fears for her life. In 1974, she published a memoir of her life with William, *It Gave Everybody Something to Do*, in which she described herself as a young, working-class Chicago woman swept up by a rich and charming man who turned out to be something of a psychopath, a man who sought exciting distractions from the tedium of his aristocratic life and found what he was looking for in firearms and violence.[66]

SNIPERS, ARMS RACES, armed radicals marching on state capitols, rich playboys amassing personal arsenals—"war" was an inexact description for whatever it was the Donald Lobsingers and Black Panthers and William Thoresens were doing in 1967, but gun control advocates like Dodd, and by 1968

President Johnson himself, thought it was an efficient metaphor for understanding America's contemporary gun problem. Increasingly they defined the twentieth-century US gunscape as a battlefield. They equated gun deaths in the United States with US war deaths overseas up through their present. In his message to Congress the day after Robert Kennedy's murder, for instance, Johnson acknowledged the "750,000 Americans dead since the turn of the century. This is far more than have died at the hands of our enemies in all the wars we have fought." (This claim checked out if you counted only combat deaths—"at the hands of our enemies.") Attorney General Ramsey Clark made the same point in a letter to Congress in early September, claiming that since 1900 firearms had killed "more than 800,000 Americans, exceeding all our war casualties from the revolution through Vietnam." He was mistaken to include wars before the twentieth century—the number of soldiers killed in the US Civil War alone approached 750,000—but the precision of these estimates mattered less than the intention in citing them: the American gunscape was a war zone in ways the everyday landscapes of other "civilized" nations were not. The administration's political goal was not rigorous accuracy; instead, the regular repetition of numbers in the range of 750,000–800,000 gun deaths across the twentieth century, along with accompanying figures on international comparisons, was meant to draw Americans' attention to the unique nature of their gun problem across time and space. What metaphor could be more appropriate for a landscape overflowing with guns and littered with the victims of the violence guns had enabled than a battlefield?

As Americans geared up for domestic war in 1967, the NRA asked, "Who guards America's homes?" The organization's answer was that the American citizen did, armed and prepared for any threat that might appear at one's doorstep. The armed citizen was a "community stabilizer," tasked with guarding "the doors of American homes from senseless savagery and pillaging." Soon thereafter the NRA would clarify that it did not "advocate the formation of armed posses to handle civil disturbances." But NRA president Franklin Orth did not balk. He told Congress in 1968 that the stockpiling of firearms in Detroit had kept the city's belligerents in check, functioning as nuclear weapons did, as a kind of deterrence or mutually assured destruction in which each side hesitated to pull the trigger because it knew the other was armed.[67]

Orth's was another metaphorical way of conceiving of the evolving gun country. But on the ground in Detroit, residents watched nervously as their neighbors acquired arsenals and extremists like Lobsinger promised to turn the Motor City into an armed camp. In May 1968, a group of civic and business leaders collaborated for an advertising campaign that aimed to promote

rational, cool thinking amid the emotions of the arms race. They called them-
selves Men United for Sane Thought (MUST). Their ads drew attention to
Detroit as a new war zone. "If you were stuck stateside in '43, missed Korea
and are too old for Vietnam," said one, "maybe you can win your medal in
Detroit this summer. Posthumously." Another connected the veterans of US
overseas campaigns to the citizens arming to defend their neighborhoods:
"Willie made it through Normandy, Seoul, and DaNang. He doesn't need the
Purple Heart for Detroit." Small type identified Willie as Black (at Normandy
he would have been in a segregated unit), noting that "some people would
have you and me believe that every normal, average, red-blooded American
Negro is looking forward to a riot in Detroit this summer." Willie, however,
was a career US Army officer—not the kind who brought his sniper training to
the streets of American cities—a father and a husband who enjoyed fishing on
the weekends, just like "the normal, average, red-blooded American white."[68]

"With the change in the enemy's color from red to black," wrote the authors
of the first-ever federal report on gun violence in 1969, "right-wing extremism
is apparent not only in paramilitary groups, such as the Minutemen, but also
in the proliferation of neighborhood protective associations," such as Breakthrough and many others that formed in reaction to the rebellions of the late
1960s. "Now arms are stockpiled 'in the home' as well as 'in the hills.'"[69]

Millions of Americans thought about that stockpiling in militarized terms:
these firearms were not for hunting or sport shooting or collecting. Prepped
for years by Senator Dodd for just such an occasion, the politicians had ready
explanations: "The lethal but militarily outmoded hardware that Europeans
have been dumping on our market since the end of the Second World War,"
said Representative Robert C. Nix, a House subcommittee chair investigating gun sales in the midst of the violence of the summer of 1968, "has finally
made its potential for horror a reality."[70] But the 1969 report also concluded
that firearms had not yet played a significant role in urban uprisings. Sniping
reports were exaggerated and most gun injuries and deaths came at the hands
of police or military. "Yet the civil disorders have stimulated gun buying and
the growth of black and white extremist groups," the report warned, "leave
this country with a dangerous legacy: the highly explosive combination of fear
and firearms."[71] Stockpiling cheap guns was an insurance policy against what
Donald Lobsinger called "the next one." These guns meant war.

CHAPTER 4

WALTHER
PP MODEL

Caliber .22 L.R. $62.50
Caliber .32 ACP $7.50
Caliber .380 ACP $7.50

CIVILIZATION AND GUNS

IF THE URBAN UNREST OF 1967 prompted you, like millions of your fellow Americans, to go handgun shopping, chances are you'd come across the Roscoe. It was a small, snub-nosed revolver, always .22 caliber, sometimes stamped "Rosco" or "Roscoe Blue" (for the supposed color of its dark steel). It could be yours for as little as ten dollars, though if you were buying it off the street you could expect to pay two or three times that. The Roscoe was cheap, and it felt like it. The metal might actually melt in your hands if you squeezed off too many rounds—ballistics specialists struggled to trace bullets fired from these cheap guns because their barrels actually changed shape slightly with each round fired.[1]

Police officers could also tell you that if they had to get shot, they'd rather it be by almost anything other than a Roscoe. Better to catch a bullet from a high-quality, higher-caliber handgun, something like a .38 or .45 made by a company like Smith & Wesson or Colt, than an imported .22. Cheap handguns fired small rounds at lower velocity, meaning that if you were struck by a bullet, it had less of a chance of passing through your body quickly. A cheap .22 handgun bullet "does a hell of a job inside of your guts, and it tears your intestines and ricochets over the bones," a Chicago officer told Congress.[2]

Senator Tom Dodd, along with the municipal and police officials who persistently pressed him for action, had long known about the Roscoe. But all they knew of its provenance was that it was a "cheap foreign gun," a phrase Dodd snarled with derision whenever he denounced America's limitless firearms bonanza. They had heard stories of factories seemingly thrown up overnight across Western Europe, in Spain, Italy, and West Germany, to cash in on Americans' unending appetite for cheap guns. But nobody had ever traced the firearms to their sources, company by company, factory by factory, gun by gun. It took until the fall of 1968, when President Lyndon Johnson was already about to sign the Gun Control Act, a law that expanded the provisions of Title IV of the Omnibus Crime Control and Safe Streets Act, which passed Congress just days after Bobby Kennedy's assassination.

In a sense, Americans did gun control backward. They banned cheap handgun imports before they really knew the full story of where they came from or the problems they caused. After Bobby Kennedy's killing, Johnson appointed Milton Eisenhower, a former college president and the brother of Dwight Eisenhower, to lead the National Commission on the Causes and Prevention of Violence. The Democratic president charged the Eisenhower Commission with interrogating the broad historical and contemporary forces responsible for the escalating violence and social conflict of the 1960s. The commission in turn appointed a Firearms Task Force (FTF) to conduct what would become the most thorough investigation yet of guns and gun violence in the United States.[3]

Americans felt trapped by their own pathologies in the summer of 1968—much of the rest of the world saw the same—and officials across the administration sought to better understand US gun culture in historical and global contexts. While the White House worked to pass new laws, Secretary of State Dean Rusk drafted a telegram to be sent to every US embassy requesting that local diplomatic staff investigate and report back whatever could be learned about each individual country's gun laws. He had a long list of questions, driven by the Johnson's administration's new legislative imperatives: licensing and registration. Rusk also requested that personnel gather and report back local statistics on gun-related crime.[4] The result would be the first comprehensive collection of data cataloging global gun control.

Rusk's first question, about whether a country had any gun laws at all, proved provincially American: virtually every nation had some kind of gun law, and as the many telegrammed replies to the request revealed, most of them had much more stringent controls than the United States. In fact, gun critics' oft-repeated claim that the United States was the only "civilized" country in the world that allowed its citizens to stockpile firearms with few or no restrictions belied a more expansive truth revealed in the many telegrammed replies: almost all countries, even those that many white Americans considered on the edges of "civilization," had stronger gun laws than the United States. This dichotomy of civilized and uncivilized, which could also substitute adjectives like *advanced, developed,* or *modern,* borrowed language from the modernization theory popular in the State Department and among elite thinking about the world in the 1960s. It was the same sort of logic that drove US policies in places like Latin America, where the US government devoted billions of dollars to development projects, but also in Vietnam and elsewhere. The central idea was that there was a normative path of development along which all societies proceeded to reach modernity, though many factors, from local culture to alien ideologies like communism, could pervert or distort that development.[5]

In 1968, gun critics in the United States borrowed the language of modernization to describe their own country's gun pathologies. By identifying the United States as backward, barbaric, nonadvanced, undeveloped, unmodern—uncivilized—they aimed to shame their fellow Americans into doing something, anything, to align the country with much of the rest of the world's gun control philosophies and policies.[6] In this period we find the origins of a discourse on American gun culture and violence that would ring over the next half century. When President Barack Obama, in the final year of his administration, made another push for "common-sense steps to save lives," he noted that the United States was "the only advanced country on Earth" that confronts mass gun violence with such alarming frequency. "It doesn't happen in other advanced countries," he said. "It's not even close." "In the greatest, most technologically advanced nation on Earth," he concluded, "there is no reason for this."[7] Such common remarks from gun control proponents in the twenty-first century drew on the language of modernization and civilization that gun critics first articulated in the 1960s.

Despite Tom Dodd's years of work, Americans only collectively tried to make sense of their gun culture for the first time in 1968, as a series of assassinations and violent crises battered the nation. In that moment of vulnerability, leaders sought cures for American pathologies in the ways other countries regulated gun consumerism and responded to gun violence. Modernization theory was a Cold War way of looking at the world, an ideology that could simplify the world's complexities to make them easier to explain, but the Cold War confidence necessary to apply it to others was crumbling, and critics turned the microscope on American society. Americans only started puzzling out the rot that gun capitalism had wrought in 1968, when, as the Firearms Task Force would conclude, it may have already been too late.

RHETORIC INTENDED TO CONTRAST the "civilized" world with an uncivilized United States obscured the extent to which modern countries from West Germany to Japan contributed to US gun violence by selling Americans cheap guns. The infamous Roscoe represented a Cold War bond, one built during the Allied occupation of Germany, nurtured under the US nuclear umbrella, and dependent on an economic relationship in which the United States encouraged rapid growth in West Germany and opened its domestic markets to German goods.

The FTF set out to learn as much as it could about the Roscoe and other "cheap foreign guns." It subpoenaed and collected records from gun importers across the country, and those unpublished reports reveal just how diffuse the import problem was. Guns came from many places where there was no US oversight over their production, and they ended up in countless locations across the United States, after importers in dozens of states distributed to them to thousands of dealers nationwide, who in turn sold them many through the mail to millions of customers. Records showed gun shipments, some as small as a few dozen, others in the tens of thousands, coming from Japan, Germany, Spain, Italy, Brazil, France, Belgium, Norway, Switzerland, and elsewhere. They went to big-time dealers, like Sam Cummings's infamous Interarms, its warehouses parked just down the Potomac from Washington, DC, but also to importers sprinkled throughout the country, with innocuous names like Blumenfeld Ice & Coal Co. (of Memphis, Tennessee) and Berent Steel (of New York City).[8]

Data from the Department of Commerce provided an overview of the national-level origins of imported guns for 1967. Importers brought a total of 1.2 million firearms into the country for sale on the civilian market that year, four times as many guns as had been imported a decade earlier and a total equal to about 50 percent of domestic civilian production. More than 60 percent of imports—747,000 of them—were handguns. That figure represented the largest increase of any category of gun, over 45 percent more than 1966's total, and more than 800 percent over the previous decade. Alarmingly, 1968 figures were on pace to double 1967's. By far the biggest supplier of handguns was West Germany, which sold 335,000 of them to the United States, followed by 131,000 from Italy, and then Brazil (93,000), Spain (91,000), and Belgium (80,000).[9] (Surely it was conspicuous that three-quarters of handgun imports came from the former Axis powers and their largest nonbelligerent ally.)

The FTF knew a lot about importers like Interarms, but it wanted to know more about the foreign firms doing the exporting. Staff members asked the State Department to contact embassies in several countries with the goal of gathering as much information as they could. What they learned from the US embassy in West Germany, the largest international source of cheap handguns, was startling. The plethora of brand names stamped on German guns had led Dodd and gun critics to believe that there was a vast, decentralized, unregulated industry manufacturing cheap handguns and competing for US dollars. But embassy staff discovered that there were, in fact, only a couple of major producers in the whole country. The largest of these manufacturers was Röhm GmbH (Rohm, sans umlaut, for its US customers, or RG), a tool engineering and manufacturing firm founded in the early twentieth century. Since the 1950s, Rohm had sold guns to US importers under a dizzying variety of brand names. The ones investigators could trace included Romo, Eig, Thalco, Omega, Viking, Galef, Liberty, Vest Pocket, Shorty, Pinker B, York, and Rosco or Roscoe, that plague of urban police forces and victims' insides. In 1963 Rohm started branding its own guns with a simple letter and number, such as the RG 7 model, but it continued manufacturing guns on order for at least nine large US importers, stamping the importer's brand name on the gun rather than RG's—the Omega Import Company, for instance, sold handguns in the United States stamped with Omega, but Rohm manufactured these in Germany on Omega's behalf.[10] Gun critics may have imagined a dispersed European industry of fly-by-night factories, but at least in the case of West Germany, the continent's biggest exporter of cheap handguns, a surprisingly centralized production regime hid behind consumer branding.

Most of the handguns researchers worried over were newly manufactured by firms like RG. But war surplus firearms also popped up in crimes and urban uprisings. The FTF discovered this when its researchers attempted to trace the origins of guns seized by Miami police in the street battles that had erupted during the Republican National Convention in August 1968. They sent lists of serial numbers to US embassies in Europe, asking them to contact local manufacturers. The embassy in Bonn reported connecting some of the guns with Rohm. Other weapons confiscated, though, included German Walther and Luger handguns that had been manufactured before the Second World War. These gunmakers' records were destroyed during the war, making it impossible to identify the handguns' precise origins. Investigators ran into the same problem with handguns manufactured in Spain. They wanted to know about the "Libia" that police occasionally encountered, for instance, which they discovered was manufactured by Beistegui Hermanos of Eibar, a Basque town in northern Spain that was virtually obliterated, along with all of the manufacturers' records, during the Spanish Civil War.[11] Guns like these were not easy to get on the streets of most European cities in the 1960s, and yet such war refuse haunted Americans in their urban conflicts. To many, this was what the failure of modernity and the collapse of civilization looked like. Liberal politicians would embrace that rhetoric in the coming years.

PRESIDENT JOHNSON USED the language of civilization and modernity as his administration made Dodd's gun control agenda its own and tried to advance it beyond the senator's ambitions. In a message to Congress criticizing its perennial inaction to restrict "lethal weapons to be hawked by the same mail order techniques used to market frozen steaks and baskets of fruit," Johnson said that a "civilized nation cannot allow this armed terror to continue."[12] Less than a year later, as his rival Bobby Kennedy lay dead, he wrote Congress again. "Alone among the modern nations of the world," the United States "remained without the gun control laws that other countries accept as an elementary need and condition of life." After the passage of Title IV, which restricted war surplus firearms and cheap handguns, Johnson wanted more, including systems for registering gun purchases and licensing their owners. Noting the discrepancies between US and foreign gun violence rates, he urged Congress to pass "common-sense safeguards which any civilized nation must apply for the safety of its people."[13]

Tom Dodd echoed the language of modernization and civilization. In the days following the riots that erupted in April 1968 after a white supremacist used a rifle to murder Martin Luther King Jr., the senator from Connecticut toured Washington, DC. The city's uprising, he said, "can be directly traced to the uncivilized approach this country takes to the sale and possession of lethal weapons." "We are the only civilized nation on this earth that allows such mail order madness," Dodd told a group of young Democrats in Hartford a month later. And in the hours between news breaking of the shooting of Bobby Kennedy and the New York senator's death, Dodd had already released a statement connecting the incident to a larger problem of American backwardness: "I think the time has come when we shall have to follow the example of other civilized countries and make registration of all guns compulsory."[14]

Beyond simply rejecting the barbarity of gun culture, proponents of gun control affirmed a faith in modern technology's ability to solve persistent social problems. "We need registration, we need information, we need computer data on all the guns," Ramsey Clark told members of Johnson's cabinet after Robert Kennedy's killing. He praised the California state registration system that enabled officials to identify within minutes the gun that assassin Sirhan Sirhan used. Two weeks later a Johnson aide circulated a memo boasting of the ability of new computer technology to sift through the registration records of more than 100 million guns in seconds, and a few days later the FBI sent a cost estimate for such a system ($11.5 million, plus regular maintenance and network expansion costs).[15]

Through the language of civilization and modernity policymakers and commentators would wrestle with ideas about manhood and control. Both gun control advocates and opponents used gendered language to portray the opposition as unmasculine. The traditional notion of manhood connected to firearms remained powerful. In a lengthy screed published just after the passage of the GCA, for instance, *American Rifleman* editor Bill R. Davidson proclaimed that American men "still like blood sports, and practice the old skills, and have a hardcore contempt for softness and excessive emotionalism. They prefer to kill their own snakes." "Our female-dominated, spastic, society has been working overtime for a generation or more to discredit manhood," he concluded.[16]

But gun critics also wielded manhood in defense of their ideas. The rational promotion of gun control was often set against an emotional, barbaric attachment to guns, implicitly coded as an effeminate lack of control in a Cold War world demanding discipline from both the individual and the nation. In the 1960s, in particular, the link between guns and masculinity was contested ground. "Politics and social struggle for most of the decade had a distinctly masculine cast," writes historian Robert O. Self. "Manhood was the sixties' cultural currency."[17] Gun control advocates used the language of modernization, with its assorted masculinist assumptions, to criticize gun rights proponents. "Far from hitting America in its manhood," wrote Johnson's attorney general, Ramsey Clark, "gun control will show we have men who will stand up for the clear and urgent public interest." To Cold War liberals like Clark and Tom Dodd, masculinity meant controlling one's emotions, resisting emotional calls of extremists on left and right, and practicing self-discipline to know when best to deploy one's might.[18]

Dodd's rhetoric was emblematic of the way Cold War liberals portrayed gun control as a masculine, civilizing, modernizing enterprise. Reflecting on his decade-long effort after the passage of the Gun Control Act of 1968, Dodd said that he "had underestimated the psychological and emotional attachment which some gun fanciers have for their weapons." He titled his unpublished reflections on his conflict with the gun lobby "Showdown at the Congressional Corral," demonstrating his understanding of the "showdown" as two clashing visions of masculinity taking place on an imagined frontier.[19] He nevertheless dismissed the "emotional reversion to romantic images of the frontiersman" that his opponents like the NRA promoted.[20] Dodd accused the gun lobby of "hysteria" when Congress took up gun control in the wake of John F. Kennedy's assassination; the NRA had resorted to "highly emotional appeals" about disarming the citizenry.[21] He denounced an angry gun rights crowd in the Connecticut State Capitol, where he had gone to testify in favor of proposed state gun control legislation, as "emotionally unstable." In this sense he understood gun control to be a civilizing, modernizing mission, even if it was not uncommon to hear his opponents wield the same language of emotion.[22]

Even purportedly distanced, bipartisan analyses of the gun debate framed the problem in terms of emotional and psychological fragility. Johnson's Commission on Law Enforcement and Administration of Justice, which published an extensive report in 1967 with a range of progressive recommendations for reform, dismissed conservative fears of disarming the public and opening the door to subversive or foreign conquest as the "most emotional position" toward gun control.[23] An unpublished draft of the Eisenhower Commission's report on guns and gun violence contained a section, excised from the final version, that offered an early gender analysis of gun culture, grounded in a superficial reading of Freudian theory, titled "Firearms and the American Psyche." It reflected on the belief that "guns are symbols of power or masculinity," that guns could embody sexual desires or anxieties. The authors of the report quoted none other than Ian Fleming, creator of James Bond, from *The Man with the Golden Gun* (1965): "the pistol . . . has significance for the owner as a symbol of virility, an extension of the male organ, and . . . excessive interest in guns (e.g., gun collections and gun clubs) is a form of fetishism." As one psychologist said, the gun "is both a source of fear and fascination and for some it takes on a magical quality. . . . To young men it is very much alive."[24]

It's possible "Firearms and the American Psyche" was redacted from the final report for its lack of social science rigor compared to the rest of the report, rather than its provocative nature. But it nevertheless demonstrated a kind of Cold War liberal understanding of gun "fetishism" rooted in modernization theory, which represented gun culture as backward, emotional, unsophisticatedly obsessed with virility and inanimate objects. It was not uncommon for liberals to talk about "gun nuts" in language analogous to that used for Vietnamese peasants or Central Asian nomads. As Americans who believed in the modernization mission of the early Cold War, the word *control* mattered as much as *gun* in *gun control*. Such policies would impose control on the emotions and passions of a population that hadn't quite yet met the conditions of modernity.

While gun control is identified almost exclusively with liberal politics in the twenty-first century, it's important to acknowledge just how much *control* appealed across the political spectrum in 1968. Many among the "silent majority" who would vote for Richard Nixon in November saw gun control as one component of a broader campaign of social control necessary to tame the worst excesses of the 1960s, excesses attributed to the permissiveness of liberalism and Johnson's Great Society. The tidal wave of letters sent to Congress and the president—Dodd alone claimed to receive 50,000 letters of support in the weeks after RFK's murder—testified to the popular impulse to control guns in order to control populations.[25] If many conservatives before 1967 chaffed at proposals to expand the federal bureaucracy to surveil gun owners and their purchases, by the summer of 1968 gun control suddenly went hand in hand with "law and order" politics. "Due to recent events which include the assassinations of Senator Kennedy and Martin Luther King, the riots in our cities, and the increased crime rate," wrote one of Dodd's constituents in a typical letter, "I urge passage of an extremely restrictive gun control law." Writers often mentioned recent Supreme Court decisions, like *Miranda v. Arizona* (1966), that expanded the rights of the accused, convicted, and incarcerated.[26] Popular patience with perceived criminals and "thugs," social constructs frequently racialized, wore thin. Johnson's pollster explained that even those liberals who tended to see socioeconomic problems at the root of violence were inclined to "hard line or conservative approaches" in response. Telegrams implored the president to take a strong stand, to push for "the most imaginably stringent gun control law," "an absolute prohibition against private ownership of firearms." As a friend wrote to a Johnson aide, "I don't think that many of us are in a half-way mood just now."[27]

MUCH OF THIS LANGUAGE CONNECTING GUNS and civilization, modernity, control, and backwardness came from the work of a journalist named Carl Bakal, whose 1966 book *The Right to Bear Arms* functioned as a foundational text for the postwar gun control movement. Bakal was also a founding member of the short-lived National Council for a Responsible Firearms Policy (NCRFP), the first gun control advocacy group to aspire to challenge the NRA at a national level, and would be among the first journalists the NRA attacked for advocating gun control, questioning his credentials, knowledge of firearms, and even his war record.[28] Bakal started investigating guns in the United States in the late 1950s and had done extensive research on comparisons between US patterns of ownership and systems of control and their foreign counterparts. By 1967 his book seemed to be on the night table of every Johnson administration official working on crime and violence. Dodd called it "the most complete source book on the firearms problem available today," and urged all members of the Senate to read it.[29] Ramsey Clark used the book to gather data for congressional testimony. Clark's own book, *Crime in America* (1970), in which he wrote, "Every civilized nation but one has acted to control guns," demonstrated the influence of Bakal's thinking on guns.[30] And Bakal was among the list of invitees to attend the White House signing of the Gun Control Act in October 1968.[31]

In *The Right to Bear Arms*, Bakal describes the plethora of guns in the United States as a "strange and peculiarly American plague," and throughout he uses the language of disease and pathology—threats to the civilized order over which modern nations must impose control. From the outset, Bakal portrays America's gunscape as alien in a world full of nations more sensible—more civilized—in their approach to deadly firearms. The book's opening chapter frames American gun violence in a global context, introducing ideas that would be common among control advocates by 1968: "no other modern nation makes death-dealing weapons so freely and cheaply available," and the US death toll from gun violence in the twentieth century exceeded that of all the country's wars over the same period (the latter figure he pegged at 530,000).[32] Bakal tells readers everything he had discovered about gun laws in other countries, mostly European, and how their restrictive systems kept their populations safe. He filled the book with dozens of accounts of odd gun incidents that he portrayed as uniquely American—a teenage girl pulling a gun on her friend in a dispute over an Elvis fan magazine; Russian rifles shipping to Klan members in Mississippi; a sixteen-year-old Texas boy hijacking a plane to fly it to Cuba, just to show communist sympathizers how bad Castro really was.[33]

Bakal, like the Democratic politicians who would push most aggressively for gun control in the lead up to the GCA of 1968, wanted to spur action by shaming Americans. Though grounded in research, Bakal's book was also hyperbolic in service of his larger goal. His claim, for instance, that his fellow Americans were "probably much safer practically anywhere out of this country than in it," willfully ignored conflict zones, like the one where his own country waged war in Vietnam. He had no patience for the National Rifle Association, which he referred to as the "Vigilante on the Potomac," and which he described as conducting, "for nearly four decades," "one of the most intensive and imaginative lobbying operations witnessed in Washington."[34] In that sense, *The Right to Bear Arms* was a clear work of activist journalism. It gave a nascent gun control movement the language it needed not just for understanding but for action. And, crucially, it established the framework for making sense of America's gun problem as one of comparative modernization.

The National Council for a Responsible Firearms Policy was the first group to claim to be a nationwide gun control organization. It drew heavily upon modernization theory to frame US public policy failings. While it never attracted a large membership, its prominent supporters gave it outsized influence in the first postwar decade of serious gun control politics. Its gravitas came from its first president, James V. Bennett, a liberal New Deal penal reformer who served as director of the US Bureau of Prisons from 1937 until his retirement in 1964. Bennett arrived at gun control advocacy through his own international work: he was a delegate to the UN Congress on the Prevention of Crime and Treatment of Offenders, where he met crime and prison experts from around the world. His participation in these conferences "enabled me to learn that the United States has fewer enforceable restrictions on the purchase and ownership of handguns than most other nations of the world," he explained to the subcommittee, noting that "Japan goes so far as to prohibit entirely the private ownership of handguns."[35] (Bakal, who served in the occupations of both Germany and Japan, noted that after the war US troops disarmed both populations and US officials wrote laws that restricted or prohibited gun ownership.)[36]

The NCRFP claimed only about a thousand members, a tiny fraction of the 1 million that funded its nemesis, the NRA. Despite Bennett and other prominent supporters, like New York City mayor John Lindsay, the NCRFP couldn't match the NRA's $5 million annual budget (more than $40 million in 2022 dollars).[37] But while it could not mobilize a massive grassroots campaign, the NCRFP did have a powerful ally in Dodd. Indeed, from the moment Dodd was appointed chair of the Juvenile Delinquency Subcommittee, Bennett offered his services in addressing the gun crime problem; eight years later, after the GCA had passed, Dodd wrote to Bennett, "I am certain that much of the committee's success is due to your untiring efforts."[38] It would not be a stretch to say that the NCRFP was a nongovernmental adjunct to Dodd's subcommittee. While it aimed to counterbalance the NRA, its goal was never to build a nationwide grassroots movement for gun control. Rather, it sought to leverage the power of its well-connected leadership to push for legislation and agitate for it through media connections.

Like a lobby, the NCRFP produced policy assessments for legislators and pamphlets. It also ran a series of provocative ads in national newspapers in 1968, including one that critiqued gun consumerism in big bold letters: "More and more people are buying guns to protect themselves from more and more people buying guns." Its approach to confronting the NRA was to take a middle ground, to appeal to an imagined constituency of gun owners who felt turned off by the increasingly anticonciliatory rhetoric from the gun lobby. One pamphlet took a shot at both rioters in cities and the NRA's "community stabilizers" line: "The tendency to resort to sniping and other military techniques as a means of political expression—and, in retaliation, widespread belief in the gun as a 'community stabilizer'—add up to a growing danger of anarchy."[39]

Like Dodd, the NCRFP imagined a center that had to hold at a time when left and right appeared to be pulling the country apart. And it was also a product of modernization thinking: wise liberal reformers, like Bennett, who had overhauled the federal prison system in the image of the New Deal and then exported that system to occupied Germany, could brainstorm policies to control those populations too vulnerable to exercise control themselves, whether they be teenagers or Black urban populations.[40] Failure to control these populations' access to guns threatened to derail normative social development. The NCRFP also expected white men to be rational actors who made prudent ("responsible") decisions about gun ownership and use. It did not lobby for restrictions on handgun or long gun ownership. In fact, after the GCA passed in 1968, the NCRFP would retreat from advocating more restrictive gun laws and instead encourage individual gun owners to reflect upon their need for a gun, a position that limited the group's influence in the 1970s, when new grassroots gun control organizations pushed for more ambitious reforms.[41]

AS THE ADMINISTRATION PREPARED its ill-fated legislative effort for licensing and registration in the fall of 1968, the National Commission on the Causes and Prevention of Violence—the Eisenhower Commission—went to work. Johnson charged the commission with a task imaginable only in an era when Americans believed that their combined economic, intellectual, and military might could be wielded to make the world a better place, or at least one more amenable to American interests. The commission's Firearms Task Force would produce a report that embodied the height of American modernization thinking, turning the magnifying glass from Third World societies overseas to domestic life. To counter the pathologies of violence, the FTF would offer some truly radical suggestions for halting the arms race playing out in countless locations across the country.

In his signing statement creating the commission, Johnson emphasized the significance of its cause in the context of the recent assassinations: "This troubled world will long remember the scar of the past week's violence, but when the week is remembered, let this be remembered, too: that out of anguish came a national resolve to search for the causes and to find the cures for the outbursts of violence which have brought so much heartbreak."[42] He asked its commissioners, staffers, and researchers to explain American violence across time and space and offer solutions to its contemporary manifestations.

By 1968 the problem seemed as intractable as building a spaceship and flying it to the moon. That the Nixon administration summarily ignored its various conclusions, issued in published reports throughout 1969, the year of the Apollo 11 mission—that the commission was, indeed, unremembered, just a year after its appointment—demonstrated that such an era had reached both its apex and its terminal crisis.

At the height of this "age of great dreams," as historian David Farber has described it, a confident United States had launched wars on poverty and crime to build the Great Society.[43] But as the decade came to a close, cynicism began to replace confidence, which many Americans came to believe had been hubris all along. And now Johnson asked a commission—yet another of his quixotic commissions—to solve the thorniest, most abstract social problem of all. "My charge to you is simple and direct," he wrote to the commissioners. "I ask you to undertake a penetrating search for the causes and prevention of violence—a search in our national life, our past as well as our present, our traditions as well as our institutions, our culture, our customs and our laws."[44] As with the Kerner Commission, the Eisenhower Commission's Firearms Task Force would offer answers and prescriptions for which the nation was not politically or socially prepared.

But where to start? Johnson appointed commissioners from the political, legal, and academic worlds. They ranged across the political spectrum, from liberals like Senator Philip Hart to conservatives like Senator Roman Hruska, who had for the previous decade served as Thomas Dodd's chief sparring partner on gun control legislation on the Juvenile Delinquency Subcommittee. (Johnson aide Larry Temple later speculated, "I think that the president put Hruska on there with the idea of converting him [to gun control] and maybe the conversion of Hruska would be the impetus to getting gun control legislation.")[45] The commissioners appointed an executive director—respected Washington, DC, attorney Lloyd N. Cutler—who then divided the work into seven task forces, each assigned two directors, one a lawyer and one a social scientist. The task forces would cover assassinations, group violence, individual violence, law enforcement, media, firearms, and US history. The staff of each task force would consist of a mix of attorneys from private practice, law school faculty, and social scientists. The commission assigned the Firearms Task Force to George D. Newton Jr., a lawyer from Washington, DC, and Franklin E. Zimring, a young law professor at the University of Chicago and one of the few criminologists studying guns. Newton and Zimring recruited a staff of nine researchers, including two women, and five secretaries, all women.[46]

In his letter to Milton Eisenhower, Johnson insisted that the country "must learn more about the deadly role that firearms play in our national life." He offered questions for the commission to consider: "What are the historical and contemporary attitudes of American citizens toward guns and gun control?" "What is the relationship between the easy availability of firearms and violence of all types?" "What technological, criminological and other developments will permit the rapid and easy identification and control of guns and gun use?" Johnson's charge to Eisenhower ended with an explicit request to gather data on how the rest of the world had addressed gun violence. He wanted the commission to investigate what the United States could "learn from the experience of other nations."[47]

Commission directors and staff felt that their work would offer real material solutions to intractable problems, demonstrating the trademark American confidence in the social sciences at its postwar peak. Noted sociologist Marvin E. Wolfgang served as codirector of research for the commission. As he tracked the FTF's progress in the fall of 1968, Wolfgang expressed the same faith in the social sciences to find solutions that US elites placed in modernization theory's ability to transform the Third World. What this political problem stretching back to the beginning of the decade needed, Wolfgang argued, was good objective social science. "Much of the recent controversy about the various schemes to control firearms can best be resolved by research," he wrote. "To date, arguments to support or oppose specific kinds of gun control legislation have been based less on evidence than on emotion," Wolfgang asserted, claiming the masculine ground of rationality for the social sciences.[48]

The FTF's researchers were, in fact, shocked to discover how little empirical research existed on issues like gun production, distribution, sales, and violence. Modern criminology was a rich field linking sociology and legal studies, but little work existed on questions specifically related to guns, crime, and society. In praising a draft of the FTF's report, eminent criminologist Leon Radzinowicz, director of the Institute of Criminology at Cambridge University, observed that it was "one of the first, if not the first attempt to give a comprehensive view of the problem." Radzinowicz did recommend, however, that the report be "more incisive and persistent" in identifying the "pressure groups resisting control," but he suggested that it do so "without being too emotional about the whole thing."[49]

FROM THE OUTSET THE FTF ADOPTED a global perspective on the problem of gun violence, looking both outward toward other nations' attitudes and experiences and inward at the impact of imports.[50] Staffers examined what the world was saying about the US gun problem. Surveying international reactions to the Robert Kennedy killing, *Time* observed that much of the world saw the country as a "blood-drenched, continent-wide shooting range where toddlers blast off with real rifles, housewives pack pearl-handled revolvers, and political assassins stalk their victims at will."[51] The US Information Agency (USIA), on behalf of the State Department, digested foreign press reactions to events at home. The agency reported "sensationalist headlines" around the world in the days after the uprisings in Detroit and Newark, including "Racial War Explodes in U.S.A." from *La Nación* of Chile and "12,000 U.S. Soldiers Fail to Contain Negro Revolution" from *Al-Rai al-Am* of Sudan.[52] The summer of 1968 brought widespread commentary, "unprecedented in recent years," according to USIA, on the deep rot guns had wrought in American society. Soviet media, of course, saw the forces of "monopolistic capital" at work, "extreme rightwing forces . . . in favor of a militarization of the country" and an "arms race."[53]

Friendly nations struggled to comprehend recent events. "Never before has America had more doubt about itself," said a West German radio correspondent, reflecting on the "severe sickness" of social and political violence. In the United Kingdom, newspapers across the political spectrum condemned the failure to implement even the mildest of firearms controls. "Americans and their Congress should be under no illusions about the universal dismay and contempt caused by the present permissive attitude to the purchase and ownership of deadly weapons," wrote Edinburgh's *Scotsman*. "It is a sorry and frightening situation when the richest, the most powerful and the most technologically sophisticated nation on earth refuses to alter a situation that can just be described as uncivilized and insane."[54]

The FTF was inspired by global reactions and potential global solutions. Staff researchers got a lot of mileage out of the data gathered from Dean Rusk's request for information on gun laws around the world in the immediate aftermath of Bobby Kennedy's slaying.[55] The nearly 120 telegrammed responses accounted for almost every independent country in the world. Some were as short as a page or two, but many were lengthier and included attachments such as published laws relating to firearms. The State Department's collection of telegrams finally provided some evidence to test critics' pronouncements about gun control in "civilized" countries and unspoken assumptions about the "uncivilized" world.

The FTF discovered that, if anything, the critics hadn't gone far enough. Americans had fewer restrictions on access to guns than the citizens of virtually any other society on earth, a condition the gun boom of the postwar era had intensified. What was so striking about the telegrams was not how they confirmed contrasts between the United States and other wealthy industrialized countries but how they revealed how nearly universal gun control laws were throughout the world, even in the many countries that Americans implicitly denigrated when they divided the world between "civilized" and "uncivilized."

The outliers were countries that had few or no national gun control laws, as opposed to those that did. Thus a telegram from the US embassy in Kabul, Afghanistan, stands out from others in the collection for observing where no gun control regulations existed. In the frontier region on the border between Afghanistan and Pakistan, among Pashtun groups, embassy staff reported, "possession of firearms is [an] accepted symbol of manhood and [an] expression [of] independence," a description that surely echoed in liberal American ears. Embassy officials did note, however, that elsewhere in the country the government imposed restrictions on handguns and required permits for other kinds of weapons.[56] Afghanistan presented a rare analogy to the US patchwork of laws, permitting unrestricted ownership in some places and tight restrictions elsewhere. The Kandahar region was Afghanistan's Arizona, while Kabul was its Washington, DC.

Mostly, however, the telegrams noted that nearly all countries, from Algeria to Zambia, maintained some sort of restrictions on gun possession. These restrictions took one of two forms: licensing, a means of controlling the people who could access guns; and registration, a means of controlling the guns people could access. Most countries had some combination of the two. The United States did, too, of course, in some states and at the federal level in the mildest of ways—the 1934 National Firearms Act used Congress's power to tax to limit the kinds of guns citizens could own (restricting machine guns and other "gangster guns"), and the 1938 Federal Firearms Act delineated classes of people who could buy and sell them (prohibiting convicted felons, among others). But telegrams relayed that gun laws around the world placed far greater restrictions on ownership than the United States, where virtually any gun below a certain caliber and lacking automatic fire capabilities was easily purchased. At one point during the research process, FTF staff collated all the comparative information that could be gleaned from telegrams from about a hundred countries. More than 90 percent of them had clear national laws or statutes with regard to firearms, and even some that didn't, like Australia and Switzerland, had federal governmental systems wherein individual states or provinces could (and most often did) create their own local gun laws.[57]

The existence of gun laws did not mean, however, that gun violence did not exist, or that gun ownership and use was restricted in practice. Laws are only as strong as the states that attempt to enforce them. In countries with strong states and restrictive laws, like Japan, gun violence rates were remarkably low—the country of 100 million people experienced a "peak" of fifty firearms homicides in 1963 but brought that figure down to just twelve in 1965.[58] Elsewhere, weak states with restrictive gun laws could not enforce them. Embassy staff in Laos noted that Laotian gun laws were "stringent on paper" but "practically non-existent with constant smuggling of all types of weapons across various borders." A weak state ensnared in a civil war also meant that data on gun violence crimes were "highly questionable," and no data existed for the years before an attempted coup in 1965, when "previous statistics were destroyed."[59]

THE SOCIOLOGICAL QUESTION of how societies can prevent gun violence is not any great mystery today, and it wasn't in the 1960s either. Societies prevent gun violence by restricting the population's access to guns. Mountains of data demonstrate that fewer guns mean fewer gun deaths.[60] Of course such a conclusion does not mean that societies are less violent when there are fewer guns; it means only that violence results in fewer deaths when guns are harder to find. Guns are, simply, the most lethal common tool of personal violence, far more so than knives, which are nevertheless used in violent crime with greater frequency. Critics in the 1960s frequently cited the statistic that gun attacks were five times as lethal as knife attacks.[61]

But acknowledging that more guns leads to more gun violence does not necessarily mean that the answer to the US gun violence problem lies in restricting access to guns. In a sense the United States is simply too far gone for that solution. However many guns there are in the United States in the third decade of the twenty-first century—most estimates put the figure well over 400 million—there are simply too many to try to restrict access to them. In that way, at least, the gun lobby was successful. It knew that ownership could reach such levels nationwide that the persistent question of restricting access, which was commonly deliberated in the 1960s, would become irrelevant. The debates over rights and laws were a distraction, a delaying tactic, while stockpiles accumulated; debating the individual's right to own a gun in the twenty-first century would be like debating the right to own a car or a phone, perhaps even more futile, given the US Supreme Court's confirmation of that right in *District of Columbia v. Heller* (2008), *McDonald v. Chicago* (2010), and *New York Pistol & Rifle Association, Inc. v. Bruen* (2022). The 1970s' debates on whether private citizens should be able to own handguns have devolved into arguments about the right to own "weapons of war" (an argument Tom Dodd knew well). Every year since the Gun Control Act in which millions of guns went onto the civilian market and Congress did nothing to stop it was a triumph for the gun lobby. There is simply no practical way to reduce the nationwide private firearms arsenal to levels that could make a significant impact on annual gun violence death rates. Consider even a 20 percent reduction—eliminating, say, 80 million out of 400 million guns—and you're still left with 320 million guns in private hands, as much as a third of them handguns. US ownership rates would still be significantly higher than not just other peer countries but any other country, period.

Researchers studying the gun problem in the 1960s had no illusion about the obvious solutions to gun violence problems either, though they tended to be more sanguine about the possibilities for reform. Celebrated Columbia University sociologist Amitai Etzioni told the White House in 1968 that if gun control were to be effective it could not be half-hearted and piecemeal. "The ultimate purpose of the various measures," he wrote in a policy memo, "ought to be clearly and openly stated: to reduce the amount of firearms to that present in other leading democracies."[62] To much of the rest of the world, America's gun mystique was no mystique at all: Americans simply had too many guns. But for the United States in the twenty-first century, reducing "the amount of firearms to that present in other leading democracies" is simply inconceivable. Compare the United States to Great Britain. A gun data clearinghouse at the University of Sydney put gun ownership in the United States in 2017 at 120 guns per 100 people. In Great Britain it was 5 guns per 100 people.[63] How can any society eliminate 115 guns per 100 people in a country of 330 million people?

The numbers game was at the time, and will always be, a distraction, because whatever the precise number is, it will be too high in historical and comparative contexts. The Firearms Task Force came to the same conclusion in its published 1969 report. It settled on the number of 90 million total guns in civilian hands, knowing that common estimates ranged from 50 million to 300 million (one might even hear estimates as high as a billion, depending on the speaker), but that the best data, culled from federal agencies and gun manufacturers, put it somewhere between 80 and 100 million.[64] The precise number, however, "makes little difference to any public policy question about firearms," the FTF wrote. "By whatever measure, the United States has an abundance of firearms."[65] The task force hesitated to say "too many," but you didn't have to read deeply between the lines to get the point.

Ultimately the FTF hedged its inferences based on observations of foreign systems but nevertheless concluded that the United States needed to get rid of handguns, which were strictly controlled in almost every country in the world with a stable government. "Firearms control systems that appear to work well in other countries with cultures and traditions different from the United States would not necessarily help to lessen the American problem of firearms mis-use," the final report said. "Yet it would be unwise to ignore what other nations have accomplished in controlling firearms violence."[66] There were good rea-sons to be skeptical of simplistic comparisons of laws in different countries but it was also hard to ignore the universal data demonstrating that "control systems that substantially reduce the number of guns are effective in reducing the level of gun violence."[67] Note the careful wording: the FTF did not say that gun laws reduce gun violence, but that gun laws *that effectively decrease the number of guns* reduce gun violence. By definition, gun violence can't exist where there are no guns.

The Firearms Task Force produced a landmark study of a perennially con-troversial issue, the most thorough government-sponsored one of its kind to date, and yet it has been barely a footnote in the literature on guns and gun violence in the last half century. In contrast, its contemporary, the Kerner Commission, published its report in a paperback that made the bestseller lists, and is still sold today in an edition annotated by prominent scholars.[68]

Why the contrast? The study's comparative nature, collecting data from around the world to assess which public policy approaches to guns and gun violence worked and which didn't, meant that its conclusions were intended to represent a series of global best practices, rather than policies specifically intended to address the problem in the unique constitutional and cultural con-text of the United States. The FTF called upon the US government to initiate what likely would have been the most extensive, expensive, and controversial civilian disarmament program in world history. "We have concluded that the only sure way to reduce gun violence is to reduce the number of handguns in civilian hands in this country," the final report read, acknowledging some 24 million in private hands. "We recognize this will be a massive and expensive task. But, the price is one we should be prepared to pay." They arrived at that conclusion not because the FTF's staff members were eager "gun grabbers" but rather because they observed how the rest of the world addressed the myriad problems presented by guns, especially handguns—cheap, plentiful, easy to use, concealable, incomparably deadly. They were Cold War liberals who believed that social science pointed toward universal best practices for modern democracies. What was good for the Japan or West Germany that US modernity reconstructed after the Second World War, and where the United States wrote new laws restricting firearms ownership, was good for the United States. Modernization could be a two-way street. The FTF recognized the tre-mendous resistance handgun confiscation would encounter, acknowledging that "no other country has ever attempted to control handguns with over 24 million such guns already in circulation. The success of any such undertaking must depend upon public understanding and support." Handgun ownership should be regulated by a "federal standard of restrictive licensing to confine handguns to persons who need them and to substantially reduce the number of handguns now in civilian hands." The goal was to reduce the number of guns in civilian hands by 90 percent, the remaining 10 percent in the hands of those who needed firearms for professional reasons.[69]

If the FTF envisioned a massive, costly, and unprecedented handgun confiscation program as the only effective solution to gun violence in 1968, when there was roughly one handgun for every twelve people in the country, what would its researchers say in the 2020s, when there is likely one handgun for every three?

To understand what went wrong after 1968, and how the Eisenhower Commission's recommendations were ignored and its predictions fulfilled, we have to appreciate what came to be called "the loophole."

CHAPTER **5**

THE NEW GREAT WESTERN

Single Action
THE DEPUTY

. . . has a full ramp sight of unique design with micrometer adjustment for windage and elevation. This new model is made in the Service Type with 4" barrel and in a Target Model with 6" barrel.

$75.00 .22 and .38 Spec. .357 ATOMIC
        CALIBERS   At $98.95

THE LOOPHOLE

AS 1968 CAME TO A CLOSE a federal bureaucrat named Harold A. Serr sat in his office and contemplated how much more complicated his job was about to get. Serr directed the Alcohol and Tobacco Tax Division (ATTD) of the Treasury Department's Internal Revenue Service (IRS), which had been charged with the administration of federal gun laws going back to the first wave of federal legislation in the 1930s. The 1934 National Firearms Act controlled guns through the federal government's taxing authority. It didn't ban guns outright but instead imposed heavy fees and registration burdens on machine guns and other "gangster guns" that plagued interwar America's urban landscape. Federal tax officials like Serr, then, also functioned as federal gun control officials.

When Lyndon Johnson signed the Gun Control Act into law on October 22, 1968, however, the ATTD's responsibilities expanded: it would now oversee gun imports into the United States, a task formerly administered by the State Department's Office of Munitions Control (OMC). Given its expanded purview under the GCA, the ATTD became the Alcohol, Tobacco, and Firearms Division (ATFD, and later, the Bureau of Alcohol, Tobacco, and Firearms [BATF]), and Serr became its new head. The Johnson administration charged Serr's ATFD with restricting the importation of all guns deemed "unsuitable for sporting purposes," a subjective criterion, to be sure, but one that the ATFD would define using a scoring rubric that assigned points for various characteristics of every gun imported—guns earned points based on barrel length, frame construction quality, weight, caliber, safety features, and various accessories.[1] As far back as 1958 members of Congress had urged the OMC to use its statutory authority to regulate gun imports; the office had, for the most part, demurred, but now responsibility for imports fell to Serr, and Congress had given him a set of criteria with which to execute it.

With all this on his mind in late 1968, Serr sat in his office and listened as a "small importer of handguns" pleaded his case.[2] The importer had just purchased a new overseas cache of cheap handguns, but while it was crossing the Atlantic the GCA went into effect and the new rules prohibited the importation of these firearms with no "sporting purpose" when they arrived in the United States.

"What am I to do? I'll go bankrupt if I can't bring them in," the importer explained.

"Why don't you dump them at a loss in some foreign market?" Serr asked.

"Where?"

"Try Cuba, Central America," Serr suggested. The importer shook his head.

"What about South America? Asia?" Again, no luck.

"Africa?" Serr had run out of suggestions. Wasn't the world outside America's borders full of people who wanted cheap guns?

"Mr. Serr," the importer said, "don't you know that the United States is the only country where there is an open market for guns? I couldn't give these guns away in practically any other place in the world."[3]

As head of the ATTD and then the ATFD, Harold Serr almost certainly wasn't ignorant of the importer's predicament in late 1968. Rather he told this story to Congress a couple of years after the fact because he knew that it effectively illustrated the point gun control legislators and federal officials like Serr had made for years: the United States was the dumping ground for the world's cheap guns, the preeminent surefire consumer market for them, and until the US government did something to stanch the flood, the country would continue to be plagued by the social consequences of mass arming at cut-rate prices.

The first federal gun control legislation in thirty years intended to address that problem by establishing a six-month deadline for imposing the new "sporting purposes" criteria for gun imports. Many of the guns importers had brought into the country throughout the 1960s, guns that had helped build a mass consumer market and arm an increasingly anxious population, would be ineligible as of December 16, 1968.[4] The clock was ticking, for Serr's importer and dozens of others like him, eager to stock their warehouses for a forthcoming era of famine after a decade of feasting.

Tom Dodd knew what the importers were up to. The chief legislative architect of the GCA pressed President Johnson and Attorney General Clark to respond to a marked increase in importing activities. Not only had the urban upheavals of the previous year created greater demand for cheap guns, particularly handguns for "self-defense," but importers had foreseen the inevitability of new federal regulations and scaled up their business while it remained legal. In just the first half of 1968, the State Department had issued 1.6 million import licenses, a total that already far exceeded the 1.2 million issued for all of 1967. Total handgun sales for 1967, from both domestic and foreign sources, were nearly 1.7 million, more than double the total from just three years earlier.[5] Dodd worried that without immediate action, 1968's import total could exceed 3 million guns. "It was never my intention," he wrote Johnson, "to give importers ample time to import millions of weapons that will be used to kill, maim and rob citizens of the United States during the years to come." Dodd asked the president for an executive order that would impose the new criteria and shut the doors immediately. He also pursued a legislative route, submitting an amendment to Title IV in the Senate that would push up the effective date for the law to August 1. He castigated the "gun runners" who were "attempting to make a last-ditch effort to flood the United States with as many as three million lethal weapons before December 16." Allowing "these gun runners six months to flood the nation with cheap foreign-made and military surplus firearms, and to put more guns into the hands of criminals" would violate Congress's intent to slam the door shut on imports.[6] Dodd knew it had taken Congress nearly a decade to pass gun legislation; such a glacial pace was unsuited for the acute problems the country faced in 1968.

Dodd was right that the importers moved quickly to bring in as many guns as they could before the door slammed shut. But the smartest of them, like Sam Cummings, always two steps ahead of Dodd, had been planning for years for just such a contingency. Cummings's Interarms imported about 250,000 guns annually in the years before 1968; its warehouses in Alexandria burst with enough supply, as many as 1 million small arms (Cummings boasted that he could arm several nation-states at the drop of a hat), to last at least a half decade on the US market. Still, the 1968 law would eliminate upward of 95 percent of Interarms' domestic sales by prohibiting the importation of war surplus firearms—the guns that had made Cummings rich, if not the international armaments that had made him infamous. He continued to sell guns on the US market as the American agent of a number of foreign gunmakers, and he also operated his own manufacturing facilities in Virginia and Alabama, but the GCA brought the halcyon age of America's golden gun runner to an end.[7]

Yet other entrepreneurs demonstrated that gun capitalism could always find a way. While the legislative victories on gun control in 1968 may have been a turning point, they ultimately proved to be more symbol than substance. The

GCA banned the cheap handgun imports that politicians blamed for gun violence, preventing upward of 750,000 from entering the US market each year.[8]
But the law also contained what critics called "the loophole," which was really
two related loopholes: the GCA neglected to prohibit the importation of most
gun *parts* as well as the domestic production of cheap handguns. As a result
the supply of the very weapons the GCA sought to constrain barely hiccupped
in the early 1970s, and by the middle of the decade many American cities suffered their worst gun violence rates of the postwar era, abetted by the inexora-
bility of gun capitalism.

Out of the loophole came a new gun control movement, one emerging at
the grassroots level in cities like Chicago and Detroit. The loophole taught
gun control advocates that the gun problem was not rooted in some vague
notion of criminality, in a horde of masked bad actors seeking guns for nefarious purposes. Instead the problem was the materiality of guns: there were
too many, and there would always be too many if the legislative response to
that reality was to tiptoe around the booming consumer market. But the GCA
didn't acknowledge the problem to be too many guns; instead it assumed that,
regardless of how many guns there were, the state needed to ensure they were
kept from bad people.[9] The 1960s gun control debate constructed a virtuous
gun buyer and owner, the "law-abiding citizen," and counterposed his rights
against the unvirtuous criminal and radical, all the while accommodating to
the virtually unchecked expansion of gun capitalism. It was the very diagnosis
that the NRA and the gun manufacturers offered. As they had wanted, the
GCA legislated around the problem of plenty. By attempting to triangulate a
path between commerce and culture, the architects of 1968's legislative victories passed the problem off to future generations of lawmakers. But the loophole showed gun critics that legislative tiptoeing would not work, that gun
capitalism would continue to arm an eager population for the social and political conflicts of the present and the future.

FEW PEOPLE SAW THE LOOPHOLE COMING until it was too late. Within six
months of the Gun Control Act of 1968's taking effect, officials in the Treasury
Department and Dodd's subcommittee staff spotted it, as did keen observers
in the press, but somehow, after six years of testimony—many dozens of witnesses, many hundreds of hours, many different bills negotiated and rejected
and eventually accepted and passed—none of them had anticipated it.

The GCA prohibited the importation of firearms "not suitable for sporting
purposes," which, in the eyes of its architects, would stymie the flood of Saturday Night Specials, those cheap handguns, like the Roscoe, manufactured in

factories in West Germany, Italy, Spain, and elsewhere that could be had for as little as ten dollars. Nobody hunted with a cheap handgun; nobody used one for shooting sports. True target pistols were manufactured in Europe, no doubt, but they looked nothing like their Saturday Night Special counterparts: even small-caliber target pistols had relatively long barrels, and if they weren't manufactured to exacting standards using quality materials, they wouldn't meet the accuracy needs of sport-shooting enthusiasts. High standards meant they were expensive. Target pistols met the "sporting purposes" criteria of the GCA. But nobody saw target pistols as the problem.

They saw Saturday Night Specials as the problem, and they assumed that the GCA's provisions would block their importation, meaning fewer cheap guns would flood into urban areas, where potential criminals or rioters and looters or even revolutionaries could access them. The gun manufacturers supported the import ban, and so did the NRA. The "gun lobby" recognized that these cheap handguns, which only ever made the news for killing and maiming people, were bad for business and the future of gun ownership in the United States, even if old-line gunmakers increasingly saw the market opportunities in the 1970s for small concealable pistols and revolvers. In fact, critics of the GCA said that the new law was a gift to the firearms industry: it eliminated a major competitor, one that had gobbled up market share and driven prices down. The traditional handgun manufacturers—Colt and Smith & Wesson were the largest—could now monopolize the handgun industry without competition from a slew of bargain brands that ate up market share and gave good guns a bad name.

But the entrepreneurs who saw the loophole would take advantage of its two related omissions: first, while the GCA prohibited the importation of guns "not suitable for sporting purposes," it did nothing to prohibit the importation of most gun parts, parts that might be used to assemble any kind of gun. The GCA did prohibit the importation of unsuitable gun frames or receivers—these are typically the largest of the many parts that make up a handgun—but even those parts might be assembled from smaller component parts that could be imported.[10] The loophole's other significant oversight was that cheap gun frames—in fact, whole cheap guns identical to their imported counterparts—could simply be manufactured in the United States without restriction.

Just months into 1969 critics noticed these flaws. Not only had the GCA failed to eliminate foreign competition in the handgun market, they observed, but it had inadvertently created a lucrative domestic market for the production of cheap handguns. The prices would go up, to be sure—those ten-dollar handguns might be twenty or twenty-five dollars now, because manufacturing and labor costs in the United States were higher than in Germany or Italy—but the difference between a $25 handgun and a $100 one from a top gunmaker like Smith & Wesson meant that a two-tiered market would continue to exist and would flourish. Sharp-eyed entrepreneurs saw what was coming with the GCA, and by 1969 they were ready to crank out the cheap handguns domestically now that the law had killed foreign competition. Congress created the loophole and gun capitalism jumped through it.

The press first reported on the loophole in the spring of 1969 and Dodd's committee scrambled to meet and address it that summer.[11] At hearings before Dodd's committee, IRS commissioner Randolph W. Thrower, who oversaw the newly minted ATFD, delivered the numbers that demonstrated the seriousness of the loophole. On the one hand, the GCA really did dam the flood of cheap imported handguns into the country. In the two months before the GCA's various provisions went into effect, roughly 1 million foreign-made handguns came into the United States, a rate of 500,000 per month. On average, in the first six months of 1969, only about 45,000 handguns entered per month. "Our experience has shown that we have been successful in keeping out of the United States cheap foreign-made firearms," Thrower told Dodd's subcommittee. Surely Dodd welcomed that statement after six years of working to just such an end. On the other hand, Thrower continued, "we have found that the importation restriction has resulted in a substantial increase in the domestic production of these cheap weapons."[12] Dodd and his subcommittee had missed the loophole, but the gun importers hadn't.

Thrower estimated that domestic production of Saturday Night Specials in 1968, before the GCA went into effect, was no more than 75,000, a total almost negligible compared to import figures. As best Treasury officials could tell, that number was on pace to increase by 1,000 percent in just a year, and by 1970, domestic production of these cheap and dangerous handguns could reach 1 million units annually.[13] Dodd fumed. "We wrote that ban on imports into the law very purposely to stop the dreadful numbers of these weapons which were pouring into this country every day," he said in the summer of 1969. "And I don't think it ever occurred to us that the domestic producer would pick it up, and in effect, just continue the problem."[14] He never saw the loophole coming.

GUN DEALER SAUL EIG HAD SEEN THE LOOPHOLE, months before anyone else, and all he wanted was for everyone to leave him the hell alone about it. In contrast to Sam Cummings, he tended to answer questions about his work with a quick "None of your business." When Neil Sheehan of the *New York*

Times called in 1969, Eig told him, "We don't want publicity." Another journalist looking into Eig's work a year later noted, "The secrecy under which Saul Eig conducts his business is reminiscent somehow of a James Bond novel." When a team of journalists investigating cheap handguns for the *Miami News* showed up in 1981, Eig shooed them away; the reporters observed that Eig had "never been one to trumpet his commercial achievements." At that point Eig was a fifty-something retiree living a comfortable life in his $350,000 home in Miami's ritzy Coconut Grove neighborhood, almost a decade removed from the gun business. But now, thanks to John Hinckley Jr., the man who shot Ronald Reagan just two months after the new president's inauguration, the press had some uncomfortable questions about Eig's commercial connections to the assassination attempt.

In the course of their investigation, the *Miami News* reporters learned that Eig had once been the country's most prolific handgun dealer. He was the Sam Cummings of the smallest small arms, an ambitious and wily entrepreneur who struck gold first with handgun imports and then, when the GCA closed the import doors, by exploiting the GCA's loophole. For his efforts, the *Miami News* team dubbed him the "Henry Ford of the $14.95 revolver."[15]

Eig might have disappeared into obscurity if not for Hinckley. Hinckley's gun, an RG-14 six-shot revolver with a two-and-a-half-inch barrel, purchased in October 1980 for forty-seven dollars at Rocky's Pawn Shop in Dallas (he had bought two of them), inspired the journalists to put together a series of articles titled "Handguns: The Snub-Nosed Killer." When Americans imagined handguns, they were likely to think of a weapon made by Smith & Wesson or Colt, something iconic and masculine, if not conspicuously phallic, like the S&W .44 Magnum carried by Detective Harry Callahan and, later, Yoshi Hattori's killer, Rodney Peairs. *Dirty Harry*'s title character, played by Clint Eastwood, describes his Magnum as "the most powerful handgun in the world," a firearm so potent and unwieldy that even the NRA in the 1930s had supported restricting these "freaks."[16] Hinckley's RG-14 presented a stark contrast: easy to conceal, not just in a pocket but in a large hand; a quarter of the weight of the Magnum, it looked like a toy by comparison. Where the .44 Magnum boomed, the RG-14 snapped. But that snap was powerful enough to send a bullet crashing into Ronald Reagan's ribs on March 30, 1981. (Before the shooting Hinckley wrote a poem, "Guns Are Fun!" about his diminutive RG-14: "This gun gives me pornographic power. / If I wish, the president will fall / and the world will look at me in disbelief, / all because I own an inexpensive gun.")[17] Soon thereafter, the press wanted to know about the RG-14, which didn't look like anybody's idea of a real handgun, but which, once they started looking, seemed to be everybody's actual handgun.[18]

The RG-14 handgun, manufactured in Miami by RG Industries, that John Hinckley Jr. used to shoot Ronald Reagan in 1981. (© Brad Trent)

The RG in RG-14 stood for Röhm Gesellschaft, the very same Rohm that had flooded the US market in the 1960s, under a variety of brand names, including Roscoe, with more cheap handguns than any other foreign manufacturer. In 1968 the GCA effectively shut Rohm's imports out of the country. Very few of the hundreds of thousands of guns the company made each year would pass muster under the most generous definition of "sporting purposes." If Rohm had any chance of keeping the money flowing from the United States, it would need some help.

Enter Saul Eig, at the time of the GCA's passage a "slim, baldish," forty-two-year-old businessman from Miami who had been, for more than a decade, the biggest US buyer of Rohm's cheap guns. Rohm had been an engineering firm, manufacturing parts for drilling equipment, when it began making cheap starter pistols in 1951 at its factory in Sontheim, a small town in southern West Germany. As Günther Röhm told it (he owned the company, along with his brothers Heinrich and Peter), US soldiers stationed in Germany bought these cheap starter pistols as novelties and souvenirs and brought them home, where they caught the eye of an entrepreneurial importer from San Francisco, who told Günther and his brothers in 1955 that, if they could manufacture the same guns but with live ammunition barrels, they all stood to make a lot of money from American gun buyers. A year later, Saul Eig, proprietor of Eig Cutlery, at the time a knife and scissors distributor, showed up in Sontheim, looking to buy cheap guns with his own name stamped on them. He would return twice a year thereafter, until 1968, each time arranging for huge shipments of handguns. All total, Rohm would export about 1.5 million handguns to the United States between 1955 and 1968, and about a third of them went to Saul Eig stamped with the "Eig" brand name.[19]

As for Eig, in the dozen years before the GCA passed, he imported about 1.5 million handguns, stamped with his name or others, according to Alcohol, Tobacco, and Firearms (ATF) records the journalists from the *Miami News* acquired through a Freedom of Information Act request. That total likely made him the single biggest US importer of handguns, accounting for one in every ten imports in the decade before the GCA and "13 per cent of all the handguns brought into the U.S. in the last 51 years," according to a 1969 Associated Press report. In 1967 he had licenses to bring in 368,000 handguns; in just the first six months of 1968 he was authorized to import 695,000 more, 60 percent of all US handgun imports over that period.[20] Like Cummings, he saw the door closing and hustled to get in as much product as he could before it slammed shut.

Eig's guns became infamous among law enforcement. In Chicago in the late 1960s, the two top gun makes seized by police were Rohm and Eig.[21] Rohm was "one word everyone in the homicide department knows how to spell," a Cleveland police official told Congress, "believe me."[22] In Eig's hometown of Miami, one homicide detective estimated that as many as 40 percent of the city's homicides were committed with what the department called an "Eig-type gun." "It's the gun that has killed more people in this country than any other brand," one Washington, DC, gun expert said.[23] Both statements were likely unintentional exaggerations—given Eig's prominence in the Miami market, any off-brand Saturday Night Special could be an "Eig-type gun"—but Eig nevertheless already had something of a reputation by the time the GCA passed.

Eig imported and sold all of his cheap handguns through 1968 so inconspicuously that the Eisenhower Commission's researchers only discovered his existence months into their work. Recall that the Firearms Task Force first learned in 1968 that a dozen or more cheap handgun brand names, including Eig, all traced back to Rohm. When FTF researchers attempted to trace cheap handguns back to their European sources, they sent an eleven-page list of guns, with serial numbers, to the US embassy in Bonn to pass along to what they believed was a German manufacturer named Eig, requesting that the company provide whatever data it had on those guns. The State Department forwarded to the FTF its correspondence with Bonn in which embassy staff explained that Rohm had, in fact, manufactured the guns, stamped them with Eig's name, and shipped them to the Miami importer.[24] From Eig's perspective, it was a minor miracle that he had eluded serious scrutiny not just from the Eisenhower Commission but also from Dodd's high-profile subcommittee. It was no wonder he never wanted to talk to anyone.

In the months after Title IV passed, banning the imported guns that had made him wealthy, Eig offered the Röhm brothers a proposition: they could continue making and selling their handguns under the RG brand name if they relocated assembly to Miami, where he would manage operations to keep the guns and profits flowing. Eig intended to take advantage of the GCA's loophole allowing for the importation of gun parts other than frames. He found a local metalworker to produce frames for forty-three cents each, using a cheap metal alloy called Zamak. He would simply import the other thirty-one parts for each RG handgun from Rohm's Sontheim factory. In October 1968 he spent $45,000 to purchase the Pentecostal Holiness Church and School in northwest Miami, not far from the airport, and converted it into a factory to assemble guns (an irony lost on no one who noticed). According to one account, by the end of 1969 he was paying minimum wage to fifteen Cuban immigrants to assemble 300 guns a day in the former church. Just a year after the GCA went into effect, Saul Eig's RG Industries, the name the Röhm brothers and Eig gave their new company, was already manufacturing guns at a rate of 100,000 per year.[25]

Eig found and exploited the loophole before anyone else. But then, just a couple of years into the life of Miami's new RG Industries, he decided he'd had enough. The Röhms found other local managers to continue running the business, which produced more than 100,000 cheap handguns a year when John Hinckley Jr. bought two from a Dallas pawnshop. At the end of the 1970s RG Industries was the third-largest domestic handgun manufacturer, behind New England gunmakers Smith & Wesson and Sturm, Ruger. Eig sold off his personal stock of guns to a company called Firearms Import & Export, an importer and distributor (and sixth-largest US handgun producer) in nearby Hialeah run by New York transplant Al Bernkrant. Bernkrant built his own business on Eig's model, sourcing cheap frames from local manufacturers, buying parts kits from overseas, and assembling handguns in a local factory. His bestsellers included the .25-caliber Titan pistol, well known to police officers who worked

street crimes. Bernkrant's big European supplier was Fabbrica d'Armi Tanfoglio Giuseppe, a gunmaker in the northern Italian city of Brescia, a traditional arms manufacturing center. (Bernkrant's loquacious brother boasted to
a reporter that it was "the Italian town Napoleon bought his arms from.") The
1981 *Miami News* investigation learned that Tanfoglio had doubled the size of
its operations, building an entire second factory, just to meet Bernkrant's gun
orders.[26]

When Hinckley shot Reagan and the *Miami News* came knocking at Eig's
Coconut Grove door, then, Eig had been out of the gun business for almost
a decade. (There was, it seems, a short-lived effort in 1974 to get back in, at
which point Al Bernkrant sued Eig and a partner for attempting to steal trade
secrets.)[27] He died just a year later, in 1982, at age fifty-six, the "Henry Ford
of the $14.95 revolver," who, "like a latter-day Sam Colt" (another historical
analogy from the *Miami Times*) stamped his name on postwar American gun
culture by helping to expand the mass market for cheap guns. And yet in a
way Eig got what he wanted, as almost no trace of him remains today: online
searches turn up scant mentions, and the comprehensive *Guns in American
Society* encyclopedia has no entry for Saul Eig. (He ought to appear between
"Eddie Eagle" and "Elections and Gun Control.") Several years after his death,
his widow Lois endowed a scholarship in his name at Miami Dade College,
where the annual announcements never mention the award's provenance in
the cheap gun trade.

FOR NEARLY TWO DECADES, out of the complex of buildings built around
that former church, not far from Miami International Airport, RG Industries
produced about 4 million cheap handguns in total, operating so far beneath
the radar that a full year passed before the press even knew the company had
ceased operations in early 1986.[28] Eig eschewed publicity and RG continued to
follow his lead after he left. The company remained intensely secretive until it
closed its doors, no longer able to afford liability insurance after a series of lawsuits. An RG executive blamed the company's troubles on an excessively liti-
gious culture—"Even the Boy Scouts are having trouble getting insurance," he
said—but nearly two decades of producing cheap guns universally condemned
as unsafe in anyone's hands left RG vulnerable to legal troubles for the dangers its firearms presented to both users and victims. Costly lawsuits included
one by a Miami police officer wounded when he accidentally dropped a confiscated RG-25 and it discharged twice.[29] But before RG closed up shop, one
crafty young journalist managed to get an exclusive inside look at its production facility and to hear firsthand from its managers, who knew all too well that
their work represented the lucrative dregs of gun capitalism.

Steven Brill was just out of Yale Law School in 1976 when the Police Foundation hired him to evaluate gun data gathered from police departments in ten cities.[30] The Police Foundation, headed by former New York City police commissioner and liberal reformer Patrick V. Murphy, was founded with funds from the Ford Foundation in 1970—the same Ford Foundation funding modernization projects across the Third World—with the goal of using research and analysis, that is, the tools of modernization, to improve domestic policing. Brill's study began with the sobering reality of policing in the 1970s: "So huge is the domestic arsenal of privately held firearms that American police must be aware that a firearm may be at hand in any situation they encounter."[31]

Brill didn't just process data from police departments, however. He did undercover work to learn more about the shadowy origins of many of the handguns making life miserable for both police and city dwellers in the 1970s. One important conclusion of his study was that the impact of Saturday Night Specials was overblown: his data revealed that the most common handguns used in crimes and subsequently confiscated by police were made by Smith & Wesson and Colt, each accounting for about 11 percent of guns seized, followed by Harrington & Richardson, a traditional manufacturer in Massachusetts, at about 9 percent. Nearly a third of confiscated guns, then, came from just three manufacturers, and their products were not likely to be called Saturday Night Specials. So many of these "good guns" popped up in crimes because many of them were stolen, Brill concluded. Numbers four and five on the list, however, rang bells in the ears of anyone who had studied gun violence since the 1960s. Rohm and RG Industries each accounted for more than 8 percent of guns seized.[32] Brill wondered how it was that, in the decade after the Gun Control Act, this infamous West German manufacturer of Saturday Night Specials popped up in one of every six crimes recorded in his study. Hadn't the Gun Control Act curtailed Rohm's exporting business?

Brill didn't know about Saul Eig, who'd left RG Industries a half decade earlier, but he did find the warehouse and factory Eig built—"so small, so underground, so fly-by-night-looking."[33] Brill posed as a sporting goods dealer from New York and got a tour of the facility from RG's hapless director of sales. The executive told Brill many things he likely wouldn't have said in front of a congressional committee, let alone a reporter. The 1970s had treated the company well: "We really can't make enough guns to meet our demand." In 1976 it shipped nearly 200,000 units of just a single model, its top-selling RG-14 .22-caliber revolver (retail $30.50, wholesale $21.80), the gun Hinckley would use to shoot Reagan. But the sales director didn't think of the RG-14 as a choice weapon for presidential assassins. Rather, "if your store is anywhere near a ghetto area," the executive assured Brill, "these ought to sell real well.

This is most assuredly a ghetto gun." Another model, the RG-25, sold well but "between you and me," the executive confided, "it's such a piece of crap I'd be afraid to fire the thing." Based on the data he used in the Police Foundation report, Brill estimated that each year 30,000 of RG's guns were used in US crimes.[34]

"This gun is a real piece of trash," one gun expert told the *Washington Post* when it investigated Hinckley's "Saturday Night Special from Miami."[35] Among the lawsuits that eventually shut down RG Industries were two filed by James Brady, Reagan's press secretary, who was left paralyzed after the shooting. Out of that tragedy was born the activism of Brady's wife, Sarah, who would become perhaps the country's best-known gun control advocate by the 1990s, leading Handgun Control Inc., the largest grassroots gun control organization in the country, which would be renamed the Brady Campaign in 2000. In these ways, as the following chapters show, gun dealers like Saul Eig helped create the very forces that tried to bring their industry to an end.

THE EISENHOWER COMMISSION was wrapping up its work just as legislators started to learn about the loophole. The Firearms Task Force had completed months of research and was preparing its report. Before Dodd's committee, Milton Eisenhower succinctly summarized the FTF's conclusions, and he pulled no punches. There were too many guns, especially handguns, in civilian hands. He acknowledged that most gun owners used guns responsibly, and that guns did not cause but rather facilitated violence. They were dangerous nonetheless, potential gasoline dumped on a fire. The dramatic growth of handgun sales, quadrupling in a mere half decade, "must be attributed to the rising fear of violence that the United States has recently experienced." Fear created a population armed against its perceived enemies. Echoing the FTF's published report, Eisenhower emphasized the threat of "neighborhood protective associations" that "share the fears of right-wing paramilitary groups, with the result that firearms are now being stockpiled in homes as well as 'in the hills.'" "A new wave of American vigilantism could result from these activities," he warned. What could the federal government do? The GCA had too many blind spots, and it did nothing to control the tens of millions of handguns already on America's streets. Given its disproportionate use in crime, "the time has come to bring the handgun under reasonable control," Eisenhower concluded.[36]

The FTF's directors, Washington attorney George D. Newton Jr. and University of Chicago law professor Franklin E. Zimring, came before Dodd's committee to answer questions. Not yet thirty years old, Zimring was already one of the most prominent legal scholars studying guns and crime, with several significant publications on an otherwise understudied subject.[37] Newton and Zimring told the committee the blunt conclusion of the FTF: if the federal government wanted to reduce gun violence, it would have to reduce the number of guns in civilian hands, especially handguns. Only the federal government could accomplish such a task, as plenty of evidence existed that lax laws in one state easily undercut another state's or municipality's attempt to impose tight controls.[38]

A full handgun ban would have to wait, however. Dodd and the committee had a more immediate problem: the GCA was supposed to curtail the trade in Saturday Night Specials, and its loophole inadvertently created a new domestic industry for these cheap handguns. Newton explained that there was "no special technology in making them. In fact, one of the reasons they are so cheap is that they are so simple to make." Zimring called the technology "extremely crude" and noted that higher labor costs in the United States vis-à-vis West Germany might increase a cheap handgun's retail price 50 percent, but "the problem will still be the same." What should Congress do about such guns then? "Ban them," Zimring said. But how could you ban a category of handguns? Dodd wanted to know, in effect, what determined cheapness—who would be the arbiter of cheap, and what criteria would they use to define it? For Zimring, the answer was fairly simple: let police departments decide. In other words, write a law that would require every handgun sold for civilian use to be certified for police use. If law enforcement officers weren't comfortable using it or having it on the streets, then civilians wouldn't be able to buy it.[39] It was the sort of savvy policy proposal that would characterize Zimring's work in the decades to come, but not one with which Congress was prepared to grapple, especially in light of the taxing fight required to pass the GCA, a tepid bill compared to any that might ban whole categories of handguns.

Zimring's proposal aligned with how many law enforcement officers saw the problem. Cheapness really did matter. Big city police chiefs, who had been lobbying Congress for a decade to do something about the proliferation of cheap handguns, suggested that there was a connection between gun crimes and segmentation within consumer markets. Cheap guns were especially dangerous not only because they could injure a shooter or a victim but because they were so ephemeral: they changed hands frequently, and because they were such a low-cost investment a person who committed a crime with one felt no regret abandoning it. In contrast to an expensive, well-crafted firearm, a cheap handgun inspired no "pride in ownership," Kansas City police chief Clarence Kelly told Congress in 1971. Criminals thus had "little reluctance to throw it away in a river"—the cheap handgun equivalent of Sam Cummings's quip about leaving a Carcano out in the woods after bagging a deer. "We find in police circles," Kelly said, "that if the crime is committed with a valuable and fine handgun there is a good chance that the owner will retain it and thereby enable investigative bodies a better chance to link the gun with the spent bullets."[40] It was a creative if ultimately futile appeal to gun crime as a component of the growing gun consumer culture, an inventive gambit to get Congress to act on an intractable problem that its 1968 political compromise failed to address.

DODD'S 1969 HEARINGS were the first to wrestle with the GCA's failures. Throughout the 1970s Congress would consider a variety of gun control bills that would have banned the production, distribution, or ownership of cheap handguns, now regularly called Saturday Night Specials. Yet, despite the fact that such firearms had few public defenders, and the GCA already expressed legislative intent to control them, Congress never passed a bill to do anything about the loophole. Why?

First was the messy question of definition. Though "Saturday Night Special" was, in fact, a law enforcement term of art dating back to the early 1950s, the common understanding of it by the 1970s was that it was a "journalistic" phrase that didn't have any precise grounding in either industry or law. No company claimed to manufacture Saturday Night Specials. Even if executives at RG Industries believed they made "ghetto guns," they said so only behind closed doors and would never have marketed them as Saturday Night Specials. It was a derogatory term, like a car manufacturer boasting of building a clunker or a lemon. Who got to define Saturday Night Specials, then, if restrictions on them became law, and how would they be defined? Would Congress use industry or law enforcement definitions? Would definitions hinge on price, size (i.e., "concealability"), caliber, accessories, quality of materials? When the GCA gave the Treasury Department the authority to restrict imports, the department convened a meeting of law enforcement and industry insiders to craft the criteria by which guns would be assessed. Critics said that the industry basically wrote the rules about what would and wouldn't come in.[41] So there was reason to think that if Saturday Night Specials were on the chopping block, it would be the industry once again writing the rules in its favor. As it had before, gun capitalism would find a way around whatever modest limits Congress imposed, because ultimately those limits would continue to recognize the fundamental legitimacy of a consumer gun market.

With Dodd gone from the Senate after the 1970 election (the NRA liked to claim gun voters defeated him, but Senate censure over financial improprieties

sank his reelection campaign before it began), the chairmanship of his influential subcommittee fell to Indiana Democrat Birch Bayh, a young moderate
midwestern liberal with presidential ambitions. Bayh proposed legislation to
close the loophole in 1971. His definition of Saturday Night Specials was broad
enough to require interpretation—"those small caliber, relatively inexpensive
pistols and revolvers that have no sporting use, but which are widely used in
crimes of violence"—and the devil would be in the details. His bill proposed to
apply to domestically produced handguns the same "sporting purposes" criteria, as defined by the Treasury Department, that the GCA applied to imports.
Dodd's old sparring partner on the committee, conservative Nebraska senator
Roman Hruska, applauded Bayh's effort and noted that he had as far back as
1966 argued that if a certain kind of gun was dangerous, it should be prohibited, regardless of country of origin. Hruska admitted that the "loophole was
fashioned primarily because of an antipathy toward the foreign-made gun,"
but, "unfortunately, the wrong remedy was applied." He did wonder, though, if
the committee was "overemphasizing the question of price or 'cheapness,'" and
how anyone might come up with criteria to define it.[42] Was a gun inherently
more dangerous if it cost twenty-five dollars rather than seventy-five dollars?
Was it possible to ban a product simply because it was "cheap"? Could Congress, for instance, ban certain cars or mattresses simply because they didn't
cost as much as others? If so, where was the line?

The NRA, of course, had some ideas. In principle it opposed cheap handguns. The organization had done so as far back as Dodd's earliest bills targeting
imports. Despite its aggressive political lobbying in the 1960s, the group in the
early 1970s still staked its reputation on its advocacy of sportsmanship and
gun safety rather than the defense of unrestricted gun rights. And no serious person argued that a .22-caliber RG-14 served any sporting purpose. But
the NRA, like Hruska, believed that the "sporting purposes" criteria were too
subjective, too open not just to interpretation but to exploitation by a particularly authoritarian Treasury secretary. (Dodd had laughed off this concern
throughout this 1960s.) "That Saturday Night Special is a magic phrase," said
NRA president Maxwell Rich in 1972, "but I don't know what it means."[43] The
organization urged Congress to develop and adopt an "objective" set of "safety
standards" to which all guns produced in the United States and imported into
the country would have to adhere. In fact, when the Juvenile Delinquency Subcommittee, now under Bayh's direction, met in the fall of 1971, Nixon's Treasury Department had already contracted with H. P. White Labs of Maryland
to conduct tests on a variety of handguns in order to establish an objective set
of safety standards that would replace the current "sporting purposes" criteria.
The lab told Treasury that "it is feasible and possible to establish a handgun

safety test that is objective and effective, inexpensive and rapidly concluded without being repressive or burdensome to the manufacturer or the consumer." (Al Bernkrant of Firearm Import & Export wrote Congress to oppose these "handgun torture tests.")[44] The Nixon administration had dragged its feet in 1969, unwilling to rile up gun defenders or cooperate with gun control liberals, but now it appeared ready to ally with the NRA in the name of consumer safety. If gun critics could stake out ground on the field of consumerism, so too could gun defenders, adopting the 1960s language of rights, especially consumer rights, to protect gun capitalism.

In addition to its argument that cheap handguns were a danger to consumers, the administration also claimed that the current law violated US international trade agreements under the General Agreement on Tariffs and Trade (GATT), essentially concurring with the protests several nations lodged in 1968 when the GCA passed. Nixon's Treasury Department argued that the United States unfairly protected a domestic industry in restricting the importation of guns that could be manufactured legally in the country. The administration claimed this damaged trade relations with Cold War allies: "Why, the embargo on Italian guns has turned some areas of that country into a poverty-stricken Appalachia," a Treasury official told journalist Robert Sherrill. "Communities that depended on gun exports to the US have become ghost towns," and regions of Spain and West Germany had experienced similar hardship. But officials from all three countries denied the claim to Sherrill, and an Italian diplomat offered a corrective: while the embargo had a small economic impact, no region was consequently "ghostlike," and "there are too many really important things in GATT to worry about guns right now."[45] After all, even several hundred thousand cheap guns sold annually accounted for only several million dollars in revenue, a drop in the bucket for big trading partners. Cheap handguns on American streets had a social impact disproportionate to their relatively small value in international trade. But the administration nevertheless offered another Cold War argument in favor of gun capitalism.

No objective safety standard would be adopted in the months and years to come, and despite various legislative proposals to control or ban Saturday Night Specials over the next half decade, Congress would pass no such law. Whether the Nixon administration or the NRA were serious about establishing "safety standards" in order to impose real restrictions on consumers' access to handguns, or whether the effort to rewrite such criteria was merely a delaying tactic until this particular gun control effort inevitably ran out of legislative steam, it's difficult to know. Even Bayh's sincere commitment was questioned: some suspected that his push for a Saturday Night Special bill in 1971 was merely an effort to pad his resume, knowing he would need it for a 1972 Democratic presidential primary contest against a senator who didn't need to prove his gun control bona fides, Ted Kennedy (and perhaps New York City mayor John Lindsay, who called for a complete national handgun ban).[46]

Other gun control advocates were ambivalent about the "safety standard" idea. Harold Serr, for instance, believed "sporting purposes" was clear enough and stronger than the criterion of "safety." If, for instance, Rohm took its cheap RG-14 and strengthened the barrel and frame so that the gun wouldn't occasionally explode in a shooter's face, it could pass a safety test, but it wouldn't make the gun any less concealable or any more "sporting." Bayh agreed: "I am afraid that such an approach would merely insure [sic] the criminal's gun was safe and reliable."[47] If anything it would improve the tool's criminal effectiveness. For Serr, Bayh, and many gun critics, the more concealable a firearm was, the deadlier it was, and there was no connection between how safely a shooter could fire a gun and how easily he could conceal it.

Sherrill, the journalist, went further: the NRA and its allies in the Nixon administration tentatively supported proposals to ban cheap handguns as a gambit to affirm the gun consumer market as respectable and legitimate after a decade of attacks against it. If Congress established a safety test that every gun on the market had to pass, it would be an explicit seal of approval for unrestricted gun consumerism. After all, if critics argued guns were inherently unsafe, Congress could write safety, or at least the illusion of it, into law. An objective, universal safety standard would mitigate against future federal control efforts. A new standard to replace "suitable for sporting purposes" would also reopen the doors to war surplus guns, which by their very nature, built for high performance on battlefields, made them "safer" than cheap guns produced for quick profits. "Actually," NRA legislative director Jack Basil told Sherrill, "some of the foreign military-surplus stuff is excellent quality." "This surplus military stuff never dies, you know," said John Sipes, who headed the Office of Munitions Control in the 1950s and 1960s. "Nobody ever buries the damn things."[48]

Sherrill also argued that the unspoken motivation for gun control legislation was race, that the GCA "was passed not to control guns but to control blacks." But because Congress was ambivalent about the former and "too ashamed" to admit the latter, it accomplished neither. It was not a straightforward argument to make, however. The fact that southerners in Congress largely voted against the GCA and resisted further proposals throughout the 1970s demonstrated that voting for gun control was not a simple calculation of voting to limit Black rights. Instead, Congress had in 1968 and in the early

1970s continued to code ideas about race in terms of cheapness. Congress, Sherrill said, "probably associated cheap guns with ghetto blacks and thought cheapness was peculiarly the characteristic of imported military surplus and the mail-order traffic."[49] As a speculative argument it likely went too far toward imparting intentionality and simplistic rationalizing that didn't exist. But Sherrill did inadvertently draw attention to the broader liberal impulse to use the tools of modernity to impose order on society. That Cold War impulse would continue to wrestle with the nature of gun consumerism in the United States.

IF THE ULTIMATE GOAL OF THE GUN CONTROL ACT was to reduce gun crime and violence, it didn't work. Nor did it lessen the number of guns on American streets. Gun deaths rose precipitously and manufacturers and dealers added millions of guns to the civilian stockpile each year. Assessing the law in 1975, Franklin Zimring noted that nobody was happy with it: "Each side has already decided that the 1968 Act failed, and each group uses the Act's presumed failure to confirm views already strongly held." Zimring's lengthy analysis, while equivocal, nevertheless deduced that "the potential impact of the Act is quite limited when measured against the problems it sought to eliminate." And he did not hold much hope for a correction anytime soon. "Whatever the future holds," Zimring concluded, "Congress is unprepared to make intelligent policy choices."[50]

Congress couldn't stop the arms race because it refused to disarm the combatants, as Zimring and the FTF had urged in 1969. Rather with the GCA it had simply legislated new rules for stockpiling, rules that were always destined to be broken. Like Tom Dodd, Ramsey Clark, and Lyndon Johnson before them, critics continued to use war metaphors and parallels to draw attention to the crisis. "Coincidentally," journalist Carl Bakal observed, "our 9,400 firearms homicides in 1969 equaled exactly the number of Americans killed in combat in Vietnam that year." Framing it another way, Bakal pointed out that the annual total of US gun deaths (including homicides, suicides, and accidents), around 23,000, was equal to half of all US deaths in Vietnam over the previous decade.[51]

Taking stock in September 1971 of the carnage since the GCA passed, journalist Flora Lewis noted that more Americans had been shot dead on US streets the week before she wrote than had been killed in Vietnam. One victim stood out to Lewis for having witnessed the horrors of an earlier war. Candy store owner Beno Spiewak survived Nazi concentration camps, but he did not survive two armed men who demanded apple pie in the early morning when Spiewak only had Danish pastry to offer. "That's the way it is at war," Lewis observed. "Men go crazy over petty frustrations and use the weapons they are carrying because they are at war." "How high does the weekly toll have to go before the country decides the regular casualty lists are intolerably long?" Lewis asked. "Does there first have to be a Tet offensive on the streets of America before a decision is made against more escalation?" She continued to push the analogies to America's disastrous contemporary war: "The war in Vietnam costs more money, but the undeclared gun war on the streets of the US takes many more American lives. The disarmament pact most urgently needed now is among the citizens of the United States."[52] The GCA didn't address disarmament, which is what the Eisenhower Commission's Firearms Task Force had called for. But in the 1970s, new voices in the gun debate, especially those coming from the grassroots, would take up the call.

Disarmament was also Patrick V. Murphy's preferred metaphor for fighting America's undeclared gun war. Murphy had spent the late 1960s on the front lines of law enforcement's response to urban unrest. He was in Washington, DC, in the aftermath of King's slaying, as the city descended into days of rage fueled by white racist violence and police brutality; he then spent a short stint as the commissioner of the Detroit Police Department, which was still recovering and rebuilding from the 1967 riots. In 1970 Mayor John Lindsay recruited him back to his native New York City, where he had previously served on the force, to rebuild the department in the wake of the fallout from the corruption unveiled by whistleblower Frank Serpico (who was, incidentally, shot in the face with a Saturday Night Special in 1971). Murphy's reputation as a reformer brought him to a place desperate for reform.[53]

He arrived in the fall to take over a police department beset by urban violence. In his first two months on the job, Murphy buried three officers, all shot to death in the line of duty.[54]

Gun crime rates in New York had skyrocketed over the previous decade. Going back to the early twentieth century, the city boasted the nation's strongest gun regulations, which included the Sullivan Act, a 1911 law which prohibited possession of a handgun without a permit issued by the NYPD. And although it always had its share of violence, through the 1960s New York's gun violence rates were lower than those of cities with few or no local gun restrictions. In Dodd Committee hearings, gun control advocates had compared New York's gun murder rate favorably to that of cities with few regulations, like Dallas and Phoenix.[55] The Sullivan Law's critics, such as the NRA, pointed out that the strictest local gun control law in the country didn't make New York a less violent place, but while New Yorkers did indeed fear violent crime in the early 1960s, they were also less likely to be wounded or killed by a gun than their counterparts in large cities with few or no controls. But by the late 1960s even the best local ordinance couldn't hold off the tide of cheap guns washing over American cities in the second half of the decade. In 1965, guns were used in about a quarter of New York City's murders; by 1970, they were used in half of them.[56]

Speaking at a national convention in Washington, DC, in late 1970, Murphy went on the offensive. He called for a "strong uniform policy of domestic disarmament," a campaign to "take away the guns from the people." "For too long we have indulged the gun maniacs," he said, "both criminal and law-abiding." He minced no words when he placed blame for the carnage on the NRA and its supporters: "Under the deceptive guise of freedom and the belief that citizens must be armed to resist tyranny, the American people tolerate and abet assault, robbery, murder and street crime at gun point." "If this is freedom in its final form," Murphy concluded, "it is also freedom in its final hour." Murphy pleaded with Congress for national leadership and a federal solution.[57]

Murphy's forceful rhetoric represented a turning point because he rejected the GCA's regulatory approach, which had accommodated to postwar gun capitalism in the belief that, with some tweaking of the right inputs, Americans might dial in a balance between gun rights and gun control that would output an acceptable level of violence and armed insecurity. Instead Murphy was candid that one solution would be to "take away the guns from the people." It marked a new era in gun thinking, one driven less often by politicians and institutional reformers and more by grassroots organizations, which would target the material culture of the gun in the United States, rather than abstract notions of criminality, as the root of this singular American pathology. Murphy's choice of the word *disarmament* to describe his vision for gun control was intentional, a reflection of the Cold War world in which the United States perpetrated violence abroad (and implicitly or explicitly threatened it even more) and Americans stockpiled guns at home in anticipation of a domestic civil conflict. Increasingly peace activists spoke of disarmament in the 1950s and 1960s, hoping to convince leaders of the superpowers to step back from the brink of nuclear annihilation. By the 1970s the nascent gun control movement had also adopted the word as a way of framing the US gun problem in universalist, modernizing terms. Indeed, the unsung founder of the modern grassroots gun control movement emerged out of the Cold War—she stood at the center, in fact, of the birth of the nuclear world, asking her fellow Americans to abandon their frontier mythologies and accept the control demanded by modernity and civilization.

CHAPTER **6**

WALTHER
PP "SPORTER"

Caliber .22 L.R. (6" or 8¾") $74.75

LITTLE OLD LADIES
IN TENNIS SHOES

WHEN LYNDON JOHNSON signed the Gun Control Act in October 1968, nothing like an organized grassroots gun control movement existed. The closest thing to it, the National Council for a Responsible Firearms Policy, founded in 1966 by longtime penal reformer and former chief of the US Bureau of Prisons James V. Bennett, never had more than a thousand members and functioned essentially as an insider's lobby—Bennett was a friend of Tom Dodd and advised and testified before the crusading senator's influential subcommittee.[1] The GCA gave the NCRFP most of the modest reforms it wanted, though into the 1970s the organization would continue to produce educational material and promote "responsible" gun ownership as the nation's gun crisis deepened. The era's other notable gun reform group, the Emergency Committee for Gun Control, came and went in a flash—established in the days after RFK's killing and headed by his friend, astronaut John Glenn, it was an entirely elite affair, consisting of prominent politicians and celebrities who mastered the art of the press release but had little effect on gun control legislation. It vanished at the end of 1968.[2]

While plenty of public officials were interested in controlling guns in the 1960s, and state and local governments had imposed regulations on firearms as far back as the early nineteenth century, the gun control *movement*—a national, grassroots, organized mass movement of private citizens—only emerged in the 1970s.[3] It started in a dozen or more cities around the country, where local groups connected to each other and then to activists in Washington, DC, where they aimed to unify local movements into a national force.

The grassroots gun control movement of the 1970s was sparked not by rising violent crime itself—that spike started well before the 1970s and peaked in 1974, when the control groups were only just beginning to organize.[4] Rather, it was the failures of the Gun Control Act, which hopeful reformers had watched work its way through Congress for half a decade only to see it prove impotent within months of its enactment. Congress sputtered in the face of clear evidence of the law's shortcomings. Frustrated grassroots groups decided gun policy was too important to leave to the politicians. The most ambitious found inspiration in global movements for disarmament and abolition.

The founder of the Civic Disarmament Committee (CDC) of Chicago interpreted the US gun problem in light of her experience working for nuclear peace and universal human security in the early Cold War. As the spouse of Enrico Fermi, the Nobel Prize–winning physicist who conducted the first successful experiments in nuclear fission at the University of Chicago in 1942, Laura Fermi had witnessed the birth of a new global order. Like Enrico and many of the scientists who contributed to the Manhattan Project, Laura Fermi became active in the nuclear peace movement after the bombing of Hiroshima and Nagasaki. Fermi learned to organize activists first in the peace movement and then, beginning in 1959, as a local environmentalist, years before the cause gained national attention.[5] At the end of the 1960s she turned toward disarming civilian populations and abolishing handguns, reasoning that disarmament was as feasible for American citizens as limiting nuclear proliferation had been among nation-states. Others working in nascent gun control groups marveled at her incomparable wit and humor and her tireless passion for peace. She liked to tease audiences that they should "never underestimate the power of little old ladies in tennis shoes."[6]

But just as her vision for a movement against handguns started to take shape, the national activists who assumed leadership of it abandoned Fermi's goals of disarmament and abolition in favor of policy compromises triangulated to draw in supporters and dollars. Out of Fermi's and the CDC's work emerged the National Council for the Control of Handguns (NCCH), the first national gun control lobby, which would evolve into Handgun Control Inc. and then today's Brady Campaign. Fermi's vision had inspired the movement, but by 1975 gun control advocates turned away from her idealism and toward what they believed to be the best way to attract money and attention quickly: direct confrontation with the National Rifle Association.

Already in the early 1970s the NRA was the sun around which orbited the gun politics galaxy: politicians, federal agents and bureaucrats, other gun rights groups, the nascent gun control organizations—all adjusted their goals,

Laura Fermi, 1961. (Hannah Holborn Gray Special Collections Research Center, University of Chicago Library)

strategies, tactics, and expectations to accommodate or confront the "vigilante on the Potomac," as journalist Carl Bakal labeled the NRA in 1966.[7] It's a truism of the twenty-first century that the NRA dominates gun politics, but it bears emphasizing for the decade after the passage of the 1968 Gun Control Act as well. Scholars and activists have crafted a popular narrative of the NRA's history that hinges on an aggressive political turn at the "Revolt in Cincinnati," a leadership coup engineered by a group of hardliners, led by longtime NRA board member Harlon Carter, who seized control of the organization at its 1977 annual convention.[8] To be sure, Carter would sharpen and magnify the NRA's dedication to unrestricted gun rights, but narratives that presume that the pre-1977 NRA was committed to hunting culture and firearms education and only occasionally and uncomfortably engaged in political activity misrepresent the reality of gun politics in and after 1968.[9] And such narratives do the NRA's work for it: since the 1970s it has wanted Americans to believe that a growing gun control movement backed it into a corner after 1968 and forced the NRA to stand up for the Second Amendment when no one else would. But such narratives belie the reality of the 1970s NRA juggernaut.

Nascent gun control organizations, perennially underfunded, understaffed, unfocused, and uncoordinated, invariably responded to the NRA's agenda. Indeed, it would not be inaccurate to say that some early grassroots gun control activists did not consider guns a problem per se as much as they considered the NRA a problem. Their every move was an attempt to outmaneuver the NRA, rather than build their own organizing visions. Such an approach meant that organizations struggled to get any traction in their first years. But the allure of confronting the NRA was powerful, especially for the men who would build out the gun control movement after Laura Fermi, drawn to the masculinist rhetoric of competition between gun rights and gun control. In the process they wrote the little old ladies in tennis shoes, with their greater ambitions of challenging gun capitalism and popular mobilization for social conflict, out of the history of American gun control.

MARK BORINSKY WAS a psychology graduate student at the University of Chicago in 1972 when, out with a friend one night, three young men approached, flashed a gun, and demanded money. As they held their victims at gunpoint, the perpetrators debated killing them to eliminate the possibility of being identified. It was a traumatic experience for Borinsky, no doubt, but not unusual for a large city like Chicago during this era. Nationally in 1974, the peak year of a violent decade, guns were used in more than 325,000 violent crimes, with Chicago accounting for about 5,000 of them, an average of 14 every day.[10] Borinsky survived and graduated soon thereafter. He moved to Washington, DC, to work as a psychologist. There he got the idea for a national gun control lobby, surprised to find that nothing like it existed. Borinsky believed the country needed a counterweight to the NRA, and he would create the National Council for the Control of Handguns to serve that purpose.

The *Guns in American Society* encyclopedia identifies Borinsky as the activist who "started the modern gun control movement" when he founded the NCCH. The two-volume encyclopedia also offers entries for Borinsky's two successors at the organization, Edward O. Welles and Nelson "Pete" Shields. Shields would become one of the movement's first national political celebrities, leading the NCCH, which became Handgun Control Inc. in 1979, through the 1980s before passing leadership to Sarah Brady, wife of Ronald Reagan's press secretary James Brady, who had been gravely injured in the 1981 attempt on the president's life.

You won't find Laura Fermi in the encyclopedia. She has no entry, and not a word about her appears in the entries for Borinsky, Shields, or Welles, even though she was instrumental in the creation of the NCCH, and all these men acknowledged her role in founding the movement. She has been written out of its history.[11] Fermi, as both an immigrant and a "little old lady in tennis shoes," was easily cast aside as the NCCH gained national attention in the mid-1970s, part of the movement's compromise with widespread civilian firearms ownership produced by the explosion of postwar gun consumerism.

Laura Fermi's gun control work was the last act of a remarkable polymathic life. Born Laura Capon in 1907, her father, Augusto Capon, was an admiral in the Italian navy who would be among the 7,500 Jews deported from Italy to death camps in 1943.[12] She met Enrico Fermi when she was sixteen and he twenty-two. He did not impress her, though surely her wit made a mark on the brilliant young physicist who was already the talk of his nation's scientific community. Laura recounted a friend telling her that "of men like Fermi only one or two are born each century," and with her characteristically dry humor she replied, "This is certainly an exaggeration."[13] Marrying a prominent scientist in interwar Italy meant postponing her own intellectual and professional aspirations for the role of mother and homemaker. As scientists the Fermis' lives were wrapped up in tight-knit scholarly communities largely disinterested in politics. When the family moved to Rome in early 1938, Laura recalled, Mussolini's fascism "so far had been a mild dictatorship and had not interfered with the private life of people who, like us, did not put their criticism and disapproval into action." But that fall Italy passed its first antisemitic laws, and the family immediately made the decision to leave. They used the opportunity of the Stockholm awards ceremony for Enrico's Nobel Prize to flee Europe for the United States.[14]

Though she had coauthored a popular science book in Italian, *Alchemy of Our Times*, in 1936, and had helped Enrico write a high school physics textbook (uncredited), during the war she by necessity dedicated her life to caring for the Fermi children while Enrico worked for years in secrecy on the Manhattan Project, traveling back and forth to Chicago from the family's home in New Jersey.[15] The Fermis moved to Chicago permanently after the war. In 1954 she published *Atoms in the Family*, a memoir of her time with Enrico, who that same year had fallen ill with stomach cancer and passed away. The simultaneous publication of a bestseller and Enrico's death "changed Laura's life profoundly," her friend recalled. She commenced a prolific and diverse intellectual second life that began with her transformation into "a grande dame of the atomic age" and a celebrity in the movement for nuclear peace.

In 1955 she was invited to serve as the official historian for the International Conference on the Peaceful Uses of Atomic Energy, an Eisenhower-era initiative to promote the president's international vision of "atoms for peace." She recorded her observations in *Atoms for the World* (1957). "Progress belongs to all," she wrote, reflecting the optimism in the international scientific community for the peaceful sharing of nuclear research across borders, "and secrecy cannot long restrict it within limited boundaries."[16] She published three books in 1961 alone: a biography of Mussolini; another, coauthored, of Galileo; and a children's book on atomic energy.[17] She spent years researching an exhaustive study of the many European intellectuals who, like she and Enrico, had fled fascist Europe and migrated to the United States before the war.[18] As the 1970s dawned she had begun work on a history of fifteenth-century Italian women, but as her health deteriorated she set the project aside to devote her energy to gun control.[19] As her fellow historian, Alice Kimball Smith (who, like Fermi, followed her scientist spouse to Los Alamos), recalled at a memorial service at the University of Chicago in January 1978, Laura's approach to "difficult projects" was, "Why shouldn't I be the one to do it?"[20]

The question was a testament to the others who joined Fermi in envisioning disarmament and abolition. Many of the women who would join the CDC were not only married to prominent scientists but were also refugees from fascist Europe, leaving behind family and friends who suffered under torrents of state violence and total war. CDC cofounder Lilla Fano's husband Ugo Fano had worked under Enrico Fermi in the 1930s at the University of Rome, where Fermi conducted the experiments that won him the 1938 Nobel Prize in Physics. Ugo went on to a prolific career at the University of Chicago, making critical contributions in atomic physics and training generations of graduate students into the 1990s.[21] Founding member Judy Roothaan was married to Clemens Roothaan, a pioneer of quantum chemistry who spent much of World War II in a Nazi prison camp, having been arrested for his brother's association with the Dutch resistance.[22] Other members had similar stories. For many of them, their first experience of violence had not been in an American context. With their own eyes they had seen societies mobilized for war.

In *Illustrious Immigrants: The Intellectual Migration from Europe, 1930–1941* (1968), her last book project to make it to print, Fermi included a section on the "wives of intellectuals." She noted that many women intellectuals emigrated and found professional success in the United States. But there was "another group of women whose intellectual output is more difficult to evaluate, though the indications are that it is not negligible," she wrote. "They are women who came to this country as the wives of European intellectuals and have remained very much in their husbands' shadow but at some time or other have engaged in intellectual occupations."[23] She offered several examples, but, of course, she was also describing herself.

Association with some of the world's brightest minds of two generations at the University of Chicago shaped the CDC and its approach to gun violence, a problem that was both local and national, even global, in origin. Direct experience with the Second World War and the Cold War molded CDC members into who they were. But these conflicts also helped create the problem the nascent CDC set out to solve, while offering language and logic for understanding the problem and solutions for addressing it.

THE UNIVERSITY OF CHICAGO helped produce the Cold War through research, and through massive infusions of government funding it was a product of the Cold War. But it was also a place made by its local urban environment. Situated in Hyde Park, a predominantly white, upper-middle-class South Side neighborhood surrounded by Black working-class neighborhoods like Woodlawn, the university influenced how scholars elsewhere came to understand cities.

Chicago's rapid growth in the century's first decades, built by a wave of immigrants from Southern and Eastern Europe, created conditions ripe for the study of human interactions in modern societies. The city's second major wave of immigration came not from Europe but from the US South, as African Americans moved northward to flee Jim Crow and search for work. "By midcentury," writes historian Andrew Diamond, "Chicago had become the case study for the rest of the nation."[24] The 1950s alone witnessed rapid demographic change, where one in four Chicagoans would be Black by 1960, up from 14 percent just ten years earlier; put another way, Chicago's population actually declined by 2 percent in the 1950s, as a result of suburbanization and white flight, but the African American population increased by 300,000.[25] This most American of cities offered the university's pioneering sociology department a singular laboratory.

Hyde Park, home to both the university and the CDC, was on Chicago's South Side but not of its South Side. Over the century's middle decades the South Side evolved into the city's "Black Belt," where a majority of Chicago's Black residents lived. By 1970 all of the communities bordering Hyde Park were predominantly Black, while the university's neighborhood remained majority white. Chicago's Democratic machine politicians referred to residents of white Hyde Park, wealthier and with more formal education than many of their counterparts throughout the city, as "lakefront liberals."[26] When Laura Fermi and the CDC started to receive hate mail from NRA members (an NRA publication mentioned these "anti-gun crusaders" in 1976), writers criticized the group for living in "well-protected high-rises," keeping their distance from commonplace street crime in Black neighborhoods below. (The CDC met monthly in Laura Fermi's fifteenth-floor home in a high-rise overlooking Lake Michigan designed by noted architect Ludwig Mies van der Rohe.) Such letters implicitly or explicitly defended gun ownership against a pathologized blackness—there was no "gun problem," one angry correspondent wrote, but "there *is* a Race Problem!"[27] For white gun owners afraid of Black urban rebellion or violent crime, the neighborhoods bordering Hyde Park represented their worst fears, fears borne out for white Chicagoans in the uprisings in the city following the April 1968 assassination of Martin Luther King Jr.

The city additionally offered a unique purview on violence, one delineated along racial lines. At the turn of the century muckraker Lincoln Steffens dubbed Chicago "first in violence," and that reputation persisted in the postwar era.[28] In reaction to the Great Migration, white populations used violence to define the boundaries of de facto urban segregation. As white Chicagoans moved to the suburbs, many neighborhoods, especially on the city's West and South Sides, became predominantly African American. Jobs left with white flight. Factory employment in the city dropped from nearly 700,000 in 1947 to fewer than 300,000 in 1982; over the same period the city's share of metro-area jobs crashed, from 71 to 34 percent.[29] This process of deindustrialization, coupled with de facto segregation and white retreat to surrounding suburbs, left vulnerable Black populations trapped by poverty, subjected to a potent mix of aggressive policing and rising crime.

By the 1970s it was obvious to the CDC, and anyone who studied crime and violence in Chicago, that the easy availability and concealability of handguns exacerbated Chicago's violent tendencies, especially in Black neighborhoods crushed by white flight and deindustrialization. The city recorded 669 gun murders in 1974, the peak year of a decade with more than 5,000 gun killings in the city; 90 percent of them involved a handgun.[30] Gun murders more than doubled from 1967 to 1974; armed robberies tripled. Fatal shootings during robberies increased nearly tenfold.[31] The violence was acutely concentrated among young Black men, especially those on the West and South Sides, members of the gangs that had once tried to lead young people in community development during the civil rights movement, tackling issues as intractable as poverty and inequality, but which also increasingly battled for turf and resources in communities starved of economic opportunities and tax revenue.[32]

In 1975 the *Chicago Reporter* published the results of a study of how two dissimilar Chicago neighborhoods experienced crime. Jefferson Park, on the city's northwest edge, sat in a police district where residents were 95 percent white and brought in solidly middle-class incomes. It had the lowest population density and crime rate of any of the city's neighborhoods. Just two miles to the southeast was the neighborhood surrounding Garfield Park, sometimes called Fillmore. Compared to Jefferson Park, it was one-sixth the size, three times more densely populated, 98 percent Black, and had half the median income. The disparities became most stark in the experiences of violent crime. Fillmore's 115,000 residents were 100 times more likely to be shot and 37 times more likely to be the victim of any kind of violent assault. "The Fillmore district is a virtual war zone," concluded the *Reporter*. "The chances of being a fatality in this war are enormous."[33]

While levels of gun violence escalated on Chicago's streets, the city's police department could hardly argue that it struggled to secure the resources it needed to counter that escalation. The city budget appropriation for the police department doubled from 1965 to 1970, while the number of officers on patrol increased from about 7,000 to 9,000. "Thus, while the urban crisis wreaked havoc on Black Chicago's education infrastructure, housing markets, and employment sectors," writes historian Simon Balto, city leaders continued to invest more resources in aggressively policing those neighborhoods.[34] The growth in crime rates in the 1960s coincided with the tenure of noted police reformer Orlando Wilson, who served as Chicago police superintendent from 1960 to 1967 and who implemented a range of reforms to "modernize" and professionalize the department. Among those reforms was an updated approach to crime data gathering and reporting, which inadvertently led to enormous leaps in the annual reported crime rates in the early 1960s. Chicagoans weren't committing significantly more crimes, but earlier recording systems hadn't counted certain crimes, like those attempted but not executed. However misleading, the headlines of surging crime rates nevertheless created a citywide sentiment that crime was out of control and needed aggressive police intervention. As Balto observes, Wilson's reforms preceded the actual significant increases in violent crime beginning in the late 1960s, demonstrating that the superintendent's modernization programs "were largely rooted in concepts and ideas of what policing should look like, not material conditions on the ground in Chicago." "As policing became *more aggressive* in Chicago," Balto concludes, "it correlated with the city becoming *less safe*," especially in Black neighborhoods, which were, as one Black Chicago police officer put it, the "most over patrolled and under protected in the city."[35] In others cities, too, Black rebellions in the late 1960s and early 1970s responded to rather than provoked aggressive, violent policing.[36]

THERE WERE RADICAL RESPONSES to aggressive policing, of course, led by groups like the Black Panthers, headed in Chicago by their charismatic young chairman, Fred Hampton, who was murdered in his bed during a Chicago police raid in December 1969. Hampton's assassination by government agents was powerful evidence for many of the need for the very communal self-defense the Panthers advocated. With good reason, such groups were suspicious of any disarmament proposal that began with civilians, and that would inevitably target Black Americans first and most aggressively, rather than with heavily armed state forces, which increasingly wore the gear and adopted the tactics of the US military's overseas counterinsurgency campaigns.[37]

Because of the ever-present threat of state violence, Chicago's Black community was hardly united on the question of disarmament—a calculation that the mostly white women who organized for gun control in Hyde Park (and in the North Shore suburbs, as we'll see in the next chapter) never had to make. And as everyday crime increased in the 1970s, some in the Black community argued that guns were necessary to defend from threats within as well as without. If disarmament was the goal, why should Black Chicagoans be disarmed first? They found themselves trapped, detractors argued, between street crime, on the one hand, and, on the other, white police and residents who had systematically brutalized the city's Black population for decades.[38] By the 1970s, Balto argues, the "entanglement of underprotection and overpolicing" had come to "full fruition."[39]

In the space between underprotection and overpolicing, the Coalition of Concerned Women in the War on Crime (CCWWC) tried to carve out a middle ground. Founded in 1974 by a group of forty prominent Black women active in local political, business, and community organizations, they were led by Ethel Payne, a seasoned journalist and editor at the *Chicago Defender*, the most prominent Black newspaper in the country; Cardiss Collins, the first Black woman to represent the Midwest in Congress; and Connie Seals, executive director of the Illinois Commission on Human Rights.[40] While they acknowledged the structural conditions that helped create violent crime in Black communities, and while they condemned the police brutality and corruption that led communities to mistrust law enforcement, the CCWWC ultimately attempted to hew to a middle ground of bourgeois respectability politics. "It is only through mutual respect between law enforcement officials and citizens," the group wrote, "that we can be assured of some freedom from fear." The CCWWC would work with police officials, including Superintendent James Rochford, to "get maximum protection from the police . . . and to [require police to] carry out their duties as required by the Law." The women of the CCWWC drew the common conclusion that "too many areas of our city are over policed and under protected."[41] Their solution was to work with the police for reform.

The CCWWC calculated that it couldn't make the Chicago Police Department more responsive with radical rhetoric, so they met the conservative "law and order" rhetoric of the era in the middle. As one member told the *Defender*, "We've got a right to live without being harassed either by the police or the criminals." "We want to get rid of the misfits on the police force," said Connie Seals, "but we also know that we have to deal with the misfits among us who are ripping us off."[42] While the CCWWC attempted to build a coalition of neighborhood groups, it also rejected radical politics. "Coordinated social pressure intelligently applied can often gain quicker and more enduring results than riots or revolutions," group leaders explained.[43]

The CCWWC's approach was grassroots community engagement. The group sought to recruit an "army of volunteers," using the *Defender* as a platform. In large, bold type, ads resembling military recruiting posters asked readers, "TIRED OF LIVING IN FEAR? TIRED OF POLICE BRUTALITY? TIRED OF BEING RIPPED OFF BY THIEVES? AFRAID TO WALK THE STREETS? WORRIED ABOUT YOUR CHILDREN'S SAFETY? WANT TO DO SOMETHING ABOUT IT?" The ads included an application declaring "I WANT TO JOIN THE WAR ON CRIME" to be filled out and mailed to the CCWWC. By September 1974 more than 700 people had responded to the ads. Soon after the CCWWC's launch, the *Defender* ran a series of articles by the group with practical tips for reducing crime and minimizing the chances of becoming a victim.[44]

By the summer of 1974, the CCWWC had joined Superintendent Rochford along with Laura Fermi's CDC and the gun control group on the North Shore in calling for an "all-out ban on the manufacture, sale, possession and distribution of handguns, handgun ammunition and component parts—throughout every spectrum of society—nationwide, excluding law enforcement officials."[45] More so than members of Chicago's mostly white gun control groups, the women of the CCWWC had direct experience with gun violence, with "tragic incidents that had personally occurred with members of our organization."[46] But while the group would support abolition proposals in the 1970s, it was pulled in too many directions to concentrate its energies on gun control. And ultimately the group believed gun violence was a symptom rather than the disease. "Even if you pass gun legislation," Ethel Payne asked the women of the CDC at a June 1974 meeting, "will it have any impact on our community?" (The CDC newsletter characterized this as a "pessimistic remark.")[47] The CCWWC pushed not only for the reduction of violent crime through gun control "but also for the elimination of the socio-economic conditions that encourage and perpetuate these deadly crimes." Such violence, in the CCWWC's diagnosis, was "nurtured by many things—the callousness of high public officials, bigotry and racial discrimination, the collapse of public morality and the disruption of the home."[48] What often went unspoken in such critiques was the burden of emotional labor this work imposed on the women of the CCWWC.[49] In the years to come the group would continue to criticize institutional racism and state violence but would direct its energies to community development programs intended to improve cooperation with police and the war on crime.[50] It was an "all-of-the-above strategy," as James Forman Jr. has described similar contemporaneous efforts in Washington, DC. But, as Forman has argued, Black community leaders who tried to pair the social justice initiatives of the 1960s with the tough-on-crime rhetoric of the 1970s inadvertently opened the door to the mass incarceration crisis, allowing for new mandatory minimum sentencing laws that would disproportionately lock up people of color.[51]

WHILE THE CCWWC concentrated on the many causes of violence, the group shared the perspective of reformers around Chicago that the easy availability of cheap guns made violence deadlier. And the city's streets were flooded with guns in the 1960s.

It was hard to know in 1970 just how many guns there were in the city of more than 3 million people. Chicago had a handgun registration law, but urban law enforcement knew that most handgun owners were unlikely to register them. The Chicago Police Department had an office of handgun registration, which employed fifteen people to register guns; by one estimate, the paperwork and processing involved to register a single gun cost the city $4.46.[52] City officials said that there were more than 500,000 registered guns in the city, and that accounted for about 90 percent of the total guns in Chicago.[53] That claim made little sense in light of an ATF study in 1976 that found that, of 9,000 guns confiscated in crimes in Chicago, more than 90 percent of them came from outside the city; 30 percent came from Mississippi alone.[54] The whole point of buying guns from Mississippi was to avoid the scrutiny of the state. How could city officials know how many guns *weren't* registered? It would not be a stretch to infer that city officials in infamously corrupt Chicago inflated the numbers of registered guns to bolster Mayor Daley's gun control bona fides. A more reasonable estimate of the gun stockpile would be at least a million, a figure similar in ratio to the half million police officials in Detroit estimated, and less than the informal estimate of 1.3 million for New York City, where the state's Sullivan Law made almost every one of them illegal.[55]

There was a point at which this numbers game became moot. As the Firearms Task Force said, precise figures made little difference to public policy; there were, whatever the differences at the margins, too many guns. Any policy that accepted the legitimacy of a largely unregulated civilian firearms market, one that attempted to distinguish between the virtuous "law-abiding citizen" and the unvirtuous criminal, would never stop the juggernaut of gun capitalism. Given the context, it was a radical proposal, but for Laura Fermi and the CDC, abolition and strict prohibition of handguns—in other words, eliminating the civilian market—was the only way to stem the surging tide of gun violence.

In early 1975 the CDC invited Dan Cox, director of the local Chicago ATF office, to join the group for a meeting. It was not uncommon for the CDC to invite law enforcement officials, judges, state legislators, congressional representatives, and even mayors to join them at Fermi's apartment, and many obliged. Cox asked the CDC for questions beforehand so he could prepare answers and bring some literature. The CDC fired off a long list of inquiries, some of them technical, about handguns in Chicago. Where did they come from? How many violations of the 1968 Gun Control Act had the ATF prosecuted in the city? How many "men-years" did the office expend "in auditing the records of gun transactions (on form 4473)"? The questions stumped Cox and he demurred. Several weeks later Laura Fermi wrote to the ATF's national director Rex Davis: "Mr. Cox called us on the telephone to cancel the meeting, saying that our questions were too technical to be researched by his limited staff and that we should send them to you."[56]

Some months later the CDC newsletter announced that henceforth there would be no more speakers at monthly meetings, "both because of the great amount of work involved, and because we feel we already know most of what the present authorities on the subject can tell us."[57]

The incident was indicative of the polymathic intellect, endless curiosity, and fierce persistence that the visage of the "quiet little Italian lady" masked. Fermi was the nuclear core that powered the CDC to do the kind of research on gun policy that only a handful of researchers in the United States were doing. The CDC left behind folders of correspondence with scholars, state and federal agencies like the BATF, and even foreign governments. This was hardly a social club for "little old ladies."

But the image of Laura Fermi as such was important because it contrasted with the evolution of the gun control movement she helped found. By the 1980s, that movement would be national, high-profile, corporate, and driven not so much by a desire for a greater understanding of human problems but the never-ending need to draw in money to challenge the NRA. And arguably such an outcome was a result of that goal, the most significant flaw built into the movement from the outset. As its leaders articulated the movement's mission, and in many ways as they continue to do, the gun control movement has existed as a negative force, opposed not just to guns—in some ways, not even opposed to firearms at all—but to the influence of the NRA. Toward the end of her life Laura Fermi saw the movement evolving in that direction, and, as her health declined, she retreated from her national activism and support of the organization she helped Mark Borinsky create, the NCCH.

The CDC's goal at the outset was ambitious and national in scope—"the complete outlawing of the manufacture, sale, and possession of handguns," with exceptions for law enforcement and military—but the group began its work at the local level, a manifestation of the 1970s dictum, "Think global, act local."[58] During the group's first meeting, in November 1971, at Fermi's posh lakefront apartment, members haggled over issues like the group's name, officer elections, and finances. They "juggled" with words to get the name of the organization just right—"Committee, Organization, Citizens, Firearms, Guns, Handguns, Restriction, Control, Education, Disarmament, Anti-violence, Crime." While they settled on the Civic Disarmament Committee, some members thought the word *disarmament* too controversial, echoing the highly charged politics of "nuclear disarmament." (In 1974 they would amend it to the Civic Disarmament Committee for Handgun Control; one early suggestion, mercifully rejected, was "United Now to Ban All Neighborhood Guns," or UNBANG.)[59] At that first meeting, University of Chicago law professor and Eisenhower Commission research director Franklin Zimring attended and told members about the lacuna of research on gun violence and the efficacy of gun control legislation.[60] Zimring would be an important conduit to the organization for the latest research on guns, crime, and policing, a thread linking the sober conclusions of the Firearms Task Force to early grassroots activists.

At the next meeting, members formed committees—one to study legislation; another to write a questionnaire to be distributed to local high school students; one to arrange visits to city courts "in which firearms cases are tried, and learn about law enforcement and its difficulties"; and another to "study the laws of other countries and . . . to ascertain whether the high rate of crime by guns in the United States is due to poor laws or to tradition."[61] Over the year that followed the committees went into action. The group polled nearly a thousand local students on "gun attitudes and knowledge," finding that while students saw guns everywhere, recognized the dangers, and wanted greater controls, they were cynical that anything would be done. The CDC used the results to develop a lecture and brief film for Chicago schools. Members visited local criminal courts to watch the proceedings on gun cases, observing that the judge "seemed more concerned with protecting people against police stop-and-frisk tactics than with protecting society from guns." They then invited the judge to visit with the group; he explained his position that the United States "can't go against history by trying to make citizens give up their guns," and insisted that "the beginning of effective gun control will start when respect for police officers is restored." Members also found themselves arguing for gun control on local talk radio and television programs. Two CDC members even joined the NRA to learn more about the organization.[62]

Additionally, the CDC in 1972 was already influencing policy positions at a national level, if indirectly. In June, the US Conference of Mayors, a national liberal organization representing the chief executives of cities larger than 30,000, passed a resolution demanding that Congress "outlaw possession of handguns." It did so after lobbying from Chicago's Richard Daley, the country's most powerful mayor. Daley, in turn, had adopted the idea from the Chicago City Council, which had passed a similar resolution that February. Councilman Leon Despres had coordinated with Fermi and the CDC, his constituents, to get the language just right, before bringing the resolution before the council. The CDC wrote to dozens of mayors of large cities around the country urging unified action on handguns. Soon thereafter the Conference of Mayors would establish its Handgun Control Project. The CDC's influence on the conference's resolution was an example of grassroots activism pushing progressive ideas from the neighborhood level up to the highest reaches of national politics. But Daley took credit for the resolution while neglecting to acknowledge the CDC's work.[63]

Fermi undoubtedly understood that men would take credit for the work of the movement she created. She was no stranger to the gender politics of activism. The CDC's members knew that, as in so many other social and political contexts, women faced a double standard. On the one hand, women were expected to be nurturing, to care for the ill and wounded, and in this sense, their identity as women lent power to their cause. They could be mothers tending to wounded children, scarred or terrified by gun violence, or wives discouraging husbands from rash, violent actions. "What is this mighty force which has been lying there awaiting recognition?" asked the CDC newsletter. "It is clear the women have a weapon in 'expending their might': it is their heart. Let us see who will win in the conflict that will ensue: the women with their hearts or the gun advocates with their guns!"[64]

On the other hand, masculinity was the currency of gun politics. Manly men knew how to care for and wield guns, the gun rights groups said; manly men knew how to exercise *control* over their environment, including its guns, the gun control politicians said. It was not a political space for women. Nobel laureate physiologist George Wald, a Harvard professor active in the nuclear peace movement and a friend of Fermi, was enthusiastic about the CDC because of the authority its members could command as women in a time of social change. "You are just the ones to handle gun legislation," he wrote Fermi in 1974. "The whole feminist movement needs to get into it." Gun culture's masculinity called for an appropriate counterweight. Handguns were "substitutes for male sex organs," he continued. "So what you are up against is in large part machismo." He suggested—or, perhaps, mansplained—that the CDC ought to "work that line to mobilize women and to make those guys feel a little self-conscious."[65]

The CDC, however, never saw itself as a feminist organization or part of the larger women's movement, even if its members held corresponding sympathies. Most of the women were middle-aged or older. They adhered to the gendered social conventions of the pre–women's liberation era. Fermi, for instance, signed her letters as "Mrs. Enrico Fermi," and the CDC membership rolls listed women's names similarly. The women of the CDC recognized gender as both inescapable in gun politics and an issue that could distract from their narrow if ambitious goal. And despite evidence that women were disproportionately affected by gun violence in the home, the CDC did not by and large present gun violence as a gendered problem.

MARK BORINSKY, THE MUGGING VICTIM TURNED NCCH founder, met Fermi through Donald Fiske, a prominent psychologist at the University of Chicago, one of Borinsky's graduate school professors, and a friend of Fermi's who knew her passion for gun control. She and the CDC "gave him the encouragement he then needed to start going," she said, with characteristic modesty.[66] "Encouragement" was an understatement.

It's hard to exaggerate the extent to which Fermi was responsible for the NCCH's creation, and thus, if the *Guns in American Society* encyclopedia is to be believed, also "started the modern gun control movement." She was the organization's first board member. She helped fundraise, wrote checks, taught Borinsky all she knew about the gun problem, kept in touch regularly, counseled him on paths forward, and, crucially, contacted her own organization's members to build the NCCH's membership and mailing list. Borinsky updated her frequently on his progress and to solicit her advice. The pair had a symbiotic relationship, Borinsky using Fermi's knowledge and connections to launch his organization and Fermi using Borinsky as an operative in Washington, where she simply couldn't spend much of her time and energy as she approached the eighth decade of her life, beset with a heart condition that would eventually take that life from her at the end of 1977.

Before Borinsky even had a name for his organization or any kind of mission statement, he relied on Fermi for her expertise and connections. He began drafting a proposal for a "national lobby to limit possession of handguns" in the spring of 1973, sending drafts to Fermi and the CDC for feedback. Building a membership base would be essential—"The single most potent political technique will be a large responsive membership," he wrote. The NRA was powerful, he reasoned, because it wielded a single-issue membership of 1 million gun owners to control a voting bloc. The lobby he envisioned would have a single issue, and it wouldn't be gun control broadly but specifically "promoting legislation to restrict private possession of handguns."[67]

From the outset, the NRA, the "vigilante on the Potomac," was in Borinsky's head. He organized the NCCH as much to oppose the NRA as to advocate for gun control. Over time these two goals became indistinguishable.[68] The NCCH saw the NRA's power stemming from its 1 million members and their annual dues. As a result, the NCCH would spend an inordinate amount of its time in its first years trying to raise money, seeking out "angel" donors who might offer large infusions of cash, and attempting to organize local gun control groups around the country into a network that would funnel funds upward to the NCCH as a kind of national umbrella lobby. But Borinsky and subsequent NCCH leaders also understood that the NRA's power and money came from its ability to mobilize a grassroots army of committed gun rights proponents. Borinsky believed he had to build a counterpart, following the logic of Illinois senator Adlai Stevenson III, who said, "When proponents of gun legislation are well organized and as vocal as the National Rifle Association, perhaps we will be more successful." Stevenson observed in 1976 that over the previous two years his office had received 100 letters opposing gun control for every 1 in support.[69] In that respect the NCCH's communication strategies would model the NRA's. The organization would send an "emergency dispatch" to members, mimicking the NRA's own "legislative alerts," urgent news messages that the NRA sent to members. Like the NRA's missives, the NCCH's expressed urgency: "Time is short. This vote is crucial. Act Today."[70]

The relationship between the CDC, driven by Laura Fermi's commitment to disarmament and abolition, and the NCCH was largely one of compromise and moderation. In the NCCH's first years Fermi's vision set the NCCH's agenda: gun control meant handgun control, and handgun control meant getting handguns out of private hands. Fermi understood that such a task would require an unprecedented federal initiative to confiscate or buy back tens of millions of guns, and persuading Americans of the need for such a drastic measure would demand lots of money and energy. But the NCCH had to survive in the cutthroat world of capitol politics. While congressional representatives, like Chicago's Abner Mikva, occasionally submitted bills proposing to ban civilian ownership of handguns, such bills had little chance of getting a hearing before a committee, let alone a vote on the floor. The bills that might draw broad bipartisan support instead came from the same pool of tepid ideas from which Tom Dodd and the 1960s reformers drew: proposals to ban certain narrow categories of guns, like Saturday Night Specials, that were universally decried as dangerous and unworthy of sports enthusiasts, while affirming a commitment to protecting the rights of "law-abiding citizens." The NCCH didn't have to spend much time in Washington to realize that it would struggle to get support from prominent political figures if it called for an outright ban on handguns. Without the support of big names, big money was unlikely to follow.

Borinsky laid out an explicit political strategy of moderation. Gun control's albatross, he believed, was its close connection to "liberal causes" and "liberal Senators and Congressmen." "This liberal association," he wrote, "has put off support for the issue from more conservative groups—Republicans, labor unions, the 'silent majority,' etc." Attracting this sort of support would require moderating policy positions. Borinsky criticized the Massachusetts sheriff, a Republican, who led the campaign to put a total handgun ban referendum on that state's ballot in 1976 as "too uncompromising with regard to pro-gun people."[71] Compromise could draw support away from the increasingly extreme rhetoric of the NRA and toward the NCCH.

Laura Fermi was not one to compromise, however. She came from an intellectual milieu that had cracked the secrets of the atom and then wrestled with its consequences. She had worked for international cooperation to control nuclear weapons. Surely the world's most powerful nation, the one that designed those weapons, could control or even abolish the smallest of small arms, the actual weapons of mass destruction that destroyed tens of thousands of its citizens' lives each year. The CDC made clear that its ultimate goal was a "federal ban on possession of handguns by private citizens," and it insisted that "all groups working with the NCCH *must* present a common front."[72] The politics of compromise gave Americans the 1968 GCA, the CDC reasoned. It had no interest in more tepid, ineffective laws.

But the leaders of the growing movement would push gun control in a more moderate direction. Fermi's ideas, shaped by her global experience, tapped into Cold War notions of human security in a nuclear world. Instead, the liberals leading the movement would adopt a narrower vision of the NRA, rather than unrestricted gun capitalism, as a threat to American politics and society.

BORINSKY AND FERMI launched the NCCH but the organization first gained a national profile under the direction of Nelson "Pete" Shields, who took over in the fall of 1975 and who would lead the group (which became Handgun Control Inc. in 1979) until 1989, becoming gun control's first minor celebrity. As Shields became the face of the NCCH, guiding it toward his vision of a professional organization built to confront the NRA, Fermi scaled back her commitment, leaving a vacuum into which Shields stepped.

Shields's story started with personal tragedy. In April 1974, his twenty-three-year-old son, Nelson T. Shields IV, was helping a friend in San Francisco load a rug into the trunk of a car when someone shot him in the back with a .32-caliber handgun. The family would eventually learn that the younger Nelson was the final victim of the city's "Zebra murders," a spate of fourteen racially motivated gun killings of white people by four young Black men. (Police claimed that the name "Zebra" derived from the radio band they used while investigating the case, rather than the word's obvious racial overtones.)[73] Everyone expected Shields to seek vengeance, he recalled, to "get a gun and go find and kill the men who murdered my loved one." But his reaction, as he told it, was to wonder instead, "Could I do something to help my society be better?"[74]

Called to action, Shields took a temporary leave from work to attend the 1975 hearings on gun control organized by John Conyers, whose House Subcommittee on Crime toured several cities, including Chicago, that spring. Shields then asked for a year of leave from his job as a marketing executive with DuPont to work full-time for gun control. (DuPont owned rifle manufacturer Remington but agreed to the leave nonetheless.) Shields's rhetoric echoed that of Cold War liberals of the 1960s like Dodd who believed that controlling guns, rather than wielding them, was a manly responsibility in the urban civilized societies of the twentieth century: "If I couldn't take at least a year off to do this for my son, for myself, for my country," he told the *New Yorker*, "I wasn't much of a man."[75] Confronting the NRA and the gun rights movement was a masculine duty.

Shields's vision for gun control in the 1970s synthesized the marketing revolution of the 1960s—Madison Avenue's "conquest of cool," as Thomas Frank describes it—with the decade's social movement politics. Shields characterized the NCCH's work as "marketing a concept the great majority of Americans agree with."[76] He knew how to work the press, and the press returned the favor by framing Shields as the founder of a gun control movement. The word *crusade* appeared in articles about Shields, giving him the veneer of a warrior prepared for a kind of righteous battle.[77] Profiles portrayed him as a "button-down businessman—his square name is Nelson T. Shields III, Hotchkiss School and Yale University," betraying a background of privilege, growing up in Manhattan, but also serving as a naval pilot during the Second World War. Shields was a sympathetic figure, marketable, attractive, charismatic, "definitely the executive type," the symbol of postwar American bourgeois masculinity and professional success.[78] The early gun control movement would place its bets on Shields, rather than "little old ladies in tennis shoes," to beat the NRA.

Shields wanted to give the impression that he meant business—literally. If any group were to challenge the NRA successfully it would have to do so with equivalent professionalism: "we have to organize on a professional rather than a purely volunteer foundation if we're going to be really effective." And for Shields, professionalism meant money. "We can't do much of anything . . . without having money up front," he said. "That's what we need—money, money, money."[79] By the logic of nonprofit fundraising and lobbying in the 1970s, money translated into direct-mail campaigns, and direct-mail campaigns translated into growing membership numbers. His goal was to increase the NCCH's current membership, which he pegged at 4,000, a hundredfold by the end of 1977 through aggressive direct-mail campaigns. He would consider the NCCH's year successful if it sent out a million pieces of mail.[80]

If the NCCH managed to send out a million pieces of mail in a year it would still be many millions behind the NRA. The NRA launched "Operation 100,000" in July 1976, an ambitious campaign to increase membership by 10 percent (or 100,000) in just a month—and it succeeded.[81] In the 1970s the gun rights organization worked with conservative direct-mail pioneer Richard Viguerie, who coordinated a million mailings *each month* for the NRA. Viguerie had cut his teeth in politics as a director of Young Americans for Freedom, organizing for the 1964 Barry Goldwater campaign, which was doomed to a crushing defeat by Lyndon Johnson but which laid the groundwork, particularly at the grassroots level, for a conservative political revival.[82] He was among the first and most successful entrepreneurs to crack the code of political mailing lists, collecting data on donors who gave to particular causes and assembling lists for candidates. By 1973 he was coordinating fundraising for George Wallace in advance of another run at the presidency by the archsegregationist, himself the victim of gun violence in a 1972 assassination attempt. Though about half of his $14 million in annual business was "non-ideological," conservative causes got Viguerie out of bed in the morning. "I'm frustrated on any day when I haven't saved Western civilization," he told a journalist in 1975. Included in his "ideological" business was the NRA account. Each year Viguerie raised $25 million for clients who "get riled up over school busing, guns, law and order, pornography, permissive education, and the cause of Governor George C. Wallace of Alabama, whom most of them love."[83]

Gun control organizations believed they could only fight a war against the NRA with money to spend on direct-mail campaigns. Indeed, success was defined by the size of a mailing list. "I believe that if we get enough money to put out enough direct mailings," Shields told the *New Yorker* in 1976, "by the end of 1977 we'll have three hundred thousand to four hundred thousand members."[84] Undoubtedly Shields was being sanguine for the press. Behind closed doors, NCCH leaders knew the reality of direct-mail campaigns required an incredible sum of money to draw in 300,000 or more new members. Direct-mail firms provided the NCCH board with estimated returns on investments. A mailing of 200,000 pieces in 1976 would cost the organization about $30,000, and advisers predicted that such a campaign might draw in at most 3,000 new members, each paying $15 for an annual NCCH membership. Based on those simple calculations, the organization would have to spend at least $3 million on direct-mail campaigns to draw in 300,000 new members. In early 1976, the NCCH was operating with a budget deficit of about $15,000, money that Borinsky and Shields had loaned out of their pockets; Laura Fermi was the only other board member who had raised money for the NCCH. Shields estimated that the group needed at least another $150,000 just to get a serious national mailing operation off the ground.[85] At middecade some nonprofit money was available for gun violence education—the US Conference of Mayors' Handgun Control Project, for instance, received $378,000 in 1975 from the George Gund Foundation of Cleveland for two years of educational programming—but funds for direct political lobbying, which were not tax-deductible, were harder to find.[86]

Gun rights groups, in contrast, knew they could fight a counterinsurgency against gun control groups on the same direct-mail grounds. The NRA and others encouraged members to write to groups like the NCCH surreptitiously to request information and literature in order to drain the gun control groups of funds. As the national campaigns of 1976 heated up, *Gun Week* magazine told its 60,000 subscribers to "put the financial crunch on anti-gunners" by sending postcards to various gun control groups to request information. If each subscriber did so, the magazine's editors estimated, it could cost the control organizations upward of $100,000 (more than a half million dollars in 2022). That spring the Conference of Mayors' Handgun Control Project identified nearly 600 postcards it believed arrived as a result of this plea, including one "smeared with what appeared to be blood."[87]

Even with polls showing a large majority of Americans eager for greater firearms regulations in the abstract, Shields and the NCCH faced an uphill financial struggle to compete with the NRA, Viguerie's advanced data operation, and a diehard group of pro-gun citizens committed to putting obstacles in the way of gun control groups. It was that pressure to compete that led Shields to the kinds of calculations and triangulations that pushed Fermi away from the NCCH.

Shields, too, wanted a ban on handguns, but he acknowledged that, given the "law and order" politics of 1970s, which drove fearful white suburbanites—and potential donors—to gun shops, anything like it was at least a decade away. His first goal was to get Congress to act to limit the number of handguns produced annually, something that a ban on the production of Saturday Night Specials would begin to accomplish. (Shields's son was killed by an Italian-made .32-caliber Beretta, a handgun of higher quality than the typical cheap Saturday Night Special, but one nevertheless made for concealability that had been imported before the GCA went into effect.)[88] Next the organization might work for registration laws. Finally, down the road, a full ban on private civilian possession of all handguns might be possible. "We're going to have to take one step at a time," he told the *New Yorker*, "and the first step is necessarily—given the political realities—going to be very modest."[89] Shields's approach of money and modesty supplanted Fermi's abolitionism ambitions.

BY 1976 FERMI and the CDC saw the NCCH as an extension of themselves into the world of Washington politics. They had inspired the organization, provided it with a foundational set of goals and ideals, and often floated the organization money as it struggled to raise funds. "We are in constant telephone touch with them," the CDC's newsletter told members. "We could not do much at the federal level without NCCH." What the newsletter left unsaid was that without Fermi and the CDC, the NCCH also could not do much at the federal level, or much of anything at all. The CDC lobbied its own members in

Chicago and around the country to join the NCCH and pay annual dues. They sent out fundraising letters for the NCCH and reported monthly how much they had raised, sometimes as much as several thousand dollars, even when their own organization's cash on hand rarely exceeded a few hundred dollars. Fermi gave frequently out of her own pocket. The CDC paid for the postage for the NCCH's first national mail campaign in 1974 and continued to offer feedback on strategic planning. Fermi wrote to wealthy acquaintances asking for money not on CDC's behalf but on the NCCH's; one letter to a friend who headed a Chicago investment firm mentioned that she was trying to secure $15,000 for the NCCH, an organization "very close to my own heart."[90]

In its effort to create a national network to raise funds and lobby for legislation, the NCCH faced resistance from local gun control organizations dispersed across the country. Local groups believed the money they raised should stay in their communities rather than go to Washington to support the NCCH. Why should a gun control group in Detroit struggle to raise funds desperately needed in its own community just to send them off to the NCCH, hoping to eventually get some back? In early 1976 the CDC was the "only local group" that pledged support for the NCCH's fundraising drive. Local groups were already starved of funds. After the 1976 national election, buoyed by optimism regarding the new Carter administration but also chastened by the landslide defeat of the Massachusetts handgun ban referendum, the NCCH decided on a subtle but telling strategy shift: it would drop its commitment to build local and state gun control groups and instead focus exclusively on a national strategy. There were "stormy" meetings between the NCCH and local groups in early 1977. Shields wrote to leaders of one group that the NCCH "must focus all of our strength on our national legislators for national legislation and not be side-tracked or lose our focus" on local or state issues.[91] Three years into its existence, the NCCH still invested significant energy in figuring out what it was. It knew it stood against the NRA—in that same letter he noted his "strong determination not to let divisiveness give the NRA any advantage"—and that it stood for whatever abstract notion of "gun control" would triangulate the most political and financial support from the greatest number of people, but it hadn't landed on an institutional structure or clear message to maximize that calculus. More broadly, the gun control groups were so far behind the NRA, and so outgunned in terms of financial and cultural capital, that the odds of winning any battles in a war on multiple fronts—local, statewide, national— appeared daunting.

The NCCH was the first national gun control group to discover a paradox of gun control politics: it needed support and money from local grassroots organizations, but that required extracting resources the grassroots organizations

needed to be self-sustaining in a federal system in which state-level legislation could matter as much as national. Even in 1976, at the height of the first
post-1968 gun control surge, when there were as many as 100 relevant bills in
Congress and so much talk about the gun problem, the biggest national organization trying to do something about it faced an existential struggle to pay
the bills, figure out its mission, coordinate with activists around the country,
get its highest-profile supporters to show up at board meetings, and agree on
its most basic of policy assumptions. It also faced a competitive and confusing
landscape of new groups attempting to organize gun control advocates nationally. The *Christian Science Monitor* counted at least six groups with national
aspirations in 1976: the NCCH; the US Conference of Mayors' Handgun Control Project; the National Council to Ban Handguns (a project of the General
Board of Church and Society of the United Methodist Church created at an
NCCH meeting in 1975); the new National Gun Control Center (established
by Morris Dees and Joseph Levin Jr., founders of the Southern Poverty Law
Center); DISARM (founded by Johnson administration attorney general Ramsey Clark and, puzzlingly, not an acronym); and the National Council for a
Responsible Firearms Policy, the "grandaddy" group created in 1966 that continued operating a decade later as a one-man show. It was a mess. ("Surely
there are enough guns around for all to work for their control," Ramsey Clark
quipped.)[92] Confusion abounded among the millions of people these organizations sought to reach. Who wanted to ban handguns, and who wanted them
simply regulated? How did each propose to accomplish these seemingly pie-
in-the-sky objectives? Why did the National Council to Ban Handguns and
the National Gun Control Center have the same logo?[93] For the NRA, it was an
easy setup: it defended gun rights, and increasingly in the 1970s in reaction to
the gun control movement, the NRA did it without qualification.

The NCCH had also largely abandoned CDC's longtime goal of a complete
civilian handgun ban. Pete Shields's new mission statement after the 1976
election mentioned nothing about it, a point not lost on disappointed CDC
members. The NCCH had also turned toward support for registration, a moderate policy opposed by the CDC and other groups advocating for complete
disarmament. For Fermi and CDC members, a registration law would negate
their goal of getting guns out of civilian hands and off the streets of their
neighborhoods. Registration would create a "huge bureaucracy," which would
then "constitute a vested interest and hamper any possible future attempts to
ban or greatly restrict possession of handguns."[94] Surely the CDC had in mind
Chicago's municipal registration system, which documented at least a half
million guns in private hands in a city plagued with gun violence. In CDC's

eyes, a registration law, like the kind most identified in Washington with liberal gun control reformers such as Ted Kennedy, would give the NRA precisely
what it wanted: legal sanction for unlimited gun capitalism with a stamp of
approval from a federal bureaucracy. Dislodging any entrenched bureaucracy
tasked with overseeing the upkeep of 100 million or more guns seemed a truly
Sisyphean task. When Borinsky had led the NCCH, influenced by Fermi and
the CDC, the organization opposed licensing and registration schemes as a
"step in the wrong direction." An expanded gun bureaucracy was "frightening because it accepts, legitimizes and actually sets up a system to perpetuate
the arming of American society."[95] But Shields, ever the marketer, attuned to
political triangulation, oriented the NCCH toward these more tepid measures,
choosing accommodation over abolition.

FERMI RESIGNED FROM the NCCH board of directors in September 1976.
In a letter to Pete Shields she wrote, simply, "You know my reasons." Her health
was among them. A candid letter to her cardiologist six months earlier shows
that she was already living with a terminal illness and pondering what she
wanted for her final days. ("I have lived a long life and so full at times that it
seems even longer," she wrote. She asked not to be kept "attached to machines"
with little chance of recovery.)[96] She started to withdraw from intensive activities like cross-country travel. She resigned as chair of the CDC in December,
passing the torch to cofounder Lillian Kaplan, who had apprenticed with Fermi
on trips to national conferences, though Fermi continued to host monthly
meetings.[97]

But it was clear that Fermi also decided to leave because she didn't like the
direction the NCCH had taken. Upon assuming leadership, Shields had contracted with "a public relations firm, a direct mail consultant, an advertising
manager, and a volunteer fund raiser," Borinsky told NCCH members.[98] Fermi
worried that the time and energy required to raise money distracted from
the cause. She noted that the spring 1976 board meeting "was too short and
not enough vital to the gun issue was discussed to make it worth a long trip
both time and money-wise." "They are trying to give themselves a 'strong business' image," Fermi reported back to CDC members, and she worried such an
approach "might be dangerous for the 'gun cause' and may inhibit it."[99] When
Pete Shields described the NCCH's "key need" as "the seed money requirements of acquiring a significant national constituency via direct mail solicita-
tion," he parroted the kind of business-speak that made Fermi reconsider her
commitment to the organization. He was dismissive of activists he described
as "romantic about the potential of local, town-meeting politics."[100] And yet

despite the turn toward a "strong business" image, the organization struggled to get board members to show up for board meetings or fundraise. Prominent board members like Abner Mikva, Massachusetts congressman Michael Harrington (who, like Mikva, had submitted bills proposing private handgun bans), and former NYC police commissioner Patrick Murphy (now head of the Police Foundation, a research nonprofit committed to gun control) rarely attended meetings in Washington, making it difficult to achieve a quorum for voting. The April 1976 CDC newsletter informed members that, after Fermi had recently hosted a couple of fundraising dinners and some CDC members gave large donations in cash or services, the "CDC has closed its efforts to raise funds for the National Council."[101]

Fermi had come to believe that the NCCH's anti-NRA DNA destined the organization to fundraise endlessly and to relegate the issues of gun violence and unrestricted gun consumerism to secondary status. She couldn't continue giving money to the organization, and soliciting CDC members to do so, if it only ever seemed to use that money to look for more money. The CDC used its scant resources to *do things* around Chicago—why did the NCCH never seem to do anything? And the search for money required a policy triangulation that inevitably led to accommodation: while a large majority of Americans polled back to the 1930s always supported stricter controls of guns in the abstract, only a minority agreed with the CDC in the 1970s that the United States should prohibit private handgun ownership. The NCCH couldn't fundraise from that small pool of hardliners. The imperatives of money mandated modesty in political goals.

Pete Shields didn't want to lose Fermi. He wrote her in March 1976 and assured her that he shared her frustration with neglectful board members and also wanted a "strong, active board" advising him. "You are one of our strongest and most active supporters," he wrote. "I truly hope you can see your way clear to continue in this role." "Don't forget," he added, "I consider you NCCH's co-founder with Mark." It was a statement he felt he had to make explicit because six months into his tenure as director of the organization he had stamped it with his personality and business sensibility. Shields acknowledged Fermi's health problems on top of her concerns with the direction of the organization but he also knew how much her support had sustained the NCCH when it had no one else to lean on. In a handwritten postscript he added, "You are essentially the *only* board member other than myself who has raised *any* money for NCCH"—Shields had tapped his wealthy friends and acquaintances from the corporate world. "I also understand that you have raised your limit," he concluded.[102]

After Laura Fermi's death in December 1977, the members of the CDC spent 1978 debating the future of the organization. Fermi's death was "a serious blow," as she had been "essentially the center of our activities and our motivating force." Bereft of Fermi's charisma, the CDC decided at the end of the year to merge into the NCCH, donating the rest of its funds to the national organization. Pete Shields told CDC members that the NCCH "could certainly use the funds, but more importantly, I think NCCH exists today because of Mrs. Fermi's initiative and influence. . . . NCCH itself is in fact a memorial to Mrs. Fermi's idealism, humanity and courage." He concluded with a commitment to memorializing Laura Fermi: "If you do decide that NCCH is an appropriate recipient of these funds, we would make every effort to acknowledge the influence of Mrs. Fermi in the handgun control movement."[103] More than forty years later, the well-funded national organization Fermi inspired, the Brady Campaign, a "memorial" to Fermi, which reported its annual revenue for 2021 at more than $41 million, makes no mention of this foundational figure in any of its literature.[104]

Shields acknowledged Fermi as a cofounder of the NCCH but he nevertheless put his indelible stamp on the organization. He'd spent his professional career, more than a quarter century, in marketing. He brought his business acumen to the NCCH, and his decision to integrate more professionalism into the organization pushed Fermi and the CDC away. The gun control movement would not be driven by "little old ladies in tennis shoes," schooled on the great global crisis of midcentury and universal threats to human security. Instead, mostly white, middle-class suburbanites would power the movement. Shields was one face of that movement. Another was working on the other side of Chicago, on its suburban North Shore—like the CDC, a group of women dedicated to gun control, but one pursuing a distinctive strategy.

CHAPTER  7

THE MOTHERS OF TODAY

AUTHENTIC HOLSTERS
Custom made Original Authentic type holsters, Avail
now for Colt 1860 Army 1851 Navy, Colt S.A. and
Remington Army, Percussion revolvers $9.20   P.P.
Colt 1848 Pocket Model

ON FIRST GLANCE, the menu for Saturday evening, June 28, 1975, looked unremarkable for an upscale Chicago restaurant. There was a "Plat du Jour" and a "Chef's Special." But on closer inspection, the $10 "Gourmet's Delight" offered diners an odd choice: "a gun dealer's license" or "informational literature" distributed to Chicagoland schools. For $200, gastronomes could decide whether to "fully arm a street gang" or send a gun control organization to Washington, DC, to talk to President Gerald Ford. And for the true gourmand, there was the $1,000 "Millionaire's Indulgence," a choice between "thousands of hand gun bullets" or 5,000 copies of a pamphlet on gun control. "The presses are ready to roll. Won't you help?"

Flipping the menu back to its cover page, guests would find a table setting with a dish sitting on a plate: a handgun and three spent bullet casings. Opposite the menu was a form to be clipped and mailed, along with a donation, to the downtown Chicago office of the Committee for Hand Gun Control Inc. (CHC). The menu was the committee's tongue-in-cheek idea of a "Saturday Night Special."[1]

The ironic edge of the fundraising pamphlet was characteristic of the CHC, which was founded in late 1973 by a group of women who lived in suburban North Shore towns like Winnetka and Kenilworth, enclaves that were almost exclusively white and had median incomes several times the national average. The CHC briefly made national news in 1975 when it seemed to be on the verge of the impossible: it had petitioned the Consumer Products Safety Commission, a federal agency tasked with ensuring the safety of tens of thousands of products, to ban handgun bullets as a "dangerous substance." The CPSC

THE SATURDAY NIGHT SPECIAL

Fundraising flyer for the Committee for Handgun Control, 1975–76. (Special Collections & University Archives, University of Illinois Chicago Library)

rejected the petition on the grounds that bullets fell outside its jurisdiction, but when a federal judge unexpectedly ruled that the commission did indeed have the authority to ban handgun bullets, the CHC and its petition became the biggest news in the gun world for a few months, until pro-gun members of Congress struck back.

But the ban-the-bullet campaign was just one part of the CHC's work. The group's members articulated a broad approach to addressing gun violence rooted not in the kind of abstract commitment to international disarmament and "civilized" modernity represented by the Civic Disarmament Committee, their counterparts in Hyde Park, but rather in the language of gendered consumerism. "We speak for the mothers of today," they liked to say, inaugurating a long tradition of women in the gun control movement claiming maternal authority over an issue dominated by masculine claims to expertise in all directions. The CHC's approach echoes today in gun control leaders like Shannon Watts, founder of Moms Demand Action, a large and vocal group with substantial funding from Every Town for Gun Safety, the gun control organization founded by billionaire New York City mayor Michael Bloomberg. While Watts makes no mention of the CHC in her 2019 book, its title alone— *Fight Like a Mother: How a Grassroots Movement Took on the Gun Lobby and Why Women Will Change the World*—would sound at home on a clever CHC mailer. "The City Fathers say, 'There's a hand gun problem,'" read a 1975 CHC flyer. "The City Mothers say, 'Let's solve it.'"[2]

IN CONTRAST TO THE WOMEN of Laura Fermi's Civic Disarmament Committee, CHC members by and large did not worry about gun violence on the streets of the neighborhoods bordering their own. Mark Borinsky's mugging was central to the narrative of the NCCH's founding. The mostly Black members of the Coalition of Concerned Women in the War on Crime lived and worked in neighborhoods beset by common street violence. Smaller groups sprinkled throughout the country often had similar stories, like Handgun Alert of Rhode Island, founded in 1973 by Lillian Potter, a widow whose obstetrician husband Charles V. Potter had been shot to death outside the hospital where, twenty years earlier, he had been the attending physician at the birth of one of his killers.[3]

The CHC's perch in the well-off North Shore suburbs, in contrast, made the CDC of Hyde Park subtly dismissive of its counterpart. Fermi and CDC members would refer to the CHC as the "Winnetka group," the "Northside group," or the "Kenilworth Committee for Handgun Control," in a muted critique of the group's authenticity, drawing attention to their wealth and distance from the city proper and specifically its violent South and West Sides.[4] While most of the CHC's active members lived in the suburbs—an early list of fifty-four members included only nine with addresses within Chicago city limits—the group directed its correspondence to an office in downtown Chicago, perhaps attuned to the optics of fighting for gun control from the comfortable North Shore, where their tax dollars went to well-funded local schools of mostly white children while the city's urban core continued to struggle under the weight of de facto segregation, deindustrialization, and poverty.[5]

In contrast to the CDC and the Coalition of Concerned Women, the women of the CHC were motivated not by any personal experience of gun violence but by the growing national trend of violent crime and the refusal of the "gun lobby" to take any responsibility for it. The CHC confronted the NRA aggressively and directly. It was the NRA's hubris—promoting unrestricted gun ownership, encouraging the fear and anxiety that led people to believe handguns would protect them, and taking no responsibility for the consequences—that fired up the CHC's members. Founder Susan Sullivan's own gun control origin story was born out of a confrontation with the NRA. Concerned about rising crime rates in 1973, she found herself in a "telephone debate" with an NRA official, pressing his organization to accept responsibility for gun violence. Several days later, she received in the mail a cookbook with recipes for preparing wild game, courtesy of the NRA official.[6]

Sullivan took the cookbook slight as a challenge: if gun rights proponents were going to dismiss women like her as simple homemakers, then she would use the identity of "suburban housewife" to muster all the authority it could in postwar America to take on the gun lobby.[7] "They describe themselves as housewives who take care of children and do the dishes," a 1975 profile of the CHC's founders said with more than a little irony.[8] In October 1975 Sullivan and two other CHC leaders traveled to Washington, DC, for, among other things, a show of force in front of the NRA's massive headquarters. "We picked that location . . . for the symbolic value," Estelle Jacobson said. A *Chicago Sun-Times* reporter observed that the "scene called forth the Biblical story of David and Goliath—three Chicago suburban housewives against the awesome power" of the NRA. The women called themselves "the conscience of America" and "a silent majority," representing the 70 percent of Americans who perennially told pollsters they supported greater restrictions on firearms. Reflecting on the ability of just a few CHC members to challenge the powerful NRA, Jacobson quipped that it was "not bad for some suburban housewives."[9]

In contrast to the CHC, Laura Fermi and the CDC had sidestepped gender, aware of the social tensions created by the women's rights movement and

A grass-roots movement against handguns springs from suburban kitchens on the North Shore, where housewives are urging a ban on bullets. After doing the dishes and getting the children off to school, Georgene Campion, Susan Sullivan and Pat Koldyke (l. to r.) go to work at the kitchen table. (Sun-Times Photo by Jerry Tomaselli)

Left to right: Georgene Campion, Susan Sullivan, and Pat Koldyke of the Committee for Handgun Control, displaying posters for their campaign, 1975. (Jerry Tomaselli/*Chicago Sun-Times* via Special Collections & University Archives, University of Illinois Chicago Library)

tacitly believing them to be a distraction from the goals of international and domestic disarmament. The character of the "little old lady in tennis shoes" was meant to be persuasively disarming—nonsexual, nonradical, and if not nonfeminist then at least agnostic toward feminism. The "little old ladies in tennis shoes" could have no agenda other than saving lives. The women of the CHC, in contrast, boldly embraced their gendered identities as "suburban housewives" to disrupt the postwar masculinist dichotomy between manly men who *wielded* guns and manly men who *controlled* guns. If the gendered expectations of housewives in the postwar United States demanded that these suburban women exercise their protective maternal instincts, they would use those expectations to their advantage.

The role of suburban housewife was performative for CHC leaders, an opportunity to leverage cultural attitudes toward political ends. Susan Sullivan hinted at this performativity when she told a reporter, "The first time I ever testified at a formal hearing was an experience I won't forget. All those lights and cameras," she said. "I had never had such an urge to go home and bake cookies."[10] The performance, in this case, was not the testimony but the affirmation of Sullivan's identity as a homemaker, one that not only disarmed audiences of male legislators but also bestowed a kind of authority in postwar America—she testified not as a political actor but one charged with securing domestic spaces against the many dangers of consumer capitalism. After all, that's what the NRA official who mailed her a cookbook assumed her to be.

Gender performativity was a tactic in a larger strategic assault on the NRA and gun rights advocates, a struggle to define the meaning of safety in postwar America. In the early Cold War, securing the "home front" against nuclear apocalypse and communist subversion was both a national political project and a domestic social one, in the sense that domestic spaces—homes—became sites where the construction of a national security state manifested as an affirmation of the value of the nuclear family and traditional gender roles. White middle-class Americans of the atomic era turned to the nuclear family for domestic social stability and security in a perilous world.[11] The Cold War taught Americans that they had to make their homes safe from various external threats. In the first postwar decades, nuclear war with the Soviet Union presented the most visible threat. The US government encouraged Americans to prepare for nuclear war and protect their families by building shelters—and securing them from their neighbors.[12] By the 1970s, as historian Elaine Tyler May writes, the threat shifted, "the danger of red shading into the danger of black": now the threat manifested as "urban" crime, understood to be primarily Black crime, linked to the urban uprisings of the 1960s and white myths about the civil rights movement's connections to international communism. "The red menace and the black menace merged at the local level," May writes, "and crime came to be seen as two sides of the same coin."[13]

For the NRA, existential threats came from dangerous people. Guns were, like knives or automobiles, simply tools to be used for good or evil. The NRA argued that "criminals" would always get their hands on guns, regardless of the laws governments passed to stop them. No phrase more pithily captured this idea than "Guns don't kill people; people kill people," a line already well worn by the time Tom Dodd began his Senate hearings in 1963. It fell to state and federal government to ensure that Americans could defend their homes from the inevitable encounter with a criminal who intended to do harm. Homes needed to be fortified, to become fortresses—not coincidentally, conservative state legislatures began passing "castle doctrine" laws in the 1970s that bestowed homeowners with the right to use deadly force against perceived threats to their property, or "castle." (These laws would evolve into "stand your ground" laws in the 2000s, expanding the rights of gun owners to exercise deadly force legally from the private realm to the public.)[14] The NRA's shift in the 1970s toward aggressive lobbying against gun control has been well charted, but one aspect that has gotten little attention is just how much it was driven by the growth in handgun ownership for home defense.

The CHC, in contrast, saw threats coming from dangerous things rather than people—dangerous people would be less dangerous if they didn't have access to dangerous things. In the 1930s the federal government imposed burdensome taxation and registration requirements on machine guns that made them virtually illegal when Congress acknowledged that they were unsafe in almost anyone's hands. Why not restrict access to handguns similarly, the CHC asked, given that they proved to be even more destructive in the 1970s than machine guns had been a half century earlier? As for "self-defense," the CHC argued that handguns were the real threat to the home—the place where most gun accidents occurred and the site of much gun violence, with roughly three-quarters of it transacted between family members or acquaintances. Statistically they were right, as women and children were more likely to experience violence in the home at the hands of family members or acquaintances and three times less likely than men to be attacked by a stranger outside the home.[15] While the NRA claimed that domestic spaces could be secured *with* handguns, the CHC argued as homemakers that the home must be kept safe *from* handguns. They would use their claimed authority as homemakers, as women with expertise in protecting the nuclear family from unsafe things, to attack handguns.

THE CHC DEPARTED from other gun control groups' strategies in that it sought to ban handguns not through new legislation but through the regulatory regimes the modern state had constructed to keep populations safe from the dangerous products and byproducts of consumer capitalism. In the United States, efforts to protect consumers from unsafe goods dated back to the 1906 Pure Food and Drug Act, a law passed by Congress to address unsanitary industrial practices and mislabeled food products. Congress created the US Food and Drug Administration to administer the act and established the federal government in the business of regulating consumer products in the name of safety. The law would be amended and expanded over the decades and new laws enacted to protect consumers against unsafe products in fields beyond food and pharmaceuticals. Though Congress passed a number of consumer protection laws in the 1960s and 1970s, the two most significant were the Federal Hazardous Substances Act (FHSA, 1960), which required labeling of household products that could injure or kill (especially children), and the landmark Consumer Product Safety Act (CPSA, 1972), which created a new federal agency, the Consumer Product Safety Commission (CPSC), with the authority to regulate products through a variety of mechanisms, from requiring safety labeling to outright bans.[16] Congress charged the CPSC with administering both the FHSA and the CPSA.

When Congress debated the CPSA, the bill faced opposition from conservatives who feared an agency with a broad mandate to reach into citizens' private lives. And no consumer product generated such anxieties more than guns. As a result, when the CPSA passed into law, it included a provision, written by Michigan Democratic congressman John Dingell, an NRA board member and a vigorous opponent of gun control laws, that prohibited the new CPSC from exercising any control over firearms and ammunition.[17] The easiest justification was that the federal government already had an agency for this purpose, the BATF, and it made little sense to create overlapping jurisdictions (even as conservatives spent much of the 1970s trying to eliminate the BATF or cut its funding).[18]

Despite the explicit prohibition against regulating firearms, gun rights advocates nevertheless feared the CPSC might be wielded against them. While discussing the agency's wide jurisdiction at the 1973 Product Liability Prevention Conference, CPSC chairman Richard O. Simpson remarked, somewhat offhandedly, "We could probably ban bullets." In response, the CPSC received a number of protest letters, including one from Neal Knox, founding editor of *Gun Week*, and later head of the NRA's lobbying arm. The commission's counsel was forced to clarify that Simpson had simply used bullets as a hypothetical example to demonstrate that while the 1972 law created the CPSC, the agency's regulatory mandate also included administering the 1960 Federal Hazardous Substances Act. Congress exempted firearms and ammunition in the CPSA but had not done so back in 1960, because few people ever thought of bullets as "substances," even though their internal chemical components formally matched the law's definitions, and because fewer conservative legislators were sensitive to gun control before the 1960s. Simpson's point was that the CPSC could consider the few products that were excluded by the CPSA but fell within the FHSA's jurisdiction. The CPSC letter to Knox noted that, "to date, no ordinary ammunition has been determined to be a banned hazardous substance," but it made no effort to reassure gun owners that the CPSC wouldn't contemplate it in the future.[19]

Word of the CPSC's aggressive interpretation of its statutory mandate leaked into the gun press. The monthly "Washington Report" column of *Guns & Ammo* magazine lambasted Simpson's comments and warned that the

CPSC "now commands perhaps the most extensive powers ever granted a single Federal agency." The column highlighted similarly hyperbolic rhetoric from gun rights sympathizers in Congress. "I believe that the Commission may try to outlaw firearms ammunition . . . for the simple reason that the Commission seems to be very ambitious in its wielding of power," said Indiana representative Earl F. Landgrebe. He added that the CHC's powers were "inherently tyrannical." Representative Jamie L. Whitten of Mississippi quipped that the CPSC had "more power than a good man wants or a bad man should have." *Guns & Ammo* concluded ominously with a remark from Ted Kennedy, perennial gun control advocate and favorite bogeyman of the gun rights crowd, who had claimed that "strict bans on the production and distribution of ammunition would solve the gun problem in quick order."[20]

Kennedy never proposed a bill banning bullets but both he and the *Guns & Ammo* article inspired Susan Sullivan. She later said that the article gave her and the nascent CHC just the issue it needed to make a splash. "We figured if the NRA was nervous about it," Sullivan told a reporter in 1975, "then we really ought to look into it."[21] Rather than push for more gun control legislation, which, even when it succeeded, resulted in tepid measures like the 1968 Gun Control Act, the CHC could pursue a regulatory angle through the federal bureaucracy created explicitly to protect Americans from dangerous things.

When the group formed in the fall of 1973, it assessed the congressional landscape for the possibility of gun control legislation and found it bleak. A lobbyist friend told Sullivan that Congress was unlikely to pass any gun control legislation in the next decade. But this wasn't just the result of the NRA's outsized power to block or water down bills. Any legislation would also have to pass through the House Judiciary Committee, which was at that moment in the midst of the evolving Watergate crisis, debating potential impeachment charges against President Nixon. A nonlegislative path presented a chance to short-circuit a sluggish and distracted Congress, and even if the gambit ultimately proved unsuccessful, it would offer returns just by drawing attention to the issue.[22] It didn't hurt that the CHC's message was simple and crafted to attract attention: It was time to "Ban the Bullet."

THE CAMPAIGN BEGAN with a June 1974 petition to the CPSC requesting that commissioners, using their authority under the CPSA, act to ban the sale of handgun bullets except to police, military, security professionals, and licensed pistol clubs. The commission responded a month later to say that it could not do so, given the 1972 CPSA's explicit exception for firearms and ammunition. Alternatively, it could do what the group asked, as CPSC chair

Simpson had said a year earlier, under its authority to administer the 1960 FHSA. After all, bullets were already regulated under the FHSA—all small arms ammunition sold in the United States was required to have a label indicating the dangers it posed.[23]

The CPSC, it seems, was as eager to test the limits of its regulatory capacity as the gun press had feared. It would have been easy for the commission to simply deny the request as it was formally written: the CHC asked the CPSC to rule under the authority granted it in the 1972 CPSA, authority that did not exist because of the law's explicit exemption of guns and ammunition. In other words, the CHC didn't know the law well, and the commission could have rejected its request on those grounds and chosen to adhere to the status quo to avoid a patently controversial issue. Instead, commission staff took the initiative to amend the CHC's request to include consideration of the CPSC's jurisdiction under the Federal Hazardous Substances Act, a law the CHC petition had not mentioned.

The CPSC's lawyers encouraged the commission to exercise its powers and stake its jurisdictional claims. The CPSA permitted commissioners to regulate "articles," like, say, a tent or a tricycle; the FHSA authorized the regulation of harmful "substances," like various home cleaning products. A bullet could be both an article and a substance: "gunpowder is a chemical substance and is contained in a bullet," the legal office observed, and thus bullets fell within the FHSA's jurisdiction. The FHSA regulated any substances that were intended for storage or use in the home. "Given the widespread use of hand guns for home protection," the lawyers said, "hand gun bullets present no problem in meeting this requirement." Handguns were not magical objects shrouded in a mystique of tradition but widely available consumer products that federal regulators should scrutinize like any other. The lawyers reminded commissioners that neither the CPSA nor the Food and Drug Administration had previously "taken a narrow view of jurisdiction under the FHSA, and to do so now would seriously limit our potential effectiveness." The lawyers recognized that Congress probably didn't want the CPSC using the FHSA as justification for regulating handgun bullets if such items had been explicitly excluded in the CPSA. The commissioners' job was not to interpret the will of Congress, however, but to regulate according to statute, and thus the Office of General Counsel recommended that the CPSC rule that, thanks to the FHSA, "it has jurisdiction over hand gun bullets, including jurisdiction to ban non-defective bullets."[24]

The CPSC accepted the petition and scheduled a hearing for the end of September. Three weeks beforehand, however, the North Shore group received word that the CPSC had already met, "in secret," without public notice, on the night of September 5, and decided by a four-to-one vote to reverse course and reject the petition. The commission acknowledged the lawyers' argument that the CPSC had the authority to regulate handgun bullets but nonetheless was impelled to interpret Congress's intention to limit its authority over guns and ammunition. The ruling noted that "a hand-gun bullet falls within the literal meaning of the definition of a 'hazardous substance' under the FHSA, and as such, all FHSA regulatory remedies are available to the CPSC." "Nevertheless," it continued, "the Commission does not believe that Congress, in establishing the Commission and in transferring to it the authority to administer the FHSA, *intended* to confer upon the Commission the authority to ban hand-gun bullets." "The practical effect of the requested ban on hand-gun bullets," the CPSC concluded, "would be a virtual ban of hand-guns. There is clearly no authority under any act which the Commission administers to regulate hand-guns."[25]

Commissioner Lawrence Kushner offered additional remarks. He voted against the petition but he wanted it known that he believed the United States "is mistaken in permitting the relatively easy sale and ownership of hand guns that we have today." It was hard to deny, he said, that the CHC "has hand gun control as its acknowledged purpose," but its means for achieving control was through the CPSC's regulatory authority rather than through the democratic mechanisms of legislation. "I believe the petition is an attempt to circumvent the unreadiness of our citizenry to regulate hand guns through legislation," Kushner wrote. He rejected the claim that the CPSC ought to consider the petition "mechanically in terms of detailed and precise interpretation of words or phrases" on a decision "involving national policy and serious as well as emotional issues." Despite his support for the potential outcome, he concluded, "A decision should not be foisted on the public by a backdoor through an administrative rule-making."[26]

The CHC wasn't ready to accept the ruling. Members flew to Washington, DC, on September 20 and filed suit in federal court. The group argued that the "secret" September 5 meeting was "arbitrary, unreasonable and capricious," and violated their Fifth Amendment rights to due process. The CHC also found fault with the CPSC's argument: if the commission acknowledged that bullets were a danger, and it acknowledged that it had the authority to regulate bullets as a dangerous "substance," an authority previously exercised by the Food and Drug Administration (which had administered the FHSA until 1972), then it was shirking its duty to the public by refusing to acknowledge that authority. After all, the CHC was not asking—at least not yet—for a ruling that handgun bullets were dangerous. It simply wanted the CPSC to decide that bullets fell within its jurisdiction and then begin the process of debating regulations or prohibitions. The CHC included in its motion for judgment letters from physicians attesting to the danger of handgun ammunition along with letters of support from a half-dozen big-city chiefs of police, including Detroit chief Philip Tannian and Chicago superintendent James Rochford. Tannian described handguns as a "very serious menace that undermines the very fibre of our democratic heritage," while Rochford noted that the handgun's "only function is the killing or maiming of human beings."[27]

The CPSC contested the CHC suit. The commission presented three main arguments to US District Court Judge Thomas A. Flannery. First, Congress never explicitly granted the CPSC jurisdiction to ban handguns, and even a cursory reading of the statute indicated that Congress did not want the CPSC to do any such thing. Second, even the FHSA did not grant the CPSC the power to *ban* ammunition; by explicitly regulating it with labeling, the 1960 law implicitly sanctioned its regulated legal ownership and use. The commission interpreted the goal of the CHC petition as not simply to ban ammunition but "to effectively ban the use of hand guns," a reasonable conclusion given the CHC's organizational mission. Third, even if the CPSC did have the authority to regulate handgun ammunition, its refusal to do so was properly adjudicated through the commission's regular functions. Commissioners had discussed the matter and voted to reject the petition.[28]

The women of the CHC were as surprised as anyone when on December 19 Judge Flannery handed down his decision: ammunition qualified as a hazardous substance under the FHSA and the CPSC had the authority to regulate or ban it. Flannery ordered the CPSC to consider the petition and vote on it within sixty days. The commission decided not to appeal the decision and to begin soliciting public comment in early 1975. Commissioners reasoned that Flannery hadn't ordered them to regulate handgun ammunition; rather he concluded that the CPSC could not reject the petition on jurisdictional grounds, though the commission could rightfully vote against it after consideration.[29]

Meanwhile, the NRA filed a motion to intervene with a consumerist counterargument. The organization asked that Flannery ignore the question of whether ammunition was a hazardous substance and instead consider that bullets were "intended for use in the open, in woods, in fields and on shooting ranges" and were "*not* intended or suitable for household use," a criterion necessary for regulation under the FHSA. It was an awkward argument for the gun rights organization to make as it increasingly focused on the right of homeowners to use handguns for self-defense. Flannery rejected the NRA's motion. On the legislative front, Senator James McClure, a conservative Republican from Idaho, following a request from the CPSC commissioners for clarification

of Congress's intent, introduced a bill to remove ammunition from its juris-
diction. Leading Senate conservative and former presidential candidate Barry
Goldwater asked to cosponsor the bill, he wrote in a response to CHC member
Estelle Jacobson, because "what this comes down to is backdoor gun control."[30]

The CHC mobilized its network of supporters in the greater Chicagoland
area to write the CPSC and amplify the group's message during the period of
public comment. As the *Chicago Tribune* put it, the unanticipated success of
the CHC, "composed largely of suburban housewives," was like "something out
of one of those droll British comedies in which members of a block club bring
parliament to a halt."[31] The CHC faced tremendous odds, and its members
knew it. Commissioners had already expressed their disagreement with the
petition. Writing public officials in opposition to gun control was right in the
NRA membership's wheelhouse, and the CPSC would report that the overwhelming majority of letters it received opposed any ban or special regulation
of handgun ammunition. Some writers to the CPSC copied their letters to the
CHC, which were several degrees more polite than the opposition letters
the CHC typically received. "The immediate outlook is not encouraging," said
the CHC newsletter, as the group waited for news from the commission.[32]

Despite the David-and-Goliath setup, and despite the clear advantages of
the opposition, the CHC got some significant support. The J. Walter Thompson Company, one of the country's most iconic advertising firms, provided
the CHC with a pro bono marketing campaign through its Chicago office. The
firm built the campaign around the slogan, "We Need Bullets Like We Need
a Hole in the Head." Each ad showed a framed face, akin to a mugshot, with a
hole superimposed in the forehead of one of the several people who modeled
for the ads, women and men, Black and white. At the bottom the ad explained
the dangers of handguns and how interested readers could help the CHC's
campaign. The agency also helped the CHC create other kinds of promotional
merchandise, like pins and bumper stickers that echoed the campaign slogan
or others that read, "Warning: Hand Guns Are Dangerous to Your Health!"
The agency's creative presentation to the CHC listed other slogans that didn't
make it into the final campaign, like "Support Your Right to Arm Bears."[33]

The women of the CHC also got a boost from the national press, which
tended to view gun control proposals sympathetically. A brief article in *Time*
magazine in early March focused on Sullivan, "a housewife in Winnetka," who
was "trying a new and imaginative approach to the problem that might be
summed up: If you can't ban the gun, ban the bullet." "There is no way we
can lose," Sullivan told *Time*, surely knowing there were plenty of ways the

CHC could lose. She appealed to Americans who believed in the government's responsibility to keep the home safe: "How can they talk about bicycles and medicine cabinets and pins being dangerous, and not bullets?" The CHC corresponded with consumer journalists to ask them to write features on the petition. Through women's magazines such writers could reach millions of women who, like CHC members, saw domestic spaces as their jurisdiction. Chicago media outlets, attuned to the impact of gun violence in their city, also supported the CHC. Local television station WMAQ ran an editorial that questioned why the CPSC was so eager to ban fireworks or aerosol sprays for the dangers they presented to consumers but hesitant to act on guns. "There does seem to be an inconsistency here, doesn't there?" the editorial mused. "If forced to make a choice, we would much prefer a whiff of a spray with vinyl chloride to the blast of a bullet."[34]

It was a message the CHC emphasized in its own literature. As citizen-consumers, CHC members demanded that the government act to protect lives. "Is the [CPSC] listening to consumers or to the gun lobby?" the group asked in April. "Are caps and projectiles from toy guns more hazardous than bullets?" The CHC critiqued the CPSC's spending; the commission had burned through $60 million in its first twenty months and had requested from Congress an annual budget over $50 million. "What kind of protection are we getting for these tax dollars?"[35]

The commission's answer, ultimately, was none at all, at least not when it came to dangers of handguns. The CHC's petition campaign ended with the intervention of Congress—the very intervention that CPSC chair Simpson wanted, despite his initial confidence in the commission's mandate. He ran out the clock on Flannery's order, and then continued stalling while congressional conservatives debated. By July the Senate had passed a bill explicitly stripping the CPSC of its authority to regulate firearms and ammunition at the same time that it denied the commission similar power over tobacco and pesticides—other controversial consumer products that Simpson believed would be better controlled (or not) through legislation rather than bureaucratic fiat. The House passed a similar bill in October but ultimately it wouldn't become law until 1976 in the form of the Consumer Product Safety Commission Improvements Act.[36]

INEVITABLY THE CHC attracted the attention of gun rights advocates. Members' names started to appear in NRA publications and magazines like *Guns & Ammo* and *Gun Week*.[37] The organization's most visceral experience with such people came in the form of hate mail, and lots of it. The CHC's records, which it donated to the University of Illinois at Chicago, contain many hundreds of letters attacking members. Some of those letters tried to engage sincerely on political and social questions. But most didn't. "You should see my obscene file," Susan Sullivan said to a reporter. "Many people consider us radicals. They really maintain that if you take away their guns, the Communists will take over."[38] One collection of letters is apparently so beyond the pale that the group requested it not be made available to researchers.

How do we reckon with these self-described "gun nuts"? They can't be dismissed simply because they weren't broadly representative of "gun culture," whatever precisely that was. It is true that they did not represent most the tens of millions of people in the United States who owned guns, but for groups like the CHC, and the many of other prominent groups in the country that have worked to do something about gun violence, these "gun nut" letters represented their visceral frontline experience with the most vocal of gun owners. They were the sort of communications congressional staffers stuffed into what they called the "You Commie-Jew-Bastard" file.[39] When NRA leaders wrote editorials denouncing groups like the CHC, they did so knowing the hell they were bringing down upon them. The NRA publicly disavowed "gun nut" letters, but its leaders knew well their value as weapons of intimidation. Women especially bore the brunt of these attacks. It took tremendous courage for the women of the CHC to read some of the letters they received and then to leave their homes to speak at press conferences and testify before legislatures, knowing that the letter writers were out there, watching, seething. The term *hate mail* implies that these letters came from cranks animated by irrational hatreds; but no word other than *hate* so succinctly describes the emotions their words conveyed and the harms they wished upon their recipients.

According to the gendered logic of hate mail writers, the women deserved scorn because they were women attempting to intrude on a masculine preserve. "I can't stand women who need a cause to keep them going so they can get some publicity," wrote one "red-blooded American," who imagined punishing the women for their crimes with racist fantasies of sexual violence. One man who saw Susan Sullivan on *The Today Show* in 1974 offered a typical comment when he said that she "impressed me as being a highly emotional woman who stumbled across a few statistics and began to rant and rave without first finding out what is really going on."[40] Writers suggested that the women of the CHC failed to appreciate how good their lives were in the United States, thanks to freedoms like the right to keep and bear arms, and that they should move to another country. Mixing misogyny and anticommunism, many writers suggested the women move to communist countries, where they would be stripped of their rights but where they could nevertheless work on behalf of the cause closest to their hearts. Writers commonly speculated that the women held ulterior, sinister motives. One correspondent took one of the ads from the "We Need Bullets Like We Need a Hole in the Head" campaign—with the image of a young white woman with a hole in her head—fired several real rounds through it, and mailed it to the CHC, with the salutation, "Dear Assholes." "We need you like we need communism," he wrote. "You can take my guns but you'll have to take me first!"[41]

Fantasies of sexual violence pointedly illustrated the extent to which the political and social upheavals of the era created conservative anxiety about the instability of the domestic home front, both in the national and the personal sense. In these letters the home is a sacred space that criminals seek to penetrate. Writers wished sexual violence and death upon CHC members. Quite a few imagined graphic fantasies of Black men raping the women and killing their families because they, or their husbands, had failed to protect themselves with guns. They speculated that the women used sex to win men (like Judge Flannery) to their policy positions.

The CHC's clash with the NRA and gun rights advocates hinged on clashing understandings of domestic "safety" and protection of the home. CHC members claimed authority as mothers and as consumers with the responsibility to ensure that the products of industrial capitalism that crossed the threshold of the home were safe for the family's consumption. The gun rights vision of domestic safety, in contrast, was premised on the assumption that a safe home was one in which adults (usually but not always men) used firearms to protect the family from outside threats, often framed as random, violent criminals who intended to break into a home to harm or kill the family during a robbery, or, more sinisterly, for the sadistic pleasure of it. Gun advocates' letters to the CHC were filled with wild fantasies of sadism, often racially coded. The domestic sphere was the refuge of the white nuclear family from the ravages of Black crime and rebellion that soft liberal politicians and judges refused to prosecute and punish. The women of the CHC, in turn, deserved punishment as traitors to their country and race.

THE EMERGENCE OF THE GUN CONTROL MOVEMENT prompted the hardline turn of the gun rights movement—and not the other way around. Histories of gun rights and gun control organizations neglect the dialectic that developed between the two in the decade after the Gun Control Act passed. Organizations like the NCCH and the CHC tried to confront the NRA as much as they attempted to do something about guns. Such groups, in turn, gave the NRA a foil more specific and arguably more valuable than the occasional anti-gun politician or the vague specter of government regulation. Now the "gun grabbers" had names, and their faces started to appear in the media. Groups with words like *ban* and *control* in their names provided the NRA with endless fodder for fundraising campaigns. In his increasingly hardline rhetoric, Harlon Carter, future NRA executive vice president and the organization's chief ideologue in the 1970s, framed such groups as emblematic of the crisis of liberalism, which had caved to the influence of feminism and the women's movement, coddling criminals and punishing men who wanted nothing more than the right to defend their families.

Carter's personal history embodied the NRA's whitewashing of American gun violence. When he was a teenager in South Texas, he chased down and shot and killed a Mexican boy he suspected of attempting to steal his mother's car. He was found guilty though the conviction was later overturned on a technicality, and although he would conceal this story for most of his life the press discovered it in the early 1980s. (Changing his name from Harlan to Harlon helped conceal his violent past.)[42] In addition to growing up on the borderlands of the Southwest he also made his professional mark there, serving in the US Border Patrol and, during the Second World War, as a regional director for the internment of Japanese Americans. After retirement from the federal government he became a top NRA official in the 1960s and served as president from 1965 to 1967. (The NRA president has traditionally been a ceremonial position, in contrast to the executive vice president, who runs day-to-day operations.) He then retired from the organization and wrote regularly for the gun press, only to be drawn out of retirement in 1975 to lead the NRA's new Institute for Legislative Action, "a powerful new lobbying unit designed especially to defeat anti-gun and anti-hunting legislation," as *American Rifleman* described it to NRA members that June.[43]

As soon as the Gun Control Act passed, Carter emerged as a stalwart opponent of all gun control legislation, one who toured the country addressing gun rights audiences and frequently took to the popular gun press to broadcast radical views about gun ownership, views that would move to the mainstream of conservative gun politics in the years and decades to come. Carter and other hardliners found inspiration in groups like the CHC, which they believed represented not just a liberal threat to gun ownership but a national existential one.

Carter railed against gun control advocates in the early 1970s and used the gun press to test out a range of defenses for gun ownership premised not on

protecting traditions of hunting or sports shooting but on a full-throated, absolutist interpretation of the constitutional right to own a firearm with almost
no restriction. In June 1974 he defended the black sheep of the gun industry,
the Saturday Night Special. He had no love for these unsavory handguns—he
argued that it was better for criminals to wield these cheap, inaccurate weapons, potentially more harmful to the shooter than his target, than a well-made
firearm from a respected manufacturer—but he believed that ceding this
ground meant giving in to an opponent that would not rest until "the manufacture, sale, distribution, ownership, possession and use of firearms in this
country is ended." "There will never be a time when strident voices among
our opponents will not be after our last six-shooter—then our rifle—then our
shotgun," he warned. "Don't ever doubt it."[44] To give an inch was to cede a mile.

Carter used his regular column in *Guns & Ammo* magazine—at once a
popular forum and just off the radar from the more respectable publications
of the NRA—to test other ideas that might have seemed extreme a decade
earlier. In a line that infuriated gun control organizations, which would use
it in their marketing, Carter told Congressman John Conyers's committee in
1975 that allowing criminals to own guns and injure and kill people was simply "a price we pay for freedom." He had introduced that line of thinking in a
column earlier that year: "It may be said the right to preserve one's life, to keep
and bear arms, costs lives," but "more lives are saved by guns in good hands
than are lost by guns in evil hands." In a confrontation with evil, government's
response could not be to strip Americans of their rights: "These rights may
not be infringed upon by the government because they are difficult or because
they are socially inconvenient or because they may, as a matter of fact, be painful at times."[45] To Carter, gun ownership was analogous to speech: instances
abounded of which society did not approve—hate speech or pornography, for
example—but the right remained inalienable, steadfast against mercurial popular opinions or fads.

The idea that the United States was undergoing some painful convulsions
was central to Carter's worldview, and he infused it into the organization he
would run. Evil lurked in American society in new and startling ways. In gendered language, Carter wrote that Americans could not hide behind the skirts
of government. They fearfully turned to gun control as a "cure-all for a soft-
boiled society." He blamed parents for coddling postwar children, a trend he
identified with child-development pioneer Dr. Benjamin Spock, who encouraged parents to see children as unique individuals in need of affection. He
mocked the parents of the "Spockian generation," who would "prefer to build
their homes like fortresses and deprive everyone of guns" just as they denied

children access to household consumer products that could harm them. He denounced the feminization of society and the abandonment of masculine ambitions on all fronts:

> Our most popular music contains only jaded and drug inspired dreamy songs. Military glee clubs go over the country and sing songs marked by soft, girlish voices. Nowhere is there a strong, thunderous, inspiring appeal to action, to production and to accomplishment. This continual enervation of the arts is the corruption of our national soul. It is pollution in its most malevolent form. Its design is to produce a passive, cringing, mewling society which, when presented with great issues, can only make a whimpering, whining response.[46]

Carter's anxiety over the feminization of society was an implicit rejection of both the CHC's claims to authority as mothers and consumers and the idea that guns could be treated as just another aspect of consumer society, that Americans ought to think about them as dangerous consumer products to be regulated like tricycles or oven cleaners. Self-defense was a sacred, masculine right, not a cheap product to be negotiated and regulated on the consumer market. When Carter told Conyers's committee that allowing dangerous people access to guns was "a price we pay for freedom," the CHC countered by turning back to guns as part of a consumer marketplace: "We can't help but ask what kind of freedom we are buying and at what price."[47] The rejoinder demonstrated the CHC's and Carter's clashing visions of gun culture, the CHC framing it as a material one, a part of modern industrial consumer society that should be regulated as any other part; Carter, in contrast, saw it as sacrosanct, a masculine domain to be defended from the feminization of society that threatened to undermine basic values like the nuclear family and male authority.

In May 1975 Carter sat on a stage in Los Angeles to speak on a panel at the invitation of the pro–gun control US Conference of Mayors. He knew he had an unfriendly audience, and he pulled no punches explaining why the gun control advocates sitting before him were fighting a losing cause. He wasn't there to tell them that Americans were buying so many guns because they were innocent hunters. Instead, gun stores were doing such good business because Americans were preparing for the breakdown of the social order, because they believed the political and legal systems had abandoned them. "I suspect it is fear," he said. "I suspect it is a lack of confidence in society." Politicians who harped on guns would "continue in this country to do nothing effective about evil men, to do nothing effective about criminals," and in the process would "eventually cause every household in America to be armed—lawfully or not— and like it or not." "We are denied freedom from fear," he told the audience. "And fear, most often, makes people go out and buy a gun who would never have done so otherwise." He described urban-dwelling Americans living a "besieged existence" where "marauders possess the streets at night." Nothing was better for gun sales, he admitted, than nightly news reports of violent crime. "Go out and ask the neighborhood gun dealers in this country and they will tell you that after heinous crimes have been committed . . . there has been an increase in gun sales."[48] He almost dared gun control advocates to pass more laws; they just didn't seem to get the point that Americans were terrified and would go out and buy guns one way or another. What Americans saw when they turned on the news or opened the newspaper was seemingly more crime and few consequences for it.

> Now, explain that if you can to the ordinary taxpayer and the voter; and explain it to the ordinary man in the street, and try to convince him that the judiciary system is working and that the instruments for an orderly society are in good shape. Try to tell him that after showing him what the facts are. He would probably laugh at you and then he would probably go out and buy a gun. And it wouldn't matter whether I approved of it and it wouldn't matter whether you approved of it. That is the way things are.[49]

While Carter and the CHC—Laura Fermi's CDC too—agreed on almost nothing, they shared an appreciation for what the gun buying boom of the previous two decades had done to society. For the CHC and the CDC, there was an urgency to action to restrict access to these weapons, handguns especially. They didn't say when, but in their understanding of the problem the United States was rapidly approaching a horizon at which it would thereafter be impossible to do anything about handguns. Any systems established to regulate them would be overwhelmed and banning them would be inconceivable. Rather than accommodate to this potential future, they wanted to eliminate access to handguns in their present, so that over time the stock would be depleted. Harlon Carter, of course, had no interest in restricting access to handguns. But he did implicitly agree that in the 1970s the US gun problem—if "problem" was even the best word to describe it—was connected to the unprecedented abundance of guns offered in the United States, and he agreed with the CHC and CDC that people often bought guns because they were afraid. Liberals were fools, he thought, to try to control the supply of guns because there were already so many available on the market that even if they were "banned" it would not be hard to meet demand, legally or otherwise. Gun control proved the great fallacy of liberalism: a political philosophy ostensibly committed to the protection of individual rights took as its approach to guns the idea that, first and foremost, people needed to be controlled.[50]

The CHC's "Ban the Bullet" campaign helped to radicalize Harlon Carter and a generation of gun rights advocates who came to believe that not only would gun controllers ceaselessly petition Congress and statehouses for legislative victories but they would also use "backdoor" opportunities offered by the vast federal bureaucracy to restrict gun rights undemocratically. In that sense they weren't wrong. The CHC attempted to circumvent democratic lawmaking and to short-circuit state and federal regulatory regimes for gun control. They did so for good reasons: they saw madness around them, fear overtaking reason. To say that the gun control movement helped produce the post-1960s gun rights movement is not to blame the gun control movement but to understand the symbiosis that mutually constituted the two. Rather than gun control emerging simply as a response to an already-existing gun rights movement, a growing chorus of voices in favor of control in the 1960s and 1970s catalyzed the emergence of the "gun nut" as a political and cultural force.

THE CHC WOULD NOT REPLICATE the "Ban the Bullet" campaign's success in terms of drawing national attention but the group's leaders nevertheless continued to push for change through innovative approaches to gun capitalism. In March 1976 the organization filed a complaint with the Federal Trade Commission against gun manufacturers who ran what the CHC argued were deceptive and dangerous advertisements in gun magazines. The CHC targeted ads in *Guns & Ammo* magazine, like one from TDE Marketing that, in the language of the ad, claimed to manufacture the "World's Smallest 380 Auto," a nonsporting handgun "approved by law enforcement." The ad offered no evidence of support by law enforcement, the CHC said, and many law enforcement officials were on record opposing cheap, easily concealed handguns. Colt marketed a .22-caliber handgun to compete with cheap and plentiful Saturday Night Specials, and the CHC found fault with marketing statements like "a good gun is a safe gun" and "shooting is for fun." Even the NRA published a twenty-five-point checklist for ensuring safety for firearms stored in the home, the CHC observed. Any attempt to market guns as "safe," they argued, was inherently deceptive.[51]

In attacking advertising, the group used the same strategy it had deployed in its CPSC campaign: it framed its opposition to gun culture in terms of its members' authority as mothers to police the boundaries of consumer culture, as caretakers charged with keeping the home safe from dangerous products. They addressed a common counterargument—why worry about guns when cars killed nearly twice as many people each year?—by arguing that cars provided value to consumers that guns lacked: "No one was ever unemployed because of no hand gun to drive to work. No one ever suffered for lack of a hand gun to get to a doctor." "Our entire nation would be paralyzed without the automobile," the CHC said. "We are hard pressed to think of a single contribution the hand gun has made to our society."[52] (Satirist Art Buchwald wrote that a gun lobbyist friend had asked him to write something nice about handguns. "Handguns are good because they're cheap," Buchwald wrote, obligingly. "They cost less now than they did 10 years ago, and since there are more than 40 million of them, you can get a used one for practically nothing.")[53]

The CHC also saw the shift in advertising in the 1970s toward self-defense as a symptom of a disturbing pathology in which gunmakers promoted the idea that guns were effective and valuable because they could injure and kill people. As the CHC wrote,

> The advertisements and the gun magazines prove that the multi-million dollar firearms industry is not satisfied with a market in legitimate sporting weapons. With crass and irresponsible disregard for human life, this powerful group thwarts all reasonable efforts to control hand guns—even cheap Saturday Night Specials. This group wants the right to sell any and all firearms, indiscriminately, to the fit and the unfit, regardless of the consequences. And more, the gun industry, through the type of advertising we have cited, promotes a gun cult—a sick fascination with deadly weapons that has no place in the true sportsman's creed and certainly no place in civilized society.[54]

The gun cult was growing into a death cult, the CHC argued. "Maybe this will make the gun manufacturers more responsible in how they promote guns," said CHC member Sally Campbell, "and also make people aware of the sick stuff that is in these gun magazines."[55] It took almost a half century, but eventually gunmaker Remington would be held liable for advertising—in 2022 it agreed to a $73 million settlement with the families of the children murdered in Connecticut in 2012 by a twenty-year-old man carrying a Bushmaster rifle that had been advertised with the slogan, "Consider your man card reissued."[56]

The CHC continued to press federal officials for action. In January 1976, CHC member Georgene Campion testified at the Chicago session of the White House Regional Conference on Consumer Representation Plans. The Ford administration organized this series of public meetings to hear from consumer groups regarding the president's plan to "beef up consumer representation in 17 federal agencies."[57] The CHC wanted to make sure the administration heard its message of gun violence as a consumer safety issue. "We speak for the mothers of today and the children of tomorrow," Campion said, once again staking her organization's authority on maternal ground.

The CHC wanted to see the Treasury Department step up its protection of consumers from the guns Congress charged it with regulating under the GCA. The group once again insisted that the federal government use its regulatory powers to establish rules to protect consumers from the most manifestly dangerous consumer products. The CHC wanted increased dealer licensing fees, limits on multiple gun sales, more oversight of private nondealer sales, stronger import criteria for all firearms, and a tax on handguns like the one on machine guns that made them prohibitively expensive to own. Government already protected consumers "against financial losses resulting from fraud," but it did not protect them against "death and injury and financial loss resulting from violent crime made possible and attractive by the ready availability of hand guns." The CPSC regulated lawnmowers, which killed thirty people a year, but was powerless to do anything about many thousands of gun deaths; now the federal government was even considering protecting citizen-consumers against secondhand cigarette smoke, but it still demurred on doing anything about bullets.[58]

Campion also asked administration representatives why "the ordinary citizen" ended up footing the hospital bill for "the innocent victim" of gun violence—"Why not the gun manufacturers, dealers and gun owners take this responsibility?" It was a provocative question. Gun manufacturers could, and increasingly were by the early 1980s, held legally and financially responsible when their products malfunctioned and harmed the user. It was why RG Industries closed its doors in 1986. But the idea that anyone in the gun industry would be held responsible for a handgun working *as it was designed*—to harm or kill a targeted human being—was novel. Not until the 1990s would gun control groups coordinate with cities around the country to attempt to hold the gun industry liable for the widespread uncontrolled distribution of its deadly products working as intended.[59] But the CHC had the idea much earlier. Not long after the "Ban the Bullet" campaign ended, CHC leaders were already brainstorming a strategy. The group's lawyers prepared a memo to this effect. "It is our opinion that all such guns are inherently dangerous products," attorney Michael Hausfeld wrote to Susan Sullivan. "As such, the manufacturers should be absolutely liable for any injuries and deaths resulting even from the 'safe' use of such a product." "Under such a theory," he continued, "any victim or surviving spouse of a victim injured or killed by a handgun could institute an action or bring a wrongful death suit against the manufacturer for the injuries or death sustained." He concluded with the kind of argument that appealed to the CHC: "Combining elements of compensatory and punitive damages for the deliberate manufacture of such an inherently dangerous product could result in the self imposed restriction of the manufacture and distribution of handguns. In other words, it would become economically unfeasible for manufacturers to produce and distribute handguns."[60]

The memo was speculative and the CHC wouldn't pursue it further. (The group owed Hausfeld's firm money, which took on the CPSC case pro bono but billed the organization for this other work, which remained unpaid a year later.)[61] But it did reveal the CHC's continued attempts to think about the US gun problem as one of buyers and sellers. Everyone ought to be held as accountable for the harmful social and economic impacts of their products as the manufacturers of refrigerators or toasters.

THE CHC HAD BIG PLANS on the first weekend of May 1977. It had been designated the local coordinating group for a program called Survival Days, organized by the National Coalition to Ban Handguns, an educational group based in Washington, DC, created by the United Methodist General Board of Church and Society. (The National Council to Ban Handguns would become today's Coalition to Stop Gun Violence.) The plan for Survival Days was to coordinate among dozens of religious institutions in Chicago, New York, San Francisco, and Atlanta to allow gun owners to turn in unwanted handguns, no questions asked. Officials from the ATF agreed to pick up collected firearms, local police forces would supervise in each location, and US Steel was enlisted to destroy the collected guns. In Chicago, the CHC arranged for the collected weapons to be deactivated and given to a local sculpture artist, John Kearney, who would incorporate them into a new work.[62]

Hopes were high for a strong showing. Local media outlets in Chicago advertised the event. The council spent a great deal of money on national promotion. But when the weekend ended, Survival Days proved a flop. In Atlanta, volunteers collected five guns; in San Francisco, three; in New York City not a single handgun was turned in. The CHC's efforts in Chicago bore the most fruit—seventy-five guns were collected, then handed over to Kearney, who welded the deactivated handguns to a 100-year-old plow to create a sculpture titled, " . . . And They Shall Beat Their Swords into Plowshares." But even

Chicago's showing hardly scratched the surface of a city handgun stockpile hundreds of thousands deep. Some CHC members and national gun control leaders laid the blame on the BATF. At the last minute the agency withdrew its participation without explanation. When pressed, an official said that the Treasury Department made the call after it "had been notified by the authorities in one state that the program would violate the laws of that state"—some speculated New York, with its strict state handgun laws, was the culprit. "So far," commented Chicago-area congressman Abner Mikva, "the score is NRA 1, ATF a big 0."[63]

Elsewhere in America that same May 1977 weekend, Harlon Carter and a cadre of gun rights hardliners plotted the future of the NRA. They believed the organization had retreated in reaction to the emergent national push for gun control. It was time for a course correction, a counteroffensive. In the "Revolt at Cincinnati," Carter and like-minded allies engineered a coup to overthrow and replace the NRA's old-guard leadership. Their success there and thereafter, coupled with the disappointment of initiatives like Survival Days, demonstrated how America as a gun country increasingly resembled Carter's vision rather than the CHC's: a nation armed, terrified, and convinced that the state could not protect it as well as an ever-growing mass movement packing cheap, plentiful, deadly weapons.

CHAPTER 8

THE NEW
GREAT
WESTERN

DOUBLE
BARREL   DERRINGER

. . . chambered for the .38 S&W
C.F. cartridge, blue satin finish, black
checkered grips as on the original
model. $49.95

THE COLD WAR'S
SECOND AMENDMENT

LIKE THE GUN COUNTRY ITSELF, the gun rights movement of the twenty-first century also has mythological origins. The story frequently begins at the famed "Revolt in Cincinnati," where, at the NRA's annual convention in 1977, former president Harlon Carter led a small army of disaffected hardliners in a coup to seize power from the traditional moderate leadership of the organization. The hardliners believed NRA leaders were trying to distance the organization from the contentious gun politics of the 1970s and reorient it toward hunting and sports shooting. In Cincinnati they would use the NRA's own bylaws and procedures to engineer a takeover, a "gentlemanly bloodbath," as one former NRA official described it.[1]

Carter stood at the head of a new generation of NRA members who saw handgun ownership and self-defense as the organization's future and its present task as fighting the "gun grabbers" who would deny them. Michigan congressman John Dingell "set off the revolution" in the days before the meeting with a fifty-seven-page memo to the NRA board complaining of a "crisis of confidence" in the leadership's ability to defend the association's "fundamental purpose: the preservation of firearms rights." The organization's leaders, like Executive Vice President Maxwell Rich, had recently planned a new, massive "National Outdoor Center" at a property in New Mexico, a kind of Disneyland for outdoorsmen, and had pursued grants from liberal funding agencies like the Ford and Rockefeller foundations for wildlife education programs. Dingell, Carter, and other insurgents, like the fiery editor Neal Knox, thought such plans foretold a path toward political moderation and compromise. "The previous administration was singing an uncertain song," Carter said a week after Cincinnati. "We are fighters around here."[2]

Almost from the moment the insurgents snatched control, they started crafting their own mythology. But the truth of the NRA's rightward turn in the 1970s was a bit more complicated. The organization had already opposed various gun control proposals on principle for years, if not decades, and only began to shift toward what appeared to Carter and the rebels as a new, apolitical course in the mid-1970s.[3] Carter, once described as "Moses, George Washington, and John Wayne rolled into one," led not so much a revolution as a restoration of an old regime, one that, like those of Europe in the nineteenth century, proved even more reactionary than its forebears.[4] After the convention of legend, Carter would lead the NRA until 1985, setting it on course to be the uncompromising gun rights organization it became by the end of the twentieth century.

Moreover, making sense of the history of the gun rights movement primarily through the NRA misses some of the most important action happening around the country at the ground level in the 1960s and 1970s. New, bellicose grassroots gun rights organizations were not going to wait around for the NRA. Seizing the initiative to spread a radical gun rights message in the late 1960s, they reached tens of thousands of Americans with a creed of "No Compromise"—a motto one group adopted in the immediate aftermath of the passage of the Gun Control Act of 1968, a law passed with the begrudging complicity of NRA leaders.

"No Compromise" was an implicit rebuke of the NRA. In the decade after the GCA passed, grassroots gun rights activists would take up the mantle of "No Compromise" where the NRA demurred, eventually pushing the national behemoth to the uncompromising right. Harlon Carter and the Cincinnati rebels would harness the energy of these grassroots activists. And these activists, influenced by right-wing anticommunism and Cold War anxieties about domestic subversion, would challenge the NRA to adopt an explicit defense of the Second Amendment as a guarantee not of hunting or sporting privileges but of an inalienable right to own a firearm to defend one's person, family, community, and country. The NRA's own turn toward "No Compromise" in 1977, and the radicalization of gun rights ideology and activism in the decades to follow, can be unearthed in an un-NRA history of the early postwar gun rights movement.

ROBERT CHARLES STEELE was just shy of his twenty-first birthday in June 1968 when he was killed by small arms fire on patrol in South Vietnam's Quang

Ngai Province. The year proved to be the costliest for US troops. Nearly 17,000 would lose their lives. In total more than 700 of Marine Corporal Steele's fellow Oregonians would fall in the conflict. Steele hailed from Sutherlin, a small town of 3,000 situated in the southwestern part of the state, about halfway between the population centers of Eugene and Medford—a decidedly rural, conservative, and white region.[5]

What did Bob Steele die for? The numerous answers to that question fractured American society in 1968. Surely many residents of Sutherlin, like those Americans still supporting the war, believed he died defending freedom. Without his sacrifice, South Vietnam would inevitably fall to communism. (It fell seven years after Bob's death.) For the antiwar protesters on college campuses and city streets, Steele died defending, even if unwittingly, any number of unjust systems, from empire to militarism to white supremacy. For many young people, he died for nothing.

For his fellow members of the Association to Preserve Our Right to Keep and Bear Arms (AKBA),[6] a grassroots pro-gun group in southern Oregon, Steele died defending Americans' Second Amendment right to own firearms to protect their families, their communities, and their country. He even gave his life to defend the rights of those politicians and liberals eager to take his guns, "steadily and quietly doing his job to protect those who refuse to protect themselves," in the words of AKBA president S. J. "Bud" Schoon. Reporting on Steele's death to fellow Association members, Schoon saw it as a literal call to arms. "His experience as a soldier taught him the necessity of a firearm to preserve his and his country's Freedom's [sic]," wrote Schoon, connecting the US overseas fight against communism to the domestic political fight for gun rights. "His country is our country, his freedoms, our freedoms, his fight our fight. As he died to protect his right, so must we prepare to fight."[7]

Just days before Steele's death, Congress had passed the first bill that would become the Gun Control Act, drawing outrage from conservative pro-gun Americans who had foretold of such a day for years. To gun rights activists like Schoon, it was the beginning of a slippery slope. Now the Johnson administration was pushing for a bill to license gun owners and register their firearms. "History tells us that no country has remained free for long once registration of firearms has been completed," Schoon warned. The Republic of Vietnam required gun registration, an AKBA member with a son serving in Vietnam observed, and that meant Vietnamese were denied the right to defend their own country. "I can see helping a country that needs help," he wrote, "but I cannot see going in and doing the job for people who cannot even help themselves."[8]

Armed Citizen News

Official Publication of   NATIONAL ASSOCIATION TO KEEP AND BEAR ARMS
Box 1189   Medford, Oregon 97501

Article II. A well-regulated militia, being necessary to the security of a free state, the right of the people to keep and bear arms, shall not be infringed.

No. 36   NATIONAL HEADQUARTERS – MEDFORD, OREGON   Nov. - Dec. 1970

Nameplate of *Armed Citizen News*, formerly *The Armed Eagle*, newsletter of the National Association to Keep and Bear Arms, 1970. Note the prominence of the Second Amendment, here labeled "Article II." (Hall-Hoag Collection of Dissenting and Extremist Printed Propaganda, Brown University Library)

Such rhetoric—linking the advance and retreat of freedom overseas to its domestic counterpart, connecting gun control at home to the global march of tyranny and US commitments to contain it—was characteristic of the ideology of groups like AKBA, one of a handful of grassroots pro-gun organizations, mostly unknown or forgotten today, that emerged in the late 1960s in response to various federal gun control initiatives. They were founded and flourished in the decade before the Cincinnati coup. Their history is the prehistory of that moment in 1977, their cause the one Carter and the rebels would advance. Their context—the Second World War, the Cold War, Vietnam, the war on the streets in the 1960s, and the seemingly limitless bounty of gun consumerism—radicalized them, and they in turn radicalized gun culture. Their ideas about guns in American society, and specifically about the Second Amendment, would be mainstreamed in the decades to come.

Anticommunism supercharged popular understandings of the Second Amendment; the Cold War radicalized them. Early gun rights activists, alongside their compatriots in right-wing groups in the 1950s and 1960s like the John Birch Society, saw communism and freedom as antithetical. Communism denied freedom; resistance to communism was a struggle to preserve and advance freedom, which included the sacred duty of defense of self and community. "Firearms and Freedom: These terms are synonymous," proclaimed AKBA, "for citizens who lose one, will surely lose the other."[9] Such ideas transferred the Cold War logic of containment, in which the United States pledged to halt the spread of global communism anywhere it appeared, to the realm of domestic politics and society.[10] Bob Steele's war in Vietnam was AKBA's war on liberal gun grabbers. For right-wing gun groups, freedom—an inevitably contentious, amorphous term—was anchored by the logic of anti-communism. In contrast to liberal anticommunism, their anticommunism was aggressively nationalist, anti-internationalist in its hostility to the United Nations and other international organizations, xenophobic, and suffused with notions of American exceptionalism. From this cauldron of ideas emerged the postwar logic of the Second Amendment as an unrestricted individual right to own firearms for "security," of both the individual (i.e., self-defense) and community ("the security of a free state"). None of these ideas was particularly new to the postwar United States, but Cold War anticommunism magnified them.

By the late twentieth century, the "individual rights theory" of the Second Amendment would be the centerpiece of the NRA worldview—the idea that this constitutional provision, for so long obscured in American life, granted the individual an inalienable right to own firearms independent of military or militia service. Beginning in the 1970s, a wave of legal scholarship, some of it NRA-funded, would push this "Standard Model" from the margins to the mainstream of legal interpretation.[11] Most Americans neglected the Second Amendment until the 1970s. Courts understood it as a limited statement, one that merely prohibited the federal government from disarming state militias, until the landmark Supreme Court decision in *District of Columbia v. Heller* (2008), which affirmed the individual rights theory.[12] Because these changes can be traced in law school journals, we can explain the shift in legal interpretation over time. But we know less about intellectual change at the popular level, where pro-gun conservatives in the 1960s and 1970s were not reading esoteric legal scholarship.

It was not a coincidence that the individual rights theory of the Second Amendment gained traction when it did. This expansive, absolutist articulation of an unrestricted right to own guns offered an ideological refuge rooted in imagined traditions just as the Cold War state's promises of security appeared to fracture overseas and at home, for Bob Steele, for his friends back in Oregon, and for millions of Americans. Black uprisings across the country in the second half of the 1960s served as evidence that the global communist threat had achieved new breakthroughs. The grassroots Second Amendment—the Cold War's Second Amendment—borrowed a Manichaean, black-and-white worldview of enemies everywhere and security only in endless vigilance. Decades after the Cold War's end, that understanding of the Second Amendment persists in American gun culture.

THOUGH THE CONTEMPORARY gun rights movement portrays itself as the inheritor of a sacred civic tradition dating to the Minutemen of the revolutionary era, it is in fact a very new political entity, born during the Cold War and armed with tactics and rhetoric borrowed from the social movements of the 1960s. Further, the postwar gun rights movement was a creation of the gun *control* movement. After feasting on the postwar bounty of the gun market through the 1960s, it was only the stirring of efforts to limit that bounty at the state and federal level that finally inspired gun rights activists to organize and radicalize.

Right-wing gun rights groups found their sense of purpose by vigilantly policing everything the gun control politicians and organizations did and using it all as fuel for organizing and fundraising. "Can These Public Officials Be Trusted with Your Guns Rights?" asked the Tennessee-based American Pistol & Rifle Association in the mid-1970s. APRA, another grassroots pro-gun group dating to the late 1960s, listed position statements supporting handgun control from a dozen civic organizations like the US Conference of Mayors, the League of Cities, and the National District Attorney's Association.[13] Gun rights groups often took their cues from their political opponents while imagining they took them from the founders and the Second Amendment. As Second Amendment historian Saul Cornell puts it, "One of the many embarrassing truths about the debate over the right to bear arms is that neither side wishes to admit that gun rights ideology is the illegitimate and spurned child of gun control."[14]

What inspired gun rights activists to action in the 1960s and 1970s was their belief the NRA was not taking the threat of the gun control movement seriously. Gun rights advocates worried the NRA had done too little to stave off the Gun Control Act and continued to hide its head in the sand in the face of a growing, popular movement for gun regulations in the early 1970s. It was first in smaller grassroots groups like AKBA and APRA that gun rights activists became radicalized and found like-minded citizens; later, professional organizers would harness their energy in well-funded national groups further to the right of the NRA, like Gun Owners of America, the Second Amendment Foundation, and the Citizens' Committee for the Right to Keep and Bear Arms.

A constellation of pro-gun groups saw the NRA as too weak or compromising to hold the line; their mission was to be radical when the NRA couldn't. The handgun issue especially radicalized these groups, because they came out in defense not of hunting and sportsmanship but their inherent right to defend themselves, with whatever weapons they saw fit, from a government that would try to take that right away from them. "The real issue is not recreation," wrote APRA's John L. Grady, "it is freedom and survival!"[15] It was the emergence of a grassroots gun control movement, which coordinated with liberal NGOs to promote gun control focused specifically on handguns, that really brought these groups out of the woodworks. "No Compromise" was a message to both the "gun grabbers" and the leadership of the NRA.

Compromise, retreat, appeasement, slippery slope—these words and concepts peppered the rhetoric of gun rights activists. Many were too young to have witnessed the gun control debates of the 1930s, which had led to the first federal laws regulating firearms. But they had internalized the "Munich analogy"—don't give an inch to authoritarians or they will take a mile, as Hitler had done when he met with his European counterparts in September 1938. As young men, many had fought overseas in the Second World War and in Korea. They returned to a country of seemingly limitless possibilities, especially for white men. They indulged in the bountiful and largely unrestricted gun market of the first two postwar decades, a golden age for not just collectors, hobbyists, and hunters but also extremists of all types. Liberals started debating restrictions on that bounty, portending an end to the golden age. With the assassinations of 1968, those liberals "no longer need[ed] to keep their true aims under cover," as the *Armed Eagle* put it.[16] Pro-gun minds latched on to convenient analogies for repression from their own lifetimes. The GCA was only the beginning, they believed. They could no longer retreat, appease, compromise, risk a slippery slope. In the words of an *Armed Eagle* headline in June 1968, "Registration—Taxation—Confiscation—Hitler?"[17]

Registration especially was on the minds of many gun rights advocates by the late 1960s. After the passage of the GCA in the summer of 1968, the Johnson administration, led by Attorney General Ramsey Clark, tried to push through a bill for the licensing of gun owners and registration of their firearms. Tom Dodd supported it publicly but behind closed doors had reservations. He wondered about the logistics—Treasury officials spoke of enormous computers costing tens of millions of dollars to track just as many guns and gun owners— but, more important, he worried such a bill was an example of the perfect being the enemy of the good.[18] Maryland senator Joseph Tydings instead led the effort in Congress. And while it wouldn't pass—by the fall the administration had run out of gas and Johnson out of political capital—various registration proposals would be revived in the 1970s by senators like Ted Kennedy and Birch Bayh and representatives like Chicago's Abner Mikva and Detroit's John Conyers. Having seen defeat in the GCA's provisions, registration became to gun rights advocates the line from which they could not retreat.

ONE OF THE LOUDEST VOICES AGAINST compromise was Harlon Carter's. Only a month after the GCA went into effect, Carter started railing against

Cartoon from *The Armed Eagle*, 1969. Early gun rights groups like AKBA scorned federal gun control agencies and efforts years before the NRA's 1977 hardline turn. (Hall-Hoag Collection of Dissenting and Extremist Printed Propaganda, Brown University Library)

the new gun law and, attuned to the grassroots outrage, encouraged right-wing gun activists to organize against it. In January 1969, he addressed the Arizona Wildlife Federation, an organization with a seemingly apolitical name but whose leadership had waded into gun politics years earlier. Carter knew his audience would be predisposed to suspicion of the federal government and even the mildest regulations on gun ownership. These were westerners, after all, hunters and sport shooters from a state with a mythology of individual self-sufficiency and a legacy of white settler frontier violence. Carter's address was notable for its prescience: its uncompromising attitude, encouragement of grassroots organizing outside the purview of the NRA, and rhetoric framing the movement's "enemies" as dangerous zealots portended changes years and even decades in the future. The hardline NRA was already lurking on the margins in 1969—it just wasn't on the national leadership's agenda yet; instead it was diffused among the membership building their own parallel grassroots movement.

As Carter told the story, he had tried to compromise. During his tenure at the NRA, the organization worked with Senator Tom Dodd and his Juvenile Delinquency Subcommittee to craft legislation that would be acceptable to "law-abiding gun owners." "I once belonged to the majority of Good Americans," Carter told the crowd. "I was a nice guy." He believed in finding common ground among people with divergent views. "I once thought honest and sincere compromise was the essence of good American law making," he explained. "I once thought that sportsmen could support reasonable gun legislation and that our opponents would leave us alone. Nonsense!" He learned the hard way that "compromise is not available to us in this controversy with unreasonable zealots."[19]

Carter's rhetoric grew increasingly confrontational as he spoke, narrating his own radical turn. He presented America's gun owners as reasonable people willing to negotiate on the details so long as constitutional rights remained secured. "Our opponents have deprived us of any prospects of compromise," however, "because they seek the elimination of the private ownership of firearms." (Not one pro-control politician or group professed this goal in 1969.) Gun owners' fears were justified: "We are being led down a one-way street to the confiscation of our guns" by those politicians Carter described as "our enemies in high places." In an era before NRA leaders were prone to such hyperbolic declarations, this claim surely caught the attention of the gathered activists. "Now the question is before us—what are we going to do about it?" In short, fight back. "We must fight our enemies unwaveringly," he implored. "If we must lose, let's force them to beat us the hard way." Carter had some suggestions for how to do as much, ideas that would transform the gun rights movement over the next two decades:

> The solution is in grass roots [sic] politics by ordinary good citizens like us—the kind who never yield. We must organize and work especially hard in election years. The NRA cannot do this indispensable job. . . . You can, however, and your vote. You count the most. . . .

The initiative is ours. We do not have to lose. The elections in
America normally are won by very small numbers. Only 500,000
people decided recently who was going to be President of the United
States, and we are millions—literally and correctly. Yes, indeed, we
already have the strength, we already have the numbers assembled, the
numbers which are enough for us to win.

It was a theme Carter would again articulate when he seized the position of
NRA executive vice-president in 1977. He accused the old leadership of being
too concerned with public relations, imaging, and accommodation in an effort
to attract "liberal money." The new combative NRA would not compromise.
"To survive in the modern political world," Carter repeated, "we have to be
fighters."[20]

The pro-gun grassroots organizations were listening: AKBA's *Armed Eagle*
published excerpts from the speech, with passages the editors found most
resonant running in all caps. The group read it as a both an affirmation of
their work and a rallying cry. More broadly, Carter's ideas were of a kind with
those that would catapult "movement conservatism" into the mainstream by
the 1980s: organized at the grassroots around issues like abortion, education,
sexuality, and, of course, guns, and institutionalized in the 1970s by groups
like Phyllis Schlafly's Eagle Forum and Jerry Falwell's Moral Majority; for gun
rights, it was not just the NRA but aggressive lobbying groups like Gun Owners of America and the Citizens Committee for the Right to Keep and Bear
Arms.[21] The professionalization of gun radicalism in the late 1970s by such
groups, and eventually the NRA, drew energy from a hardcore grassroots
movement that arose to oppose the GCA.

JACK MARLOW MOVED to rural Josephine County, Oregon, from the Los
Angeles area in the early 1960s to "get away from the glut," as he told it. In 1971
he was a sixty-year-old maintenance worker at the county fairgrounds and
chairman of AKBA's Josephine County "arm"—the word the organization used
for its chapters. Marlow oversaw the arm's 450 members, a significant number
in a county with just 35,000 people. There were likely several thousand AKBA
members in southern Oregon alone by 1971. Add to that dozens of "arms" in
states throughout the union and it's fair to say that membership reached the
low five figures, with literature like the *Armed Eagle* (which became *Armed
Citizen News* in 1971) reaching even more.[22]

Marlow told a local reporter that AKBA was a "rightwing group," "founded
primarily to uphold the Second Amendment. . . . We believe in Constitutional

law and order and we stand for God and country." "We are trying to keep the country armed," he continued, "because we think it should be armed." He explained that groups like AKBA encouraged an armed population because of the ever-present threat of "subversive groups" eager to see American citizens disarmed while stockpiling their own caches of weapons. The upheavals of the 1960s radicalized Marlow and others like him. The only way to maintain freedom from communism, they concluded, was to arm patriotic Americans. Indeed, the right to own a firearm was synonymous with freedom: "We believe that freedom will be lost when the citizen's power to defend it is lost. The citizen's power is the guaranteed right to keep and bear arms."[23]

Radical pro-gun groups like AKBA and APRA articulated a defense of individual and collective liberties distinct from the democratic liberalism of the nineteenth century. They located freedom not in the will of a democratic populace but in the vigilance of an armed citizenry. "We must stand ready and able, as did the men of Lexington and Concord, to defend our Freedom if the need arises," said an AKBA pamphlet.[24] Firearms protected freedom, and freedom required firearms. Indeed, the fact that the United States had "the largest armed civilian population the world has ever known" made the country the "strongest remaining repository of relative freedom in the world"—a reality of which gun rights proponents boasted while it kept gun control advocates awake at night. "The bullet should never be used in place of the ballot," the *Armed Eagle* said, hedging on advocating revolutionary violence. "But history has proven the bullet, used in defense of Liberty, must be used to gain and preserve the right to use the ballot."[25]

At a time when conservative white Americans felt traditional values to be under assault as never before—a perpetual state of social and political crisis they would maintain into the twenty-first century—AKBA's uncompromising attitude distinguished it from the NRA and other organizations too concerned with side issues like hunting and sporting rights and appealing to a wide mainstream constituency. Marlow believed the moment called for radicalism in light of what the 1960s showed was possible: "Everybody says 'No, this won't happen' and 'It can't happen here' and all of this, but the fact remains that there is a lot of things happening here that I wouldn't have believed even five years ago."[26] He didn't say what "this" or "it" was, but it didn't take much reading between the lines of right-wing gun literature to understand that he saw the upheavals of the 1960s—the Black freedom movement, the antiwar protests—as communist-inspired and existential threats to a free America.

Unlike the elite political operators who ran the NRA or who would create thriving and well-funded organizations like the Second Amendment

Foundation and Gun Owners of America, the grassroots warriors for gun rights were everyday men with working- or middle-class jobs. Today they don't have Wikipedia pages. They didn't leave their personal papers to university archives. Only traces of the lives they lived can be found in local newspaper obituaries or on genealogy websites. Many of them were war veterans, who were, as a whole, more likely to own firearms than nonveterans.[27] Arthur J. Hollowell, one of the founders and an early president of AKBA, served in the Korean War, attended the University of Montana, and worked as a forester in Medford, Oregon, where he then started a business "selling precious metals and health foods supplements." His successor, S. J. "Bud" Schoon of Sutherlin, served in the Marines in the Second World War, attended South Dakota State College, established a flooring business in Oregon "selling and installing Torginol seamless floor systems," and later ran unsuccessfully for county commissioner under the slogan "Vote for a Straight Shooter." Richard Lee Worley was a 1950 graduate of West Point, a decorated infantry officer who saw combat in Korea, and a civil engineer in North Carolina, where "he devote[d] much of his spare time to studying the Communist Conspiracy and attempting to alert his fellow Americans."[28] A few minutes of searching for the names that appear in this early literature turns up similar stories. These were ordinary men with extraordinary ideas about guns, ideas that would increasingly become mainstream within the gun rights movement by the end of the century.

These were also ordinary men who believed in their manly duties to safeguard freedom with firearms. Their families and communities depended on them to be the last bulwark of a free society. They were early manifestations of what sociologist Jennifer Carlson calls "citizen-protectors," men who decide to arm themselves to protect their communities from what they perceive as broad patterns of social collapse and government failure.[29] To acquiesce to the mildest gun control regulations was the beginning of an Orwellian slippery slope that ended when "the calked heel of Godless Communist tyranny comes smashing down."[30] "What Do You Tell Your Children?" the *Armed Eagle* wanted to know, as the Johnson administration's registration proposal sat before Congress in the fall of 1968:

> How do you tell them you stood complacently by while your government registered, taxed and then confiscated firearms? . . . How do you tell them that the policeman on the corner is no longer a friend—he has been replaced by a tyrant from the steppes of Asia or from the jungles of Africa? How will you tell them that the America your fathers gave to you has been lost? . . .

What will you say when your little son . . . asks you why don't you take a gun and go out to set things straight? What will you say when your teenager asks you what you have done to prevent this takeover? Will you tell him you played golf, or went fishing, or learned to water-ski, or worked in the garden, or learned to make ceramics, or hiked in the hills, or a million other things, while our nation went down the drain?? . . .

What will you say if they ask you if they should continue to adore God, despite the ultimatum of the New Order? . . .

Will you admit that you dismissed all efforts to halt the loss of freedoms and the drift toward socialism and communism as Right-Wing extremism and that you helped smear everyone who tried to point out the danger?[31]

Coded language about race, gender, and class pervaded the increasingly panicked discourse of gun rights groups. Warnings of a "tyrant from the steppes of Asia or from the jungles of Africa" revealed that anxieties about the instability of white supremacy encompassed both the US urban uprisings of the 1960s and global decolonization. Men who "worked in the garden, or learned to make ceramics," caved to contemporary challenges to traditional masculinity, and the golfers or water-skiers among them had chosen bourgeois comforts over vigilance.

Grassroots gun rights organizations also saw their activities as supporting the self-defense rights of women, who were increasingly in danger in a world full of not just communists but also criminals eager to take advantage of liberal gullibility. Talk of restrictions or bans on Saturday Night Specials in the early 1970s provoked them to action. Calling these small and cheap handguns "a girl's best friend," AKBA warned that any legislation targeting them would "either **DISARM** or make **OUTLAWS** of millions of good women." The men of AKBA had to act to protect "our mothers, wives, and sisters." The group published a couple dozen brief news clippings of incidents in which women armed with handguns protected themselves from criminals. Every story began with a woman confronted, either in a home or a business, with an assailant, none of whom is described as armed. The woman pulls a pistol or revolver, fires a warning shot or shoots the would-be criminal, and all of the "thugs" either flee or are wounded or killed. The one exception was a woman in Key Largo, Florida, who awakened from a nap to find a "young intruder" forcing his way through a window into her kitchen; she called the police and held him at gunpoint with her .32 pistol. When he indicated he was hungry, she made him a peanut butter sandwich.[32]

THE *ARMED EAGLE* defined compromise as "surrender on the installment plan"—every time gun right supporters accepted even a moderate limitation on their right to keep and bear arms, they put a down payment on an ultimate surrender of their freedom.[33] To the gun absolutists of the late 1960s, NRA president Franklin Orth, a member of the organization's old guard, committed to hunting, sports shooting, and marksmanship training, sold out their movement with his support for the GCA. As various federal proposals made their way through Congress, Orth affirmed the NRA's commitment to a "positive, specific and practical program for reasonable and proper firearms controls"— something AKBA members didn't believe existed—and argued that the NRA could not maintain an "'ostrich' attitude toward firearms legislation," acknowledging that the "dynamism and complexities of modern society [have] create[d] new problems which demand new solutions."[34] It was the very language the "gun grabbers" in the Johnson administration had used to push the GCA through.

In the decades since, uncompromising utterances have become iconic, or infamous, depending on one's perspective, and the NRA has embraced them unreservedly. NRA president Charlton Heston in 2000 holding aloft a rifle and challenging liberal politicians to take it "from my cold dead hands"; longtime executive vice president Wayne LaPierre in 2012 doubling down in the aftermath of the slaughter of twenty children and six teachers at Sandy Hook Elementary in Newtown, Connecticut, claiming, "The only thing that stops a bad guy with a gun is a good guy with a gun." This uncompromising NRA emerged after the 1977 Cincinnati coup. Previously, the organization's old guard leadership consisted of figures like Orth and Maxwell Rich, a retired US Army major general who was ousted from power by Harlon Carter and the hardliners. Dating back to the first federal gun control legislation of the 1930s, the old guard attempted to rein in aggressive legislative efforts but also met with congressional committee staff and offered suggestions for moderate bills that NRA leaders believed would not violate the rights of "law-abiding citizens." All the way back to the passage of the National Firearms Act in 1934, the NRA had accepted limitations on certain firearms in exchange for the exclusion of others from regulation.[35] In other words, it compromised.

That said, groups like AKBA typically avoided calling out the NRA's compromises by name. To group members after 1968, they didn't have to—the meaning of "no compromise" was clear enough to anyone who followed gun politics. But such groups also recognized that the NRA had a role to play, that hewing to the center allowed the organization to appeal to a wider mass of moderate Americans, keeping distance from and yet opening up space on the right for more radical approaches while building a mass membership base with real power in Washington.

Even after 1977, smaller grassroots groups to the right of the NRA continued to push the big national organization to adopt an uncompromising approach. Reginald Shinn, a retired Air Force officer and IRS attorney, was a life member of the NRA, Gun Owners of America, and the American Pistol & Rifle Association, serving as California chairman of APRA, the most radical and least compromising of the three groups.[36] (In the 1990s APRA would be among a handful of groups investigated by the FBI as white supremacist domestic terror organizations.)[37] Shinn attended the 1979 NRA annual convention in San Antonio and left unimpressed with the national organization's commitment to right-wing causes, even in the wake of what he called, with a hint of snark, "the Great NRA Revolution of 1977 in Cincinnati." The convention failed to consider a single resolution on the agenda at the meeting. Shinn and APRA members especially favored a resolution condemning the development of a "federal police force" through the Law Enforcement Assistance Administration, a federal agency created by the 1968 Safe Streets Act that funneled resources to local and state police agencies.[38] Shinn and APRA wanted a more confrontational NRA. He concluded that APRA was "the only effective organization in the nation today that is hitting at the heart of the gun control movement." "No compromise where our rights are in question"— APRA's own motto—"becomes more important and apparent every day."[39] What distinguished APRA, AKBA, and others from the NRA was not just their uncompromising attitude toward gun rights but also antigovernment subtexts lurking beneath the surface. That subtext evolved into text in the years to come, channeled through the militia movement of the 1990s, and eventually that text would bleed into the NRA's own script.

Groups like AKBA and APRA recognized the NRA's need to appeal not just to a broad spectrum of possible members—including those hunters and sport shooters generally uninterested in political activism whose money supported the organization—but also to legislators on Capitol Hill. The grassroots groups could tolerate NRA moderation knowing that they filled the vacuum of radicalism, even of the antigovernment variety. These kinds of relationships between the NRA and the smaller, more aggressive gun rights groups would become institutionalized in the coming years with the founding and growth of organizations like the Second Amendment Foundation and Gun Owners of America, which were much savvier when it came to fundraising and lobbying. Not only would such groups take public antigovernment positions that might alienate political moderates who continued to see the NRA as serving a civic function, but they would also function as a buffer for radicals who might otherwise taint the NRA with unsavory connections. Larry Pratt, for example, longtime head of Gun Owners of America and one of the country's most prominent Second Amendment absolutists, has been credited as a founder of the militia movement of the 1990s and infamously ran in circles with white supremacist and neo-Nazi groups.[40] While publicly professing different views, Pratt's GOA and the NRA worked symbiotically in a greater gun rights ecosystem.

THE GRASSROOTS GUN RIGHTS GROUPS' conception of the Second Amendment differed from how pro-gun organizations like the NRA perceive it today. AKBA did not hide from the "militia" clause, as the NRA did when it carved only the amendment's final words (" . . . the right of the people to keep and bear arms, shall not be infringed") into the wall in the lobby of its national headquarters.[41] For AKBA and many other early postwar grassroots gun rights advocates, the Second Amendment articulated both a right and a duty. Gun owners had not only a "right to keep and bear arms" but also a duty to use those arms to protect the nation from enemies within and without. The duty of armed citizenship came into particularly sharp relief during the Cold War, when right-wing conservatives believed that the United States faced an unprecedented existential threat from the Soviet Union abroad and its communist sympathizers at home.

In that sense, this earliest gun rights organization, unlike many of its counterparts today, adhered to a traditional understanding of the Second Amendment, one dating to the era of the founding. As historian Saul Cornell has written, our contemporary debates about the amendment conferring either an individual right to own a gun independent of service in a militia or a collective right of the people to organize a "well-regulated militia" for collective defense miss the more authentic, hybrid understanding of the right from the late eighteenth century: it was a civic duty in the sense that citizens had the right to keep and bear arms in order to meet their obligations to participate in a well-regulated militia. As Cornell puts it, it was "less individualistic than most gun rights people assume, and far more martial in spirit than most gun control advocates realize."[42] Even within that framework, however, the founders could disagree on who benefited from the meeting of rights and obligations. Was the militia, as the Federalists understood it, a tool of the new federal government, to be used to secure the young republic against external and internal threats? Was it, as the Antifederalists held it, the ultimate guarantee of individual state sovereignty against the federal government? Or was it, as the insurrectionists associated with antigovernment uprisings like Shay's Rebellion and the Whiskey Rebellion believed, a popular right to organize against and resist a tyrannical government, either at the state or federal level? Cornell says the founding generation tolerated a "pluralist model" for understanding the Second Amendment. Groups like AKBA took the third interpretation—the Second Amendment as a popular right and a duty to be armed in order to resistant tyranny and oppression—as a kind of gospel (indeed, frequently blending in Christian imagery), inspired by the anticommunism of the twentieth century.

That gospel contained a mix of common ideological commitments among right-wing groups in the 1950s and 1960s that framed the early gun rights groups within a larger political galaxy. The masthead for *American Challenge*, a typical right-wing newsletter produced in Birmingham, Alabama, put it succinctly: "Constitutional Government / Rights of the States / Free Enterprise / Gospel Christianity."[43] Left-wing politics motivated the most infamous and commemorated gun rights demonstration of the 1960s—the Black Panthers' march into the California State Capitol in May 1967—but the more substantive popular armed organizing was taking place in right-wing circles, among groups like AKBA and APRA. Such groups could tap into more than a decade of right-wing activities in the white suburbs and exurbs of America, where groups like the John Birch Society thrived. As Donald Lobsinger's Breakthrough group in Detroit showed, such activists could draw on white resentment and anxiety in the late 1960s to organize quickly.

What groups like AKBA also learned from the John Birch Society was grassroots organizing, a central facet of their approach to gun politics that distinguished them from the national, elite-led NRA. Among AKBA's most important activities was the creation and organization of new "arms." As early as 1968 the *Armed Eagle* contained an explanation of "How to Organize a Local Arm" that advised finding a dozen or so people "whom you know and can depend [on]" to form a steering committee, which would meet with an AKBA regional director, elect officers, organize committees, raise funds, and conduct meetings in the appropriate fashion (including an opening prayer and the Pledge of Allegiance). Each arm should aspire to create a Public Meetings Committee, Membership Committee, Political Committee, and Educational Committee.[44] Newsletters emphasized the importance of organizing at the grassroots level, an effort that accelerated through 1968, as the passage of gun legislation in Congress appeared imminent. AKBA collected signatures on petitions and mailed newsletters to everyone who signed—at least 20,000 by May 1968, a considerable monthly expense. "You are asked to carry and sell memberships to all your friends and acquaintances," the *Armed Eagle* urged as bills made their way through Congress. "This is a dire necessity! The battlelines have been drawn." What AKBA needed was not a passive membership waiting for a national organization to take the initiative but grassroots leaders: "We need *Oxen at the Yoke*, not *Asses in the Cart*."[45]

Absent organizational records, it's hard to determine just how many oxen and asses populated AKBA's membership rolls. The operation was small and local as of February 1968, with only forty dues-paying members in the greater Medford area, and prospective members could sign up at only a single location.[46] But a flurry of activity boosted the group's profile quickly. At the end of March, the group held a rally at the Josephine County Fairgrounds, where, according to a local news report, more than 800 people came to hear group president A. J. Hollowell of Medford give a speech titled "Americans Beware." He urged listeners to arm themselves and their families—he praised a recent program in Orlando that trained thousands of women in armed self-defense— for a coming social conflict.[47] A spring issue of the *Armed Eagle* advertised about fifty locations around southern Oregon where locals could now join an "arm." Interest in the organization grew rapidly in and after 1968, spurred by the GCA's passage. Each newsletter boasted of arms established in states across the country in every region, and by 1973 the group operated as far east as Massachusetts.[48] It had breadth to match the NRA, if not the depth. But its membership across the board was more steadfastly committed to an absolutist defense of gun rights.

THE GRASSROOTS GUN RIGHTS imagination did not stop at US borders. When activists looked out on the contemporary world they found plenty of evidence for why Americans could not surrender their gun rights. Surrender meant the end of freedom and the triumph of dictatorship and totalitarianism. For the grassroots pro-gun movement in the 1960s, the history of the twentieth-century world taught them that the existential threats of a Cold War world demanded an unbending approach to the defense of freedom. The right-wing worldview was hardly parochial but rather was rich with historical analogies and allegories, even if adherents played fast and loose with historical truth.

The movement's understanding of the world and its recent history fit neatly into a tradition of American exceptionalism. America's gun rights, as guarantors of individual liberty and national sovereignty, made it exceptional in the world. Activists mobilized evidence from every civil and international conflict of the previous half century to support their claims that guns protected freedom and authoritarians feared armed populations. And they let the would-be gun grabbers know it. "I've been called everything from Lenin to Hitler, which is quite a span you know," quipped Milton Eisenhower, reflecting on the many "abusive letters" he received as a consequence of his commission's conclusions about guns.[49] Activists interpreted every suggestion that the United States might benefit from adopting the gun regulations of other developed countries as a communist or totalitarian plot to undermine American constitutional government and disarm the civilian population. The McCarthyite fears of the "international communist conspiracy" were alive and well in the rhetoric of right-wing gun rights groups in the 1960s and 1970s.

The communist menace offered plenty of examples of the danger of disarmament. As far back as 1922, the NRA's monthly publication, then called *Arms and the Man*, connected New York's Sullivan Law, which imposed licensing requirements on handgun owners, to "Bolsheviki Russia" as a "disarmed people."[50] Popular in postwar right-wing circles was the "Rules for Revolution," a document purportedly dating from the Bolshevik takeover, which listed the ten rules by which communists could overthrow liberal democracies. It included "Corrupt the young," "Get control of all means of publicity," and "Divided the people into hostile groups." Most tantalizing for gun activists was rule 10: "Cause the registration of all firearms on some pretext, with a view to confiscating them and leaving the population helpless."[51] In 1970 the *New York Times* investigated the document and labeled it a "durable fraud," created sometime after 1945, but that didn't stop conspiracy theorists from sharing it or the occasional House member from publishing it into the *Congressional Record*.[52]

Events in Hungary in 1956, when the Red Army crushed a nascent democratic uprising, and Czechoslovakia in 1968, when Soviet leaders ordered a Warsaw Pact invasion of the country to halt the blossoming reform movement known as the "Prague Spring," loomed large in the right-wing imagination. If only the forefathers of the Czechoslovak state had provided for the right to keep and bear arms, mused Louisiana's John Rarick on the floor of the House in January 1969, they could have done more than cower in fear with "Russian tanks and soldiers squatting in their city parks." The *Armed Eagle* told of "some Americans who were there" and who had asked the people of Prague "if there wasn't something they could do." "We have no guns, there is nothing we can do," the trapped residents of the city were alleged to reply, as if off the pages of a Hollywood screenplay. Marion Kimmet of Roseburg, Oregon, published a poem in the *Armed Eagle*—AKBA had a surprising affinity for pro-gun poetry—that opened with the lines, "The Czechs registered their guns, /

Radical gun rights organizations drew analogies between gun control policies and the Nazi occupation of Europe. Here an image of a murdered anti-Nazi partisan is appropriated for a 1974 flyer with accompanying text that recycles gun rights slogans like "When guns are outlawed only outlaws will have guns" and "Register communists, not firearms." (American Opinion Bookstore via Special Collections & University Archives, University of Illinois Chicago Library)

So did the Hungarians and the Poles, / So let's not be taken in by gun controls." For twenty-five cents, AKBA sold a "The Czechs Registered Their Guns" bumper sticker, alongside perennial favorites "Guns Don't Kill People, People Kill People," "When Guns Are Outlawed Only Outlaws Will Have Guns," and the George Wallace–inspired "Register Communists, Not Firearms."[53] (In the aftermath of the Communist government's imposition of martial law in Poland in 1981, Gun Owners of America would offer members a "Poland Has Gun Control" bumper sticker.)[54]

APRA used the world's most prominent Soviet dissident, Nobel laureate Aleksandr Solzhenitsyn, as evidence for the righteousness of an armed populace. The group asked, "Should Americans Give Up Their Guns?" and quoted a passage from *The Gulag Archipelago* (1974) in which Solzhenitsyn speculated how Stalin's repression might have had a different outcome if the Soviet people had committed to violent resistance every time the secret police showed up at the door. Each officer may have rethought his commitment to the job if, whenever he went out for an arrest, he "had been uncertain whether he would return alive." "Had he been met with an ambush of half a dozen people with axes, hammers, pokers, or whatever else was at hand," then "the cursed machine would have ground to a halt." "Remember," said APRA in bold capital letters, "the man who wants to take your guns is your enemy."[55]

Cuba proved another instance, according to pro-gun thinking, in which gun control laws led to communist dictatorship and the loss of freedom. In this narrative, pro-American dictator Fulgencio Batista had implemented a restrictive firearms registration law years before 1959, when an insurgency led by Fidel Castro overthrew his regime. As a result, "law-abiding" Cubans had registered their guns; Castro and his guerrilla army, being the rebels they were, did not register theirs. When Castro seized power, he and his comrades could simply comb through the rolls of registered guns and confiscate them to ensure no armed opposition could organize.[56] (No one seemed to notice the irony that Castro did precisely what groups like AKBA and APRA advocated— he refused to register his guns and took up arms against a corrupt, tyrannical government that had imposed gun control.)

Every international conflict appeared to be evidence of the disastrous consequences of an unarmed or disarmed population. The people of Northern Ireland were under siege because gun laws prevented them from defending themselves. The people of Bangladesh were subjected to the "butchery" of the Pakistani government because they were not allowed to own firearms.[57]

These instances of disarmament and oppression demonstrated the centrality of firearms and the threat of popular violence, rather than just democratic ideals, to ensuring freedom. "In all civilizations past or present," wrote

AKBA's Richard Lee Worley, "the denial of a citizen's right to arm himself has resulted in slavery for the unarmed citizen." "How much freer would the Chechs [sic], Poles, Hungarians, Cubans, etc. be if we sent each of them a hundred, a thousand, or even a million copies of our Constitution and the Bill of Rights[?]," asked AKBA vice president William Peters. "Maybe a little warmer as their leaders burnt them, but certainly no freer." What distinguished Americans in a world of free and unfree was not just "the desire to remain free" but also the material means to ensure that the Constitution's restrictions on the powers of the federal government "never be over-stepped and those God given rights re-asserted in the Bill of Rights never be infringed."[58] "As long as the people of America have guns in the home America will never fall as other countries have fallen in our own time when their weapons were taken from them," warned *The American Challenge.* "It can happen here, it has happened in other countries."[59] Other countries might have constitutions; only America had the Second Amendment.

SEVERAL NATIONAL GUN RIGHTS GROUPS emerged in the 1970s to harness the grassroots energy of organizations like AKBA and APRA, seeing in them a source of political power and fundraising. These grassroots groups proved that an uncompromising message could have a national reach. Organizations like the Second Amendment Foundation (SAF, along with its lobbying arm, the Citizens Committee for the Right to Keep and Bear Arms) and the Gun Owners of America (GOA) fundraised aggressively—not unlike their gun control counterparts—and built a roster of advisers and board members from among conservatives in Washington's ruling class, a group sweeping into the capital during the "Reagan Revolution" of the early 1980s. The gun groups' own revolution was a political movement built on a grassroots social one. Gun Owners of America, for instance, was founded in California in 1975 by H. L. "Bill" Richardson, a brash Republican state senator, NRA board member, one-time member of the John Birch Society, and former advertising executive who aimed to raise money for pro-gun candidates using the kind of aggressive rhetoric of groups like AKBA. "We're not defensive, we're attack oriented," he said in 1976, the year he created the "Target '76" fundraising campaign for the presidential election. "Our object is not to stop legislation; our object is to get new legislators."[60] Richardson, along with longtime GOA head Larry Pratt, applied polish to the rough edges.

Though groups like GOA and the SAF were often identified in the press as the radical alternatives to the NRA, it's important to note that they were in many ways as professional and bureaucratic as their much larger counterpart.

Ultimately they existed to raise money for lobbying efforts within a wider spectrum of right-wing groups using new mail-order techniques, like those pioneered by Richard Viguerie (who worked both with the NRA and smaller groups like GOA), to harness the grassroots energy of white backlash and emerging evangelical politics. They were wildly successful almost from the start. In the 1978 midterm elections, only three years into operations, the Gun Owners of America Campaign Committee spent more than a half million dollars on pro-gun candidates (something its gun control opponents could only dream of), while the NRA Political Victory Fund contributed just under $200,000, according to the gun control activists who tracked money spent on pro-gun lobbying.[61] The SAF and its tandem lobbying organization, Citizens for the Right to Keep and Bear Arms (CCRKBA), together raised roughly $5 million annually by the early 1980s.[62]

The SAF and the CCRKBA were both created in the mid-1970s in Bellevue, Washington, by Alan Gottlieb, a "buccaneering entrepreneur with a remarkable knack for cashing in big on right-wing causes," as a rare 1994 journalistic profile described him.[63] Gottlieb spent his youth in Los Angeles and Queens and headed to the University of Tennessee in 1966 to study nuclear engineering. There he clashed with student radicals as campus chair of the Young Americans for Freedom, at one point suing to keep the institution open when administrators considered closing it because of antiwar protests. He started a "Committee for Peace on Campus," which sounded innocuous enough but was in fact an effort to turn opinion against confrontational protest groups like the Students for a Democratic Society.[64] In doing so he caught the eye of conservative icon William F. Buckley, who helped create the YAF in 1960 to promote conservative values among students. Buckley met with and brought Gottlieb on to the YAF student board. When he graduated in 1971, Gottlieb struggled to find a job because, as he told it, the US government had decided to shift away from the development of nuclear power in the face of the growing environmental movement, even though nuclear was, according to Gottlieb, "the wave of the future to ensure an energy-free and independent America." Unsure of his own future, Gottlieb turned his work with the YAF into a full-time job, relocating to Seattle in 1972 to become a regional director for the organization.[65]

In addition to his duties as director for the Pacific Northwest, Gottlieb was appointed director of the YAF's small ad hoc group, Students for the Right to Keep and Bear Arms. The job was eye-opening. As he put it, "I saw there was a vacuum and a void, in the gun movement," a space for more aggressive direct pro-gun lobbying. There was the NRA, of course, but its public identity was still mostly that of a hunters' and sportsmen's civic organization, its leadership mostly uncomfortable with aggressive, confrontational politics before 1977. But he knew from his conservative contacts on college campuses around the country that there was grassroots energy to be harnessed into an organized, well-funded pro-gun movement. Gottlieb grew Students for the Right to Keep and Bear Arms from a fledgling branch of the YAF into an operation rivaling its parent group. In 1973, the YAF encouraged an amicable split between the two organizations, and in early 1974 Gottlieb incorporated the new Citizens Committee for the Right to Keep and Bear Arms to "operate exclusively for the purpose of defending the Second Amendment to the United States Constitution."[66] He claimed 60,000 members in early 1975, boasting of going through a "super-growth stage." "The NRA doesn't do anything but make a lot of noise," Gottlieb told the *Baltimore Sun*. Its energies were pulled in too many directions. But the CCRKBA was devoted exclusively to lobbying for an expansive interpretation of the Second Amendment: US citizens had the constitutional right to own a firearm, full stop.[67]

Gottlieb proved as shrewd as the NRA when it came to building institutions and raising money. The CCRKBA was a registered lobbying group and donations to it were not "charitable" and thus not tax-deductible. Professional fundraisers knew that this could limit a new group's income. Shortly after creating the CCRKBA, Gottlieb founded the Second Amendment Foundation, an organization with nearly identical aims as the CCRKBA but one that would engage in "educational" initiatives rather than political lobbying, thus allowing donors to write off gifts as charitable donations. Knowing that such groups relied on increasingly sophisticated direct-mail operations to solicit funds, Gottlieb created Merril Associates (using his middle name), a for-profit company that would handle all of the CCRKBA's and SAF's mailing campaigns. Eventually Gottlieb would also purchase the property that housed the headquarters for the CCRKBA and SAF and rent the space out to the group at inflated rates. And while this arrangement proved wildly successful—the two gun groups were bringing in millions a year by the early 1980s, making Gottlieb rich and politically influential in the process—it didn't happen without drawing legal scrutiny: in 1984, Gottlieb was convicted of tax evasion and spent ten months in prison. (As a convicted felon he couldn't own a firearm until he successfully petitioned the BATF for restoration of his gun rights.)[68]

Even Gottlieb's enemies described him as a "direct-mail genius," and in that regard he matched up the new professional communications strategies of the 1970s with the visceral white conservative backlash against the upheavals of the 1960s. He especially mastered the "Dear Friend" fundraising letter.

The language was at once folksy, playing up traditional conservative values ("I'm a proud man and I'm not used to asking for financial support from others") while ratcheting up the potential threat over the course of many short, punchy paragraphs. As he explained in a 1993 book on organizing against the environmentalist movement—another cause close to his heart and bank account—direct-mail letters "must appeal to three base emotions: Fear, Hate and Revenge." They also "must present you with a crisis—a problem won't do, because only a crisis carries a *sense of urgency*. . . . That crisis must *frighten* you. . . . If you are not frightened, you won't send money."[69]

Early SAF letters played up that sense of crisis and urgency by targeting the nascent gun control movement, singling out groups like the National Council for the Control of Handguns and Chicago's Committee for Handgun Control and their legislative allies. A mailer from 1976 warned of "new and radical laws outlawing the use of guns" making their way through Congress and state legislatures that would "directly affect your right to a safe home." Gottlieb predicted that if "radical and outspoken pressure groups" got their way, "your safety and the safety of each and every person in your neighborhood will be in jeopardy." After warning of a threat to the home, then one to the local community, Gottlieb escalated the potential horrors to the national level: "I don't believe we can sit back and allow the 'Gun Confiscation' people in this country to pass laws that would set the stage for the *most terrifying crime wave ever to occur in modern history*."[70] Such hyperbole would define the SAF and similar gun rights fundraising groups for decades to come.

Gottlieb described his organization as the "gun lobby's lobby."[71] He stoked popular fears and anxieties to bolster support for the gun industry and the NRA in the kinds of direct appeals that would have soured mainstream voters and legislators who were willing to entertain the gun lobby as a good-faith negotiator in addressing gun violence. He harnessed the radical pro-gun, and often antigovernment, attitudes of the grassroots movement from the 1960s, steeped in the anticommunist and anti-internationalist paranoia of the John Birch Society and fixated on the Second Amendment as an all-encompassing safeguard against tyranny. Disarmingly diminutive, smiling, sporting a neat mustache, glasses, and a suit and tie (later he would favor bowties), Gottlieb professionalized Second Amendment radicalism in ways that a forester or a maintenance worker couldn't have done without significant time and money.

The SAF's annual report for 1979 conveyed the extent to which Gottlieb had professionalized gun radicalism in just a few short years. The group had launched the "first weekly, pro-gun radio program," *On Target*, which was broadcast on 130 radio stations. Among its "educational" activities, the SAF published the "first comprehensive, fully documented study of the BATF's police-state tactics," a 117-page report, *The BATF's War on Civil Liberties: The Assault on Gun Owners*, that purported to document "entrapment, false arrest, illegal searches and seizure, and perjury, all directed against law-abiding gun owners." The report listed a variety of "legal aid" activities in support of firearms owners and businesses that had allegedly been abused by the BATF. Gottlieb claimed to have nearly won the American Civil Liberties Union over to the SAF's cause, convincing an ACLU committee to recommend dropping the group's gun control positions, but losing in a close board vote. The SAF hosted a lavish annual Committee of One Thousand Dinner, a celebration of those donors who had given at least $1,000 to the SAF. And in perhaps the ultimate marker of mainstream political success, the SAF boasted of expanding its Congressional Advisory Board from twenty-five to fifty members in 1979, including the addition of seven new US senators alongside notable freshmen congressmen Dick Cheney and Ron Paul.[72]

Such success made Gottlieb, in the words of two Seattle-area journalists who sat with him for a series of lengthy interviews in 1994, the "most successful" fundraiser for "conservative candidates and causes" beyond the Washington Beltway. Reflecting back on two decades of work, Gottlieb boasted that his efforts were responsible for the NRA's rightward shift since the 1970s. "I prod them a whole lot," he said. "What happens is that things get innovated here [at the SAF and CCRKBA] and the NRA is then forced to copy it." He had made the "gun movement more of a civil-rights type thing," he claimed, a claim that wasn't wholly untrue, but one that did obscure the grassroots energy already fermenting in the conservative white pro-gun backlash to the civil rights movement, the Great Society, the antiwar movement, and the Gun Control Act of 1968.

By the 1980s there was an established pro-gun movement independent of the NRA. Born out of the grassroots movement of the 1960s, firmly rooted in a Cold War understanding of the threats posed to American society and unequivocally committed to an interpretation of the Second Amendment shaped by it, the movement was then professionalized and institutionalized by political opportunists in the 1970s. Thus, when Yoshi Hattori knocked on Rodney Peairs's door in October 1992, the battle lines drawn two decades earlier had already calcified, limiting the possibilities for how Americans might respond to an international tragedy in Baton Rouge.

CHAPTER 9

AMERICA'S WORST DISEASE

ALAN GOTTLIEB, EXPERT fundraiser and provocateur, never missed an opportunity to capitalize on the conservative outrage du jour. In May 1993, he alerted the Second Amendment Foundation's sizable mailing list to the latest threat to America's guns and freedom: Japan. "YOU *must* ACT NOW," the letter's envelope warned. "JAPAN LAUNCHES 'SNEAK ATTACK' ON YOUR GUN RIGHTS." This Pearl Harbor redux came in the form of "750,000 petition signatures" presented to the US embassy in Tokyo "calling for a ban on guns in our country." Gottlieb unspooled a fantasy in which President Bill Clinton along with longtime gun control proponent Senator Ted Kennedy and Brady Bill sponsor Senator Howard Metzenbaum—a rogue's gallery of the Second Amendment's greatest enemies—had "allied with gun grabbers in Japan in an effort to destroy our gun rights."[1] Why were they so intent on banning guns? To remake the United States in the image of other nations and hasten the establishment of a "new world order," a phrase that had echoed in right-wing conspiracy thinking for decades.

Japan's waxing economic superpowerdom of the 1980s and early 1990s presented a new international challenge to the United States and an opportunity for fundraisers like Gottlieb to exploit racist fears and unearth the ghosts of a bloody past.[2] "We must put Japan on notice that they are not going to take away our firearms freedoms," he declared. "We didn't let them do it after they bombed Pearl Harbor and we're not going to let them do it now." He encouraged his audience of gun consumers to abstain from consuming Japanese products like the televisions and stereos that lined department store shelves. He reminded his readers of past sacrifices: "My father didn't risk his life in World

War II to have Japan or any other country dictate away our Bill of Rights." "When we make Japan back down," he concluded, "all Clinton, Kennedy and Metzenbaum will have left is 'sushi' on their face"—as punchlines go, this one fell flat, but it nevertheless punctuated a pugnacious provocation.

Despite the bluster, Gottlieb had observed a legitimately new phenomenon: a foreign country, or at least a significant number of its citizens, had entered the fray of US gun politics. It was certainly not the first time that Gottlieb's audience *believed* such a thing had happened—right-wing gun rights activists had been disseminating conspiracy theories about Soviet, Chinese, and UN plots to undermine US gun freedoms for decades. But this time, while there was no insidious plot, Japanese citizens really were trying to enact changes in US gun culture. By the end of 1993, nearly 2 million of them would sign a petition asking their government to urge the United States to do something, anything, about the 30,000 people killed annually with firearms.

When Japanese activists connected with their US counterparts to create a transnational movement, it provided right-wing provocateurs like Gottlieb with plenty of ammunition to stoke the rage of gun rights proponents who continued to pour millions of dollars each year into the "gun lobby." What Gottlieb and his audience got wrong, however, was that there was no grand international plot or conspiracy to undermine the US Constitution. There was, instead, only a dead sixteen-year-old Japanese boy in Louisiana and his heart-broken and determined family and friends who insisted his death not be in vain.

Yoshi Hattori was one of more than 30,000 people killed with guns in the United States annually by the early 1990s. His killing was ordinary in a nation too accustomed to it. And yet it also became extraordinary for its national and international ramifications. For Americans, as one writer put it, "Another culture held up a mirror to ours, and for a moment, we were shocked."[3] What was at first a local tragedy only became a national story after inspiring inter-national dismay at evidence of a rot within the American republic. Gun capitalism had flooded the country with firearms for decades; a population taught to see enemies everywhere found few restrictions to accessing guns and building arsenals for the imagined conflicts of the future. "The gun lobby says this is a matter of freedom, to have a gun," observed Tokyo Broadcasting System anchorman Tetsuya Chikushi. "This is America's worst disease, I think. Guns everywhere—it's like a cancer."[4]

YOSHIHIRO HATTORI GREW UP IN NAGOYA, Japan, an automaking city 225 miles southwest of Tokyo, but he loved America. It was the most exciting country in the world. He loved pizza, basketball, and dancing to American music. When he arrived in Baton Rouge, Louisiana, in the summer of 1992 as a sixteen-year-old exchange student, Yoshi charmed many of the Americans he met. He supplemented his developing English-language skills with a disarming playful physicality. "I will never forget how Yoshi moved through space," recalled Richard Haymaker, his host "father" in Baton Rouge. "He would walk so gracefully, almost dancing through the house."[5]

(Later, Rodney Peairs's defense attorney, Lewis Unglesby, would use Yoshi's physicality against the dead teenager in court, telling the jury that Yoshi had "an extremely unusual way of moving," which Unglesby described as "aggressive," "kinetic," "antsy," and "scary.")[6]

Yoshi loved America, and he somehow even managed to love the sights of Baton Rouge, a midsize city squeezed along the eastern bank of the wide and muddy Mississippi, where the most prominent landmarks as one headed east across the river were oil refineries and the thirty-four-story Depression-era State Capitol, a monument to the ambition and arrogance of Louisiana's most infamous politician, Huey Long. "Good! Wow!" Yoshi uttered repeatedly the first time he drove past these landmarks, trying to remember other superlatives he'd learned in English class.[7]

Yoshi was "completely infatuated with Americans," reported T. R. Reid—"right up to the moment one of them shot him to death."[8]

ONLY ONE PERSON LIVED to see Rodney Peairs emerge from his carport door on October 17, 1992. Webb Haymaker, Yoshi's "host brother," was only sixteen himself, a junior at McKinley High School in Baton Rouge, which sat just blocks from Louisiana State University, where his parents, Holley and Richard, worked as professors. Accompanying Yoshi on that fateful night, he saw Peairs's gun, recognized the danger, and shouted to Yoshi, but it was too late.

Eighteen months later Webb stood on the other side of the world, in Nagoya's Asahigaoka High School, Yoshi's school, recalling the trauma of that evening. Five other students and three teachers from McKinley traveled with him, touring the school and answering questions about the lives of teenagers in the United States. Inevitably the conversation turned to US gun violence and the stark contrasts between the United States and Japan, where gun regulations were so strict that few citizens owned them legally and annual gun death figures never reached three digits, let alone five. McKinley principal Clarence Jones thrilled the audience with sensational accounts of drug and gang violence in Louisiana's poverty-plagued capital, including stories of "eleven-year-olds selling drugs on the corner." "To the Japanese," wrote the *Washington Post*'s T. R. Reid, who had followed Yoshi's story since the shooting, "this description sounds like a different planet." One McKinley student tried to clarify that "very few Americans have actually seen a shooting," but it turned out that three of the six young Americans had. "What I've noticed is that in Japan if someone gets killed, that's really big," said McKinley senior Angela Chang. "But in America, it's common to hear of someone being murdered. And when you think about it that's really scary about our country."[9]

As if to serve as evidence for these Japanese teenagers' stereotypes of the United States, on the morning the McKinley students arrived at Asahigaoka High, news broke of the shooting deaths in Los Angeles of two young Japanese men, Takuma Ito and Go Matsuura. They had been studying filmmaking at Marymount College until they became victims of a carjacking gone wrong in a Ralphs supermarket parking lot in San Pedro. The killing of Japanese students in America once again made front-page news across the Pacific. The press reported that Ito's mother hadn't wanted her son to go to the United States because Yoshi's killing had terrified her. Observers again noted the possibility of cultural misunderstanding. "They went to the supermarket, as they would go to a convenience store at night in Japan," observed Kazuo Kubota of the Ikebukuro Institute of Multicultural Understanding. "I think no American would go out at night."[10]

The murders of Ito and Matsuura accompanied Yoshi on a growing list of high-profile shooting deaths of Japanese nationals in the United States, and given the negligible gun death rates in Japan, every such killing became high-profile. Iwao Matsuda, president of Nagoya's Chukyo University, had been shot to death in his Boston hotel room eight months before Yoshi. In February 1991, a woman shot and killed Chiharu Tango, a twenty-two-year-old Tokyo native and student at Oklahoma City University, after Tango had dinner with the woman's ex-boyfriend. Masakazu Kuriyama was a twenty-five-year-old exchange student who was shot and killed at a train station in Concord, California, in 1993. Kei Sunada was twenty-two years old when he was robbed and murdered in Queens, New York, in 1994. After Yoshi's death, the Japanese press seemed to report more frequently on foreign tourists, even non-Japanese, killed in the United States. In just the half decade before Yoshi's killing, the press observed, the number of Japanese tourists victimized by crime overseas doubled (though the number of overseas travelers almost doubled as well). Family members in Japan created an "Association of Survivors of Murder Victims in the U.S.A."[11] With good reason, images of American violence were never far from Japanese minds in the 1990s.

The students from McKinley High found themselves in the grim position of once again having to account for their country's violence, incomprehensible to much of the rest of the world. "Everywhere we've been in Japan, we've mainly had to answer questions about the Los Angeles murders," Webb Haymaker said. "All you can do is apologize." Americans living in Japan faced questions from Japanese friends and acquaintances who planned vacations or whose children hoped to study overseas: "Do you know a safe neighborhood in New York? How is Tacoma? Do you think my son will be all right in Minnesota?" President Clinton offered a rare formal apology for the deaths of Ito and Matsuura through Ambassador Walter Mondale in an effort, as the *Asahi Evening News* put it, "to counter Japan's growing certainty that the United States is a nation of gun-wielding maniacs, unfit for tourism or study." Mondale insisted that these kinds of killings "give an entirely distorted picture of life in the United States."[12]

The editors of the *New York Times* didn't think Yoshi's death distorted the reality of American life. Seven months after Yoshi's death, when a Baton Rouge jury found Rodney Peairs not guilty of manslaughter, they explained to Japanese readers trying to understand American gun culture: "Just think stupidity, intolerance, a warped interpretation of the 'right to bear arms,' and a refusal to learn anything from the deaths of several famous Americans, countless ordinary ones and, now, Yoshihiro Hattori."[13]

BY THE EARLY 1990S, Rodney Peairs's Smith & Wesson .44 Magnum revolver was just one of the country's estimated 200 million guns, a total more than double that of the stockpile of civilian-owned weapons that had so worried the Eisenhower Commission back in 1968. The growth of handguns, which the commission's Firearms Task Force identified as the most troubling of personal weapons, unsuitable for hunting, easily concealed for nefarious purposes, and responsible for three-quarters or more of gun deaths annually, had risen to roughly 80 million.

Throughout the 1970s and 1980s, the gun industry and its gun rights allies attempted—quite successfully—to naturalize the handgun as a standard firearm, alongside the rifle and the shotgun, in the red-blooded American man's arsenal. A robust consumer culture emerged around a gun once seen as contemptible. New publications like *American Handgunner*, first published in 1976, brought handguns middle-class respectability.

No gun represented this shift better than Peairs's Smith & Wesson .44 Magnum revolver, one of the most powerful handguns on earth. Designed earlier in the century to handle more powerful ammunition, Magnum models were shunned by law enforcement and the NRA in the 1930s as too unwieldy and dangerous for the average shooter.[14] But the romance with larger and more powerful handguns took off in the 1970s, inspired by, among other things, Hollywood's portrayal of vigilante white men, like Clint Eastwood's *Dirty Harry* (1971) and Charles Bronson's Paul Kersey (*Death Wish*, 1974), bucking a corrupt and complacent legal system to dispense real justice to heartless street criminals. The growing fetish for handguns included new combat pistol courses for men to develop their "tactical" ability to handle street crime that rarely affected people outside of certain zip codes and socioeconomic groups.[15] More commonly, though, people simply bought handguns and tucked them away in nightstands, dressers, glove boxes, and closets.

Although the Magnum was too large and cumbersome for most shooters, Rodney Peairs, at more than six feet tall and 180 pounds, likely handled its heft without much trouble. There was nothing unusual about guns in his lower-middle-class white neighborhood of Central, which sat at the northeastern edge of Baton Rouge, bleeding suburban tract homes, gated communities, and trailer parks into the more rural areas of southern Louisiana—the places that epitomized the state's motto, "Sportsman's Paradise," a slogan meant to draw hunters to the state's unique ecology. A rifle or a shotgun would have been a standard accessory for a white man, even a necessary one, in the centuries of settler colonialism, slavery, and white settlement in the area before the late twentieth century. But by the time Yoshi Hattori knocked on Peairs's front door at 10311 Brookside Drive (Yoshi and Webb were looking for 10131 Brookside, a few houses down), a quarter century of anxiety about crime rates and Black urban uprisings made a handgun in the bedroom a new essential element of the white logic of safety and security.

"He showed it to me once," Ford Bevens told a local reporter when asked about Rodney Peairs's .44 Magnum only a couple of days after the killing. "He said he had a beautiful gun to show me. It is a beautiful weapon." Bevens was Peairs's neighbor. His wife Sandra had mopped up the blood that had poured from Yoshi's chest and stained the Peairs's carport driveway.[16]

Peairs claimed to have bought the gun for deer hunting, and while many handguns would seem impractical for the purpose, and traditional hunters might have scoffed at the idea, a well-placed shot from such a powerful weapon could do the trick, aided by an aftermarket 4 × 8 mm mounted telescopic sight. This was no Saturday Night Special. Despite the magical aura *Dirty Harry* gave the .44 Magnum, the gun was unsuitable for a real-world combat situation, impossible to conceal, and its muzzle flash could blind you at night and leave your ears ringing for days.[17] The complete package of Peairs's

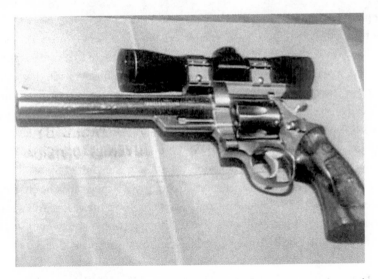

Rodney Peairs's .44 Magnum Smith & Wesson, 1994. (Christine Choy and Film News Now Foundation, *The Shot Heard 'Round the World*)

large shiny revolver and sophisticated scope gave his firearm a science-fiction silhouette that might not have signaled danger to Yoshi as effectively as the profile of a common handgun. The courtroom gasped when it was displayed. "When I looked at it," Richard Haymaker recalled, "it was a legitimate issue to even know what was being pointed at you. . . . It is just not that clear: Is this some kind of contraption?"[18]

It's hard to know how many of these handguns purchased for self-defense ever actually performed that function. The category of "defensive gun uses," instances in which a gun is brandished or fired or even just displayed in what a gun owner interprets as a successful act of self-defense, is inherently contentious, and annual estimates of incidents range from the high five figures to several million a year.[19] But what mattered was less the statistical reality of handgun self-defense and more the subjective feeling that a handgun was, for tens of millions of Americans, a necessary tool for daily survival in the United States. This phenomenon was new to the post-1960s United States, when handguns shifted from the weapon of choice of outlaws and gangsters in popular imagination and became the tools of personal and social violence at scale, abetted by a booming consumer market.

To the 120 million people of Japan who saw or read the news of Yoshi's killing in October 1992, however, it made no sense that a handgun would be a necessary tool, a consumer commodity no different from an automobile or a telephone or a television, for thriving in a modern society. "America seems to be trapped in a vicious cycle," the *Nikkei Weekly* observed after Peairs was indicted. "More crime involving guns causes more people to purchase guns to defend themselves against crime involving guns"—an observation that echoed gun control ads from a quarter century earlier. The Japanese newspaper urged Americans to not dismiss the case as one of "cultural difference" embodied in the word *freeze*, the warning Peairs shouted and Yoshi apparently misunderstood. In a globalizing world, cultural differences smashed into each other all the time, but among advanced economies, only in the United States did they result in shooting deaths with alarming regularity. "Americans should stop to think about how their gun-dominated society looks to the rest of the world."[20] It was a message adopted and preached by the gun control movement inspired by Yoshi's life and death: American gun exceptionalism was killing Americans.

DAYS AFTER YOSHI'S DEATH, his parents, Mieko and Masaichi Hattori, expressed frustration not with the individual actions of Peairs but with the society that allowed him to keep a deadly weapon at hand and to wield it on his doorstep—a society where, as defense attorney Unglesby explained it after his client's acquittal, "You have the absolute legal right . . . to answer your door with a gun."[21] The tragedy occurred "because in this country possession of guns is legal," Mieko told the Baton Rouge press. "Maybe this is something the society will now reconsider." She and Masaichi decided on their flight back to Japan, with Yoshi's body in the hold of the plane, that they would take action and start a petition to advocate for abolishing private US handgun ownership. The following weekend they held two days of funeral services in Nagoya; 300 friends and relatives came to remember Yoshi. Mieko and Masaichi distributed a thousand petitions to the crowd, asking each mourner to find twenty people to sign. The petitions urged Japanese prime minister Kiichi Miyazawa to press President George H. W. Bush to consider a law "to prohibit Americans from carrying or possessing handguns."[22] Just ten days after the shooting, Mieko and Masaichi were on a mission to turn heartbreak into action.

But the Hattoris soon discovered a wide gulf between their advocacy goals and the realities of gun ownership in the United States. Mieko and Masaichi said repeatedly during Peairs's trial and after that they would fight for policies that would prohibit private handgun ownership in the United States, which sounded quixotic to Americans accustomed to living in a country with more than 200 million firearms, at least 40 percent of which were handguns. Japanese citizens were (and remain) generally prohibited from owning guns, with fewer than a million (most of them long guns) among a population of 130 million in the 2020s. The Hattoris would learn the consequences of that contrast in the coming years. In a telling moment during a 2000 visit to Hawaii, Masaichi said to a small crowd, "We hope to see Hawaiʻi become one of the first states for the elimination of guns." Mieko leaned over to him and whispered something, at which point Masaichi qualified his wish: "Gradually. The gradual elimination of guns."[23]

For American activists, working with the Hattoris meant negotiating between the couple's hopes and the reality of gun life in the United States. Even allies in the United States sympathetic to the Hattoris' cause understood that Mieko and Masaichi would have to moderate their message if they hoped to reach many Americans. They initially called for the complete abolition of civilian gun ownership, then for the abolition of handguns, and then for prohibitions against keeping handguns in the home. (In Japan, many guns are required by law to be stored at local police stations and signed out for recreation.) Local US activists like the Haymakers and others, including those in the Japanese American community, helped the Hattoris craft a message that might be palatable to a country with tens of millions of gun owners who increasingly believed in a constitutionally protected right to own firearms.[24] But the initial message of handgun abolition—moderate by Japanese standards but radical by American ones—came from a former enemy nation, perversely giving credibility to Alan Gottlieb's sensationalist claims about a "sneak attack" from Japan.

While they were steadfastly opposed to private gun ownership, the Hattoris were remarkably conciliatory toward Rodney Peairs, and rather than anger toward the United States, they spoke frequently of the sadness they felt for a society in which people were so terrified that they believed they needed to be always armed. The Hattoris believed that Peairs was, like Yoshi, a "victim of a gun society," as Mieko said the day after a Baton Rouge jury let her son's killer go free. "The thing we must really despise, more than the criminal," the Hattoris said in a statement at Yoshi's Nagoya memorial, "is the American law that permits people to own guns"—a variation on the American Christian credo "Love the sinner, hate the sin." After the criminal trial, Mieko published an open letter in the Japanese press in which she reasoned, "When an innocent child is shot by mistake and the guilty party is let off scot-free, we can only conclude that such a society is sick." Twenty years later, Mieko again offered thoughts for Peairs: "He is also a victim of this shooting." Peairs shared in the tragedy: he lost his job, his wife left him, the civil trial bankrupted him. The safety and security that gun culture had promised him proved a lie. The Haymakers admired Mieko's grace toward Peairs, her sadness that "his life is now changed forever because of the accessibility of guns."[25] They observed the "grace, compassion, and fortitude" the Hattoris showed from the outset. Holley Haymaker wrote a friend of the Hattoris' "compassion for their son's killer, for he too is a victim of a society in which guns are too easily available and too easily used." (Of Mieko, she wrote, in Laura Fermi–like fashion, "Women never cease to amaze me with their humor, humanity, and ability to survive.")[26]

Though Rodney Peairs was acquitted in a May 1993 criminal trial, he would be found responsible for Yoshi's death and ordered to pay $653,000 in a September 1994 civil trial. Afterward, the Hattoris made him an extraordinary offer: hand over the gun and keep the money. The Hattoris knew that Peairs, who had worked for years as a butcher in a local Winn-Dixie supermarket—a job he lost after the shooting—would never be able to pay his share of $553,000, the remaining balance after his insurance company paid out $100,000. They made it clear they were uninterested in the money. Peairs's insurance company reportedly offered a six-figure settlement before the civil trial, but the Hattoris refused, hoping instead that a victory would provide what they really wanted, legal acknowledgment of Peairs's wrongdoing. Mieko and Masaichi hoped that they could make Peairs's gun "a symbol of the U.S. gun-control movement." They wanted the gun destroyed, an idea they may have gotten from the Haymakers' minister, Steve Crump, who had suggested that "the gun that was once used to kill, be rendered useless for killing ever again."[27]

His lawyer claimed Peairs never formally received such an offer, but Peairs decided anyway that he did not want to be part of a gun control campaign; in the same way, he claimed to have rejected entreaties from the NRA as well as lucrative offers from the media to tell his story.[28] As for the Hattoris, with the insurance money they received they created Yoshi's Gift, a nonprofit fund that offered small grants to gun control organizations and sponsored exchange student trips to Japan.[29]

THE HATTORIS' PASSION and grace inspired the Haymakers in turn to take up gun control activism in the United States. They were both well-respected professors at Louisiana State University, Holley a physician teaching in the medical school and Richard a physicist in the physics department. Their campaign attracted much attention, connecting the Haymakers with thousands of gun control advocates in the United States, Japan, and around the world. They tapped their professional and social networks, linking to activists in the academic and medical professions as well as those in religious organizations, through the local Unitarian Church. Richard Haymaker took leave from his job during the 1993–94 academic year to commit fully to organizing. The Haymakers toured the country to talk about the issues, and they visited Japan

Mieko and Masaichi Hattori hold a photograph of Yoshi at the conclusion of the civil trial, 1994. Richard Haymaker stands to the back left, while Yoshinori Kamo, a sociologist at LSU and the Hattoris' translator, is to the right. (Christine Choy and Film News Now Foundation, *The Shot Heard 'Round the World*)

several times. They built a transnational gun control movement of nongovernmental actors connecting across borders and pressuring governments for reform. Their goal in building such a network was to push the United States to learn from the successful policies other nations, like Japan, had enacted to curb gun violence.

The Haymakers resisted the mythology of American gun exceptionalism, the idea that the unique gun history and culture of the United States made foreign approaches to gun control unworkable. Following the Hattoris' lead, the Haymakers were already articulating ideas about American gun violence in a global context just two weeks after the shooting, when they published an op-ed in the *New York Times*, "Another Magnum, Another Victim." "Americans must learn to think of guns as reserved—without exception—for hunting," they argued. They encouraged their fellow citizens to leave behind the "imperatives of an unpoliced frontier," the mythologies of the nineteenth century, "when a homeowner couldn't lock his door and dial 911, as Mr. Peairs might have done." They echoed not only the Hattoris' and other Japanese commentators' critiques of American-style modernity, but also their US gun control forebears of the 1960s and 1970s: "We hope and pray that the time is near when our civ-ilization will attain a new maturity."[30] For the Haymakers, the *New York Times* piece and the encouraging responses to it (the discouraging ones aside) felt like an important moment and the seed of a possible movement for change.

For Richard Haymaker, inspiration came not just from the tragedy of Yoshi's life cut short but also from the Hattoris' graceful and impassioned response. He had a deep personal stake in the success of the campaign, as if he did not want to let the Hattoris down. Even if Peairs was to blame, or, as the Hattoris told it, American gun culture was ultimately culpable, Yoshi died under the Haymakers' care. Buried beneath the political fights they embraced lay deep heartbreak. Richard Haymaker channeled heartbreak into energy for organiz-ing within the gun control movement.

Unlike many Americans who chafed at the idea that Japan would dictate American customs and values—the *Daily Yomiuri* reported that one juror at Peairs's criminal trial "said she did not like foreigners to tell Americans what to do"—the Haymakers saw international empathy in the Japanese campaign.[31] Richard believed Americans could capitalize on that sincere human senti-ment. "The reason I feel such a huge personal stake in this effort," he wrote an American compatriot in Japan, "is the belief that the huge outpouring of effort in Japan can be really effective only if WE in the US respond adequately. Then the Japanese effort can be interpreted as a message from THEIR HEART to the HEARTS of AMERICANS, and the AMERICANS RESPOND. That is my dream."[32]

Richard Haymaker pursued that dream full-time during his year of leave, founding and directing Louisiana Ceasefire, integrating the new group into a national network linked to the Coalition to Stop Gun Violence (the former National Coalition to Ban Handguns).[33] He aimed to build a campaign to match the outpouring of Japanese sentiment. Ever the physicist, he framed his goal as "a quantum change in awareness and attitudes," inspired by Japan's call for domestic peace and disarmament. "We are seeking something much farther-reaching than the next gun-control law," he explained. While the Hat-toris started collecting signatures at funeral services for Yoshi a week after his death, Richard began a month later, over the Thanksgiving holiday. "In the tradition of theoretical physics, working in isolation," he wrote Michael Armacost, a friend from college days who happened to be US ambassador to Japan until 1993, "I tried to dream up ways to reach national organizations that might distribute it to their members." He sent "about 20 letters," hoping they would reach the right people to have a viral effect to match the Hattoris' signature-collecting efforts. He described it to a friend as a "numbers game trying to catch the impossible number of Japanese signatures."[34]

Haymaker believed grassroots organizing was his strength and the move-ment's goal. He found wanting the strategies of the big-money national gun control organizations, like Handgun Control Inc., the former NCCH, now headed by Sarah Brady. "Continuing as we are to fight tooth and nail for the smallest steps such as the Brady Bill," a modest bill implementing waiting peri-ods and background checks, he wrote, "is just not good enough." In contrast to such piecemeal national campaigns, he believed the Yoshi movement should "speak from the heart. We do not emphasize cold statistics. We try to reach other hearts directly."[35] He aimed to "reach enough good hearts" in the United States to match the "enormous success" of the Japanese campaign and its nearly 2 million signatures. Haymaker wanted just as many US signatures, identify-ing them as a "top priority." Indeed, he worried that if the campaign in Japan dwarfed its American counterpart, it would give credence to "possible criticism that the Japanese are trying to have an undue influence" on US gun politics.[36]

ON TUESDAY, NOVEMBER 16, the Hattoris and the Haymakers met with President Bill Clinton at the White House. It was six days shy of what would have been Yoshi's eighteenth birthday, November 22, a day when Americans were also set to commemorate the thirtieth anniversary of the Kennedy assas-sination. Five months earlier, Clinton had traveled to Japan for a G7 summit and while there had a ten-minute phone call with the Hattoris. Masaichi asked if they could visit the White House with the Haymakers on Yoshi's birthday. The Haymakers tapped their professional networks to make contacts within the White House. The meeting eventually happened a week earlier than the anniversary of the Kennedy assassination because Richard Haymaker worried that commemorations would mute press coverage of the Hattoris' visit and a planned concurrent gun control conference in the capital.[37]

Clinton's inauguration in January 1993 was a welcome development for gun control, as Richard Haymaker saw it. "President Clinton offers the great-est hope this country has ever had," he wrote in a Japanese newspaper on the first anniversary of Yoshi's death, "that we can, at last, join the rest of the world in our attitudes and laws on gun violence." He praised Clinton for speaking "forcefully many times about how we are out of line with the rest of the world in our laws and attitudes about guns," and he appreciated that Clinton shared his belief that handguns made homes less safe. Haymaker saw Clinton's value as a communicator, a leader who could transcend the gridlock of Congress and speak directly to the American people. Surveys consistently showed that the public favored greater restrictions on civilian guns than Congress's decades of dithering reflected.[38] Haymaker recognized the significance of a fellow south-ern liberal who might transcend the party divide.

Haymaker composed an open letter to Clinton a week before the conference in Washington, when it was still unclear whether the president's schedule would allow for a meeting with the Hattoris. He called on Clinton to "help formulate a comprehensive national strategy to combat gun violence." He identified himself as one of those Americans who, thirty years earlier, in the wake of John F. Kennedy's assassination—and then again five years later with those of Robert Kennedy and Martin Luther King Jr.—had believed national tragedy "would lead to a turning point in this country in our attitudes and laws on firearms." Instead, in the last quarter century, the United States had become "an anomaly in the world," the most violent nation not at war. He told Clinton about Yoshi and revealed that the day before his death, the teenager had attended a rally for candidate Clinton in Baton Rouge, where "Yoshi patted you on the shoulder" and took some photographs that he never saw developed.[39]

The Hattoris and Haymakers presented Clinton with those photographs on November 16, along with a recording of a song called "Yoshi," with lyrics written by Mieko and music composed by Japanese musician Akemi Mano. The Japanese signatures were their most important delivery: the Hattoris handed the president 1.8 million of them—a figure equal to about 1.4 percent of Japan's entire population. The Haymakers added 250,000 signatures from the United States, far short of what Richard Haymaker had hoped for but still, according to one journalist, a "record high for a U.S. gun-control petition."[40]

At the time the Clinton meeting felt like a triumph and perhaps the start of an expansion of the gun control movement. Only days earlier the Brady Handgun Violence Prevention Act, better known as the Brady Bill, finally passed Congress after years of debate, and two weeks after he met with the Hattoris and Haymakers, Clinton signed it into law, with polls showing 88 percent support among the public. When the president said that "millions of Americans face streets that are unsafe, under conditions that no other nation—no other nations—has permitted to exist," he spoke the Haymakers' language.[41] But rather than the kind of transcendent political change the Haymakers hoped for, the Brady Bill's modest provisions merely addressed some of the loopholes of the Gun Control Act, the most important of which was mandated federal background checks for all guns purchased from licensed dealers. Gun control advocates found more reason to cheer Clinton when, less than a year later, he signed into law the Federal Assault Weapons Ban (AWB), a subsection of a far-reaching omnibus crime bill. Once again the law's aims were modest: it banned the manufacture and sale of select "assault weapons"—mostly semiautomatic rifles—with certain military-style aesthetic characteristics, like pistol grips and barrel shrouds, and also high-capacity magazines, but permitted ownership and transfer of any prohibited firearm or magazine manufactured before the bill became law. The bill also contained a ten-year sunset provision, due to pressure from the NRA, and President George W. Bush and a Republican Congress would allow it to expire in 2004.

The modest goals of these two Clinton-era bills, which accommodated rather than confronted gun capitalism, led to predictably modest outcomes. At the end of the decade, gun violence researchers found that the Brady Bill had no measurable effect on homicide rates. Most guns used in crime are not acquired legally through a federal firearms licensee.[42] A study published a decade after the AWB passed concluded much the same, that the ban had little effect, in part because it didn't last long enough to have one.[43] The meeting with Clinton, then, felt like the beginning of something big but instead proved to be the end of a quarter century of federal gun control lawmaking. The Brady Bill and the AWB were the only federal gun restrictions passed for nearly three decades, until a massacre of children in Uvalde, Texas, prompted similarly modest bipartisan legislation intended not to reduce civilian stockpiles but instead to provide funding for more mental health interventions and oversight of gun transactions. In the debate, which required at least ten Senate Republicans to sign on, any discussion of limiting gun capitalism or rethinking the gun country's unparalleled stockpiles was a nonstarter.

LIKE THE LIBERAL POLITICIANS who needed conservative votes to get gun bills passed, the Haymakers necessarily triangulated too, not around gun rights sensibilities but instead around race. Despite their own commitments to antiracism, the Haymakers worried that a gun control narrative taking took cues from Japanese accusations of American racism would forestall efforts to reach millions of white Americans accustomed to media images of Black urban crime. To many Japanese, even those not swayed by nationalist anti-American rhetoric (itself on the rise in the 1980s, fueled by Japan's meteoric economic growth), there were "obvious elements of racism" in the shooting and the verdict, a friend wrote to Haymaker from Japan. If Americans learned of such Japanese reactions, he wondered, "is there any danger that white Americans who initially felt sympathy towards Yoshi and his family would change their mind and lose all interest in gun control?"[44]

Haymaker had of course thought about the intersections of gun violence and racism, an unavoidable crossroads for anyone working for US gun control in the early 1990s, especially for an activist in Baton Rouge, a majority-Black and de facto segregated city. "I guess I do think that a public call from Japan about racism could be explosive and could backfire," he admitted. He made the point, however, that while Rodney Peairs and his lawyer (and even Louisiana governor Edwin Edwards) denied race had any effect on the incident, "the defense was the first to inject racism" into the case, trying to convince the jury that Yoshi's darker skin made Rodney's wife Bonnie, who described it as "darker-colored" at trial, rightfully afraid when Yoshi appeared at her doorstep.[45]

The issue of race—ever-present in conversations about US gun violence, especially in the early 1990s, when it spiked mainly among young Black men in urban communities—was complicated in this instance by xenophobia and racial nationalism.[46] Holley Haymaker laid out what she saw as the "backlash toward Japan theme" to an editor: "Remember Pearl Harbor" and "What are those guys doing telling us how to live?" were common refrains. "Actually," she wrote, "the don't-tell-me-how-to-live theme plays itself out on every level here: Japan to the US, the Northeast to the South, the national press to the local, government to the individual."[47]

The Haymakers had good reason to worry about a racist backlash—that's precisely what happened, and precisely what cynical gun rights fundraisers like Alan Gottlieb counted on. The Haymakers' transnational activism provoked anger and fear in Americans ready to spew xenophobia, anti-Japanese racism, and conspiracy theories. Why did the Haymakers spend their time criticizing US laws and institutions, letter writers asked, when Japanese society was among the world's most violent and oppressive? This line of reasoning focused on both the historical Japan and on the contemporary nation. Hate mail writers (many of them anonymous) told the Haymakers about everything from Japanese soldiers' Pacific War crimes to the most fantastical fables of a global torture and sex slave trade directed by the present-day Japanese government. Some correspondents composed vicious, stinging letters that tried to exonerate Peairs and blame the Haymakers for Yoshi's death. They should have known better, these letters argued, than to allow an exchange student with poor English skills out at night in a city where crime left people on edge. "Tragic, but it was Yoshi's fault!," one wrote. "He should have known better English." Another suggested that the Haymakers' energies would be more productively directed at ensuring "that all foreigners coming to the US can speak enough of the English language to save their own lives."[48] Like gun control activists before them, the Haymakers became accustomed to frequent anonymous, cruel hate mail. Racism was a common theme in much of the hate mail activists received; in the Haymakers' correspondence, the Japan element added a new bogeyman for racists and xenophobes.

CYNICS LIKE GOTTLIEB stoked racist fears of a former enemy turned ally, but an alternative discourse on Japan and guns had gone back decades: Japan showed what a gun-free society looked like. As early as the 1960s, gun control proponents had used the East Asian nation as a primary counterexample to the growing US gun violence problem. During the many Senate hearings Tom Dodd chaired, it was not uncommon to hear Japan mentioned positively alongside Western European countries for minimizing gun ownership and thus gun violence. Japan was among the countries that the Eisenhower Commission's Firearms Task Force highlighted favorably. In the first cabinet meeting after Bobby Kennedy's assassination, as the Johnson administration discussed a legislative response, Attorney General Ramsey Clark pointed admiringly to Japan's strict laws and few gun killings. Debate over the Gun Control Act in 1968 sparked interest in the press over "what other countries do," and Japan was frequently in the conversation alongside other "advanced" countries. John Glenn's Emergency Committee for Gun Control noted in the aftermath of Bobby Kennedy's killing that Japanese laws on gun ownership were "so strict" that US television stars making personal appearances in costume in Japan were "only allowed to wear cap pistols." At the height of the debate in 1968, James Bennett, founder of the National Committee for Responsible Firearms Policy and longtime director of the Bureau of Prisons, explained to the *New York Times* that "in Japan only a couple of dozen people other than policemen are permitted to own handguns. . . . In my business I like that idea very much. But for this country that's an extremist position."[49]

The first grassroots gun control organizations in the 1970s had also been fascinated with Japan's strict regulations on guns. Laura Fermi and the Civic Disarmament Committee corresponded with Japanese officials to acquire copies of firearms laws and statistics. They received a thick packet of records in return, which a Japanese-speaking friend translated.[50] Meanwhile, the North Shore's Committee for Handgun Control wrote to embassies from many countries in search of information on handgun controls and violence rates, and the group kept an entire separate research file on Japan.[51]

Japan's streets were famously safe—in 1970, Tokyo counted 3 handgun murders, compared to 538 in New York City—but its manufacturers quietly benefited from the sale of guns to the United States that had no legal civilian market in Japan.[52] In 1975, Japan accounted for 13 percent of total US firearms imports, ranking fourth behind West Germany, Italy, and Brazil.[53] The country appeared frequently in conversations about guns in the United States as a positive example of effective public policy, but Japanese manufacturers were occasionally the subject of implicit criticism for their contributions to unrestricted American gun consumerism. The abundant pre-1968 war surplus market was flush with Japanese firearms like Arisaka rifles and Nambu pistols, which the Japanese government sold off at clearance prices to US importers.[54]

The scope affixed to Lee Harvey Oswald's Italian-made Mannlicher-Carcano rifle was stamped "Made in Japan."

Further, anecdotal evidence pointed to a kind of Japanese fascination, even a fetish, especially among men, for American gun culture. This could be observed at shooting ranges in areas frequented by Japanese tourists or business travelers. About a third of all business at the Los Angeles Gun Club, a few blocks from Little Tokyo, was Japanese, according to one worker whose job was to translate for the Japanese speakers who came to shoot. The business was decorated with posters of iconic figures of American popular gun culture like John Wayne, Clint Eastwood, and Bruce Willis. Japan's strict gun laws "combined with romanticization of gun violence in Western films" drew Japanese tourists to the club, reported the Japanese American newspaper *Rafu Shimpo*. A brochure for Japanese tourists enticed them with tours of San Francisco and Los Angeles, where they could visit gun ranges and "experience 200 types of firearms." Reflecting on this appeal, gun control researcher and activist Tom Diaz described the United States as "a kind of underdeveloped moral Third World, a place where the rest of the world can indulge its gun lust."[55]

YOSHI'S KILLING AND PEAIRS'S ACQUITTAL provided an opportunity to view American gun violence from the outside. For many Japanese, these events demonstrated America's regression into a backward and uncivilized society. At the end of the US occupation of Japan (1945–52), Douglas MacArthur, who had served as an ersatz emperor of the country throughout the occupation, offended many Japanese when he referred to their nation as "a boy of twelve compared to our [US] development of 45 years."[56] Four decades later, the teacher had become the student. Japanese understood their own society to be modern, rational, and civilized, demonstrated by its safety, pacifism, and extraordinary economic growth, while the "nation of gun-wielding maniacs" had lost its postwar luster and descended into social barbarism. "I think Americans are 12-year-olds," sixty-five-year-old Yasuo Ume of Chiba Prefecture told the *Daily Yomiuri*, rebutting MacArthur. Eriko Fujima wondered how Yoshi's murder could go unpunished: "My mother told me that it could not be helped because Japan was a nation defeated in war," the thirty-six-year-old from Kanagawa Prefecture wrote. "For how many decades must Japan continue carrying the burden of having been a loser?"[57]

Kaname Saruya, a professor of US history at Tokyo Women's Christian University, pulled no punches when he described the United States as "still a Third World nation in terms of gun control," and, "being only 200 years old . . . still partly a developing country."[58] Other Japanese matched Saruya's rhetoric of development and maturity. "Most Americans may think of the present

conditions in Cambodia or Bosnia as hell," said Shinji Kakichi of Kosugi, referring to nations suffering from political violence and instability. "With respect
to the Hattori case, many Japanese feel the same way about the United States."[59]
Two weeks after Yoshi's killing, Toshio Fukuhara of Yokohama wrote to the
Baton Rouge *Advocate* to describe a recent family vacation to New Orleans
in which he "had the harrowing experience of being chased by a man with a
handgun."[60] "We will not go back again," a banker in Tokyo who vacationed in
the United States told the *Guardian*. "Nobody will kill you in Japan if you don't
understand Japanese."[61]

Even many Americans could agree with the Japanese perspective. Bill Lar-
kin of St. Petersburg wrote his local newspaper after Peairs's acquittal to decry
"another example of the joke our legal system has become." Americans had "no
fear of violent reprisal from the Oriental people," he wrote. "After all they are
a civilized people."[62]

The many Americans living and working in Japan provided a mirrored
perspective on their home country. They wrote to Japanese newspapers to
offer apologies, condolences, and explanations, though if they proffered justifications the Japanese press printed few. They described "sorrow, shame and
outrage" upon hearing the Peairs verdict. The impression, if not the reality,
of social life in the United States contrasted sharply with the kindness that
they experienced from strangers in Japan (even if it was not uncommon for
non-Japanese to report experiencing racism in the country). Former US
exchange students juxtaposed their time in Japan with Yoshi's in Louisiana.
An American in Tokyo said the jury's decision "sanctioned the deterioration
of U.S. society into a virtual war zone." Some writers urged caution in reading
sensationalized "gross misrepresentations" of the United States, where gun
laws in fact varied from jurisdiction to jurisdiction, making some places safer
than others. One American living in Shiga Prefecture acknowledged that "as a
nation, we are guilty of a sickening fascination with guns and violence," but he
also wanted Japanese readers to note that Louisiana was "not exactly famous
for its tolerance of 'outsiders'": nearly 40 percent of the electorate in 1991, after
all, had voted for gubernatorial candidate David Duke, a former grand wizard
of the Ku Klux Klan. "Don't, please, don't view this tragedy as typical of U.S.
society as a whole," he pleaded. A woman who spent a year in Osaka as an
exchange student wrote, "If we want the Japanese to have a different image of
who we are, we need to change who we are, instead of asking the rest of the
world to wear rose-colored glasses when they look at us."[63]

The *Rafu Shimpo*, a Los Angeles–based newspaper serving the Japanese
American community, the largest and oldest of its kind, spoke to locals after
news broke of Peairs's acquittal. "My initial reaction is, 'Are we that scary?'"

said Soji Kashigawa, a Nisei (second-generation) Japanese American. More than one respondent mentioned echoes of the murder of Vincent Chin, a twenty-seven-year-old Chinese American who was beaten to death outside a Detroit bar in 1982 by two white men who subsequently received lenient sentences. "They should tell Japanese not to visit the state of Louisiana," said a local Chinese American businesswoman. "Money is all mighty. Have the Japanese business there transfer to other states. . . . Let Louisiana know that you are fighting back."[64] (It would be difficult to prove causation, but there is certainly a correlation between Yoshi's death and reduced Japanese corporate investment levels in Louisiana compared with the rest of the US South.)[65]

After Yoshi's killing, the Japanese Ministry of Transportation began preparing a phrasebook for its many travelers to the United States. Rather than the common travel guide with tips on everyday phrases to help navigate an unfamiliar country and language, the new phrasebook flipped the script: it contained all manner of colloquialisms that American English speakers might use to convey danger. In addition to the now infamous "Freeze!," it explained phrases like "Back off!," "Duck!," "Stick 'em up!," "Look out!," "Get lost!," and "Cut that out!" The tourist who had been chased by a man with a handgun in New Orleans commented that the phrasebook would "probably be very valuable to those foolish enough to go to the land of guns." When asked about the phrasebook, Masaichi Hattori demurred and said that Americans "needed some training as well—about life in a society where guns are scarce." Some Japanese companies took precautions a step further and began hiring private security firms for their executives traveling to the United States.[66]

Many Japanese felt such precautions were necessary for those who had a lifetime of encounters with English in schools, often in preparation for an intense examination regimen, but little practical colloquial experience. Shortly before Yoshi's death a new television show, *Unusable English*, premiered in Japan, mocking the textbook English that Japanese students learned in schools and that was functionally useless in a world of fluent English speakers. Despite the population's general familiarity with English, a poll at the end of 1992 found that 69 percent of Japanese believed they were "very likely" or "somewhat like[ly]" to become a crime victim during a visit to the United States.[67]

RICHARD HAYMAKER UNDERSTOOD the value of these overseas perspectives on US gun violence. If only his fellow Americans could see the problem from the outside, like people in Japan or elsewhere did, they would understand how irrational it appeared. He thought Yoshi's peers could help. Not long after Yoshi's death, his classmates contacted the Haymakers to express their

A Japanese news program explains the colloquial American usage of the word *freeze*, 1993. (Christine Choy and Film News Now Foundation, *The Shot Heard 'Round the World*)

grief and commitment to preventing future tragedies. Keisuke Nishikawa, representing Yoshi's classmates in Room 202 at Asahigaoka High in Nagoya, wrote the Haymakers in English. Days after Yoshi's funeral his schoolmates had formed a committee dedicated to helping the Hattoris with the signature-collecting campaign. Students tried to make sense of the alienness of US gun culture. "Yoshi's death indeed teaches us the terror of the gun society," Nishikawa wrote just three weeks after the shooting, "and we can't help this feeling that we must try our best to exterminate guns from all the houses in the world. It might be a duty Yoshi has left us."[68]

Yoshi's classmates debated the nature of the gun country. "We still wonder if you are terribly in need of guns for self-defence [*sic*] in spite of the existence of the police & military force that protect America and keep your life safe," Nishikawa wrote after the Peairs verdict. "I think the individual ownership of firearms is too much in any society. . . . The real 'peace' must be formed when & where there are no weapons around us and we can feel that all the people in the world are friends forever."[69] These Japanese students tried to process the logic of American gun ownership, the idea that having a gun protected you from other people who also might have a gun. "All of my friends," Nishikawa wrote, "are disgusted at the American's [*sic*] common sense."[70]

Haymaker tried to connect Yoshi's classmates with US editors who might be interested in the students' ambivalent perspectives on the United States—they condemned US gun culture, but, like Yoshi, they admired and idolized so much else. Keisuke Nishikawa's "Letter to America" appeared in *Tell* magazine a year after Yoshi's death. Yoshi had written to friends describing what it was like to drive past "magnificent sights exactly like what I've seen in American movies." "I was just uttering 'Good!' or 'Wow!' though," he told them, "because you know I can't find a good way to express my feelings in English yet." Reflecting a broader Japanese view, Nishikawa wrote, "We immensely wonder why and how some of you stand in need of such guns to protect yourselves despite the laws made to guarantee your safety." Calling on Americans with guns to "throw them away forever," he repeated the conclusion he'd come to when he first wrote Richard Haymaker: "Yoshi has left us a serious duty—to eliminate firearms from all the houses of not only the U.S., but also the world."[71]

TO MANY IN JAPAN, the solutions to the gun problems of the United States seemed so simple. But 7,000 miles away in Baton Rouge, the problem's intractability divided the local community. The injustice of Yoshi's killing was compounded by the fact that twelve of Rodney Peairs's peers from East Baton Rouge Parish agreed with his self-defense claims. Many residents also wrote to newspapers or called in to radio shows to express support for Peairs. To Holley Haymaker, the response demonstrated two different Baton Rouges, and perhaps two different Americas. The Haymakers' Baton Rouge was a diverse, cosmopolitan state capital, the home of a flagship public university that embraced the world's differences, and a place in which guns posed dangers and ought to be regulated heavily and limited to recreational activities; Peairs's Baton Rouge was racially segregated, conservative, and fearful of difference, a place where guns protected against the world's endless dangers. The Peairses' and the Haymakers' divergent worldviews seemed as different as stereotypical American and Japanese, even though the two families' homes were separated by just a dozen miles. "I think it is important to Mr. Peairs to understand that Richard and I come from a world where we are really curious about people," she explained. "We don't have the same world view he does, that differences are threatening." The Haymakers, she said, believed in opening their home to people who were different—Yoshi was not the first exchange student they had hosted. Peairs, in contrast, believed that "the home is to be protected from people."[72]

Those divergent worldviews were best illustrated in the Peairs's refusal to see Yoshi's death as anything but an unfortunate accident, not emblematic of a broader American pathology. At the end of the trial, Peairs asked to meet privately with the Hattoris. He wanted to express his regret for the incident, even if he still didn't believe himself criminally culpable. The meeting never happened. Lawyers had arranged for it to occur at the local WAFB television station, but Peairs's lawyer, Unglesby, called it off at the last minute because the Hattoris would not agree to keep it off the record. A shouting match between Unglesby and Yoshinori Kamo, the Hattoris' translator and an LSU sociology professor, erupted, and both sides left without meeting. Rodney and Bonnie nevertheless wanted to convince the Hattoris that ultimately cultural misunderstanding caused the tragedy. Bonnie approached Kamo and asked him to interpret "just one thing" for Masaichi Hattori: "Does he understand that if it were an American boy, he would have stopped when my husband shouted 'freeze' and 'stop'?" It was inconceivable to the Rodney and Bonnie that racism shaped the question, let alone the answer.[73]

At the Baton Rouge memorial for Yoshi, held at the Haymakers' Unitarian Church just days after the shooting, minister Steve Crump did not mince words. He declared it was "time for an American Confession." "We run body counts as if we were at war because we *are at war with ourselves and our passions and our fears.*" "Guns in every neighborhood, guns in the homes, guns in every room. Guns, guns, guns, guns, not enough guns. When will private citizens have enough guns?"[74]

Yoshi's death came at a moment when the residents of Baton Rouge were increasingly attuned to the impact of gun violence in their communities. A year after the shooting the local newspaper, the *Advocate*, published a series called "Making a Difference," which included articles about city residents working to address skyrocketing levels of gun violence. Louisiana held the unenviable position of national leader in homicide rate. Baton Rouge passed its own annual homicide record just eight months into 1993; killings were up 41 percent in just three years, and all violent crime was up 62 percent. In 1989 there were 1,387 shooting incidents in the city; three years later there were 4,299.[75] Articles covered activists in Baton Rouge's Black communities, where homicide rates were the highest and on the rise. They pointed to the links between gun violence and drug activity, and observed a dramatic increase in the number of murder suspects who were children, a trend duplicated in cities throughout the country.[76] Occasionally the stories struck a sensationalist tone: "Whether you live in one of Baton Rouge's comfortable, upscale subdivisions or a drug-infested combat zone, your chances of being a victim of violent crime are greater than ever." In one discomfiting image covering much of the top half of a page, an eighty-eight-year-old Black man, James Harris, lays on his

Cartoonist Dale Stephanos demonstrates the frustration many Americans
felt at what the gun country had become after Rodney Peairs was acquitted in the criminal trial in 1993. (© Dale Stephanos)

bed shirtless in boxer shorts, wearing an oxygen mask, alongside a pistol and a
shotgun. Harris said the violence had grown so bad he could not sleep without
these firearms beside him.[77]

The *Advocate* series clearly communicated the racialized representation
of gun violence in Baton Rouge: it was a Black problem, but increasingly it
crept into "safe" white neighborhoods. "It was not until a bullet hit our congre-
gation," said Unitarian minister Crump, that members of this predominantly
white, middle-class community recognized the personal toll of gun violence.
Crump's church became a headquarters for gun control activism in the Baton
Rouge community, much of it coordinated by Holley and Richard Haymaker.
One congregant summarized the church community's reaction to Yoshi's killing: "We don't live in neighborhoods that are riddled with drugs and crime.
We basically live in secure, middle-class neighborhoods. It was like something
happening to us that happens to other people."[78]

Baton Rouge also became an unlikely location where increasingly tense
US-Japan relations played out. In 1994, Mayor-President Tom Ed McHugh

proposed building a small memorial to the city's victims of gun violence. The design included a plaque with Yoshi's likeness and the words, "He came in friendship." (A year earlier, Baton Rouge created and donated a similar plaque to Nagoya.) McHugh appointed a commission, which included Richard Haymaker, that studied the possibilities and recommended placing the memorial near a fountain at the Riverside Centroplex (a shopping and entertainment complex, today called the River Center, that sits alongside the Mississippi River near downtown Baton Rouge).[79] The memorial would be a small part of the cityscape visible from the river bridge that left Yoshi searching for superlatives when he arrived in America.

The proposal provoked an emotional debate. Frank Masanz, a former commissioner of the Louisiana Naval War Memorial, which rested on the river across the street from the proposed site, spoke against the plan. As a World War II veteran, Masanz and others were upset that a plaque memorializing a Japanese boy would be placed so close to the USS *Kidd* memorial, a museum housed in a destroyer from the Second World War that had been named for Admiral Isaac C. Kidd, a casualty of the Japanese attack on Pearl Harbor and the first-ever US admiral killed in action. Masanz claimed the media was "trying to make the public feel guilty" about opposing the plaque, and he questioned why there were no plaques "for the victims of Japan's innumerable misdeeds," a common sentiment among those opposed to the plan.[80] The *Advocate* also printed responses to what memorial proponents labeled racism and "Japan-bashing." John Lewis of Baton Rouge, also a veteran, exhorted his community to "see a kinship between" Yoshi and the battleship. "This instrument of war and young American lives were on the line so that future generations could be free to live in a democratic society." "Yoshihiro Hattori's history is part of ours," Lewis wrote. "To commemorate him is, in a way, a way to commemorate our dedication to healing."[81]

Early plans for the plaque included a quote from the novelist Mary McCarthy: "In violence, we forget who we are."[82] Though Richard Haymaker approved of the line and had served on the commission that drafted plans for the plaque, it was an ironic choice. The implicit argument of the Haymakers' campaign was that, to the contrary, in gun violence, Americans found out who they were and who they weren't—they weren't a people ready to change, despite powerful evidence demonstrating the need for it.

CHAPTER 10

FRENCH M35A
7.65MM FRENCH LONG
NRA
GOOD
ONLY
$23
Design features of
Browning, Petter and
the Neuhausen auto.   AMMO
8-rd. mags. $3.00. $7.00/100

GLOBAL GUN GRABBERS

FIVE YEARS AFTER Rodney Peairs murdered Yoshi Hattori, Japan remained a bogeyman for the US gun rights movement. But the nation of purported pacifists—Article 9 of the 1947 Japanese Constitution prohibited war as an instrument of national policy—had moved beyond polite petitions and into a global governing forum, the United Nations. Or at least that was the gun lobby's narrative, crafted to provoke maximum outrage. The Japanese were "try[ing] to export their brand of firearms regulations throughout the rest of the world," complained Tanya Metaksa, an influential NRA lobbyist. A nascent global effort to regulate illegal international firearms transfers, coordinated by the UN, emerged in the mid-1990s, but the NRA claimed to see the shadowy hand of Japan behind a more sinister scheme to make domestic gun control policies more like its own, all in a bid for a seat on the UN Security Council, which would provide geopolitical muscle to back up its surging economic power. The country funded the UN effort, the NRA said, as well as a recent gun buyback program in South Africa. "The primary people are the Japanese, who have no firearms in their society," said Thomas Mason, the NRA's chief UN lobbyist, "so when you're talking to the Japanese, it's like being from Venus and they're from Mars. It's extremely hard to work with them."[1]

As with Alan Gottlieb's accusation that Japan was trying to intervene in US gun politics, the lobbyists' claims began with a nugget of fact. The UN did coordinate a campaign in the latter half of the 1990s to address the impact of gun violence around the world, culminating in a major 2001 conference, and Japan, along with dozens of other countries, had supported it enthusiastically.

"No, this is not some wild claim cooked up by the fevered imaginations of the militia crazies," wrote Ronald Bailey in the conservative *Weekly Standard.* The "Global Gun Grabbers" were coming for real this time.[2] As early as the 1960s, gun rights ideologues had concocted fantasies of a UN power grab with disarmament of the American people as its centerpiece, and now, in a post–Cold War world, their nightmares were taking shape.

To understand what Japan and dozens of other member states in the United Nations were doing about guns in the 1990s, it's important to consider how the end of the Cold War reshaped the international environment and conflict within it. In one sense, the Cold War was the "Long Peace," in historian John Lewis Gaddis's famous phrasing.[3] Conflict between the world's great powers was notably lacking in the half century following the Second World War, a condition Gaddis attributed to the superpowers' nuclear stalemate, which limited global violence. Historians today are skeptical of the argument; there was, after all, a great deal of horrific violence around the world during the Cold War, especially outside the West, and much of it driven by superpower intervention in the Third World.[4] But Gaddis's was a common sentiment at the Cold War's end—it was even a kind of nostalgia for the certitudes, however potentially apocalyptic, of the "Long Peace"—and observers worried that the dissolution of superpower global competition would mean uncontrollable regional conflagrations driven by old hatreds, like nationalism and religion, that the Cold War had tried to bottle up.

Evidence for this perspective appeared almost immediately in places as diverse and far-flung as Yugoslavia, Afghanistan, and Rwanda. Ethnic and religious conflict filled the vacuum left by the end of competition between liberal capitalism and authoritarian communism.[5] And into those lacunae flowed the Cold War's arsenals—not nuclear weapons but millions of what came to be called "small arms and light weapons" (or SALW, in the literature of the time): any tool of violence that could be easily transported and wielded by an individual, from a machete to a landmine. And the most important, plentiful, and deadly SALW were guns.

The guns came from many places, including from the one-time Second World: former Soviet republics and China, mostly, which looked to offload aging arsenals of Cold War–era SALW and found willing markets in the Third World. More often than not, they came from the same general source of Americans' personal arsenals, from the legal trade conducted by states or international businesses, despite unease about shadowy black market arms dealers fueling conflict around the world. As Sam Cummings had said a half century earlier, there was no reason to obscure his business as an international arms trader because it was easy enough to get rich without touching the black market. Why go to the trouble of selling a few thousand guns to guerrillas in Central America when Americans were buying them, legally, by the millions? Gun capitalism remained a safe bet in the 1990s, as it had been for Cummings in the 1950s.

Absent superpower competition in the postcolonial world, even a small number of small arms could mean big trouble in countries or regions short on political stability. Such guns were cheap, plentiful, easy to access and transport, and most important, deadly. For the cost of a modern fighter plane, a country, or an insurgency, could buy hundreds of thousands of modern assault rifles, and few insurgencies needed that many to threaten "human security," a phrase on the lips of many NGO officials in the 1990s. Compared to major weapons systems, assault rifles were inconspicuous and discrete. They were also durable. "Virtually all of the weapons of ethnic warfare were designed decades ago," explained political scientist Aaron Karp in 1994. "Today's battlefields look more like a museum than Silicon Valley." The guns of wars from decades past could continue to circulate through international networks so long as they had regular cursory upkeep. Military firearms like the AK-47 could be purchased in conflict zones for the price of a Saturday Night Special in Miami in the 1970s. In the words of political scientists Jeffrey Boutwell and Michael Klare, who were among the first to study the SALW issue systematically, "With a few hundred machine guns and mortars, a small army can take over an entire country."[6]

Karp, Klare, and Boutwell were part of a small but dedicated international cohort of scholars conducting research on and drawing government and NGO attention to the SALW issue in the 1990s. The group hosted and attended conferences, produced academic volumes, and connected with NGOs eager to direct donor money to the problems of human security in the post–Cold War world. By 1999, activist and scholarly effort had led to the creation of the International Action Network on Small Arms (IANSA), a London-based umbrella organization that coordinated activities among hundreds of NGOs in dozens of countries. IANSA served as a clearinghouse for research and activism in the lead-up to the 2001 UN conference. One of the most significant contributors to the evolving scholarly understanding of the SALW issue was the Small Arms Survey, a Geneva-based think tank funded by grants from governments around the world. Beginning in 2001 the organization produced its annual *Yearbook*, an invaluable source for data and analysis of international trade in and stockpiles of arms.[7]

The truth was that social scientists knew little about global SALW stockpiles and trade. Only in the 1990s did they attempt to fill this lacuna. They discovered that the global trade in major weapons systems declined after the Cold War but the sale of SALW remained strong, amounting to $10 billion globally, with only 30 percent of it conducted on the black market. In the context of annual global military spending in excess of $850 billion, $10 billion was a drop in the bucket, but $10 billion worth of guns could have a disproportionate impact on political violence in unstable regions. The political scientists offered startling examples of the impact of small arms, how an AK-47 could be had in Angola for as little as fifteen dollars or a "large sack of maize," or how Liberian dictator Charles Taylor seized power in 1990 with just 100 solders armed with AK-47s—perhaps less than $20,000 worth of firearms. The largely unregulated "global deluge of surplus weapons" into conflict zones was responsible for most of the 5 million deaths—90 percent was the most cited figure—in more than 100 conflicts around the world between 1990 and 2000; in 1996 the World Health Organization labeled violence a pandemic, while the International Committee of the Red Cross said, "Weapons are bad for people's health."[8] Among the biggest contributors to the destabilizing proliferation of SALW were US companies: in 1998, they sold nearly $500 million worth of small arms to 124 countries, and in at least five instances sold them into conflict zones where those weapons would be used against US troops or UN peacekeepers.[9]

In 1995 UN secretary-general Boutros Boutros-Ghali first drew international attention to this largely unregulated flow of guns into conflict zones. He celebrated the superpowers' achievements in ending the Cold War and crafting agreements toward nuclear disarmament and limits on the proliferation of weapons of mass destruction. But now, he said, was the time for "micro-disarmament," or "practical disarmament in the context of the conflicts the United Nations is actually dealing with and of the weapons . . . that are actually killing people in the hundreds of thousands."[10] Nuclear weapons hadn't killed anyone in a war zone for a half century, but the annual death toll attributed to SALW was at least a half million. Boutros-Ghali had in mind weapons in those conflict zones where UN peacekeeping missions operated, nations like Somalia, Liberia, Rwanda, and Mozambique, countries with weak or nonexistent states where even a relatively small number of SALW, purchased on the black market for a fraction of the cost of a tank or warplane, could create havoc and threaten human security.

Boutros-Ghali made no mention of Americans' guns, or any other private firearms legally owned in peaceful societies. The impetus for "micro-disarmament" came not from gun ownership or violence in the United States but from the political violence resulting from the breakdown of civil society in countries half a world away. But what would emerge from the UN process by

2001 would be an implicit critique of US gun culture and capitalism, a widespread consensus among most of the world's governments on several basic points that contradicted US gun ideology: there was such a thing as too many guns; civilian populations did not need guns for "self-defense"; and because almost all "illicit" firearms started as legally made and distributed weapons, it was impossible to address the problem of the former without regulating the markets of the latter.

Despite this consensus, over the two decades that followed Boutros-Ghali's call to action, the international community would fail to produce an agreement that would put any substance behind his plea. In the end it was the United States that stood in the way. As the United Nations initiated and coordinated an international conversation about the global SALW problem, no country would play a more determinative role in shaping the outcome, and the US "gun lobby" would be at the center of that process. At home the NRA and more extreme gun rights groups spread misinformation and stoked outrage. On the international stage, the NRA, supported by the George W. Bush administration, would neuter the UN effort to create a significant and effective treaty. As the new millennium began, America's politicized gun culture went global.

BY THE 1990S, fears of an international plot to disarm Americans, coordinated by the UN, were widespread in right-wing political circles. The burgeoning militia movement described "black helicopters" swooping in to impose a "New World Order," which would disarm patriotic Americans who resisted. NRA chief Wayne LaPierre capitalized on the fears, publishing a book titled *The Global War on Your Guns: Inside the UN Plan to Destroy the Bill of Rights* in 2006, in which he warned, "The United Nations wants your guns. They want all of them—now—and they've found a way to do it."[11]

This rhetorical bombast was common by the turn of the century, but the origins of conspiracy theories about "global gun grabbers" traced back decades, to the early 1960s, and to a series of steps taken by the John F. Kennedy administration to address the nuclear arms race. In a narrow sense we find here one unexplored origin story for the militia movement of the 1990s as well as an unexamined source of a new understanding of the Second Amendment—rooted in international fears, inspired by the Cold War, and only later to be mainstreamed as the "individual rights theory" and the "Standard Model."

In 1961, at the behest of the new Kennedy administration, Congress passed the Arms Control and Disarmament Act. The State Department's new Arms Control and Disarmament Agency was tasked with drafting proposals for lowering the temperature of the US-Soviet clash, which had reached a boiling point in late 1961—in the spring, the failed Bay of Pigs invasion of Cuba embarrassed the new administration; in June, Kennedy clashed with his Soviet counterpart, Nikita Khrushchev, at a summit in Vienna; and thereafter Khrushchev challenged the young president by approving the construction of the Berlin Wall as well as detonating the largest nuclear weapon ever tested.[12] The United States needed creative approaches to unprecedented challenges.

Out of the Arms Control and Disarmament Agency came two related documents. The first, presented to the United Nations in September 1961, was the "United States Program for General and Complete Disarmament in a Peaceful World," later published by the State Department under the title *Freedom from War*. A US delegation presented a follow-up document, "Outline of Basic Provisions of a Treaty on General and Complete Disarmament in a Peaceful World"—soon thereafter published by State as *Blueprint for the Peace Race*— to an April 1962 international disarmament conference in Geneva.[13] The two documents offered, in President Kennedy's words, the "most comprehensive and specific series of proposals the United States or any other country has ever made on disarmament." Kennedy challenged the Soviets and all world leaders "not to an arms race but to a peace race—to advance together step by step, stage by stage, until general and complete disarmament has been achieved."[14]

Freedom from War and *Blueprint for the Peace Race* offered some startling, even outright utopian, recommendations for achieving peace in the twentieth century. They proposed a process of increasingly ambitious steps toward disarmament, beginning with agreements to limit nuclear testing and concluding, in the "Third Stage," with nations abandoning all armaments beyond those necessary for "maintaining internal order," ending the manufacture of arms, and submitting global peacekeeping authority to a UN "Peace Force."[15]

Despite, or perhaps because of, their utopian ambitions, the two documents quickly faded into the background noise of the rhetorical Cold War. It was not novel for a superpower to call for a "peace race"—Khrushchev's analogous policy of "peaceful coexistence" dated back several years. The Kennedy administration would prioritize arms controls agreements and improved diplomatic communications but "placed disarmament largely in the realm of 'propaganda,'" according to historian Lawrence Wittner.[16] For public consumption—to win the "peace race"—the United States would utter utopian plans about nations dismantling armed forces, but no serious planning to that effect ever took place.

But official denials—or rather, conspicuous official silences—birthed conspiracy theories. Conspiracist thinking about the US government especially bloomed during the Cold War because the government really did engage in conspiracies—from the FBI's COINTELPRO initiative to infiltrate and subvert civil rights and leftist organizations to the Tuskegee medical experiments on unwitting African Americans, government agencies conspired to subvert democracy and harm Americans while attempting to hide it all. Journalistic and congressional investigations in the 1970s revealed that many Americans were not crazy to think their government was plotting against them and hatching wild international schemes.[17]

Furthermore, conspiracist beliefs about the UN were not new to the 1960s; from the organization's founding, right-wing conservatives saw something nefarious in its ambitions, be it in the its commitment to human rights, which especially rankled white southerners, or in its promotion of global scientific and cultural exchange. Throughout the 1950s, right-wing activists urged Congress to pass proposals like the Bricker Amendment, which would have limited the Senate's authority to approve international treaties.[18]

In other words, when *Freedom from War* and *Blueprint for the Peace Race* appeared there was already fertile ground on which to see the UN as a communist tool to subvert US sovereignty. Over the coming years and decades, these two Cold War footnotes would provoke a kind of political blowback for which they have yet to be credited. Very few Americans—very few historians, even— would recognize "State Department Document 7277" (the *Blueprint*), but by the late 1960s it had already entered the lexicon of right-wing gun rights circles; by the 1990s, it was a synecdoche for black helicopters and global government, fears that motivated the militia movement. After 1962, Document 7277 started appearing in conspiracy-minded letters to editors. Despite occasional journalistic efforts to debunk the theory, it persisted, as conspiracy theories are wont to do.[19]

Document 7277 allegedly described the UN as the vehicle for the imposition of a gun-free global dictatorship. Such thinking could be found as early as 1962 in the otherwise anodyne *Sports Afield* magazine (alongside articles like "Varmints! State-by-State Guide" and "Tactics for August Bass").[20] Writers assumed that when instruments of international diplomacy like Document 7277 spoke of disarmament they meant not nuclear weapons but firearms in the hands of private citizens. "Your gun is wanted by those who seek to destroy America from within and without," warned *American Challenge*, and under the infamous State Department Document 7277, "ALL DISARMAMENT IS UNDER THE CONTROL OF THE UNITED NATIONS regardless of what or who is to be disarmed and this time it is you!" Others saw Document 7277 behind the Johnson administration's push for licensing and registration.[21] The UN threat was, according to a *Sports Afield* writer, precisely why "there has never been a greater need for the Second Amendment."[22]

Fears of a UN-led world government and the end of US sovereignty did not—need it be said?—prove true. But they nevertheless threaded through the decades.[23] Such fears are often associated with the militia movement of the 1990s, as radical gun rights groups of that decade continued to press the conspiracy, inspired by the geopolitical changes of the end of the Cold War. The Second Amendment Committee (SAC, not to be confused with the larger Second Amendment Foundation, or SAF) used Document 7277 to imagine a "world army" in which US, Soviet, and Chinese forces would be merged under a new UN military force led by a Soviet commander. The SAC accused Congress of scheming to close all US military bases "except for those which will be used by the world army." (The SAC later championed the cause of Michael New, a US soldier who refused to serve under UN command in the Balkans in 1995.)[24]

In a 1995 profile of Oklahoma City bomber Timothy McVeigh, the *New York Times* described the future domestic terrorist as "living—and not alone— in a world of mysterious black helicopters, where Mongolian troops were secretly training in the mountains for the pending takeover and the United Nations plan for dividing up the country was confirmed by a child's map on the back of a cereal box." McVeigh frequented gun shows and sold kitschy bumper stickers that said, "Fear the government that fears your gun," and "A man with a gun is a citizen, a man without a gun is a subject."[25] The radical militia ideology of the 1990s had its roots in the 1960s.

Right-wing gun rights advocates used the new federal gun control laws of the early 1990s—the Brady Bill and the Assault Weapons Ban—to justify the growth of the militia movement.[26] "Anti-gun zealots in the media, White House and Congress," Alan Gottlieb wrote on behalf of the Second Amendment Foundation days after the Oklahoma City bombing, "are most to blame for the creation and growth of the militia movement." He disavowed McVeigh's act of terrorism but nevertheless claimed, "Gun laws violate rights and fuel feelings of mistrust, alienation and resentment." The US government's violence at Ruby Ridge in 1992 and Waco in 1993, two instances in which federal agents killed citizens suspected of violating federal gun laws, demonstrated that it was not accountable for its actions, so, according to Gottlieb, no one should be surprised when citizens acted similarly.[27]

"For the most part," wrote the SAF's Karen L. MacNutt of militia members, "they are good-hearted, honest, well-meaning, loyal but naive Americans who are legitimately concerned over our increasing loss of individual freedom, loss of nationality, and the growth of violent, politically inspired, law enforcement activity." Growing pockets of right-wing extremists were, she argued, a product of the gun control movement's repression of the Second Amendment.

Militia ideology was "based on a premise the anti-gun groups have pushed for years, that the Second Amendment is a collective right and only the 'militia' is guaranteed the right to have arms."[28] In other words, militia members formed militias because gun control activists insisted that the Second Amendment was about militias, and because, in the minds of militia members, it was a constitutional way of resisting what they saw as increasingly aggressive federal infringement of individual rights. The 1990s militia movement fulfilled the prophecies of the 1960s right-wing pro-gun groups.

THE NRA ACTED QUICKLY to attack the UN process in the late 1990s, recycling ideas from decades of conspiracy theories about the UN disarming Americans and installing a global police state. These provocateurs didn't have to start from scratch. As early as 1997, NRA fundraising letters warned that a UN treaty would mean a "virtual worldwide ban on firearms ownership." "What would happen," the letter asked, "if the United Nations demands gun confiscation on American soil?" The UN process amounted to a coordinated campaign of "third world dictatorships plotting through the United Nations to eliminate your Second Amendment rights." Not to be outdone on the extremist front, Gun Owners of America described the UN as a "tourniquet that is slowly being drawn around gun owners' necks." Never afraid to twist reality to serve narrow political ends, the gun lobby saw opportunity in portraying a UN threat that didn't exist.

The United Nations, in contrast, acted like the deliberative, consensus-driven body it was. In the years after Boutros-Ghali's 1995 statement, the General Assembly commissioned several expert studies of the impact of the illicit SALW trade on armed conflicts, and in 1997 the General Assembly's Panel of Governmental Experts on Small Arms recommended an international conference; in 1998, the General Assembly voted to prepare for and host a major conference on SALW, which would become the landmark 2001 Conference on the Illicit Trade in Small Arms and Light Weapons and All Its Aspects; in December 1999, the General Assembly passed a resolution establishing a conference Preparatory Committee, which then held ten public meetings with dozens of national participants and NGOs, working consistently for two years to build consensus toward a draft resolution.[29] In other words, the process that began with the secretary-general's 1995 call for "micro-disarmament" of armed conflicts in countries with collapsing states and peaked with the 2001 SALW Conference involved thousands of participants from nearly every UN country, producing hundreds of discussions, studies, and reports at the national, regional, and global levels. The idea that all this work was part of a sinister, coordinated effort to disarm Americans was absurd, but gun rights groups ran with it anyway. Stoking American exceptionalism, isolationism, and xenophobia had long proven good for business.

In an April 2001 column in *American Rifleman*, NRA president Charlton Heston ratcheted up the rhetoric. He warned members that "United Nations leaders have been meeting quietly behind closed doors for several years now to impose their anti-gun schemes on you." He accused "countries that haven't the foggiest notion of what *any freedom* means" of trying to dictate gun policy to the United States. He speculated that "small arms and light weapons" included "your Browning pistol, your Ruger rifle and your garden-variety Benelli shotgun." He admitted that the UN had no power to "unilaterally impose its will upon Americans," but he reminded readers that an international treaty could become US law if the Senate ratified it, and a "future, more anti-gun Senate could."[30]

Heston and NRA leaders knew better than to believe that any such thing was politically possible. But they also knew from experience that many of the organization's members would respond aggressively, that some relished the opportunity to harass legislators and gun control organizations and now they would do the same to UN officials. At a time when the NRA found itself under assault for its increasingly uncompromising positions, two years after the massacre at Columbine High School in Colorado, the UN conference was a welcome distraction and an auspicious opportunity to raise money and mobilize its base. The NRA's aggressive anti-UN stance also marked a public shift in just a half decade. When it came to light that Timothy McVeigh's various extremist obsessions had included firearms and UN black-helicopter conspiracies, the NRA tried to distance itself from the "paranoids crouched in their bunkers with loaded rifles just itching for UN peacekeepers to make their move," as one journalist put it. NRA publications mocked militia-movement fears that the UN, with its peacekeeping missions failing in southeastern Europe, was capable of an operation as extensive as seizing Americans' guns.[31] At the same time, there were reports that the organization quietly signaled to militia groups that they remained welcome in the NRA, even if publicly the group was forced to disavow them.[32] The years-long UN process allowed the besieged NRA to direct its energies outward to an enemy that was not the US government—a hard line momentarily discredited by the McVeigh bombing and the backlash to Wayne LaPierre's extremist rhetoric about "jackbooted thugs" in the ATF, which had led to high-profile resignations from the organization, including that of former president George H. W. Bush. Instead, the NRA could attribute the assault on gun ownership to a shadowy global cabal of unaccountable bureaucrats, drawing on decades of right-wing animosity toward international institutions, while maintaining the veneer of patriotic activism.

Heston's column provoked a flood of angry emails to the UN Department of Disarmament Affairs (DDA). The emails echoed the language and rhetorical tactics of hate-mail campaigns dating back decades. Some hinted at threats. "Hello and this is a warning," opened one email, which consisted of a numbered list of declarations like, "If you attempt to disarm America you will find we will wage war with you and drive you out!" Emailers reproduced common fears of socialist control within the UN: "WE WILL FIGHT UNTIL WE ARE KNEE DEEP IN BLOOD TO DEFEND OUR WAY OF LIFE AND TO MAKE SOCIALIST PIGS LIKE YOU LEAVE OUR LAND." Others observed that the SALW Conference would only rally the pro-gun crowd to the cause more determinedly. "This gives me time to stock up on weapons and ammunition in preparation for the inevitable invasion," wrote one; "Dear Totalitarian," wrote another, "I wish to send my thanks for helping me decide on when to purchase my next handgun." A writer who warned UN officials to "leave your filthy one world hands off my guns!!" boasted of being inspired to contribute $1,000 monthly to the NRA. Anti-UN images included in the emails showed Uncle Sam standing before the UN emblem, pointing and declaring, "The United Nations WANTS TO DISARM AMERICA." Another replaced Uncle Sam with an image of Kofi Annan, the Ghanaian diplomat who succeeded Boutros-Ghali as secretary-general in 1997, taunting, "Rich lazy American fools! I will take your guns and then you will kiss the UN's ass!"[33]

All these messages sounded at least vaguely threatening, but the UN Special Services Unit concluded that none was so specific as to require action.[34] After all, the messages were conditional: *if* the UN tried to take Americans' guns; *if* the UN attempted a takeover of the United States. Nobody at the UN had anything of the sort planned.

Officials with the DDA nevertheless found the over-the-top American reaction worth addressing and prepared a public response to counter the "active campaign" of misinformation. "We are not going to take guns away from them," the DDA's director told the press. "We are looking at small arms in an international context. We are not looking at domestic gun control."[35] The DDA's list of common misconceptions was long, demonstrating just how many wild ideas about the UN, guns, and the conference permeated right-wing media. Among the myths the organization sought to dispel: the UN wanted to eliminate the Second Amendment; the UN wanted to restrict privately owned weapons; shutting down illegal trade in guns required shutting down legal trade; the conference would produce a legally binding treaty requiring signatories to confiscate and destroy guns; nongovernmental organizations, including gun control groups, could vote on conference resolutions; the conference intentionally targeted the United States and its gun culture; the conference would build an international database of guns and owners; the conference would encourage Americans to destroy guns at "public destruction events." In all these cases, gun rights media took some real aspect of the conference—such as a few participating states proposing public events where they might destroy illegal weapons seized in their countries—and twisted it to appear more sinister.[36]

AMERICAN GUN OWNERS with genuine concern had little reason to worry once the conference began. They had on their side no less than President George W. Bush and his representative to the conference, John Bolton, a prominent neoconservative bulldog then serving as undersecretary of state for arms control and international security affairs. In 2005 Bolton would become Bush's ambassador to the United Nations, an appointment indicative less of Bolton's diplomatic skill and more of the Bush administration's contempt for diplomacy. More than a decade later Bolton's directness would appeal to President Donald Trump, a man who believed he appreciated and embodied bluntness himself but who quickly turned against anyone who told him the truth, as he would with Bolton, who served as his national security adviser for a year and a half. The pugnacious mustachioed Bolton, an unabashed champion of American military power and irascible skeptic of international cooperation, was the ideal figure to represent the United States at the UN small arms conference—if the goal was to derail the proceedings.

The Clinton administration had been sympathetic to Boutros-Ghali's vision. "Weapons of mass destruction have the potential to wipe out whole cities at a time," said John D. Holum, Bolton's predecessor under Clinton. "Small arms routinely do wipe out the equivalent of whole cities, a few people at a time."[37] But Clinton was gone and Holum with him. Bush had won a controversial election in 2000 with the vocal support of the NRA, and with his eye on 2004 he had no interest in alienating gun rights voters. Obstructionism was the strategy: the administration aimed to prevent the SALW conference from crafting an international instrument that would impose any obligation on the US government or US citizens. It also attempted to limit the extent to which the international community could even speak of imposing limits on US and global gun capitalism. Bolton had the bravado to deliver this message loud and clear.

Critics accused Bolton of taking his marching orders from the gun lobby and the NRA. His obstructionist behavior at the conference did nothing to dispel that impression. On the conference's first day, July 9, 2001, when ministers from dozens of countries offered pro forma pledges of cooperation, Bolton instead delivered a "blistering speech that literally woke up the Conference."[38] He began by praising the shared goal of addressing the *illicit* trade in SALW, that roughly 30 percent of the global trade in SALW that occurred on the black market. But the conference's mandate did not extend further than that goal, he insisted, and discussions had drifted beyond that mandate to include, with no justification, the legal trade in arms. Further, the United States did not accept the conference's broad definition of SALW; such weapons were, in Bolton's words, "the strictly military arms . . . that are contributing to the continued violence and suffering in regions around the world," a narrow definition that contrasted with the broader one the Clinton administration had accepted in earlier negotiations.[39] The United States did not recognize SALW as including hunting rifles or handguns, "which are commonly owned and used by citizens in many countries." By muddying the definition of SALW and allowing it to encompass all kinds of firearms beyond the "strictly military" variety, the draft "Programme of Action" suffered from a "diffusion of focus," blending "legitimate areas for international cooperation and action and areas that are properly left to decisions made through the exercise of popular sovereignty by participating governments."[40] Bolton was there to make sure the global gun grabbers didn't press beyond their limited mandate.

Bolton affirmed the centrality of the Second Amendment, and the Bush administration's endorsement of an individual-rights interpretation of it, to the US approach to the conference—a sharp contrast with the US diplomats who had worked with the UN process during the last years of the Clinton administration. The Bush administration was, in fact, the first in US history to endorse the individual-rights theory of the Second Amendment. Attorney General John Ashcroft did so explicitly in a letter to the NRA in early 2001.[41] Bolton channeled the new administration's pro-gun policy. Some of the main arguments of the gun rights movement since the 1960s rang through his address, mixing American exceptionalism with an affirmation of an expansive understanding of the Second Amendment and the emerging idea that gun rights were human rights. "The United States believes that the responsible use of firearms is a legitimate aspect of national life," Bolton said. "We, therefore, do not begin with the presumption that all small arms and light weapons are the same or that they are all problematic."[42]

Bolton set the tone for the conference when he announced several "redlines" across which the United States would not step in negotiations. Many of the subsequent discussions boiled down to the United States taking a defensive stance while other member states maneuvered for compromise, which was not forthcoming from the US delegation. The Clinton-era negotiators had agreed to a number of provisions for the draft "Programme" that Bolton's team rejected, including restrictions on "legal trade and manufacturing" ("The vast majority of arms transfers in the world are routine and not problematic," Bolton said); promotion of gun control advocacy; limits on civilian ownership of firearms, which would mean "abrogating the Constitutional right to bear arms"; prohibitions on sales to nonstate actors; and finally, a mandatory review conference, which would only "institutionalize and bureaucratize this process" that the Bush administration so clearly resented.[43]

Two of these redlines especially revealed the extent to which the ideology of the mid-twentieth-century gun rights movement had become US government policy in the early twenty-first. First, not only did the Bush administration reject outright any suggestion that civilian gun ownership ought to be limited, but it also proposed language that would globalize the individual-rights inter-pretation of the Second Amendment. Bolton suggested changing the language of the draft "Programme" to "establish the principle of the legitimacy of the legal trade, manufacturing and possession of small arms and light weapons"— such language would, in fact, go beyond the Second Amendment, which, even in its most expansive interpretations, said nothing about commerce.[44] The statement represented a merging of gun capitalism with Second Amendment fetishism.

Second, US resistance to prohibitions on sales to nonstate actors could, on the one hand, be interpreted as an assertion of national sovereignty by a superpower with an extensive post-1945 track record of supplying arms to antigovernment insurgencies; on the other hand, it was an expression of the idea that not just Americans but all free people or people aspiring to freedom had a right to armed self-defense. Limiting international sales solely to govern-ments "would preclude assistance to an oppressed non-state group defending itself from a genocidal government," Bolton claimed. "Distinctions between governments and non-governments are irrelevant in determining respon-sible and irresponsible end-users of arms," he concluded.[45] In other words, gun ownership was a universal human right, independent of state sovereignty. Bolton's claim called into question the legitimacy of the UN process, and even the legitimacy of states themselves—if a state can't deny or limit its people access to the tools of violence, how can it maintain a monopoly on legitimate violence? There were radical subtexts lurking beneath Bolton's statement.

Member states had expected the new Bush administration to take a recalci-trant stance toward the UN process. But Bolton's forceful speech caused wide-spread disappointment among those hoping the conference would nonetheless produce real solutions. Delegates from other member states described it as "undiplomatic" and "un-UN-like." In addition to rejecting several provisions that the Clinton administration had agreed to in the 1999 preparatory meeting, the hardline US opposition to some of the conference's central goals gave cover to countries like Russia, China, and India, which also opposed many of these goals for a variety of geopolitical reasons but had not wanted to defy international consensus so openly. The United States "ended up becoming silent partners with China, Cuba, and other 'rogue' states, rather than working with its closest allies," wrote one arms policy analyst.[46]

Critics saw the gun lobby behind Bolton's remarks. "The Bush administration might as well have sent Charlton Heston," said a *New York Times* editorial, accusing Bolton of "faithfully follow[ing] the NRA script." The paper of record sharply condemned this "American Retreat on Small Arms."[47] When asked afterward if the initial US position he outlined was too uncompromising and if it neglected the fact that any consensus statement from the conference would be nonbinding, Bolton replied, "From little acorns, bad treaties grow."[48]

An additional explanation for US intransigence came in the debate over the use of the phrase "excessive and destabilizing accumulation." Its repetition became, in the words of the *Small Arms Survey*, a "code for addressing the legal acquisition, production, and transfer of these weapons," which had been a Bolton redline. The phrase expressed global critiques of unrestricted gun capitalism. Just two years earlier, the Clinton administration had not objected to it.[49] But the Bush administration read the phrase differently. To Bolton's team, it implied that there was such a thing as too many guns in a society, a point gun capitalism could never concede, least of all to the United Nations, bête noire of gun rights nationalists. The final *Programme* used the phrase twice, but in both instances the document made clear that that it was the "excessive and destabilizing accumulation" of *illicit* weapons in conflict zones that posed a danger, and it included a footnote that pointed to an earlier document in which the phrase's meaning was debated at length.[50] Gun radicalism in the United States now shaped the language other countries could use to describe their own problems.

THE CONFERENCE NEVER recovered from Bolton's initial blow. The US redlines dictated the next two weeks of negotiations and ultimately watered down the final *Programme of Action to Prevent, Combat and Eradicate the Illicit Trade in Small Arms and Light Weapons in All Its Aspects* signed at the end of the conference. On the conference's final day the United States stood alone (though with tacit, unspoken support from a number of "rogue" states) against two points in the draft "Programme": one on civilian ownership of firearms and another on sales to nonstate actors. A bloc of African states insisted on the inclusion of these two points—their countries suffered most from the post–Cold War proliferation of SALW—but in the dawn hours of July 21 the states agreed to drop resistance for the sake of consensus. In exchange, conference president Camilo Reyes of Colombia described the African states' objections in a public statement, which expressed "disappointment over the Conference's inability to agree, due to the concerns of one State, on language recognizing the need to establish and maintain controls over private ownership of these deadly weapons and the need for preventing sales of such arms to non-State groups."[51]

Assessing the conference's achievements, or lack thereof, Human Rights Watch spoke for many once-hopeful NGOs when it called the resulting document a "Program of Inaction." The group argued that the conference failed to address "state responsibility for weapons proliferation" and focused too much on the illicit trade. "Many delegates have tried to single out shadowy gunrunners as the chief culprits," Human Rights Watch said, "while neglecting the governmental role in supplying the weapons used to commit atrocities." "Whether the fact of international measures undertaken . . . reduced the net global stockpile by even a single gun is highly questionable," said political scientist Aaron Karp.[52] Follow-up meetings and conferences failed to produce any substantive action, as they remained hamstrung by the US insistence that debate focus exclusively on the illicit trade in firearms. "The glass is still 95 percent empty," said IANSA director Rebecca Peters in 2008.[53] Eventually, in 2013, UN member states signed a watered-down Arms Trade Treaty, but by 2019 President Donald Trump had already withdrawn the United States from participation.[54]

Controversy at the conference had hinged on the inherent nature of firearms: Were they, regardless of legal status, fundamentally dangerous and destabilizing to human societies? Most member states said yes, but the most powerful member state insisted they were not—thus, at root, the disagreement over the "excessive and destabilizing accumulation" phrase. It was not just constitutional objections that drove US resistance. Global gun capitalism also figured. After all, the Second Amendment was not a statement of market freedoms. Yet one of the two primary US objections concerned the ability to manufacture and sell guns freely to anyone, anywhere, regardless of state laws and borders. Ultimately it was intransigence on this issue that prevented, and continues to prevent, any global action to limit the international trade in firearms, legal or illicit. Gun capitalism and gun culture, embodied in gun

radicalism, were mutually constitutive. The Second Amendment did not produce the unparalleled US gun market; on the contrary, the largely unregulated
and singular gun market generated a new influential interpretation of the Second Amendment that persists today.

AT THE UN SALW CONFERENCE, the NRA's posture was essentially defensive:
the organization aimed to prevent the adoption of a resolution or treaty that
might affect the US gun industry or culture of gun ownership in any meaningful way. To do so it urged the Bush administration to tap into the language
of national sovereignty and security while, ironically, challenging the state's
authority to regulate the tools of violence domestically. But the NRA also
played offense internationally in the years after Yoshi's killing. The group targeted its message to the Anglophone world in particular in an effort to globalize the insurgent right-wing interpretation of the Second Amendment as an
inalienable and unrestricted individual right to keep and bear arms independent of service in a militia. Such an offensive linked the domestic and international spheres. To fire up its most committed supporters, the NRA asserted
that the UN's international SALW process would increase pressure for SALW
control—or "gun control"—at home.[55]

The NRA attempted to establish an overseas beachhead in, among other
places, Australia, a country that shared a history of white settler colonialism.
Hunting and shooting sports had long been popular traditions there. But in
1996, when a man armed with military-style firearms murdered thirty-five
people in the small Tasmanian town of Port Arthur, conservative prime minister John Howard acted decisively. He coordinated with Australia's states to
establish uniform laws prohibiting most firearms, requiring registration of permitted ones, and initiating a buyback program that would ultimately remove
700,000 guns from civilian hands. (Like the United States, Australia has a
federal system of government that required coordination with state governments.) Howard faced a right-wing backlash, but he and his conservative coalition weathered it. Their policies proved widely popular in a country where,
despite vast rural regions, 60 percent of the population lived in an urban area.
Before Port Arthur, Australia had been the only other large democracy with
few restrictions on ownership. Now the United States stood alone.[56]

The NRA started funneling money to its Australian counterpart, the Sports
Shooters Association of Australia (along with its New Zealand affiliate), in the
early 1990s. In 1992 the association's director spoke at the NRA's national convention, and thereafter the US organization provided funds for the Australians to establish an equivalent of the NRA's Institute for Legislative Action,

its explicit lobbying arm. The NRA's longtime marketing agency, Ackerman-McQueen, visited Australia in the late 1990s to help craft advertising for the Sports Shooters Association. One result, a television commercial titled "Global Gun Grabbers," claimed that Australia was "awash in criminal violence" as a result of the firearms restrictions imposed after the Port Arthur massacre. The ad implied that Australians petitioning for tougher sentencing guidelines for violent crimes also opposed gun restrictions, prompting a rebuke from petitioners who had appeared in the commercial but who had no interest in pro-gun lobbying. The Australian attorney general wrote Charlton Heston to say that there were "many things Australians can learn" from the United States but "how to manage firearm ownership is not one of them." "Don't let me get on my high kangaroo, but they're doing us wrong," one Australian diplomat told *Salon*. "The fact is, we're not a gun culture like yours."[57]

Just a month before the massacre in Port Arthur, a gunman walked into a primary school in the small town of Dunblane, Scotland, and used four handguns to murder sixteen children and one teacher. As in Australia, the political reaction in the United Kingdom was swift and decisive: within months, the Conservative government introduced a bill that would ban all handguns above .22 caliber and limit the remnants to sporting clubs. The country already had restrictive gun laws—gun owners were required to obtain from police officials a firearms certificate that had to be renewed every five years, though reports indicated that 99 percent of applications were approved pro forma, including the Dunblane killer's. The new restrictive post-Dunblane law went into effect in 1998 and made about 70 percent of legally owned handguns illegal overnight.[58] Gun deaths across the United Kingdom declined from 247 in 1996 to 107 twenty years later.[59]

Great Britain had its own variant of the "gun lobby," though it was hardly as influential and entrenched in national politics as its American counterpart. A mass shooting in the town of Hungerford in 1987 had prompted a previous wave of gun control sentiment, but the most significant proposed reforms had been blocked by the firearms lobby, which managed to put "firearms safety" and "safer shooting" on the political agenda rather than gun control. The most prominent gun rights organizations included the British Association for Shooting and Conservation (the largest, with 115,000 members), the British Shooting Sports Council, the National Rifle Association (unlike its American namesake, concerned exclusively with rifle competitions), and the "shadowy" Shooters' Rights Association, an organization that popped up after the Hungerford massacre and was led by Jan Stevenson, an Alabama-born graduate of Yale and Oxford, firearms expert, and editor of *Handgunner, Ltd.* magazine.[60]

Such groups recycled the rhetoric of the US gun lobby. "You cannot legis-late for someone who goes off his mind," said one organization leader after Hungerford. In a "carefully-orchestrated campaign" of harassment that would have made the American NRA blush, British pro-gun groups generated out-rage when they published the names and telephone numbers of civil servants working to write new legislation. But the public outcry after Dunblane proved insurmountable. Perhaps the most convincing argument, which spanned the political spectrum, was that the British should not become like their American cousins. Commentators fired off pithy reflections. "The aim of any new laws, speedily introduced," wrote Andrew Neil in the *Sunday Times* just days after the shooting, "should be to place ourselves at the opposite end of the spectrum in this regard from the United States." "Nothing resembling the pollution of the country by firearms, in the fashion so familiar in the United States," said the conservative *Daily Telegraph*, "can be tolerated here." "If we want to import the American way of life," a former British cabinet minister said, "we've got to come to terms with the American way of death." Scotland's *Daily Record* described the American NRA as "sinister" and made up of "thousands of right-wing lunatics" who were "happy to stick their noses into Britain's business."[61]

Expansion into the Americas seemed a natural step for the NRA. Since the 1990s the organization has made inroads into Canadian gun politics, which included material support for one of its counterparts, the Canadian Sports Shooting Association. The NRA was "instrumental" in helping launch the Canadian Institute for Legislative Action, modeled on the NRA-ILA, after the 1989 murder of fourteen women at the École Polytechnique in Montreal had led to a groundswell of support for tighter restrictions on guns. NRA executive vice-president Wayne LaPierre boasted in 2010 that the NRA hoped Canada might serve as a test case for initiating pro-gun campaigns in other countries. Canadians were generally less sanguine. "The National Rifle Association is one American export Canada does not want," said Prime Minister Jean Chrétien in 1999.[62]

The hemisphere's second-most populous country, Brazil, also witnessed NRA incursions. Plagued by their own gun violence crisis—through most of the twenty-first century, only Brazil has topped the United States in total gun deaths globally—Brazilian legislators introduced a series of gun control mea-sures beginning in the late 1990s. Brazilian conservatives linked up with the NRA to map a pro-gun response. In 2003 NRA-ILA director Charles Cun-ningham toured Brazil and spoke to the National Association of Gun Owners and Retailers, Brazil's NRA equivalent, and the Society for the Defense of Tra-dition, Family and Property, a far-right Catholic association that established a pro-gun group called Pro Legítima Defesa. "We view Brazil as the opening salvo for the global gun control movement," NRA spokesperson Andrew Arulanandam said. "If gun control proponents succeed in Brazil, America will be next."[63]

Coming full circle, Wayne LaPierre denounced Canada's "irreversible ratchet" of gun control in a March 2010 *American Rifleman* column. On the page opposite the article was an advertisement from Brazil's largest gunmaker, Taurus, offering a free one-year NRA membership with the purchase of a handgun.[64]

The NRA's Anglophone and Americas initiatives were part of a campaign to build an international coalition to provide a stamp of global legitimacy to the NRA's anti-UN drive, some cover to which it could point when critics accused it of trashing multinational arms control in the name of American exceptionalism. In 1997 the NRA spearheaded the establishment of the World Forum on the Future of Sport Shooting Activities, a coalition of twenty-one pro-gun groups from eleven countries, to be headquartered not in the United States but in Belgium. The new organization held one of its first meetings on the second anniversary of the Dunblane massacre. As NRA lobbyist Metaksa explained it, "When guns are being confiscated in Australia and Britain—nations which once shared a tradition of gun ownership, hunting and shooting—NRA members must stand shoulder to shoulder to defend the Second Amendment."[65] There was no Second Amendment equivalent in Australia or the United Kingdom, of course. But the rhetorical shift was telling: Metaksa and the NRA now portrayed the individual rights they imagined inherent in the Second Amendment to be global civil rights, not just exceptional American rights. It was a notable shift from the 1960s, when pro-gun activists claimed that the Second Amendment was what made the United States exceptional, but Metaksa's revisionism would be crucial to counter what the NRA saw as the anti-gun propaganda proliferating globally through the UN process.

THE 2001 UN CONFERENCE HIGHLIGHTED the nascent global movement to address SALW proliferation and the NRA's determined effort to quash it. But the momentum for concerted international action quickly dissipated that fall with the attacks of September 11, 2001, and the bellicose US military response.[66] The actual weapons of mass destruction of the 1990s, which killed hundreds of thousands of people around the world annually, gave way to the "WMDs" of the Bush administration's Global War on Terror imagination. After 9/11, the US military would export American gun culture and the Second Amendment to Iraq. When the Bush administration launched an invasion in

March 2003, Iraqi dictator Saddam Hussein gave the invaders what gun rights extremists in the United States had practically prayed for since the 1960s: a population armed to the teeth and ready to resist an invading and occupying foreign army. Right-wing Cold War fantasies of an armed insurgency against a Soviet invasion played out in real time, only it was US troops who experienced the consequences—not to mention the people of Iraq, who suffered 200,000 deaths in the violence and countless more wounds and pervasive misery.[67] The US military exported gun culture in ways the NRA hadn't yet been able to do.

There was no better illustration of the discrepancy between WMD fantasies and the reality of small arms violence than the 2003 US invasion of Iraq. The Bush administration ordered the invasion under the pretext that Hussein harbored chemical, biological, and nuclear weapons. In a post-9/11 world, as Bush's national security adviser Condoleezza Rice famously put it, "We don't want the smoking gun to be a mushroom cloud."[68] UN weapons inspectors insisted that Iraq had no such programs. The administration countered that Hussein had figured out how to hide his WMDs from the eyes of the world and all would be uncovered when US forces and a handful of allies—the "Coalition of the Willing," as Bush dubbed it—arrived. While they focused on WMDs, however, US war planners failed to anticipate Hussein's tremendous stockpiles of conventional weapons, including many millions of SALW that quickly flooded into post-Hussein Iraq, resulting in actual mass destruction on a scale the Bush administration hadn't imagined and couldn't control. "In place of an exceptionally well-armed state," wrote the *Small Arms Survey* a year after the invasion, "the world must now deal with a heavily-armed society."[69]

Rather than a mushroom cloud, then, it would be the ever-present report of AK-47s that represented Iraq's descent into chaos.

In anticipation of the invasion, Hussein's military and security forces had scattered arms stockpiles across the country. The Iraqi dictator hoped that caches of SALW would provide the fuel to sustain a protracted popular guerrilla war against invading forces. And there was, by any measure, an extraordinary number of SALW stockpiled. As they fanned out through the country in the spring of 2003, US forces uncovered weapons caches that "dwarfed any reasonable conventional combat doctrine" and had been stashed in "every conceivable place," from mosques to schools to hospitals, according to a history written by a US Army Corps of Engineers unit tasked with collecting and destroying this incredible bounty of munitions.[70] "Many of the caches were spread across large areas virtually impossible for units to physically secure," says one study from the US Army War College, "and the sheer volume of munitions was equally daunting."[71] The *Small Arms Survey* estimated that the

Iraqi Army alone had stockpiled 4.2 million firearms—perhaps as many as ten guns for each Iraqi Army regular in 2003—all of which fell into the hands of Iraqi civilians when Hussein's regime collapsed.[72]

Once US troops started uncovering munitions sites throughout the country they quickly realized they didn't have enough personnel to both carry out the combat mission and attend to these "overwhelming" stockpiles. "There is more ammunition in Iraq than any place I've ever been in my life," CENTCOM commander Gen. John P. Abizaid told a Senate committee in September 2003, "and it is not all securable." Invading forces didn't have enough troops to guard discovered caches, let alone to dispose of them in such a way that they didn't do precisely what Hussein wanted them to do: fuel an insurgency. North of Baghdad one company of Marines captured a large storage site, nearly a square kilometer in size, with more than fifty concrete structures filled with arms and ammunition. "Literally just within this facility," said the Marine commander, "there is enough ammunition to supply a small army." One US official believed that as many as fifty similar sites existed unsecured throughout Iraq. "The whole country was an armed camp," said Lt. Gen. David McKiernan. "There were weapons and ammunition storage sites everywhere in Iraq."[73]

The United States had, in fact, discovered weapons of mass destruction, just not the ones it was looking for, the headline-grabbing biological, chemical, and nuclear weapons that administration officials warned of for months in advance of the invasion. The weapons were, instead, conventional, and some of them quite old—ammunition, for instance, that dated to 1944—but which, when distributed to millions of Iraqis living under a collapsed state, caused a specific and unanticipated sort of mass destruction. The *Small Arms Survey* described the dumping of SALW into Iraqi society after March 2003 as "the single most significant small arms stockpile transfer the world has known." The Geneva-based publication estimated conservatively that 8 million firearms flooded Iraqi society in 2003, and once Hussein's stockpiles ran dry in 2004, black-market arms from Iran and Syria continued to refresh supply to meet unquenchable demand. Gun ownership was not unheard of in prewar Iraq, though it was, for most people, prohibitively expensive, requiring a $150 government-issued license, and confined mostly to the privileged Sunni minority. Street crime was unknown under the Hussein regime. Now, 8 million firearms in a country of 25 million citizens made Iraq suddenly well armed, even if not exceptionally so on a global scale, equivalent to about one-third of US ownership rates at the time. Still, as the *Survey* concluded, "Where Iraq stands out most is not in the magnitude of its public stockpile so much as the suddenness with which it fell upon a fragile society."[74] In contrast to the United

States, where gun owners had been stockpiling firearms for decades in a relatively stable society, Iraq experienced a run on stockpiles precisely because Iraqis expected or intended to use the weapons they found there. Indeed, it was Hussein's plan.

In some ways, the situation in Iraq in 2003 was just what right-wing gun rights advocates had asked for. In 1998 economist John R. Lott had published *More Guns, Less Crime*, a provocative book that argued that those places in the United States with the fewest restrictions on gun ownership had the lowest rates of crime and vice versa. It was, to be sure, an argument that found an eager audience of gun rights activists, if also a skeptical one among many social scientists. Now Lott turned his expertise to occupied Iraq. In May 2003, Paul Bremer, the head of the US-led Coalition Provisional Authority (CPA), declared that Iraqis could keep firearms like AK-47s in their homes so long as they didn't bring them out in public without a weapons permit issued by the CPA. He also ordered that Iraqis turn in a host of other kinds of weapons that were now deemed illegal. The deadline passed in June with few Iraqis eager to hand over their weapons. Lott saw this development as a positive one. More armed Iraqis would mean a safer Iraq. Echoing popular gun rights arguments back to the 1960s, Lott claimed that "disarming law-abiding citizens actually increases crime and encourages criminals to attack because they have less to worry about." US troops would be safer in an Iraq where "law-abiding citizens" armed with machine guns could defend themselves against "bands of thugs," who would think twice about roaming the streets of Baghdad in search of victims. Only "law-abiding citizens" comply with gun bans—by definition—and not the "terrorists and Ba'ath Party members whom our troops should be concerned about."[75]

Lott translated the rhetoric of the gun rights movement since the 1960s, built around a radical interpretation of the Second Amendment, into Iraq's postinvasion context. Bremer and the CPA, installed in power by the pro-gun Bush administration, did much of the same, permitting fully automatic AK-47s to be stashed in homes for self-protection, something "law-abiding citizens" in the United States couldn't do—Americans couldn't even purchase a semiautomatic version of such a weapon in 2003, since they had been removed from the market by the 1994 Assault Weapons Ban. Of course, those AK-47s left Iraqi homes all the time, and they found their way into the hands of not only criminals but also insurgents, militia members, and a whole host of anti-US and antioccupation groups. Black-market prices for looted firearms fluctuated wildly once the regime collapsed but settled around $100–$200 for an AK-47 a few months later. Coalition officials only started to make the connection between increasing rates of political violence and the wide availability of firearms and other munitions in the fall of 2003. They read street prices for AK-47s like tea leaves, attempting to foretell planned insurgent offensives. Six months after the invasion many weapons caches remained unguarded, providing a cornucopia for insurgents, especially those crafty enough to build improvised explosive devices "made with ammunition and ordnance from Hussein's arsenal that have been 'daisy-chained' together." Press reports described black-market arms dealers who had been among the criminals Hussein freed from Iraqi prisons in anticipation of the invasion. "People have no jobs; they have no money," a former Hussein regime insider told a journalist. "But the Americans just let them loot the weapons."[76]

Bremer's rationale for a permissive firearms policy was that the invasion had unleashed a wave of criminal activity that took advantage of the collapse of authority, and "tougher restrictions would be unfair to the law-abiding majority." But many Iraqi officials cooperating with the Americans regretted the decision. "We'd be a lot better off if we didn't let people keep AK-47s in their homes," explained a police chief in a large district of Baghdad. "Under the old regime, there were a lot fewer guns in private hands, and that made our job easier and safer."[77] Even Iraqis eager for guns recognized that living by the gun was no way of life. One sixty-seven-year-old Baghdadi who'd never owned a gun and suddenly found himself with an AK-47 told the Los Angeles Times that when he felt safe again "I will throw out my Kalashnikov. But not until then."[78]

JUST AS THE IRAQ INSURGENCY MATERIALIZED, two legislative developments back home paved the way for the capitalism-driven militarization of gun culture. First was the 2004 expiration of the Federal Assault Weapons Ban, which, when it passed in 1994, had included a ten-year sunset provision to placate the NRA. The AWB stood no chance of renewal under a Republican-controlled House of Representatives and executive branch. Studies showed the AWB had done little to affect gun violence in the aggregate.[79] Mass shootings declined—the effort to pass the AWB began in response to the horrific 1989 mass shooting at a schoolyard in Stockton, California, carried out with a semiautomatic AK-47—but mass shootings were at the time (and remain) rare enough to have little effect on overall gun violence statistics, never accounting for more than a few hundred deaths out of more than 30,000 annually. The AWB targeted "military-style" firearms, an amorphous category that distinguished certain semiautomatic firearms from others less by their mechanics or lethality and more by cosmetic characteristics: a rifle with the appearance of a traditional hunting weapon might function in precisely the same ways as one with, say, a pistol grip and barrel shroud, the latter marked only by its intimidating "military-style" appearance. (The exception among the AWB's provisions was an important ban on "high-capacity magazines" that held more than ten rounds.) It was, in the words of legal scholar Adam Winkler, a "triumph of symbolism over substance."[80]

The AWB followed logically from the gun control efforts of the 1970s, which had focused on the relative aesthetic characteristics of handguns rather than on their absolute lethality. The "Saturday Night Special" was as nebulous a category as "assault weapons," saying more about perceptions of the user (poor, criminal, "urban," that is, Black) than the functions or utility of the firearm. In both cases—and in virtually all cases of "gun control" since the 1960s—the legislative goal was to define a virtuous gun user against an imagined unvirtuous one. The "law-abiding citizen" stood opposite the criminal, the child, the mentally ill, the terrorist. Liberals have long scoffed at the old gun lobby saw, "Guns don't kill people; people kill people," but the gun laws they've crafted for more than a half century have in fact been premised on that very idea. Laws that aim to keep guns out of the hands of the "wrong people," rather than out of the hands of people—period—are laws that proceed from the gun lobby's own argument that guns are simply tools to be wielded to constructive or destructive ends. Guns in the hands of the virtuous don't kill people; the unvirtuous use guns to kill people.

While the expiration of the AWB removed one mild restriction on gun capitalism, the 2005 Protection of Lawful Commerce in Arms Act (PLCAA) freed gun manufacturers from legal responsibility when their firearms were used to harm or kill. As early as the 1970s, the Chicago-area Committee for Handgun Control had debated suing handgun manufacturers for their products working as intended, that is, effectively maiming and killing human beings. The CHC ran out of money before it could pursue the idea, but it was an innovative way of approaching guns as a consumer problem: throughout the twentieth century activists had sought to use legislation and the courts to hold manufacturers accountable for unintentional injury and death resulting from dangerous ingredients or unsafe design, but in the case of guns, injury and death were the intended outcomes of a consumer product functioning as intended—a feature, not a bug. In the 1990s a number of cities, including Chicago, pressed lawsuits against gun manufacturers for flooding their streets with deadly weapons. The goals ranged from seeking compensation for gun violence victims to pressuring manufacturers to design firearms with more safety features and even attempting to bankrupt gunmakers with mountains of legal fees.[81]

In 2005 the Republican Congress and president, believing that such lawsuits attempted an end-around on legislation, came to the aid of the gun industry.

The PLCAA put a stop to most of the lawsuits that threatened gunmakers. Coupled with the expiration of the AWB, it couldn't have come at a more opportune moment. While plenty of manufacturers found loopholes within the AWB that allowed them to sell modified models of banned weapons—often with the letters "AB" in the model name, to designate "after ban," a process the industry described as "sporterization," the word Sam Cummings had used fifty years earlier—the AWB's expiration opened new possibilities for the unabashed marketing of "assault rifles" in the age of the Global War on Terror.[82] No gun would come to symbolize that shift more than the AR-15.

IT'S BETTER TO THINK of the AR-15 not as one specific firearm but as a platform upon which infinite variations of "assault rifles" can be built. That is its primary appeal as a consumer product, even if its appeal as a cultural icon remains the inextricable link with its use in militarized police units and the global US military adventures of the twenty-first century. "It's the most universal rifle platform that's ever been manufactured," said a gunmaker in Idaho. "Because there is such a standardized way it's been built, it can be reconfigured very easily."[83] The AR-15 is infinitely customizable, and a booming industry of manufacturers stand at the ready to supply countless modifications that allow owners to feel like they've built a special weapon all their own. They're "Lego sets for anyone old enough to shoot a machine designed for offensive military operations," in the words of a former industry insider; others in the industry referred to the AR-15 as the "Barbie doll of guns" because of the marketing of a multitude of mix-and-match accessories.[84] As a consumer subculture, then, AR-15s are not all that different from car culture or motorcycle culture or computer culture or even the high-stakes Beanie Baby subculture of the 1990s. This powerful consumerist appeal is one reason why the NRA calls the AR-15 "America's Rifle." It is the preferred rifle of the American consumer-citizen playacting as a citizen-soldier.

In that sense, the AR-15's connection to militarized popular culture and consumerism should not be underestimated. The post-9/11 burst of jingoism and the US invasions of Afghanistan and Iraq created a civilian appetite for stories of military adventure and heroism, which the booming video game industry, aided by exponentially increasing computer processing firepower, sought to fill. The expiration of the AWB and the passage of the PLCAA then unleashed an industry eager to market guns to young men who first encountered them in virtual worlds. Millions of gamers learned to identify the profiles and functions of dozens of contemporary military firearms from games like *Call of Duty 4: Modern Warfare* (2007), which sold 17 million copies, more than doubling the sales of its Second World War–themed predecessors. In

total, games in the series would sell hundreds of millions of copies.[85] Even
the US military produced a video game, *America's Army* (2002), intended as a
recruiting tool, that introduced players to virtual versions of the real firearms
US troops carried into combat.[86]

The twenty-first century witnessed a perfect storm of racialized gun capitalism: perpetual fear of terrorists and foreign others; endless overseas wars;
the end of the ban on assault rifles and companion legislation to protect companies that marketed them as instruments of militarized personal violence;
a stream of entertainment that fetishized weapons of war; and, in the 2010s,
the popular resurgence of the Black freedom movement in the form of Black
Lives Matter.[87] It all came at the right time for the gun industry too: the civilian
firearms market in the United States had been slumping since the 1980s due in
large part to market saturation among a shrinking segment of the US population. Crime rates had declined precipitously since the early 1990s. Without a
crime panic, fewer people saw the need for a gun in the home for self-defense;
the ratio of Americans who lived in a home with a gun dropped from one-half
in 1980 to one-third in 2010.[88] The most enthusiastic gun buyers were people who already owned guns. The industry needed product innovation and
new marketing strategies. In marketing language, it needed to shift from a
"push" model, in which products were pushed out to meet to demand, to a
"pull" model, in which appealing new products and marketing could pull in
new customers.[89]

The industry's approach, as the Violence Policy Center described it, was to
"generate demand with new and more lethal designs." "Find a market, show
them something they need and why they need it, give 'em a good price, and
they'll buy it from you," said Massad Ayoob, a longtime gun rights writer. "Capitalism in action."[90] Military-style firearms would do the trick. The industry
advertised its explicit military connections in order to turn those couch commandos into rifle owners. "As close as you can get without enlisting," boasted
an advertisement for the pricey FN SCAR 16S. "Defending homeland security
is more critical than ever no matter how you define the word home," said an ad
for a Benelli "tactical" shotgun. "Iraq. Afghanistan. Your living room."[91]

"Tactical" became the industry's codeword for military-style weapons and
accessories. There were endless variety of tactical firearms, of course, but there
were also tactical vests, tactical pants, tactical knives, tactical pens—even tactical baby gear, for the new father on the go who might need to change dia-
pers and defend against a terrorist attack. The "tactical" industry had gone to
such excess that it earned the epithet "tacticool" and an assortment of internet

memes to mock the superfluous militarization of consumer products marketed to men.[92]

But the tacticool joke obscured the deeper rot of the new "tactical gun culture," as the philosopher Chad Kautzer labels it. The pervasiveness of tactical weapons, gear, and language had blurred the lines between gun owners and soldiers—between citizen-consumers and citizen-soldiers—with many of the former "increasingly seeing themselves as de facto militia members regardless of whether they engage in paramilitary training." Kautzer identifies the mass shift from arming for self-defense to arming in defense of the Constitution and abstract notions of freedom. The emergence of a tactical gun culture has been "fueled by an individualist notion of sovereignty more dangerous than any military-grade weaponry."[93]

Fulfilling that fantasy of individual sovereignty, however, remains contingent on access to the military-grade weaponry the consumer market provides. There is a justifiable tendency to see the "tacticool" phenomenon as something qualitatively new in American gun culture. As material objects increasingly occupying public space, guns provoke singularly visceral emotions. But the consumer fascination with military-grade weaponry is hardly new to the twenty-first century. Sam Cummings, Arms Dealer Sam, his warehouses housing mountains of Mausers, Carcanos, and more, understood that obsession more than seventy years ago.

EPILOGUE

THIS AMERICAN CARNAGE

IN HIS INAUGURAL ADDRESS on January 20, 2017, Donald Trump conjured a dystopian vision of America in the twenty-first century: inescapable urban poverty, a crumbling industrial sector, a failing education system, "and the crime, and the gangs, and the drugs that have stolen too many lives." Commentators chose a variety of adjectives to capture the essence of Trump's vision: dark, grim, bleak, violent, apocalyptic. "This American carnage stops right here and stops right now," the new president warned.[1]

In the days and months and years to come, critics observed the ironies of that most notable of neologisms, "American carnage." Assessing the speech and several subsequent Trump statements, the *Washington Post* awarded Trump three out of four Pinocchios for inaccurate claims about recent shootings and rising urban crime rates.[2] A few cities—Chicago especially, a minor obsession for Trump and, relatedly, home of Barack Obama—had seen terrible spikes in gun violence in the two years before Trump's inauguration. But nationally, violent crime rates had plummeted since their peak in the early 1990s, when a Baton Rouge homeowner worried about criminals lurking in every shadow shot and killed Yoshi Hattori. Depending on what and how you measured, the America that had elected Donald Trump was experiencing crime rates as low as they had been in more than fifty years, since the beginning of the "Great American Gun War," as the eminent economist Philip J. Cook described it.[3] New York City, the onetime national capital of violent crime in the 1970s and bête noire of conservative gun rights activists—who claim restrictive gun laws are counterproductive—approached record-low homicide rates.[4]

The decline in violent crime puzzled criminologists. Nearly a half century after he coordinated research on the Eisenhower Commission's pathbreaking Firearms Task Force, Franklin Zimring described it as a "surprise," one still poorly understood decades after it began. None of the experts had seen it coming, and it was several years before anyone noticed. Political scientist John J. DiIulio had infamously imagined a generation of young Black men who would kill wantonly and remorselessly, with "no respect for human life and no sense of the future," yet he coined the "superpredator" archetype to describe this generation in 1995, when rates of urban crime had already started falling.[5]

When gun sales began to climb in the early 2000s, it was in a very different context. Sales had spiked in the late 1960s and early 1970s because of fears of crime and urban uprisings, but in the twenty-first century gun capitalism would push on consumers visions of social war in more explicit terms than ever. The first postwar decades had witnessed gunowners buying up literal castoff weapons of war, with the perennial possibility of the Cold War going hot, and with anxieties about social conflict and race war looming on the horizon. A half century later gun capitalism all but asked its customers to enlist. The 2004 expiration of the Assault Weapons Ban and the 2005 passage of the Protection of Lawful Commerce in Arms Act came just as American television screens and internet feeds were flooded with images of US soldiers carrying the latest in military firepower and sartorial chic. The industry started tooling up to meet consumer demand for "black rifles." Despite the low crime rates, gun sales boomed in the Bush years on the back of the "tactical" revolution in the gun industry.

Then, in 2008, a young Black senator from Illinois stormed onto the political scene, claiming the Democratic nomination and the presidency, and becoming what former Kimber Manufacturing executive Ryan Busse called the "best gun salesman in America." By the time Obama left office in 2017, the industry could thank him for 101 million sales tallied, a 75 percent increase over the eight years of the Bush administration, a figure equal to perhaps as much as 40 percent of the entire civilian firearms stockpile in 2001. The largest jump came in the aftermath of the 2012 killings at Sandy Hook Elementary, where a man used a Bushmaster AR-style rifle to murder twenty children and six adults.[6] Rather than flinch at the carnage and reflect on what the gun country had wrought, buyers flocked to gun stores and sellers met them eagerly.

Ironically, the surprise election of a presidential candidate who openly courted the NRA and espoused its culture war rhetoric as none had done before was responsible for the so-called "Trump slump" in gun sales.[7] Gunmakers had saturated the market with AR-15s and other "black rifles" during the Obama years, and though buying accelerated in 2016 as a Hillary Clinton victory looked likely, fears of violent crime remained at historic lows.[8] With no chance of new gun control bills getting signed into law, the market suffered a 17 percent drop in 2017. It was hard to see it as a coincidence that the NRA escalated its culture war rhetoric at that very moment, launching aggressive, pro-Trump, right-wing programming on its new television network, NRATV, and promoting confrontational culture war celebrities, like Dana Loesch, who produced inflammatory recruiting ads that looked like, in the words of the *Washington Post*, "an excerpt from North Korean state television railing against the evil Americans."[9]

As Trump's administration unfolded, gun capitalism continued to bob and weave around mild regulations and laws that recognized the basic legitimacy of the civilian consumer market for firearms. The deadliest mass shooting by a single shooter in US history took place in October 2017, when a gunman rained down more than a thousand rounds on a concert crowd from a hotel window in Las Vegas, killing 58 and injuring more than 500.[10] Just weeks later another gunman killed 26 worshippers in a church in Sutherland Springs, Texas. One online archive of gun violence charted 346 mass shootings in 2017, up from 269 in 2014. That number—an ever-contentious one contingent on different definitional metrics—would increase to 611 by Trump's final year in office. Total gun deaths not including suicide were up 56 percent nationally during the same six-year span.[11] It's difficult to claim that one president or another can directly impact gun violence rates, but Trump explicitly claimed he would do so, and if anything, his violent rhetoric, his open courting of the NRA and gun rights ideologues, and his commitment to placating gun capitalism created more American carnage than they eliminated.

The Las Vegas and Sutherland Springs killings generated the kind of cyclical discourse about gun violence that dated back at least to the 1999 killing of twelve students and one teacher at Columbine High School in Colorado. Critics described the cycle as "Grief. Horror. Inaction."[12] Leaders did take minor action to address the problem at the margins. The Las Vegas shooting prompted a ban on "bump stocks," a niche accessory that allowed the shooter to convert a semiautomatic rifle into an automatic, which could fire at a rate like that of illegal machine guns. But beyond Las Vegas, killings with bump stocks were statistically insignificant. The foundations of gun capitalism remained secure. Gun defenders recycled the "mental health" refrain, which had been used for decades to stigmatize mental illness and distract from the inexorable stockpiling of firearms. "This isn't a guns situation," Trump said of the Texas slaughter, parroting an NRA talking point. "This is a mental health problem at the highest level."[13] But even if there were some truth to that diagnosis, the Trump administration offered no prescription.

In 2018, though, young people arose to find hope in tragedy to break the discursive cycle. In February a gunman killed seventeen people and injured seventeen more at Marjory Stoneman Douglas High School in Parkland, Florida. Student survivors refused to accept the "thoughts and prayers" of politicians, mostly conservatives and Republicans, who had spent decades rejecting and obstructing any effort to restrict access to firearms. President Trump, quoting scripture, said, "I have heard your prayer and seen your tears. I will heal you."[14] But the Parkland students, joined by tens of millions of Americans, refused to believe the president had healing in mind. They wanted significant legislative action. Just a month after the shooting the students, bright and media savvy, organized a "March for Our Lives" demonstration in Washington, DC, and at hundreds of locations around the country. Their movement prompted a few state legislative victories, most notably in pro-gun Florida, though Congress remained deadlocked.[15] The students labored to convert the fleeting energy for reform into a sustained movement.

The murder of nineteen children and two teachers in the small town of Uvalde, Texas, in May 2022 generated so much outrage and grief that a few Republicans finally decided to respond to Democratic entreaties for bipartisan "gun safety" negotiations. President Joe Biden signed into law legislation that offered no new ideas for reining in gun capitalism but instead sought to strengthen existing gun control regimes, with enhanced background checks for buyers under twenty-one, new money for mental health services and crisis intervention, and more obstacles to gun purchases for convicted domestic abusers. "We've finally moved that mountain," Biden said, calling out the three decades of inaction and intransigence since the Brady Bill and the Assault Weapons Ban passed, laws he had championed in the Senate three decades earlier and which critics argued did less to reduce gun violence than they did to exacerbate the mass incarceration crisis of the twentieth and twenty-first centuries.[16]

If we might be skeptical of the 2022 law, it is because it falls too neatly within the legacy of federal gun control laws dating back to the 1968 Gun Control Act. In the rare instances when it has acted, Congress has struggled to contain and reduce gun violence because it has legislated around the problem of plenty. Gun capitalism thrives and will continue to thrive because these laws have avoided confronting it. Instead, acquiescing to conservative gun rights ideology and committed to a liberal faith in the regulatory state, lawmakers have sought to define legitimate gun market activity as much as the illegitimate, clearing space for gun capitalism to flourish and expand with the imprimatur of the state. Such political efforts have always accepted the construct of the "law-abiding citizen" as an objective reality rather than a marketing invention, a category to delineate the virtuous from the unvirtuous gun owner, the latter too easily racialized and othered. But neither gun capitalism nor the idea of the "law-abiding citizen" has ever existed in a vacuum. The political and social vicissitudes of postwar America defined their opportunities and limits.

Is it possible to break the cycle of gun consumerism and violence? Any substantive effort to do so must acknowledge the deep roots in the postwar era of our contemporary crisis. There's an irony in saying that: Americans across the political spectrum already believe their gun culture has deep historical roots, buried far down in the soil of the eighteenth and nineteenth centuries. But our guns-everywhere society would not exist without the postwar boom of gun consumerism, just as our fear-everywhere society would not exist without the Cold War and racial anxieties teaching us to fear our neighbors or our government of the people. The postwar world forged the gun country as much as did the eighteenth- and nineteenth-century developments that typically get all the credit.

Even if America always has been and always will be *the* gun country, though, there's nothing natural or inevitable about the kind of gun country it is today. The same postwar forces that produced the gun country also produced Laura Fermi's abolitionist vision and the Committee for Handgun Control's innovative use of gender and consumer identities. Despite the endless cycle of heartbreak and legislative obstruction, tens of millions of Americans continue to organize and fight for change. There is widespread popular support for several "common sense" policies and strategies—rebranded as "gun safety" rather than gun control—including universal background checks, expanded red flag laws, and "violence interrupter" programs.[17] Countries across the globe, like Japan, still offer more concrete solutions, waiting for their American cousins to confront the material reality obscured by myth.

In an American context, these ideas still seem radical. But our twenty-first-century gun politics are already radical, whether we view them from the perspectives of the founders or policymakers just a generation or two ago. My pie-in-the-sky wish list would begin with abolition, a concept that has moved to the center of leftist politics in recent years. Scholars and activists often use it to mean an end to the era of mass incarceration. More broadly it means the abolition of state violence, and that must include the disarmament of police forces. Populations with justifiable suspicion of police would not—and should not—disarm first. Abolition also ought to mean decriminalization. Federal and state gun laws have been as culpable in the mass incarceration crisis as the war on drugs. And decriminalization ought to be accompanied by destigmatization, an admittedly thornier cultural process.

My wish list would also include gun enthusiasts taking the historical Second Amendment seriously. Today's conservative Second Amendment is a product of the consumers' republic of twentieth century, not the founders' republic of the eighteenth. The founders never intended it as a statement of market freedoms and consumer choice. Instead, since the eighteenth century it has outlined a right tied to a duty, despite the Supreme Court's "faux-originalist" decision in *D.C. v. Heller* (2008), which tried to divorce the two.[18] By owning a firearm, you've implicitly signed a compact that the founders wrote for citizen-soldiers, not citizen-consumers. Second Amendment T-shirts are for citizen-consumers. Keeping and bearing arms in some form of a well-regulated militia—registering your firearms with the state, engaging in regular supervised upkeep and training—is for citizen-soldiers.

Meaningful reform is possible, but it will require confronting mythologies and material reality head on. We must stop legislating around the problem of plenty and in the service of historical obfuscation. If the gun country of the postwar era could be made, it can be unmade. Other worlds are possible.

ACKNOWLEDGMENTS

I AM GRATEFUL to the many people who have made writing a book during a global pandemic a less miserable and isolating experience than it otherwise could have been.

Archives are the foundation of this book's material, so I ought to begin with the people who made that possible. My thanks to the archivists and librarians at the following institutions: Hill Memorial Library at Louisiana State University; the Lyndon B. Johnson Library; Archives and Special Collections at the University of Connecticut; the Hannah Holborn Gray Special Collections Research Center at the University of Chicago Library; Special Collections and University Archives at the University of Illinois at Chicago; the John Hay Library at Brown University; the Ohio Congressional Archives at the Ohio State University; the Woodson Regional Library of the Chicago Public Library; the Kenneth Spencer Research Library at the University of Kansas; and Noel Memorial Library at LSU Shreveport. And special thanks to Regina Foster at Prescott Memorial Library at Louisiana Tech University for years of diligent interlibrary loan and scanning assistance.

I'm grateful to colleagues and friends at Louisiana Tech who continue to be supportive and encouraging in the most trying of conditions. David Anderson and John Worsencroft deserve special thanks for having read and commented on almost every word of the manuscript. For their gracious support I also thank Jeremy Mhire, Jason Pigg, Elaine Thompson, Ken Rea, and the late Steve Webre. The students in my "Guns in America" classes over the years have shared their experiences and opened my eyes in ways that undoubtedly improved this project. I was able to complete much of the work on the manuscript thanks to an ATLAS (Award to Louisiana Artists and Scholars) grant from the Louisiana Board of Regents.

Just as I was preparing to share preliminary thoughts on the gun country with the world, the world came to a standstill; six scheduled conference presentations were canceled in the spring of 2020 alone. I am therefore indebted to colleagues and friends in many far-flung places who gave their time and energy to read and critique this work or just offer encouragement under truly bizarre circumstances. Foremost among them are my writing group friends, the MWMWG: Katherine Rye Jewell, Arissa Oh, and Ellen Wu. I appreciate Kate, along with Kyle Burke and Brian DeLay, for thoughtful reflections on a full draft of the manuscript. For helpful suggestions on various chapter drafts I'm indebted to Alex Beasley, Carly Goodman, Richard Grippaldi, Caroline Light, Jennifer M. Miller, K. J. Shepherd, David Yamane, and the members of the Postwar Faculty Colloquium at the University of North Texas. The last thing I did before everything shut down was present an early version of several chapters at the University of Louisiana at Lafayette; I appreciate Rich Frankel, Chad Parker, Liz Skilton, and their colleagues for their generosity. For chats about Laura Fermi, my thanks to Rachel Sturges; for suggesting the book's title, Katherine Benton-Cohen; for endless sage wisdom some twenty years after I began graduate school, Richard Immerman. And thanks to Matthew Gabriele, Michael McGuinness, and Varsha Venkatasubramanian for the chance to share thoughts publicly through various media. Varsha also provided valuable research assistance, as did Jonathan Cortez.

This project began a decade ago as a conversation over a drink or two with Brandon Proia, who cultivated the manuscript from a tiny seedling to a book at a terrific press. He has my thanks, as do Debbie Gershenowitz, JessieAnne D'Amico, and the team at the University of North Carolina Press, who have once again made the experience of publishing a book truly joyful.

Finally, my thanks to my family—Jennie and Ian; my parents, Linda and Henry—for their constant support. And my apologies for the obligatory "Don't ask" response whenever one of them inquired how the book was coming. You can ask now. This book is dedicated to my grandfather, Carl E. Fazzi, who passed away many years ago. He passed on his love for history and, for better or worse, first showed me what the gun country looked like. I can almost hear him shouting about how I got everything wrong.

NOTES

ABBREVIATIONS

The following abbreviations are used throughout the notes for sources cited repeatedly.

Manuscript Collections

CDCR   Civic Disarmament Committee for Handgun Control Records, Hanna Holborn Gray Special Collections Research Center, University of Chicago Library, Chicago, Illinois.

CHCR   Committee for Handgun Control Inc. Records, Special Collections and University Archives, University of Illinois at Chicago.

ECM   Records of the National Commission on Violence, Part 1: Executive Files, edited by Robert E. Lester, LexisNexis, UP, Bethesda, Maryland, 2003.

ECR   Records of the National Commission on the Causes and Prevention of Violence (Eisenhower Commission), Record Group 283, Lyndon Baines Johnson Library, Austin, Texas.

HH   Gordon Hall and Grace Hoag Collection of Dissenting and Extremist Printed Propaganda, John Hay Library, Brown University, Providence, Rhode Island.

JHGA   John H. Glenn Archives, Non-Senate Papers Sub-Group, Ohio Congressional Archives, Ohio State University, Columbus, Ohio.

LBJC   Cabinet Papers, Lyndon B. Johnson Library, Austin, Texas.

LBF   Legislative Background Files, Lyndon B. Johnson Library, Austin, Texas.

LFP   Laura Fermi Papers, Hanna Holborn Gray Special Collections Research Center, University of Chicago Library, Chicago, Illinois.

RCP   Ramsey Clark Papers, Lyndon B. Johnson Library, Austin, Texas.

RWHC   Richard W. Haymaker Collection on Yoshihiro Hattori, Mss. 4698, Louisiana and Lower Mississippi Valley Collections, Special Collection, Hill Memorial Library, Louisiana State University, Baton Rouge, Louisiana.

LHMP   Leonard H. Marks Papers, Lyndon B. Johnson Library, Austin, Texas.

TJD   Thomas J. Dodd Papers, Archives and Special Collections, University of Connecticut Library, University of Connecticut, Storrs, Connecticut.

WHCF   White House Central Files, Lyndon B. Johnson Library, Austin, Texas.

Government Documents

F&VIAL   National Commission on the Causes and Prevention of Violence.
            Firearms & Violence in American Life. Washington, DC: US Government
            Printing Office, 1969.

FL 1975   US Congress, House of Representatives, Committee on the Judiciary.
            Firearms Legislation: Hearings before the Subcommittee on Crime, Part 2,
            94th Cong., 1st sess., 1975.

FFA 1965   US Congress, Senate, Committee on the Judiciary. *Federal Firearms Act:
            Hearings before the Subcommittee to Investigate Juvenile Delinquency*,
            89th Cong., 1st sess., May 19, 20, and 21; June 2, 3, 8, 24, and 30; July 1,
            20, and 27, 1965, Washington, DC.

FFA 1967   US Congress, Senate, Committee on the Judiciary. *Federal Firearms Act:
            Hearings before the Subcommittee to Investigate Juvenile Delinquency*,
            90th Cong., 1st sess., July 10, 11, 12, 18, 19, 20, 25, 28, and 31, and August
            1, 1967.

FFL 1968   US Congress, Senate, Committee on the Judiciary. *Federal Firearms
            Legislation: Hearings before the Special Subcommittee on Juvenile
            Delinquency*. 90th Cong., 2nd sess., June 20, 27, 28, and July 8, 9, and 10,
            1968, Washington, DC.

ISF 1964   US Congress, Senate, Committee on Commerce. *Interstate Shipment of
            Firearms: Hearings before the Committee on Commerce*. 88th Cong., 1st
            and 2nd sess., December 13 and 18, 1963; January 23, 24, and 30, and
            March 4, 1964, Washington, DC.

JD 1963   US Congress, Senate, Committee on the Judiciary. *Juvenile Delinquency:
            Hearings before the Subcommittee to Investigate Juvenile Delinquency*,
            88th Cong., 1st sess., Part 14, Interstate Traffic in Mail-Order Firearms,
            January 29 and 30, March 7, and May 1 and 2, 1963, Washington, DC.

JD 1964   US Congress, Senate, Committee on the Judiciary. *Juvenile Delinquency:
            Hearings before the Subcommittee to Investigate Juvenile Delinquency*.
            88th Cong., 2st sess., Part 15, Interstate Traffic in Mail-Order Firearms,
            March 26, and April 24 and 25, 1964, Washington, DC.

JD 1969   US Congress, Senate, Committee on the Judiciary. *Firearms Legislation:
            Hearings before the Subcommittee to Investigate Juvenile Delinquency*,
            91st Cong., 1st sess., July 23, 24, and 29, 1969, Washington, DC.

MSAX 1958   US Congress, House, Committee on Foreign Affairs. *Mutual Security Act:
            Hearings before the Committee on Foreign Affairs*. Part 10, 85th Cong.,
            2nd sess., March 25 and 26, 1958, Washington, DC.

MSAXI 1958 US Congress, House, Committee on Foreign Affairs. *Mutual Security Act
            of 1958: Hearings before the Committee on Foreign Affairs*. Part 11, 85th
            Cong., 2nd sess., March 27 and 31, 1958, Washington, DC.

SNS 1971   US Congress, Senate, Committee on the Judiciary. *"Saturday Night
            Special" Handguns, S. 2507: Hearings before the Subcommittee to
            Investigate Juvenile Delinquency*, 92nd Cong., 1st sess., September 13 and
            14; October 5 and 27; and November 1, 1971, Washington, DC.

Warren   *Report of the President's Commission on the Assassination of President*
  Report   *John F. Kennedy.* Washington, DC: US Government Printing Office, 1964.

Periodicals

AR   *American Rifleman*
CD   *Chicago Defender*
CR   *Congressional Record*
CSM   *Christian Science Monitor*
CT   *Chicago Tribune*
DFP   *Detroit Free Press*
DY   *Daily Yomiuri*
EPHP   *El Paso Herald Post*
G&A   *Guns & Ammo*
LAT   *Los Angeles Times*
MDN   *Mainichi Daily News*
MN   *Miami News*
NW   *Nikkei Weekly*
NYP   *New York Post*
NYSN   *New York Sunday News*
NYT   *New York Times*
OT   *Oakland Tribune*
RS   *Rafu Shimpo*
SB   *Sacramento Bee*
SFE   *San Francisco Examiner*
WP   *Washington Post*

PREFACE

1. There is no precise way to count guns in the United States. These figures are necessarily estimates. See *F&VIAL*, 6; Raymond W. Kelly, "Toward a New Intolerance of Crime and Violence," *FBI Law Enforcement Bulletin*, July 1993; Thomas Black, "Americans Have More Guns Than Anywhere Else in the World and They Keep Buying More," *Bloomberg*, May 25, 2022; and Jennifer Mascia, "How Many Guns Are Circulating in the U.S.?," *The Trace*, March 6, 2023.

2. I conceive of this less as a work of "gun history," which often traces the development of the technology over time, and more as a work of "guns in US history," which tries to make sense of guns in social, political, economic, and cultural contexts, and of which there is a growing historiography. For a sampling, see David J. Silverman, *Thundersticks: Firearms and the Violent Transformation of Native America* (Cambridge, MA: Belknap, 2016); Randolph Roth, *American Homicide* (Cambridge, MA: Harvard University Press, 2009); Richard Slotkin, *Gunfighter Nation: The Myth of the Frontier in the Twentieth Century* (New York: Atheneum, 1992); Kellie Carter Jackson, *Force and Freedom: Black Abolitionists and the Politics of Violence* (Philadelphia: University of Pennsylvania Press, 2019); Carol Anderson, *The Second: Race and Guns in a Fatally Unequal America* (New

York: Bloomsbury, 2021); and Pamela Haag, *The Gunning of America: Business and the Making of American Gun Culture* (New York: Basic Books, 2016). On firearms in the eighteenth-century British Empire, see Priya Satia, *Empire of Guns: The Violent Making of the Industrial Revolution* (New York: Penguin, 2018).

3. Saul Cornell, *A Well-Regulated Militia: The Founding Fathers and the Origins of Gun Control in America* (New York: Oxford University Press, 2006); Patrick J. Charles, *Armed in America: A History of Gun Rights from Colonial Militias to Concealed Carry* (New York: Prometheus, 2018); Adam Winkler, *Gunfight: The Battle over the Right to Bear Arms in America* (New York: W. W. Norton, 2013).

4. Aaron Karp, "Estimating Global Civilian-Held Firearms Numbers," Small Arms Survey, Briefing Paper, June 2018, https://www.smallarmssurvey.org/resource/estimating-global-civilian-held-firearms-numbers.

5. Jake Fogelman, "Survey: Pandemic First-Time Buyers Younger and More Diverse, Oppose Gun Control," *The Reload*, March 28, 2022; "One in Five American Households Purchased a Gun during the Pandemic," NORC at the University of Chicago, March 24, 2022, https://www.norc.org/NewsEventsPublications/PressReleases/Pages/one-in-five-american-households-purchased-a-gun-during-the-pandemic.aspx.

INTRODUCTION

1. For this narrative of the killing of Yoshi Hattori, I have drawn from court documents, including depositions from the participants. Unless otherwise cited, all material in this narrative is drawn from RWHC, box 5, folders 17–19. See also the documentary, *The Shot Heard 'Round the World*, directed by Christine Choy (New York: Film News Now Foundation, 1997), DVD.

2. At the time Central was an unincorporated neighborhood of Baton Rouge. It incorporated as a separate city in 2005. Baton Rouge's population is about 55 percent Black, while Central's is only 12 percent.

3. "Defense Depicts Japanese Boy as 'Scary,'" *NYT*, May 21, 1993; "Acquittal in Doorstep Killing of Japanese Student," *NYT*, May 24, 1993.

4. For global statistics on gun ownership and violence see gunpolicy.org.

5. T. R. Reid, "Japanese Image of U.S. Affirmed in Student's Death," *WP*, October 20, 1992.

6. Quoted in Reid, "Japanese Image of U.S. Affirmed."

7. David E. Sanger, "Acquittal in Doorstep Killing of Japanese Student," *NYT*, May 24, 1993.

8. Sanger, "After Gunman's Acquittal"; "Acquittal in Doorstep Killing of Japanese Student," *NYT*, May 24, 1993.

9. Story recounted in Daniel Todd Cohen email to Richard Haymaker, October 26, 1993, RWHC, box 2, folder 31.

10. Daniel Todd Cohen email to Richard Haymaker, October 26, 1993, RWHC, box 2, folder 31.

11. David Yamane, "What's Next? Understanding and Misunderstanding America's Gun Culture," in Craig Honey and Lisa Fisher, eds., *Understanding America's Gun Culture* (Lanham, MD: Lexington, 2018), 157–64.

12. Richard Hofstadter and Michael Wallace, eds., *American Violence: A Documentary History* (New York: Knopf, 1970), v. On the context of the collection's production, see David S. Brown, *Richard Hofstadter: An Intellectual Biography* (Chicago: University of Chicago Press, 2006), 214–18.

13. Richard Hofstadter, "America as a Gun Culture," *American Heritage*, October 1970; Janell Ross, "Obama Revives His 'Cling to Guns or Religion' Analysis," *WP*, December 21, 2015.

14. The best history of gun capitalism to date is Pamela Haag, *The Gunning of America: Business and the Making of American Gun Culture* (New York: Basic Books, 2016). Haag argues that what we often call gun culture was the invention of nineteenth-century industrialists and savvy marketers like Oliver Winchester and Samuel Colt.

15. Carl Bakal, *The Right to Bear Arms* (New York: McGraw-Hill, 1966).

16. Bakal, *The Right to Bear Arms*, 1.

17. Ramsey Clark to members of the Senate, September 10, 1968, LBF, Gun Control, box 2, folder Firearms Act (1968) (2). Clark's claim about "war casualties" was only true if one counted combat deaths and not military deaths from disease, which caused a majority of wartime deaths in the nineteenth century.

18. Michael S. Sherry, *In the Shadow of War: The United States since the 1930s* (New Haven, CT: Yale University Press, 1995).

19. Christopher G. Ellison et al., "Peace through Superior Firepower: Belief in Supernatural Evil and Attitudes toward Gun Policy in the United States," *Social Science Research*, September 2021, https://www.sciencedirect.com/science/article/abs/pii/S0049089X21000727.

20. "NRA: Full Statement by Wayne LaPierre in Response to Newtown Shootings," *Guardian*, December 21, 2012.

21. On the founders' understanding of the Second Amendment as a "civic duty," see Saul Cornell, *A Well-Regulated Militia: The Founding Fathers and the Origins of Gun Control in America* (New York: Oxford University Press, 2006).

22. On guns and global capitalism, see Satia, *Empire of Guns*; Haag, *The Gunning of America*; and Brian DeLay, "How Not to Arm a State: American Guns and the Crisis of Governance in Mexico, Nineteenth and Twenty-First Centuries," *Southern California Quarterly*, Spring 2013, 5–23. On recent historiography, see Kritika Agarwal, "A World of Weapons: Historians Shape Scholarship on Arms Trading," *Perspectives on History*, September 1, 2017.

23. B. Bruce-Briggs, "The Great American Gun War," *Public Interest*, Fall 1976, 41.

24. Historians have written extensively about these consumer goods. See, for example, Katherine J. Parkin, *Women at the Wheel: A Century of Buying, Driving, and Fixing Cars* (Philadelphia: University of Pennsylvania Press, 2017); Jonathan Rees, *Refrigerator Nation: A History of Ice, Appliances, and Enterprise in America* (Baltimore: Johns Hopkins University Press, 2016); and Michael Nevin Willard, "Cutback: Skate and Punk at the Far End of the American Century," in Beth Bailey and David Farber, eds., *America in the Seventies* (Lawrence: University Press of Kansas, 2004).

25. See Colin Campbell, *The Romantic Ethic and the Spirit of Modern Consumerism* (London: Blackwell, 1989); and Campbell, "Consuming Goods and the Good of Consuming," *Critical Review* 8, no. 4 (1994): 503–20. See also Lawrence B. Glickman, ed.,

Consumer Society in American History: A Reader (Ithaca, NY: Cornell University Press, 1999). For a thoughtful perspective on gun consumerism, see Joan Burbick, *Gun Show Nation: Gun Culture and American Democracy* (New York: New Press, 2006).

26. Kim Bellware, "Sandy Hook Families Announce $73 Million Settlement with Remington Arms in Landmark Agreement," *WP*, February 15, 2022.

27. Jennifer Carlson, *Citizen-Protectors: The Everyday Politics of Guns in an Age of Decline* (New York: Oxford University Press, 2015).

28. Kathleen Gray, "In Michigan, a Dress Rehearsal for the Chaos at the Capitol on Wednesday," *NYT*, January 9, 2021; Lindsay Whitehurst, "Oath Keepers Jury Hears about Massive Weapons Cache on Jan. 6," *AP News*, October 12, 2022.

CHAPTER 1

1. These descriptions of Cummings come from Kobler, "The Man with the Crocodile Briefcase," *Saturday Evening Post*, March 24, 1962; and George Nobbe, "Dealer in Death," *New York Daily News*, August 15, 1965. George Thayer, "Arms Dealer Sam," *Harper's*, April 1969.

2. Thayer, "Arms Dealer Sam," 92; Kobler, "Man with the Crocodile Briefcase," describes Cummings's briefcase.

3. Quoted in Sanche de Gramont, "Samuel Cummings Dates Human Affairs B.G. and A.G.," *NYT*, September 24, 1967.

4. Edwin Shrake, "The Merchant of Menace," *Sports Illustrated*, May 11, 1970.

5. Alexander DeConde, *Gun Violence in America: The Struggle for Control* (Boston: Northeastern University Press, 2001), 153.

6. Shrake, "Merchant of Menace."

7. Nobbe, "Dealer in Death."

8. Neil Sheehan, "American Does Brisk Business in Surplus Weapons," *NYT*, July 21, 1967.

9. Neil Sheehan, "Armament Sales: A Huge Business," *NYT*, July 19, 1967.

10. These rumors are recounted in a sensationalist biography of Cummings published in 1983 by journalists who had interviewed him. See Patrick Brogan and Albert Zarca, *Deadly Business: Sam Cummings, Interarms, and the Arms Trade* (New York: W. W. Norton, 1983). See also George Thayer, *The War Business: The International Trade in Armaments* (New York: Simon & Schuster, 1969).

11. "Memorandum: Ramparts: John Garrett Underhill Jr., Samuel George Cummings, and Interarmco," July 19, 1967, Mary Ferrell Foundation Archive, JFK Assassination Documents, CIA Documents Released on November 9, 2017, National Archives and Record Administration Record Number 104-10170-10145.

12. Tim Weiner, "Samuel Cummings, 71, Trader in Weapons on a Grand Scale," *NYT*, May 5, 1998.

13. Shrake, "Merchant of Menace"; John Burgess, "Alexandria Debates Whether to Give Space for Collection," *WP*, May 8, 1983.

14. "Cheap" guns were arguably important to Americans as far back as the eighteenth century. See Ellen Ruppel Shell, *Cheap: The High Cost of Discount Culture* (New York: Penguin, 2009), 8.

15. FFA 1967, 219.

16. Kobler, "Man with the Crocodile Briefcase"; "Private Arms Dealer," *NYT*, July 21, 1967; Lisa Pulitzer, *A Woman Scorned: The Shocking Real-Life Case of Billionairess Killer Susan Cummings* (New York: St. Martin's, 1999), frontmatter. In 1997, Cummings's daughter, Susan, shot and killed her boyfriend just a few months before Cummings's death from a series of strokes.

17. Nobbe, "Dealer in Death"; William Armistead, "Arsenal on the Potomac," *Guns*, October 1959. On the Alexandria waterfront, see Steve Trimble, "Alexandria's 'Merchant of Menace' along the Waterfront," *Alexandria Living*, January 14, 2022.

18. FFA Hearings, 1965, 720; Armistead, "Arsenal on the Potomac."

19. Carl Bakal, *The Right to Bear Arms* (New York: McGraw-Hill, 1966), 9.

20. Hunter's Lodge advertisement, *AR*, June 1961, n.p.

21. Hunter's Lodge advertisement, *AR*, November 1962, n.p.

22. Hunter's Lodge advertisement, *Guns*, September 1956.

23. Hunter's Lodge advertisements, *AR*, June, July, and August 1962.

24. FFA 1965, 665.

25. Hunter's Lodge advertisement, *Guns*, July 1957, n.p.

26. FFA 1965, 203.

27. "Surplus Military Rifles, Part 2 of 4," *AR*, January 1961, 42; "Surplus Military Rifles, Part 4 of 4," *AR*, March 1961, 38.

28. Klein's Sporting Goods advertisement and Hunter's Lodge advertisement, *AR*, January 1961, 2, n.p.

29. See "New England's Gun Valley, Child of the Springfield Armory," New England Historical Society, 2022, https://www.newenglandhistoricalsociety.com /new-englands-gun-valley-child-of-the-springfield-armory/.

30. Herbert Roback, Memorandum to Military Operations Subcommittee of the House Committee on Foreign Affairs, "Importation of Surplus Small Arms," reproduced in MSAX 1958, 1289–90.

31. MSAX 1958, 1287.

32. See Thomas W. Zeiler, "Managing Protectionism: American Trade Policy in the Early Cold War," *Diplomatic History* 22, no. 3 (Summer 1998): 337–60.

33. MSAX 1958, 1290.

34. Army Service Forces, War Department, *International Aid Statistics, World War II: A Summary of War Department Led Lease Activities*, International Branch, Headquarters, Army Service Forces, War Department, 1946, 46.

35. *F&VIAL*, 6.

36. Harry S. Truman, "Special Message to Congress on the Mutual Security Program," *The American Presidency Project*, https://www.presidency.ucsb.edu/node/231118.

37. *CR*, 80th Cong., 2nd sess., vol. 104, April 15, 1958, 6471; and May 13, 1958, 8502.

38. MSAX 1958, 1314.

39. MSAX 1958, 1314.

40. MSAX 1958, 1315.

41. MSAX 1958, 1316.

42. MSAX 1958, 1316.

43. MSAX 1958, 1319.

44. US Department of Commerce, Business and Defense Services Administration, Consumer Durable Goods Division, *The United States Small Arms Industry, 1954–58* (Washington, DC: US Government Printing Office, 1959).

45. Department of Commerce, *United States Small Arms Industry*, 1.

46. Department of Commerce, *United States Small Arms Industry*, 21.

47. Department of Commerce, *United States Small Arms Industry*, 18.

48. Department of Commerce, *United States Small Arms Industry*, 4; also see the report's "Addendum," 1.

49. Department of Commerce, *United States Small Arms Industry*, 25.

50. See, for instance, Kim Parker et al., "The Demographics of Gun Ownership," *Pew Research Center*, June 22, 2017; and Philip J. Cook and Kristin A. Goss, *The Gun Debate: What Everyone Needs to Know* (New York: Oxford University Press, 2020), 7.

51. MSAXI 1958, 1474–75.

52. MSAXI 1958, 1455–68.

53. MSAXI 1958, 1458, 1469.

54. MSAXI 1958, 1462.

55. DeConde, *Gun Violence in America*, 164.

56. FFA 1965, 710, 715.

57. MSAXI, 1459.

58. Brogan and Zarca, *Deadly Business*, 101; Hunter's Lodge advertisement, *AR*, April 1962, n.p.

59. Brogan and Zarca, *Deadly Business*, 251–56; on the price Crescent paid for the guns, see FFA 1965, 68.

60. Warren Report, 119.

CHAPTER 2

1. Warren Report, 79, 81. For comparisons between Mausers and modern assault rifles, see Timothy W. Luke, "Counting Up AR-15s: The Subject of Assault Rifles and the Assault Rifle as Subject," in Jonathan Obert, Andrew Poe, and Austin Sarat, eds., *The Lives of Guns* (Oxford University Press, 2019), 79.

2. Warren Report, 554.

3. Warren Report, 84, 119, 190.

4. Warren Report, 555.

5. Robert Sherrill, *The Saturday Night Special, and Other Guns with Which Americans Won the West, Protected Bootleg Franchises, Slew Wildlife, Robbed Countless Banks, Shot Husbands Purposely and by Mistake and Killed Presidents—Together with Some Debate over Continuing the Same* (New York: Charterhouse, 1973), 168. The story was later corroborated in part by the release of a cache of FBI documents that showed that Western Cartridge had produced 4 million rounds of 6.5 mm ammunition in 1954 on order for the US Marine Corps. At the time it made no sense to investigators, as no Marine rifle fired 6.5 mm ammunition. They speculated that the Marines served as a cover for a CIA order, which planned to supply allies around the world with ammunition for cheap and plentiful Carcanos. See "F.B.I. Records Trace Oswald and Bullets," *NYT*, December 2, 1977.

6. Patrick Brogan and Albert Zarca, *Deadly Business: Sam Cummings, Interarms, and the Arms Trade* (New York: W. W. Norton, 1983), 18. Cummings's colleague at Interarms, Peter Beer, told FBI investigators this story in 1964. See "Efforts to Trace Purchase of Ammunition by Lee Harvey Oswald and Related Data," May 28, 1964, Mary Ferrell Foundation Archive, JFK Assassination Documents—Central Intelligence Agency, Oswald 201 File, vol. 40, National Archives and Record Administration Record Number 1993.06.11.14:41:25:500000.

7. Warren Report, 172–74.

8. FFA 1967, 234.

9. JD 1963, 3227–28.

10. JD 1964, 3537.

11. JD 1969, 166.

12. FFA 1965, 519; "Gun Control Legislation and the Fight against Crime," Statement by Dodd on Senate floor, May 7, 1968, TJD, box 209, folder 5630.

13. "Estimated Production and Imports of Firearms in the United States, 1951–1968," undated [1968], ECR, Series 44: Research File, box 1, folder CH-1 Sources.

14. The phrase "vital center" comes from Arthur Schlesinger Jr., *The Vital Center: The Politics of Freedom* (Boston: Houghton Mifflin, 1949). On Cold War liberals like Dodd, see Kevin Mattson, *When America Was Great: The Fighting Faith of Postwar Liberalism* (New York: Routledge, 2006).

15. Eugene H. Methvin, "Crusader from Connecticut," *Reader's Digest*, September 1964, 3–4, reprint in TJD, box 216, folder 6016; "Senator Thomas J. Dodd," biographical sketch, undated, TJD, box 210, folder 5648.

16. Adam Winkler, *Gunfight: The Battle over the Right to Bear Arms in America* (New York: W. W. Norton, 2011), 248–49.

17. Methvin, "Crusader."

18. FFA 1965, 273–74; quoted in *F&VIAL*, 197.

19. Leonard K. White, "Diary Notes," May 18, 1960, General CIA Records, Freedom of Information Act Electronic Reading Room, Central Intelligence Agency, Document Number CIA-RDP76-00183R000300060024–1.

20. *CR*, August 31, 1961, 17198–99, copy in JD, box 191, folder 4546; Dodd to John F. Kennedy, November 29, 1961, TJD, box 24, folder 739.

21. Dodd, "A Personal Message to Arms Industry Employees," October 28, 1964, TJD, box 201, folder 5142.

22. Sherrill, *Saturday Night Special*, 72; Drew Pearson, "Dodd's Strange Tie to Gun Makers," *WP*, August 9, 1966.

23. Sherrill, *Saturday Night Special*, 92–93.

24. Murray Schumach, "F.B.I. Crime Data Called Misleading by Sociologists," *NYT*, March 22, 1965, copy WHCF, JL, box 26, folder JL 3 12/21/67-2/29/68.

25. Franklin E. Zimring, *The Great American Crime Decline* (New York: Oxford University Press, 2007), 58.

26. Quoted in Michael S. Sherry, *The Punitive Turn in American Life: How the United States Learned to Fight Crime Like a War* (Chapel Hill: University of North Carolina Press, 2020), 10–11.

27. See, for example, Gilbert Geis, "Crime and Politics," *Nation*, August 14, 1967, 115–16; also President's Commission on Law Enforcement and Administration of Justice, *The Challenge of Crime in a Free Society* (Washington, DC: US Government Printing Office, 1967), 5. A contemporary critique is Will Sparks, "Terror in the Streets?," *Commonweal*, June 4, 1965, 345–48. For historical critiques of crime statistics and race, see Stuart Hall et al., *Policing the Crisis: Mugging, the State, and Law and Order* (London: Macmillan, 1978); and Khalil Gibran Muhammad, *The Condemnation of Blackness: Race, Crime, and the Making of Modern Urban America* (Cambridge, MA: Harvard University Press, 2010).

28. See David Hajdu, *The Ten-Cent Plague: The Great Comic-Book Scare and How It Changed America* (New York: Picador, 2009).

29. On the juvenile delinquency panic of the 1950s, see James Gilbert, *A Cycle of Outrage: America's Reaction to the Juvenile Delinquent in the 1950s* (New York: Oxford University Press, 1986).

30. Grace Palladino, *Teenagers: An American History* (New York: Basic Books, 1996), 159. See also Eric C. Schneider, *Vampires, Dragon, and Egyptian Kings: Youth Gangs in Postwar New York* (Princeton, NJ: Princeton University Press, 1999); and Alan Petigny, *The Permissive Society: America, 1941–1965* (New York: Cambridge University Press, 2009).

31. Roy Dickerson, "Police Told Must Know Their Guns," *Marshall (TX) News Messenger*, November 8, 1955.

32. Virginia Turner, "Death by Mail! It's Easy for a Boy to Buy a Gun!," *EPHP*, March 12, 1963; Gary Turner, "Gary Tells How He Did It," *EPHP*, March 12, 1963.

33. Frank Ahlgren Jr., "'Lie about Yourself and You Get a Gun,' Says Police Chief," *EPHP*, March 13, 1963.

34. B. Bruce-Briggs, "The Great American Gun War," *Public Interest*, Fall 1976, 50, claims that the term was racist from the outset because it refers to a "n——town Saturday night," but I have found no corroboration or earlier claim, and every subsequent mention cites the Bruce-Briggs article.

35. FFA 1967, 404.

36. Lynyrd Skynyrd, "Saturday Night Special," *Genius*, https://genius.com/Lynyrd-skynyrd-saturday-night-special-lyrics.

37. The Chicago investigation is discussed in JD 1964, 3647. The Turners' experiment was replicated by other news organizations in the 1960s to demonstrate easy access to guns through the mail. In 1965, the *Paterson (NJ) Morning Call* ordered a Smith & Wesson similar to the one Oswald used to murder J. D. Trippet. The newspaper had no problem getting it, even using the name "L. H. Oswald" to make the purchase. See "Shadow of Tragedy: 'L. H. Oswald' Buys Pistol," *Paterson (NJ) Morning Call*, November 19, 1965, reprinted in *CR*, March 8, 1966, 5058.

38. "Remarks of Senator Thomas J. Dodd on the Floor of the Senate on the Introduction of a Bill to Amend the Federal Firearms Act," August 2, 1963, TJD, box 197, folder 4913.

39. "Remarks of Senator Thomas J. Dodd on the Floor of the Senate on the Introduction of a Bill to Amend the Federal Firearms Act," August 2, 1963, TJD, box 197, folder 4913.

40. "Statement by Senator Thomas J. Dodd (D-Conn.) on the Introduction of an Amendment to S. 1975, a Bill to Amend the Federal Firearms Act," November 27, 1963, TJD, box 198, folder 4960.

41. *F&VIAL*, 12.

42. On the pulps of this era, see Gregory A. Daddis, *Pulp Vietnam: War and Gender in Cold War Men's Adventure Magazines* (New York: Cambridge University Press, 2021).

43. JD 1963, 3228–29.

44. *Adventure*, December 1963, 65.

45. *Adventure*, March 1958, 77,80; *Climax*, March 1959, 74.

46. *Adventure*, May 1957, 11.

47. Jack Anderson, "It's Easy for Your Child to Get a Gun," *Parade*, March 8, 1962, copy in TJD, box 423, folder 9509.

48. JD 1964, 3536.

49. See JD 1964, beginning on 3541.

50. Dewey Linze, "He Can Sell You a War Wholesale," *Cavalier*, February 1962.

51. William C. L. Thompson, "Guns Are Big Business," *Guns*, March 1955, 4–7, 48–49.

52. JD 1964, 3546–47; "Firearms Imported as Scrap," *Capital Journal* (Salem, OR), March 27, 1964.

53. JD 1964, 3547–49, 3559.

54. FFA 1965, 160.

55. JD 1964, 3668.

56. FFA 1967, 196–98; the restoration of the OMC statistical unit is explained in Theodore B. Dobbs, "Munitions Control: U.S. Foreign Policy in Action," *Department of State Newsletter*, January 1967, 10–11, copy in ECR, Series 44: Research File, box 4, folder State Department Materials on Imported Guns. See also Memorandum, "Reasons for Variances in Statistics," August 26, 1968, ECR, Series 44: Research File, box 5, folder State Department, Office of Munitions Control Materials.

57. JD 1964, 3547.

58. JD 1964, 3550–51; Leonard K. White, "Diary Notes," March 26, 1964, General CIA Records, Freedom of Information Act Electronic Reading Room, Central Intelligence Agency, Document Number CIA-RDP76-00183R000500010007–3.

59. This didn't become public knowledge until the release of the Warren Report in September 1964. See "L.A. Mail-Order Firm Sold Murder Pistol," *Los Angeles Times*, September 28, 1964.

60. JD 1964, 3646–57.

61. JD 1964, 3646–57; "Gun Dealer to End Chicago Shipments," *CT*, April 25, 1964.

62. JD 1964, 3591.

63. Joan Burbick, *Gun Show Nation: Gun Culture and American Democracy* (New York: New Press, 2006), 68–69.

64. JD 1963, 3468–85.

65. ISF 1964, 198.

66. ISF 1964, 204.

67. FFA 1965, 570–71.

68. FFA 1965, 571.

69. FFA 1965, 694.

70. C. W. Derrenger, "Memorandum for Section Files, Re: Import Provision of the Firearms Bill," March 30, 1967; and Herbert E. Hoffman, "Memorandum for Section Files, Re: Firearms—H.R. 5384," May 2, 1967, LBF, Gun Control, box 2, folder Firearms Act—Drafting and Submission (1967) (II).

71. C. W. Derrenger, "Memorandum for Section Files, Re: Administration Firearms Bill," April 3, 1967, LBF, Gun Control, box 2, folder Firearms Act—Drafting and Submission (1967) (II).

72. See Joseph W. Barr, "Memorandum to the Honorable Lawrence F. O'Brien," July 14, 1965, LBF, Gun Control, box 2, folder Firearms Act (1968) (2).

CHAPTER 3

1. These are headlines from *DFP*, July 25, 26, and 27, 1967.

2. For overviews of the 1967 Detroit rebellion, see Sidney Fine, *Violence in the Model City: The Cavanagh Administration, Race Relations, and the Detroit Riot of 1967* (Lansing: Michigan State University Press, 2007); and Joel Stone, ed., *Detroit 1967: Origins, Impacts, Legacies* (Detroit: Wayne State University Press, 2017).

3. William Serrin, "The Sniper's Sneak Attack Is the Worst Thing," *DFP*, July 25, 1967; see also "Detroit '67," *DFP*, undated (2017), https://www.freep.com/pages /interactives/1967-detroit-riot/.

4. "LBJ Approves All-Out Drive to End Strife," *DFP*, July 25, 1967.

5. Philip Meyer, "Police Doubt Sniping Was Organized," *DFP*, July 31, 1967.

6. Meyer, "Police Doubt Sniping"; Serrin, "Sniper's Sneak Attack"; Don McKee, "Riot Victims Represented Wide Range of Detroit Life," *Shreveport Times*, July 31, 1967.

7. I've borrowed this term from Charles Fruehling Springwood, "Gunscapes: Toward a Global Geography of the Firearm," in Charles Fruehling Springwood, ed., *Open Fire: Understanding Global Gun Cultures* (New York: Berg, 2007), 14–27.

8. National Advisory Commission on Civil Disorders, *Report of the National Advisory Commission on Civil Disorders* (Washington, DC: US Government Printing Office, 1968).

9. Arnold Kotz, Harold Hair, and John K. Scales, *Firearms, Violence, and Civil Disorders* (Menlo Park, CA: Stanford Research Institute, 1968), 1, 10.

10. Danielle L. McGuire, "Murder at the Algiers Motel," in Stone, *Detroit 1967*, 176.

11. Kotz, Hair, and Scales, *Firearms, Violence, and Civil Disorders*, 26, 34.

12. Kotz, Hair, and Scales, *Firearms, Violence, and Civil Disorders*, 37.

13. Kotz, Hair, and Scales, *Firearms, Violence, and Civil Disorders*, 42.

14. *F&VIAL*, 7.

15. *F&VIAL*, 56.

16. Thomas J. Dodd, "For the Meriden, Connecticut, Record," August 24, 1967, TJD, box 208, folder 5549; "Statement Issued from the offices of Senator Thomas J. Dodd on Firearms Used in the Detroit Riot of July 1967," *CR*, November 17, 1967, S 16655.

17. "Introduction of Two Bills," Dodd speech before the Senate, March 22, 1965, TJD, box 201, folder 5180.

18. Thomas J. Dodd, "The Sickness of Violence," speech before Young Democratic Convention, Hartford, CT, May 4, 1968, TJD, box 209, folder 5628; Dodd press release, May 15, 1968, TJD, box 209, folder 5636.

19. Quinn Tamm, "The Age of Snipers," *Police Chief*, July 1967, 6, copy in ECR, Series 44, box 9, folder National Rifle Association.

20. *F&VIAL*, 70.

21. Detroit's police commissioner estimated that there were 500,000 unregistered handguns in the city by 1971. See SNS 1971, 83. On Toledo, see Stephen Cain, "Tough Laws Jam Gun Traffic," *Detroit News*, February 16, 1969, copy in ECM, reel 2.

22. Jack Shoemaker to Frank Zimring, October 28, 1968, ECR, Series 44, box 2, folder Ch-8 Sources.

23. Oral history transcript, David Ginsburg, interview 4 (IV), November 11, 1988, by Michael L. Gillette, LBJ Library Oral Histories, https://www.discoverlbj.org/item /oh-ginsburgd-19881111–4-12-08.

24. Oral history transcript, Jerome P. Cavanagh, interview 1 (I), March 22, 1971, by Joe B. Frantz, LBJ Library Oral Histories, https://www.discoverlbj.org/item /oh-cavanaghj-19710322–1-79–92.

25. Kotz, Hair, and Scales, *Firearms, Violence, and Civil Disorders*, 51–52.

26. Thomas J. Sugrue, *The Origins of the Urban Crisis: Race and Inequality in Postwar Detroit*, rev. ed. (Princeton, NJ: Princeton University Press, 2005), 210. On the long-term causes of the 1967 Detroit rebellions, see also Heather Ann Thompson, *Whose Detroit? Politics, Labor, and Race in a Modern American City* (Ithaca, NY: Cornell University Press, 2004); and Mark Jay and Philip Conklin, *A People's History of Detroit* (Durham, NC: Duke University Press, 2020).

27. Bill McGraw, "Detroit's Infamous Right-Wing Extremist Died and Hardly Anyone Knew—Until Now," *DFP*, July 9, 2020.

28. Biographical details for Lobsinger come from "Donald Lobsinger, June 23rd, 2016," *Detroit 1967 Online Archive*, http://detroit1967.detroithistorical.org/items/show/287.

29. On the John Birch Society, see D. J. Mulloy, *The World of the John Birch Society: Conspiracy, Conservatism, and the Cold War* (Nashville: Vanderbilt University Press, 2014); Edward H. Miller, *A Conspiratorial Life: Robert Welch, the John Birch Society, and the Revolution of American Conservatism* (Chicago: University of Chicago Press, 2022); and John S. Huntington, *Far-Right Vanguard: The Radical Roots of Modern Conservatism* (Philadelphia: University of Pennsylvania Press, 2021).

30. William Winkel, "In the Uprising's Wake: Reaction in the White Community," in Stone, *Detroit 1967*, 266.

31. George Walker, "Right-Winger Is Mad at World," *DFP*, March 2, 1966; Breakthrough flyer, October 9, 1967, reproduced in FFL 1968, 392.

32. Breakthrough flyer, October 9, 1967, reproduced in FFL 1968, 392.

33. McGraw, "Detroit's Infamous Right-Wing Extremist Died."

34. "Aptheker's No Danger," *DFP*, February 11, 1966.

35. "Donald Lobsinger, June 23rd, 2016," *Detroit 1967 Online Archive*; Elaine Tyler May, *Fortress America: How We Embraced Fear and Abandoned Democracy* (New York: Basic Books, 2017), 75.

36. Andrew Mollison, "Detroit's White Backlash: The Enemy Is Known as 'They,'" *DFP*, September 28, 1967.

37. Kotz, Hair, and Scales, *Firearms, Violence, and Civil Disorders*, 51; Walker, "Right-Winger Is Mad at the World"; Mollison, "Detroit's White Backlash."

38. May, *Fortress America*, 75.

39. "Donald Lobsinger, June 23rd, 2016," *Detroit 1967 Online Archive*.

40. Breakthrough flyer, October 9, 1967, reproduced in FFL 1968, 392.

41. Mollison, "Detroit's White Backlash."

42. Reproduced in Kotz, Hair, and Scales, *Firearms, Violence, and Civil Disorders*, 104.

43. Mollison, "Detroit's White Backlash"; Fine, *Violence in the Model City*, 383.

44. See, for example, the statement of Representative Henry B. Gonzalez, FFA 1967, 288.

45. Breakthrough flyer, October 9, 1967, reproduced in Kotz, Hair, and Scales, *Firearms, Violence, and Civil Disorders*, 103; Breakthrough newsletter, October 1967, reproduced in FFL 1968, 394; Mollison, "Detroit's White Backlash."

46. FFL 1968, 388–92.

47. Breakthrough newsletter, October 1967, reproduced in FFL 1968, 393.

48. "Donald Lobsinger, June 23rd, 2016," *Detroit 1967 Online Archive*.

49. McGraw, "Detroit's Infamous Right-Wing Extremist Died."

50. There is a rich historical literature on the Panthers. See Joshua Bloom and Waldo E. Martin Jr., *Black against Empire: The History and Politics of the Black Panther Party* (Berkeley: University of California Press, 2016); Robyn C. Spencer, *The Revolution Has Come: Black Power, Gender, and the Black Panther Party in Oakland* (Durham, NC: Duke University Press, 2016); and Sean L. Malloy, *Out of Oakland: Black Panther Party Internationalism during the Cold War* (Ithaca, NY: Cornell University Press, 2017). See also the literature on armed Black resistance elsewhere in US history, which includes Lance Hill, *The Deacons for Defense: Armed Resistance and the Civil Rights Movement* (Chapel Hill: University of North Carolina Press, 2005); Charles E. Cobb Jr., *This Nonviolent Stuff'll Get You Killed: How Guns Made the Civil Rights Movement Possible* (Durham, NC: Duke University Press, 2015); Timothy B. Tyson, *Radio Free Dixie: Robert F. Williams and the Roots of Black Power* (Chapel Hill: University of North Carolina Press, 2001); Nicholas Johnson, *Negroes and the Gun: The Black Tradition of Arms* (New York: Prometheus, 2014); and Akinyele Omowale Umoja, *We Will Shoot Back: Armed Resistance in the Mississippi Freedom Movement* (New York: New York University Press, 2014).

51. "State Police Halt Armed Negro Band," *SB*, 2 May 1967.

52. Thaddeus Morgan, "The NRA Supported Gun Control When the Black Panthers Had the Weapons," *History*, August 30, 2018, https://www.history.com/news/black -panthers-gun-control-nra-support-mulford-act.

53. As scholars have emphasized, the Panthers used firearms as part of a political and recruiting strategy but paired this with intensive political education, which became increasingly important after the group's violent first years. See Spencer, *The Revolution Has Come*, 43–61; and Malloy, *Out of Oakland*, 61–67.

54. "Black Nationalist Political Party to Be Established in California," *LAT*, February 20, 1967; "Background of Black Panthers," *OT*, May 3, 1967.

55. Wilson K. Lythgoe, "Assembly Unit Okays Gun Control Bills," *SB*, May 3, 1967.

56. Lythgoe, "Assembly Unit Okays Gun Control Bills."

57. Lythgoe, "Assembly Unit Okays Gun Control Bills"; "Gun Curbs Plan Moves to Assembly," *OT*, May 3, 1967.

58. Ed Salzman, "Gun Control Bill Runs into Trouble," *OT*, May 12, 1967; Richard Rodda, "'Hot Line' Is Initial Step in Tightening Capitol's Security," *SB*, May 12, 1967.

59. Descriptions in these two paragraphs drawn from "Arsenal in Mansion Here," *SFE*, April 21, 1967; "Mystery S.F. Arsenal Is Confiscated," *OT*, April 22, 1967; "Wife Silent on Arsenal," *SFE*, April 22, 1967; and "Thoresen Ruled Sane, Faces Trial for Huge Arsenal," *SFE*, May 17, 1967.

60. Daryl E. Lembke, "4 New Discoveries Deepen Mystery of S.F. Man's Arsenal," *LAT*, April 26, 1967; "Thoresen: Cannons Are Ornaments, Every Lawn Ought to Have One," *SB*, April 27, 1967; Daryl E. Lembke, "Thoresens Indicted over Vast Arms Cache," *LAT*, June 29, 1967; "Wife Silent on Arsenal."

61. "Thoresen Ruled Sane, Faces Trial for Huge Arsenal," *SFE*, May 17, 1967; "Thoresen Test Delayed," *SFE*, May 10, 1967; "Thoresen: Cannons Are Ornaments, Every Lawn Ought to Have One."

62. "Mystery S.F. Arsenal Is Confiscated"; "Steel Heir Silent about Gun Cache," *LAT*, May 14, 1967.

63. "Thoresens Have Met Cops," *SFE*, April 22, 1967; "Thoresen Jailed over Woman," *SFE*, August 22, 1967; "Thoresen Jury Selection Begins," *SFE*, March 17, 1969.

64. "Gun Curbs Plan Moves to Assembly," *OT*, May 3, 1967.

65. "Federal Agents Seize 17 Tons More of Arms in Bay Area; Hunt Continues," *SB*, April 26, 1967.

66. "Thoresens Guilty in Gun Case," *SFE*, March 19, 1969; "Thoresen Gets Jail Term," *SFE*, April 3, 1969; "Mrs. Thoresen Asking for Divorce," *SFE*, November 17, 1969; Jerry Cohen, "Millionaire Once Found Guilty in Gun Case Slain," *LAT*, June 11, 1970; Jerry Cohen, "New Arms Cache Discovered in Home of Slain Millionaire," *LAT*, June 12, 1970; "Fresno Jury Acquits Mrs. Thoresen in Killing of Gun-Collector Husband," *SB*, November 20, 1970; Judith Anderson, "Why Louise Thoresen Killed Her Husband," *San Francisco Chronicle*, January 7, 1974.

67. "Who Guards America's Homes?," *AR*, May 1967; FFL 1968, 388.

68. MUST advertisement, May 1968, reproduced in ECM, reel 2; *CR*, May 14, 1968, 13230-31.

69. *F&VIAL*, 58. Other white "neighborhood protective associations" are examined in Elizabeth Hinton, *America on Fire: The Untold History of Police Violence and Black Rebellion since the 1960s* (New York: Liveright, 2021).

70. US Congress, House, Committee on Post Office and Civil Service, *Mail Order Gun Control: Hearing before the Subcommittee on Postal Operations of the Committee on Post Office and Civil Service*, 90th Cong., 2nd sess., July 2, 1968, 1.

71. *F&VIAL*, 57.

CHAPTER 4

1. In 1971 Senate testimony Washington, DC, police chief Jerry Wilson said the metal in cheap guns "is of such low quality that the characteristics of the barrel are altered every time the weapon is fired." See SNS 1971, 110. See also Robert Sherrill, "The Saturday Night Special and Other Hardware," *NYT*, October 10, 1971.

2. SNS 1971, 224–25.

3. The FTF's report was published as *F&VIAL*.

4. Dean Rusk, telegram draft, undated (drafted between June 6 and 10, 1968), ECR, Series 44: Research Files, box 5, folder State Department, Office of Munitions Control, Materials.

5. On modernization and US foreign policy, see Nils Gilman, *Mandarins of the Future: Modernization Theory in the Cold War* (Baltimore: Johns Hopkins University Press, 2003); and David Ekbladh, *The Great American Mission: Modernization and the Construction of an American World Order* (Princeton, NJ: Princeton University Press, 2010).

6. Gilman, *Mandarins of the Future*, 13, says, "Whereas scholars in the 1950s felt good about modernity and confident that imposing modernity on the postcolonial world

would be a good thing, by the 1970s they were dubious about modernity even in their own homeland."

7. Victor Luckerson, "Barack Obama's Speech on New Gun Control Measures," *Time*, January 5, 2016.

8. These records can be found in ECR, Series 44: Research File, box 1, folder CH-1 Sources.

9. US Department of Commerce, Business and Defense Services Administration, "U.S. Imports by Country of Origin, 1967," ECR, Series 44: Research File, box 1, folder CH-1 Sources.

10. US Embassy Bonn airgram to Department of State, October 18, 1968, ECR, Series 44: Research File, box 3, folder State Department Replies re: Statistics and Serial Numbers.

11. Frederick S. York to George D. Newton Jr., November 8, 1968; and US Embassy Madrid airgram to Department of State, November 9, 1968, ECR, Series 44: Research File, box 3, folder State Department Replies re: Statistics and Serial Numbers.

12. Lyndon B. Johnson letter to Congress, September 14, 1967, LBF, Gun Control, box 2, folder Firearms Act (1968) (2).

13. Lyndon B. Johnson letter to Congress, June 24, 1968, LBJ Papers, LBF, Gun Control, box 1, folder 6 Licensing and Registration Bill—1968.

14. Dodd press release, April 8, 1968, TJD, box 209, folder 5619; and Thomas J. Dodd, "The Sickness of Violence," speech before the Young Democratic Convention, Hartford, CT, May 4, 1968, TJD, box 209, folder 5628; Thomas J. Dodd press release, June 5, 1968, TJD, box 210, folder 5651.

15. "Minutes of Cabinet Meeting, June 12, 1968," LBJC, box 14, folder Cabinet Meeting, June 12, 1968, 1 of 3; Matthew Nimetz, Memorandum, "Firearm Registration," June 24, 1968, LBF, Gun Control, box 1, folder 2; Memorandum, FBI director to attorney general, July 5, 1968, RCP, box 92, folder Firearms Testimony, July 9, 1968.

16. Quoted in Alexander DeConde, *Gun Violence in America: The Struggle for Control* (Boston: Northeastern University Press, 2001), 187.

17. Robert O. Self, *All in the Family: The Realignment of American Democracy since the 1960s* (New York: Hill and Wang, 2012), 80.

18. Ramsey Clark, *Crime in America: Observations on Its Nature, Causes, Prevention and Control* (New York: Simon and Schuster, 1970), 114. On Cold War liberalism and masculinity, see Robert D. Dean, *Imperial Brotherhood: Gender and the Making of Cold War Foreign Policy* (Amherst: University of Massachusetts Press, 2003); and K. A. Cuordileone, *Manhood and American Political Culture in the Cold War* (New York: Routledge, 2004).

19. On the frontier in twentieth-century thinking, see Richard Slotkin, *Gunfighter Nation: The Myth of the Frontier in Twentieth-Century America* (Norman: University of Oklahoma Press, 1998).

20. Thomas J. Dodd, "Showdown at the Congressional Corral," unpublished manuscript, undated draft (1969), TJD, box 141, folder 3729; Thomas J. Dodd statement on "The State Firearms Control Assistance Amendments of 1965," March 10, 1966, TJD, box 204, folder 5316.

21. "Remarks of Senator Thomas J. Dodd on the Floor of the Senate on Introduction of a Bill to Amend the Federal Firearms Act," January 6, 1965, TJD, box 201, folder 5153.

22. Dodd press release, July 17, 1968, TJD, box 211, folder 5682. For example, see Warren Magnuson's call, after the JFK assassination, for a solution not "conceived in hysteria, born of ignorance," but instead "dictated by the voices of reason, not emotion." ISF 1964, 9.

23. *The Challenge of Crime in a Free Society: A Report by the President's Commission on Law Enforcement and Administration of Justice* (Washington, DC: US Government Printing Office, 1967), 241.

24. "Final Report Draft," pp. 17-4, 17-6, ECM, reel 12.

25. Dodd, "Showdown at the Congressional Corral." The White House reported 5,000 letters on gun control in the week after RFK's death, with 90 percent supporting stronger restrictions. See Larry Levinson to Joe Califano, June 14, 1968, LBF, Gun Control, box 1, folder 3.

26. Sample letters to Dodd can be found in TJD, box 130, folder 3471.

27. The Cohen family to LBJ, June 6, 1968; Robert N. Jorgensen to LBJ, June 5, 1968; and Palmer Smith to Douglass Cater, June 7, 1968, all in WHCF, LE, box 34, folder F LE/CM/Firearms, December 11, 1965–; Fred Panzer Memorandum to the President, re: Advance Gallup for Sunday, June 9, 1968," June 7, 1968, LBF, Gun Control, box 1, folder 3.

28. Patrick J. Charles, *Armed in America: A History of Gun Rights from Colonial Militias to Concealed Carry* (New York: Prometheus, 2018), 254.

29. Thomas J. Dodd to Jerry Gross, July 19, 1968, TJD, box 128, folder 3420.

30. Photocopies of excerpts of Bakal's book can be found in RCP, box 105, folder Firearms; Clark, *Crime in America*, 105.

31. List of attendees for signing of H.R. 17775—Gun Control Act, October 22, 1968, LBF, Gun Control, box 2, folder Firearms Act (1968) (2).

32. Carl Bakal, *The Right to Bear Arms* (New York: McGraw-Hill, 1966), 1, 12.

33. Bakal, *The Right to Bear Arms*, 27, 43, 66.

34. Bakal, *The Right to Bear Arms*, 31, 8.

35. JD 1963, 3374.

36. Bakal, *The Right to Bear Arms*, 277.

37. Robert Sherrill, "High Noon on Capitol Hill," *NYT*, June 23, 1968.

38. James V. Bennett to Dodd, February 7, 1961; and Dodd to James V. Bennett, July 14, 1969, TJD, box 393, folder 8675.

39. NCRFP, "For Firearms Policies in the Public Interests," pamphlet, undated [1968], RCP, box 105, folder Gun 1968 (1 of 2); NCRFP advertisement, 1968, copy in ECM, reel 2.

40. On reformers like Bennett, see Elizabeth Borgwardt, *A New Deal for the World: America's Vision for Human Rights* (Cambridge, MA: Harvard University Press, 2007).

41. See David J. Steinberg to NCRFP members, April 15, 1977, CHCR, box 1, folder 24. On grassroots attitudes toward the NCRFP, see Laura Fermi, "Report on Detroit Meeting, November 16, 1974," November 19, 1974, CDCR, box 2, folder Minutes, 1974–1978.

42. Kyle Longley, *LBJ's 1968: Power, Politics, and the Presidency in America's Year of Upheaval* (New York: Cambridge University Press, 2018), 155.

43. David Farber, *The Age of Great Dreams* (New York: Hill and Wang, 1994).

44. "Statement by the President to the Commission on Investigating Violence," June 10, 1968, LBF, Gun Control, box 1, folder 3, Public Concern.

45. Larry Temple interview, Tape no. 3, June 26, 1970, LBJ Library Oral Histories.

46. For the makeup of the commission and the various task forces, see the commission's final report, *To Establish Justice, to Insure Domestic Tranquility: Final Report of the National Commission on the Causes and Prevention of Violence* (Washington, DC: US Government Printing Office, 1969).

47. Lyndon Johnson draft letter to Milton Eisenhower, undated [June 1968], LBF, Gun Control, box 2, folder 3, Public Concern.

48. Marvin Wolfgang, "Progress Report Draft," undated [Fall 1968], ECM, reel 2.

49. Leon Radzinowicz, "Memorandum A, Draft Report: Task Force on Firearms," February 3, 1969, ECM, reel 1.

50. Staff requested and received extensive documentation from the State Department about these issues. See "State Department," undated memo (1968), in ECR, Series 44: Research Files, box 4, folder State Department Materials on Imported Guns; *F&VIAL*, 122.

51. Quoted in DeConde, *Gun Violence in America*, 183.

52. "158. Media Reaction Analysis Prepared in the Office of Police and Research, United States Information Agency," July 26, 1967, *Foreign Relations of the United States, 1917–1972*, vol. 7, *Public Diplomacy, 1964–1968* (Washington, DC: US Government Publishing Office, 2018). See also Foreign Broadcast Information Service, Special Report on Communist Propaganda, "Communist Reaction to the Assassination of Senator Robert Kennedy," June 13, 1968, LBJ Library, National Security File, Subject File, box 20, folder Senator Kennedy Assassination, June 5, 1968.

53. US Information Agency, "Media Reaction Analysis," June 5, 1968, in US Information Agency, *Media Reaction Analysis*, vol. 7, *April—June 1968*, in LHMP, box 41.

54. US Information Agency, "Media Reaction Analysis," June 7, 10, and 12, 1968, in US Information Agency, *Media Reaction Analysis*, vol. 7, *April—June 1968*, in LHMP, box 41.

55. These telegrams can be found in ECR, Series 44: Research Files, box 4, folder State Department Materials on Imported Guns.

56. US Embassy Kabul telegram to Department of State, June 18, 1968, ECR, Series 44: Research Files, box 4, folder State Department Materials on Imported Guns.

57. List of countries and gun laws, ECR, Series 44: Research Files, box 5, folder State Department, Office of Munitions Control, Materials.

58. US Embassy Tokyo telegram to Department of State, June 13, 1968, ECR, Series 44: Research Files, box 4, folder State Department Materials on Imported Guns.

59. US Embassy Vientiane telegram to Department of State, June 17, 1968, ECR, Series 44: Research File, box 4, folder State Department Materials on Imported Guns.

60. For a good primer on social science research on gun violence, see Philip J. Cook and Kristin A. Goss, *The Gun Debate: What Everyone Needs to Know* (New York: Oxford University Press, 2020); and Philip J. Cook, "The Great American Gun War: Notes from Four Decades in the Trenches," *Crime and Justice* 42, no. 1 (August 2013): 19–73.

61. See *F&VIAL*, 44.

62. Amitai Etzioni, "Gun Control: Arms Reduction, Criminality, and Political Constraints," May 1968 memorandum to Frederick M. Bohen, LBJ Library, Office Files of the White House Aides, James C. Gaither, box 9, folder Gaither: Gun Control (1-a).

63. Data are available at gunpolicy.org.

64. The Eisenhower Commission received data from gun manufacturers in a roundabout way. The gunmakers were hesitant to share what they claimed were sensitive industry

data, so they arranged with commissioners to submit data that had been aggregated and anonymized by the industry's lobby, SAAMI. See Robert C. Zimmer, "Memorandum of Conference of Members of the Sporting Arms and Ammunition Manufacturers' Institute with the Staff of the National Commission on the Causes and Prevention of Violence," August 9, 1968, ECM, reel 2.

65. *F&VIAL*, 7.

66. *F&VIAL*, 119.

67. *F&VIAL*, 128.

68. Jelani Cobb and Matthew Guariglia, eds., *The Essential Kerner Commission Report* (New York: Liveright, 2021). Elizabeth Hinton, *America on Fire: The Untold History of Police Violence and Black Rebellion since the 1960s* (New York: Liveright, 2021), 171, says the Kerner report sold 2 million copies in paperback.

69. *F&VIAL*, 140, 142.

CHAPTER 5

1. See Internal Revenue Service form, "Factoring Criteria for Weapons," reproduced SNS 1971, 43.

2. The Office of Munitions Control reported seventy-two importing firms registered with the State Department in 1968, of which twenty-nine qualified as "major." See Robert H. Rose to Joseph Sahid, July 3, 1968, ECR, Series 44: Research File, box 4, folder State Department Materials on Imported Guns.

3. I've recreated this dialogue from Serr's account of the conversation in SNS 1971, 331–32.

4. Thomas J. Dodd press release, July 10, 1968, TJD, box 210, folder 5677.

5. *F&VIAL*, 174.

6. Dodd to Lyndon Johnson, July 6, 1968, WHCF, TA, box 15, folder TA 6/F; Dodd press release, July 10, 1968, TJD, box 210, folder 5677.

7. John W. Sipes to Dodd, July 15, 1968, TJD, box 128, folder 3420; Patrick Brogan and Albert Zarca, *Deadly Business: Sam Cummings, Interarms, and the Arms Trade* (New York: W. W. Norton, 1983), 227, 282–83.

8. "Saturday Night Specials," editorial, *NYT*, March 14, 1970.

9. For a popular assessment of the GCA and other federal gun control efforts, see Robert J. Spitzer, *The Politics of Gun Control*, 8th ed. (New York: Routledge, 2020).

10. SNS 1971, 26.

11. See, for example, Neil Sheehan, "Pistol Production in U.S. Rising, Offsetting '68 Importation Ban," *NYT*, April 30, 1969.

12. JD 1969, 46.

13. JD 1969, 46.

14. JD 1969, 167.

15. Charles Patrick, "Saturday Night Specials: The Cheap, Easy and Deadly Way to End an Argument," *Floridian*, November 28, 1971; Sheehan, "Pistol Production"; Terry Johnson King, "Business Booming for Maker of Cheap Pistols," *Orlando Sentinel*, February 15, 1970; Joseph Albright and Henry Eason, "The Man Who Made a Killing on Guns," *MN*, September 8, 1981.

16. Frank Smyth, *The NRA: The Unauthorized History* (New York: Flatiron, 2020), 54.

17. Alexander DeConde, *Gun Violence in America: The Struggle for Control* (Boston: Northeastern University Press, 2001), 215.

18. Violence Policy Center, "Where'd They Get Their Guns?," http://www.vpc.org /studies/wgun810330.htm. The six-part series, "Handguns: The Snub-Nosed Killer," was produced by a team of journalists working for Cox News Service, based in Miami and Washington, DC, and ran in newspapers across the country.

19. Sheehan, "Pistol Production"; Albright and Eason, "Man Who Made a Killing."

20. Frank Murray, "Importation of Handgun Parts Riddles Federal Arms Law," *MN*, December 17, 1969; John W. Sipes to Dodd, July 15, 1968, TJD, box 128, folder 3420.

21. SNS 1971, 124.

22. SNS 1971, 293.

23. Sheehan, "Pistol Production"; Albright and Eason, "Man Who Made a Killing"; Matt Taylor, "Gunmaker: Big Profit on Cheap Weapon," *Miami Herald*, May 11, 1969; King, "Business Booming."

24. Frederick S. York to George D. Newton Jr., November 8, 1968, ECR, Series 44: Research File, box 3, folder State Dept Replies re: Statistics and Serial Numbers.

25. Neil Sheehan, "Pistol Production"; Albright and Eason, "Man Who Made a Killing"; Joseph Albright, "There's Plenty of Profit Potential in a $39.95 Gun," *MN*, September 8, 1981; Murray, "Importation of Handgun Parts."

26. Joseph Albright, "Tiny Gun Shop Hit It Big with an Import," *MN*, September 9, 1981; "Leading Sources of Handguns, 1979," *MN*, September 9, 1981; Judith Gaines, "Gunmakers Defend Gun Law Loophole," *MN*, September 9, 1981.

27. Albright, "Tiny Gun Shop."

28. The first press reports in January 1987 noted that the company had stopped making guns and listed its property for sale a year earlier. See Nancy McVicar, "Insurance Woes Close Miami Plant That Put Hinckley Handgun Together," *MN*, January 30, 1987.

29. McVicar, "Insurance Woes Close Miami Plant."

30. Brill would create the cable television network Court TV in 1991.

31. Steven Brill, *Firearms Abuse: A Research and Policy Report* (Washington, DC: Police Foundation, 1977), vii.

32. Brill, *Firearms Abuse*, 56.

33. Steven Brill, "The Traffic (Legal and Illegal) in Guns," *Harper's*, September 1977, 37–44.

34. Brill, "The Traffic (Legal and Illegal) in Guns."

35. Pete Early, "The Gun: A Saturday Night Special from Miami," *WP*, March 31, 1981.

36. Milton S. Eisenhower, "Commission Statement on Firearms & Violence," July 28, 1969, reproduced in JD 1969, 90–101.

37. These included two well-cited articles published in 1968: "Is Gun Control Likely to Reduce Violent Killings?" *University of Chicago Law Review* 35, no. 4 (Summer 1968): 721–37; and "Games with Guns and Statistics," *Wisconsin Law Review* 4 (1968): 1113–26.

38. JD 1969, 154–57.

39. JD 1969, 166–67.

40. SNS 1971, 353.

41. In 1977 the National Council for the Control of Handguns received through a Freedom of Information Act request documents related to how "sporting purposes"

criteria were initially determined in 1968. The NCCH reported that the panel charged with developing the criteria had no gun control advocates but did include representatives from the gun industry. See "Carter Sets Handgun Control Bill on '78 Agenda," *NCCH Washington Report*, October 1977, CDCR, box 2, folder NCCH 1976.

42. SNS 1971, 26, 34–35, 131.

43. "How NRA Disarms Gun Control Efforts," *CT*, June 30, 1972.

44. SNS 1971, 133, 295.

45. SNS 1971, 132; Robert Sherrill, "The Saturday Night Special and Other Hardware," *New York Times Magazine*, October 10, 1971.

46. Sherrill, "The Saturday Night Special and Other Hardware."

47. SNS 1971, 330–32, 342.

48. Sherrill, "The Saturday Night Special and Other Hardware"; see also Robert Sherrill, *The Saturday Night Special, and Other Guns with Which Americans Won the West, Protected Bootleg Franchises, Slew Wildlife, Robbed Countless Banks, Shot Husbands Purposely and by Mistake and Killed Presidents—Together with Some Debate over Continuing the Same* (New York: Charterhouse, 1973).

49. Sherrill, *Saturday Night Special*, 283.

50. Franklin E. Zimring, "Firearms and Federal Law: The Gun Control Act of 1968," *Journal of Legal Studies* 4, no. 1 (January 1975): 134–35, 198.

51. Carl Bakal, "The Failure of Federal Gun Control," *Saturday Review*, July 3, 1971, reproduced in SNS 1971, 204–5.

52. Flora Lewis, "New York's Shooting Deaths Exceed Those of Vietnam," *WP*, September 4, 1971; SNS 1971, 171.

53. Al Baker, "Patrick V. Murphy, Police Leader Who Reformed New York Force, Dies at 91," *NYT*, December 17, 2011. See also Patrick V. Murphy, *Commissioner: A View from the Top of American Law Enforcement* (New York: Simon & Schuster, 1978).

54. Richard L. Madden, "Murphy Seeks a Policy to Disarm All Citizens," *NYT*, December 8, 1970.

55. See ISF 1964, 276–77.

56. SNS 1971, 183.

57. Madden, "Murphy Seeks a Policy to Disarm All Citizens"; SNS 1971, 185.

CHAPTER 6

1. See "Statement of Senator Thomas J. Dodd: A Tribute to James V. Bennett upon His Retirement as Director of Federal Bureau of Prisons," August 20, 1964, TJD, box 200, folder 5096.

2. See the small collection of materials in JHGA, box 53, folder 24.

3. On "gun control" in the nineteenth century, see Saul Cornell, *A Well-Regulated Militia: The Founding Fathers and the Origins of Gun Control in America* (New York: Oxford University Press, 2006); and Adam Winkler, *Gunfight: The Battle over the Right to Bear Arms in America* (New York: W. W. Norton, 2011). Histories of gun control in the twentieth century include Kristin Goss, *Disarmed: The Missing Movement for Gun Control in America* (Princeton, NJ: Princeton University Press, 2006); and Alexander DeConde, *Gun Violence in America: The Struggle for Control* (Boston: Northeastern University Press, 2001).

4. At the peak of gun violence in 1974 there were 325,000 incidents nationally, or 890 per day. See Winkler, *Gunfight*, 16.

5. Fermi founded the Cleaner Air Committee of Hyde Park and Kenwood in 1959, which she described as "one of the earliest citizens' groups to alert the public about the dangers of air pollution and work toward the abatement of pollution." Laura Fermi to unknown recipient, March 15, 1975, LFP, box 7, folder 10.

6. This line comes from a story recounted in a letter from John J. Buckley to Lillian Kaplan, undated (July 1978?), CDCR, box 1, folder Corres. w/ Legislators, 1972–1976. Michelle M. Nickerson, *Mothers of Conservatism: Women and the Postwar Right* (Princeton, NJ: Princeton University Press, 2012), xviii, observes that the "little old ladies in tennis shoes" moniker was commonly used in the 1960s to denigrate members of the John Birch Society in California.

7. Carl Bakal, *The Right to Bear Arms* (New York: McGraw-Hill, 1966), 128.

8. The most prominent example is Winkler, *Gunfight*, 65–68.

9. Recent work has emphasized greater continuity in the NRA's messaging pre- and post-1977. See Matthew J. Lacombe, *Firepower: How the NRA Turned Gun Owners into a Political Force* (Princeton, NJ: Princeton University Press, 2021).

10. Winkler, *Gunfight*, 16; Chicago Police Department, *Statistical Summary 1974*. Chicago Police Department annual reports can be found at https://home.chicagopolice .org/statistics-data/statistical-reports/.

11. See Gregg Lee Carter, ed., *Guns in American Society: An Encyclopedia of History, Politics, Culture, and the Law*, 2 vols. (Santa Barbara, CA: ABC CLIO, 2002); Gregg Lee Carter, *The Gun Control Movement* (New York: Twayne, 1997); and Robert J. Spitzer, *Gun Control: A Documentary and Reference Guide* (Westport, CT: Greenwood, 2009).

12. Emilio Segrè, Alice Kimball Smith, and Ruth Grodzins, "Laura Fermi, 1907–1977," *Bulletin of the Atomic Scientists*, May 1978, 2–3; Raul Hilberg, *The Destruction of the European Jews*, vol. 2, 3rd ed. (New Haven, CT: Yale University Press, 2003), 723. Fermi never appeared to have written about Augusto Capon's fate, though it was known during her lifetime, appearing at least as early as Robert Katz, *Black Sabbath: A Journal through a Crime against Humanity* (New York: Macmillan, 1969).

13. Laura Fermi, *Atoms in the Family: My Life with Enrico Fermi* (Chicago: University of Chicago Press, 1954), 7.

14. Fermi, *Atoms in the Family*, 116, 120.

15. "Laura Fermi," Atomic Heritage Foundation, https://www.atomicheritage.org /profile/laura-fermi.

16. Laura Fermi, *Atoms for the World: United States Participation in the Conference on the Peaceful Uses of Atomic Energy* (Chicago: University of Chicago Press, 1957), 1.

17. Laura Fermi, *Mussolini* (Chicago: University of Chicago Press, 1961); Laura Fermi and Gilberto Bernardini, *Galileo and the Scientific Revolution* (New York: Basic Books, 1961); Laura Fermi, *The Story of Atomic Energy* (New York: Random House, 1961).

18. Laura Fermi, *Illustrious Immigrants: The Intellectual Migration from Europe, 1930–41* (Chicago: University of Chicago Press, 1968).

19. CDC newsletter, undated (January 1978), CDCR, box 4, folder Newsletters, 1974–1978.

20. Segrè, Smith, and Grodzins, "Laura Fermi, 1907–1977."

21. "Physicist Ugo Fano Dies at 88," *University of Chicago Chronicle*, March 15, 2001.

22. Louise Lerner, "Clemens C. J. Roothaan, Eminent Quantum Chemist and Concentration Camp Survivor, 1918–2019," *UChicago News*, July 1, 2019.

23. Fermi, *Illustrious Immigrants*, 375–76.

24. Andrew J. Diamond, *Chicago on the Make: Power and Inequality in a Modern City* (Berkeley: University of California Press, 2017), 3.

25. Diamond, *Chicago on the Make*, 173.

26. Diamond, *Chicago on the Make*, 134.

27. Richard S. Kjarval to Laura Fermi, March 2, 1976, CDCR, box 1, folder Corres. 1976.

28. Diamond, *Chicago on the Make*, 16.

29. Diamond, *Chicago on the Make*, 222–23.

30. Chicago Police Department, *Statistical Summary 1974*. In any given year as much as 20 percent of gun homicides identified firearms of "unknown type" as responsible. It's safe to assume, following national data trends, that at least 70 percent of these unknown firearms were handguns.

31. Clarence G. Erickson to Laura Fermi, undated (August 1972), CDCR, box 1, folder Corres. 1971–1972; Robert Sherrill, *The Saturday Night Special, and Other Guns with Which Americans Won the West, Protected Bootleg Franchises, Slew Wildlife, Robbed Countless Banks, Shot Husbands Purposely and by Mistake and Killed Presidents—Together with Some Debate over Continuing the Same* (New York: Charterhouse, 1973), 125.

32. Simon Balto, *Occupied Territory: Policing Black Chicago from Red Summer to Black Power* (Chapel Hill: University of North Carolina Press, 2019), 178.

33. Douglas Longhini, "Chicago Crime Victims: A Reporter Study," *Chicago Reporter*, August 1975, copy in CHCR, box 13, folder 129.

34. Balto, *Occupied Territory*, 164–65.

35. Balto, *Occupied Territory*, 158–59, 163, 179, 1.

36. Elizabeth Hinton, *America on Fire: The Untold History of Police Violence and Black Rebellion since the 1960s* (New York: Liveright, 2021), 15. For a similar argument, see Lauren Pearlman, *Democracy's Capital: Black Political Power in Washington, D.C., 1960s–1970s* (Chapel Hill: University of North Carolina Press, 2019).

37. On the origins of federal funding of local and state police forces, which included surplus military equipment, see Elizabeth Hinton, *From the War on Poverty to the War on Crime: The Making of Mass Incarceration in America* (Cambridge, MA: Harvard University Press, 2016). On counterinsurgency and policing, see Stuart Schrader, *Badges without Borders: How Global Counterinsurgency Transformed American Policing* (Berkeley: University of California Press, 2019).

38. For examples, see "2 Support Sidearms for Private Citizens," *CD*, October 15, 1974; and "Defends Guns," *CD*, December 14, 1974.

39. Balto, *Occupied Territory*, 157.

40. On Ethel Payne, see James McGrath Morris, *Eye on the Struggle: Ethel Payne, the First Lady of the Black Press* (New York: Amistad, 2017).

41. CCWWC statement, June 2, 1975, CHCR, box 14, folder 147; CCWWC question and answer sheet, undated (1974–75), CDCR, box 3, folder Sponsoring Orgs. Corres., Publicity, Statements, 1974–1975.

42. "Women Fighting Crime Announce Next Move," *CD*, March 4, 1974; "Supt. James Rochford Urges Ban on Handguns," *CD*, June 19, 1974.

43. "Rochford and Coalition of Concerned Women," *CD*, March 18, 1974.

44. CCWWC advertisement, *CD*, March 2, 1974. The ad ran several times a week for a period in 1974. See also Jennifer Mayer, "A Review of the War on Crime," *CD*, September 7, 1974; "War on Crime: What to Do to Protect Yourself," *CD*, March 16, 1974.

45. "Supt. James Rochford Urges Ban on Handguns"; CCWWC statement, June 2, 1975, CHCR, box 14, folder 147.

46. CCWWC Statement, June 2, 1975, CHCR, box 14, folder 147.

47. CDC newsletter, June 20, 1974, CDCR, box 5, folder 2.

48. CCWWC statement, June 2, 1975, CHCR, box 14, folder 147; "War on Crime Anniversary," *CD*, February 24, 1975. Nicholas Johnson, *Negroes and the Gun: The Black Tradition of Arms* (New York: Prometheus, 2014), 14, attributes the kind of abolitionist sentiment the CCWWC expressed to the emergence of a new Black political class with real political power in places like Chicago and Washington, DC.

49. On the emotional labor related to gun violence by Black women in Chicago, see Justin Agrelo, "The Unsung Women Healing Chicago," *The Trace*, October 11, 2022.

50. For example, the CCWWC received an $85,000 grant in 1976 for a "Citizen Participation Advocacy Program" that proposed "active citizen involvement and increased understanding of the functions of rules, laws, and organization of the criminal justice system." See the materials in Abbott-Sengstacke Family Papers, box 183, folder 11, Chicago Public Library, Woodson Regional Library, Vivian G. Harsh Research Collection of Afro-American History and Culture.

51. James Forman Jr., *Locking Up Our Own: Crime and Punishment in Black America* (New York: Farrar, Straus and Giroux, 2017), 12.

52. Jon Van, "Gun Registration Meant to Cut Crime—It Hasn't," *CT*, December 23, 1973.

53. CDC meeting minutes, January 8, 1974, CDCR, box 1, folder Minutes, 1971–1974; FL 1975, 506. On Kane's views, see Francis P. Kane, "Bunkers with Guns," *CT*, April 23, 1973.

54. See Bureau of Alcohol, Tobacco, and Firearms, *Concentrated Urban Enforcement: An Analysis of the Initial Year of Operation CUE in the Cities of Washington, D.C., Boston, Mass., Chicago, Ill.* (Washington, DC: Department of Treasury, 1977); Phillip J. O'Connor, "Many Confiscated Guns Traced to the South," *Chicago Daily News*, January 17, 1977.

55. Susan Hall, "Nice People Who Carry Guns," *New York*, December 12, 1977.

56. Barbara Rosi to Dan Cox, March 5, 1975, and Laura Fermi to Rex D. Davis, March 27, 1975, CDCR, box 1, folder Corres. 1974–1975.

57. CDC newsletter, January 1976, CDCR, box 5, folder 2.

58. On citizen activism in this era, see Michael Stewart Foley, *Front Porch Politics: The Forgotten Heyday of American Activism in the 1970s and 1980s* (New York: Hill and Wang, 2013).

59. CDC meeting minutes, February 20, 1974, CDCR, box 1, folder Minutes, 1971–1974.

60. CDC meeting minutes, May 17, 1972, and November 18, 1971, CDCR, box 1, folder Minutes, 1971–1974.

61. CDC meeting minutes, CDCR, December 2, 1971, and January 19, 1972, box 1, folder Minutes, 1971–1974.

62. Various CDC meeting minutes from 1972–73, CDCR, box 1, folder Minutes, 1971–1974; "A Brief History of the Civic Disarmament Committee, 1977," CDCR box 3, folder Statements, Corres., Reports, Publicity, 1972–1975.

63. See Leon M. Despres to Laura Fermi, February 21, 1972; CDC to Richard J. Daley, June 2, 1972; and CDC form letter to city mayors, May 26, 1972, CDCR, box 1, folder Corres. 1971–1972. Also see "Statement of the Civic Disarmament Committee before the City Council Committee on Federal and State Legislation," February 24, 1972; Chicago City Council, "Resolution Memorializing Congress to Outlaw Hand Guns [sic] by Enacting S. 2815," February 24, 1972; and US Conference of Mayors, "Resolution on Gun Control," June 21, 1972, CDCR, box 4, folder Clippings and Press Releases, 1972–1977.

64. CDC newsletter, May 20, 1974, CDCR, box 5, folder 2.

65. George Wald to CDC, March 4, 1974, CDCR, box 1, folder Corres. 1973–1974. Wald had made the same point in a letter six months earlier.

66. Laura Fermi notes on NCCH founding, March 1975, CDCR, box 2, folder Minutes 1974–1978.

67. Some of these drafts can be found in CDCR, box 2, folder NCCH Corres., Statements, Publicity 1975–1976.

68. See CDC newsletter, November 20, 1974, CDCR, box 5, folder 2.

69. Adlai Stevenson III to Laura Fermi, August 5, 1976, CDCR, box 1, folder Corres. w/ Legislators 1972–1976.

70. NCCH, "Emergency Dispatch," undated (May 1978), CHCR, box 3, folder 29. On the LRS, see Patrick J. Charles, *Armed in America: A History of Gun Rights from Colonial Militias to Concealed Carry* (New York: Prometheus, 2018), 235–37.

71. Mark Borinsky to Patricia Koldyke, undated (late 1974), CHCR, box 3, folder 43.

72. CDC to "NCCH Friends," September 12, 1975, CDCR, box 1, folder Corres. 1974–1975.

73. For an analysis of the Zebra murders and race, see Christine Lamberson, "The Zebra Murders: Race, Civil Liberties, and Radical Politics in San Francisco," *Journal of Urban History* 42, no. 1 (2016): 201–25.

74. Richard Harris, "Handguns," *New Yorker*, July 26, 1976, 53–58; Donald Singleton, "Exec Who Faced Death Seeks Handgun Law," *NYSN*, September 21, 1975.

75. Harris, "Handguns"; Richard A. Ryan, "Slain Student's Father Leads Handgun Crusade," *Detroit News*, September 14, 1975.

76. See Thomas Frank, *The Conquest of Cool: Business Culture, Counterculture, and the Rise of Hip Consumerism* (Chicago: University of Chicago Press, 1998); Robert Bender, "One Father's Crusade against Handguns," *Parade*, September 18, 1977.

77. See NCCH pamphlet, undated (1976), CDC Papers, box 3, folder NCCH 1976; Ryan, "Slain Student's Father Leads Handgun Crusade"; Bender, "One Father's Crusade."

78. Singleton, "Exec Who Faced Death Seeks Handgun Law."

79. Harris, "Handguns."

80. Harris, "Handguns."

81. Hillary Johnson, "The Friendly Persuaders," *NYSN*, June 6, 1976.

82. See Rick Perlstein, *Before the Storm: Barry Goldwater and the Unmaking of the American Consensus* (New York: PublicAffairs, 2001).

83. Johnson, "The Friendly Persuaders"; Nick Thimmesch, "The Grass-Roots Dollar Chase—Ready on the Right," *New York*, June 9, 1975; Richard A. Viguerie and David

Franke, *America's Right Turn: How Conservatives Used New and Alternative Media to Take Power* (Chicago: Bonus Books, 2004).

84. Harris, "Handguns."

85. NCCH Minutes of Special Meeting of Governing Board, March 5, 1976, CDCR, box 2, folder National Coalition to Control Handguns, Corres. & Publicity, 1975–1976; NCCH, "A Proposal for Support," undated (late 1975, early 1976), CHCR, box 3, folder 43.

86. Peter C. Stuart, "Handgun Foes—Too Many Strategies?" *CSM*, June 2, 1976.

87. *Gun Week*, April 9, 1976, copy in CHCR, box 2, folder 26; CDC meeting minutes, May 12, 1976, CDCR, box 1, folder Minutes 1974–1978; *Targeting in on Handgun Control*, May 1976, CDCR, box 3, folder US Conference of Mayors Mailings and Bulletins, 1975–1976.

88. Harris, "Handguns"; Jeanne Shields, "Why Nick?," *Newsweek*, May 12, 1976, reprinted in *NCCH Washington Report*, June 1978, CHCR, box 2, folder 23.

89. Harris, "Handguns."

90. CDC meeting minutes, April 3, 1974, and May 1, 1974, CDCR, box 1, folder Minutes, 1971–1974; Laura Fermi to Sydney Stein Jr., January 20, 1976, CDCR, box 1, folder Corres. 1976.

91. CDC newsletter, February 4, 1976, CDCR, box 5, folder 2; CDC meeting minutes, January 5, 1977, CDCR, box 1, folder Minutes 1974–1978; Pete Shields to Estelle Jacobson, May 3, 1977, CHCR, box 3, folder 29. Shields had said early in 1976 that he would watch Massachusetts closely to determine the organization's direction after the 1976 election. See NCCH, "A Proposal for Support," undated (late 1975, early 1976), CHC Records, box 3, folder 43.

92. Ramsey Clark to Preston E. Cook, June 25, 1976, CDCR, box 1, folder Corres. 1976.

93. Stuart, "Handgun Foes."

94. Laura Fermi to Robert McClory, May 2, 1975, CDCR, box 1, folder Corres. 1974–1975; Lillian Kaplan to Nelson Shields, January 19, 1977, CDCR, box 2, folder National Coalition to Control Handguns, Corres. and Publicity, 1975–1976.

95. "NCCH Position Regarding Licensing and Registration," undated (1974), CDCR, box 2, folder NCCH Corres., Statements, Publicity 1975–1976.

96. Laura Fermi to Nelson T. Shields, September 1, 1976, CDCR, box 1, folder Corres. w/ Legislators, 1972–1976; Laura Fermi to Harry Fossward, March 4, 1976, LFP, box 7, folder 11.

97. CDC newsletter, December 1976, CDCR, box 5, folder 2.

98. Mark Borinsky to NCCH members, October 1, 1975, CDCR, box 2, folder National Coalition to Control Handguns, Corres. & Publicity, 1975–1976.

99. CDC meeting minutes, March 10, 1976, CDCR, box 1, folder Minutes 1974–1978.

100. Nelson Shields, "Memorandum to Guests at the U.S. Conference of Mayors June 10, 1976 Meeting," June 4, 1976, CDCR, box 2, folder Corres., Statements, Releases, 1974–1977.

101. CDC meeting minutes, April 7, 1976, CDCR, box 1, folder Minutes 1974–1978.

102. Nelson T. Shields to Laura Fermi, March 26, 1976, CDCR, box 2, folder National Coalition to Control Handguns, Corres. & Publicity, 1975–1976.

103. CDC newsletter, December 1978, CHCR, box 9, folder 91.

104. See Brady United against Gun Violence, *Annual Report Fiscal Year 2019*, available at https://www.bradyunited.org/annual-report.

CHAPTER 7

1. "Saturday Night Special" flyer, June 1975, CHCR, box 3, folder 32. At first the CHC wrote *handgun* as two words but later used both the open and closed forms. Unless quoting directly, I write *handgun* as one word.

2. CHC press release, "Why We Have Come to Washington," October 1975, CHCR, box 3, folder 32; Invitation to Conference on Hand Gun Control, Committee the for the Study of Hand Gun Misuse, undated (1975), CHCR, box 1, folder 8. See Shannon Watts, *Fight Like a Mother: How a Grassroots Movement Took on the Gun Lobby and Why Women Will Change the World* (New York: HarperCollins, 2019). For an earlier iteration of the Moms Demand Action phenomenon, see Donna Dees-Thomases, *Looking for a Few Good Moms: How One Mother Rallied a Million Others against the Gun Lobby* (New York: Rodale, 2004). Dees-Thomases organized the 2000 Million Moms March.

3. C. Fraser Smith, "'I Feel I Have to Be Doing This,'" *Providence Sunday Journal*, December 15, 1974, copy in CHCR, box 3, folder 36.

4. See, for example, CDC meeting minutes, October 15, 1974, and November 6, 1974, CDCR, box 2, folder Minutes, 1974–1978.

5. CHC membership list, undated (1974–75), CHCR, box 14, folder 150.

6. Monica Wilch Perin, "Women Take Aim at Hand Guns," *Chicago Herald*, March 15, 1976, copy in CHCR, box 1, folder 8.

7. Historians have explored several aspects of women's postwar political activism, particularly in conservative circles. See Lisa McGirr, *Suburban Warriors: The Origins of the New American Right* (Princeton, NJ: Princeton University Press, 2001); Michelle M. Nickerson, *Mothers of Conservatism: Women and the Postwar Right* (Princeton, NJ: Princeton University Press, 2012); and Donald T. Critchlow, *Phyllis Schlafly and Grassroots Conservatism: A Woman's Crusade* (Princeton, NJ: Princeton University Press, 2005).

8. Jane Gregory, "Housewives against Handguns," *Sun-Times Two*, March 4, 1975, copy in CHCR, box 6, folder 70.

9. Ellis Cose, "Illinois Gun Foes Hope to Shake Up NRA Goliath," *Chicago Sun-Times*, October 13, 1975, copy in CHCR, box 1, folder 8; Al Bernstein, "'Housewives Doing Good' in Push for Handgun Ban," *The Life* (Skokie, IL), October 26, 1975, copy in CHCR, box 6, folder 71.

10. Gregory, "Housewives against Handguns."

11. The classic work on this phenomenon is Elaine Tyler May, *Homeward Bound: American Families in the Cold War Era* (New York: Basic Books, 1988).

12. See Thomas Bishop, *Every Home a Fortress: Cold War Fatherhood and the Family Fallout Shelter* (Amherst: University of Massachusetts Press, 2020).

13. Elaine Tyler May, *Fortress America: How We Embraced Fear and Abandoned Democracy* (New York: Basic Books, 2017), 75.

14. See Caroline E. Light, *Stand Your Ground: A History of America's Love Affair with Lethal Self-Defense* (Boston: Beacon, 2017).

15. May, *Fortress America*, 136.

16. Lizabeth Cohen, *A Consumers' Republic: The Politics of Mass Consumption in Postwar America* (New York: Vintage, 2003), 360.

17. Fox Butterfield, "Limits on Power and Zeal Hamper Firearms Agency," *NYT*, July 22, 1999.

18. On the battles over BATF funding, see William J. Vizzard, *In the Cross Fire: A Political History of the Bureau of Alcohol, Tobacco, and Firearms* (Boulder, CO: Lynne Rienner, 1997).

19. See Michael A. Brown to Neal Knox, December 20, 1973, Office of the General Counsel Advisory Opinions, CPSC, https://www.cpsc.gov/s3fs-public/pdfs/blk_media_54.pdf.

20. "Washington Report," *G&A*, June 1974, copy in CHCR, box 4, folder 49.

21. Gregory, "Housewives against Handguns."

22. This was how the CHC explained its decision in an undated (likely 1975) and untitled draft of a brief history of the organization, in CHCR, box 12, folder 120. See also Sam Cahnmann, "Bullets: A Private Plea for Gun Control," *University of Chicago Maroon*, July 26, 1974, copy in CDCR, box 1, folder 6.

23. CHC to Richard S. Simpson, June 1974, and Sheldon Butts to Susan Sullivan, July 30, 1974, CHCR, box 13, folder 132.

24. Alan C. Shakin, Office of General Counsel, to CPSC Commissioners, August 28, 1974, CHCR, box 13, folder 132.

25. CPSC ruling, undated (September 1974), CHCR, box 13, folder 132.

26. "Remarks by Commissioner Lawrence Kushner on Hand Gun Control and the Petition of the Committee for Hand Gun Control, Inc., to Ban Hand-Gun Ammunition," September 6, 1974, CHCR, box 13, folder 132.

27. CHC newsletter, October 7, 1974, CHCR, box 3, folder 45; Carole Shifrin, "Group Seeks to Force Ban on Hand Gun Bullets," *WP*, September 21, 1974; *Committee for Hand Gun Control, Inc., v. Consumer Product Safety Commission*, "Plaintiff's Motion for Summary Judgment," US District Court for the District of Columbia, October 1974, and accompanying letters, in CHCR, box 13, folder 132.

28. *Committee for Hand Gun Control, Inc., v. Consumer Product Safety Commission*, "Memorandum of Points and Authorities in Support of Defendants' Motion to Dismiss," US District Court for the District of Columbia, October 1974, CHCR, box 13, folder 132.

29. Jeff Lyon, "Local Group Wins Handgun Skirmish," *CT*, January 15, 1975.

30. CHC profile draft, undated (1975), CHCR, box 12, folder 120; Barry Goldwater to Estelle Jacobson, May 23, 1975, CHCR, box 13, folder 123.

31. Lyon, "Local Group Wins Handgun Skirmish."

32. CHC newsletter, May 1975, CHC Records, box 4, folder 46.

33. J. Walter Thompson Co., "Creative Presentation: The Committee for Handgun Control," undated (early 1975), CHCR, box 8, folder 76.

34. "Ban the Bullet," *Time*, March 3, 1975; CHC letter to consumer journalists, March 21, 1975, CHCR, box 13, folder 133; WMAQ-TV editorial, October 5, 1974, CHC Records, box 3, folder 45.

35. CHC newsletter, April 1975, CHCR, box 13, folder 133.

36. "House Backs End to Control on Some Consumer Items," *NYT*, October 23, 1975; "Ford Signs Bill Reinforcing Product Safety Commission," *NYT*, May 13, 1976.

37. For example, see "Act Before It Is Too Late," *AR*, September 1974, which describes the CHC as a "fresh movement out of Chicago to undermine legitimate gun ownership"; and Maxwell Rich, NRA fundraising letter to members, May 5, 1975, CHCR, box 16, folder 171.

38. Gregory, "Housewives against Handguns."

39. Hillary Johnson, "The Friendly Persuaders," *NYSN*, June 7, 1976.

40. This correspondence, along with all the quotes cited hereafter, can be found in CHCR, boxes 4–5, folders 55–63.

41. Defaced CHC advertisement, CHCR, box 4, folder 60.

42. Chad Kautzer, "America as a Tactical Gun Culture," *Boston Review*, December 17, 2021.

43. "NRA Forms Legislative Action Unit to Check Anti-gun Moves," *AR*, June 1975.

44. Harlon Carter, "The Saturday Night Special," *G&A*, June 1974.

45. Harlon Carter, "Liberalism and Gun Control: Just Where Do You Draw the Line?," *G&A*, March 1975.

46. Harlon Carter, "Gun Control: Cure-All for a Soft-Boiled Society," *G&A*, July 1975.

47. CHC press release, March 15, 1976, CHCR, box 13, folder 138.

48. US Conference of Mayors, *National Forum on Handgun Control Proceedings*, Los Angeles, May 27–29, 1975, 19–22, copy in CHCR, box 14, folder 158.

49. US Conference of Mayors, *National Forum*, 22.

50. Carter, "Liberalism and Gun Control."

51. See sample ads, CHC press releases, and a copy of the FTC complaint in CHCR, box 13, folder 138.

52. CHC press release, March 15, 1976, CHCR, box 13, folder 138.

53. Art Buchwald, "Handgun 'Merits' Shot Full of Holes," *Washington Post*, May 1, 1975, copy in CHCR, box 2, folder 19.

54. CHC press release, March 15, 1976, CHCR, box 13, folder 138.

55. "Gun Advertising Target of Complaints," *Chicago Herald*, March 15, 1976.

56. Rick Rojas, Karen Zraick, and Troy Closson, "Sandy Hook Families Settle with Gunmaker for $73 Million over Massacre," *NYT*, February 15, 2022.

57. Dick Pothier, "Ford's Consumer Plan Is Booed," *Philadelphia Inquirer*, January 24, 1976.

58. Georgene Campion testimony before the White House Regional Conference on Consumer Representation Plans, January 13, 1976, CHCR, box 12, folder 120.

59. See Timothy D. Lytton, ed., *Suing the Gun Industry: A Battle at the Crossroads of Gun Control and Mass Torts* (Ann Arbor: University of Michigan Press, 2006).

60. Michael D. Hausfeld to Susan Sullivan, August 5, 1975 (and attached legal memo), CHCR, box 13, folder 132.

61. Michael D. Hausfeld to Susan Sullivan, April 14, 1976, CHCR, box 13, folder 132.

62. CHC press release, April 18, 1977, CDCR, box 2, folder Corres., Statements, Releases, 1974–1977.

63. CDC newsletter, June 1977, CDCR, box 5, folder 1; CHC press release, January 4, 1978, CHCR, box 10, folder 100; Bette B. Anderson to Nelson T. Shields, July 12, 1977, CHCR, box 17, folder 181; Estelle Jacobson to Laura Fermi, June 15, 1977, CHCR, box 2, folder Corres., Statements, Releases, 1974–1977.

CHAPTER 8

1. Quoted in Harry Kelly, "New NRA Chief Draws a Bead on Gun Control," *CT*, May 29, 1977. Examples of this standard narrative abound. For example, see Adam Winkler, *Gunfight: The Battle over the Right to Bear Arms in America* (New York: W. W. Norton,

2011), 65–68; Josh Sugarmann, *National Rifle Association: Money, Firepower & Fear* (Washington, DC: National Press, 1992), 46–50; Osha Gray Davidson, *Under Fire: The NRA and the Battle for Gun Control* (Iowa City: University of Iowa Press, 1998), 35–36; Joshua Horwitz and Casey Anderson, *Guns, Democracy, and the Insurrectionist Idea* (Ann Arbor: University of Michigan Press, 2009), 36.

2. Kelly, "New NRA Chief Draws a Bead"; National Council to Ban Handguns Newsletter, June 1977, CHCR, box 9, folder 94; Hugh Hough, "Mikva Hits U.S. Unit's Pulling Out of Gun Turn-In," *Chicago Sun-Times*, May 22, 1977.

3. On the NRA's opposition to gun control legislation before the 1960s, see Patrick J. Charles, *Armed in America: A History of Gun Rights from Colonial Militias to Concealed Carry* (New York: Prometheus, 2018), 194–230. For a sophisticated recent assessment of the NRA, see Matthew J. Lacombe, *Firepower: How the NRA Turned Gun Owners into a Political Force* (Princeton, NJ: Princeton University Press, 2021).

4. The Moses line comes from Davidson, *Under Fire*, 31.

5. S. J. Schoon, "Memorial to Marine Cpl. Robert Steele," *Armed Eagle*, September 1968, HH, box 46-2, folder 435/1/1; "Robert Charles Steele," Virtual Wall, https://www .virtualwall.org/ds/SteeleRCo1a.htm.

6. In 1970 the Association to Preserve Our Right to Keep and Bear Arms changed its name to the National Association to Keep and Bear Arms. To avoid confusion I've chosen to abbreviate the organization as AKBA throughout, using initials common to both names.

7. Schoon, "Memorial to Marine Cpl. Robert Steele."

8. Schoon, "Memorial to Marine Cpl. Robert Steele"; Gene Veseley, "Gun Control Is the Big Lie of the Age," *Armed Eagle*, June–July 1969, in HH, box 46-2, folder 435/1/1. As US officials at the Saigon embassy reported in 1968, the Republic of Vietnam required the registration of all firearms and the licensing of all firearm owners. See the materials in ECR, Series 44: Research Files, box 4, folder State Department Materials on Imported Guns.

9. "What Is the National Association to Keep and Bear Arms?," undated pamphlet (1971–72), HH, box N-13, folder 621.

10. "The language of containment," writes historian Elizabeth Gillespie McRae, "traveled easily between the diplomatic and domestic front." See McRae, *Mothers of Massive Resistance: White Women and the Politics of White Supremacy* (New York: Oxford University Press, 2018), 142.

11. For a critique of this development, see Charles, *Armed in America*, 279–95.

12. The most accessible works on the changing interpretations of the Second Amendment include Saul Cornell, *A Well-Regulated Militia: The Founding Fathers and the Origins of Gun Control in America* (New York: Oxford University Press, 2006); Winkler, *Gunfight*; Michael Waldman, *The Second Amendment: A Biography* (New York: Simon and Schuster, 2014); and Charles, *Armed in America*.

13. APRA flyer, "Can These Public Officials Be Trusted with Your Gun Rights?," undated [1975–76], HH, box 389 B, folder 199A:25.

14. Cornell, *A Well-Regulated Militia*, 4.

15. John L. Grady, "Communism vs Gun Ownership," APRA flyer, undated [early 1980s], HH, box 43-1, folder 1043/1/1.

16. "What Do They Really Want?," *Armed Eagle*, no. 11 (June 1968).

17. *Armed Eagle*, no. 11 (June 1968).

18. Memorandum, FBI director to attorney general, July 5, 1968, RCP, box 92, folder Firearms Testimony, July 9, 1968.

19. Excerpts from Harlon Carter speech, Annual State Convention of the Arizona Wildlife Federation, January 19, 1969, *Armed Eagle*, no. 20 (May 1969), HH, box 46-2, folder 435/1/1. In the *Armed Eagle*'s reproduction of the speech, many passages are fully capitalized. I assume this was a choice of the newsletter editors, since it was a common style in the pages of the *Armed Eagle*, so I have uncapitalized them for readability.

20. Kelly, "New NRA Chief Draws a Bead."

21. See Kevin M. Kruse and Julian E. Zelizer, *Fault Lines: A History of the United States since 1974* (New York: W. W. Norton, 2019), 88–112.

22. "National Assn. to Keep and Bear Arms: What and Why?," *Daily Courier* (Grants Pass, OR), clipping in *Armed Citizen News*, no. 41 (June 1971).

23. "National Assn. to Keep and Bear Arms: What and Why?"

24. "What Is the National Association to Keep and Bear Arms?," undated pamphlet (1971–72), HH, box N-13, folder 621. Jennifer Carlson describes this evolving understanding of guns as "not just protecting of individuals but also productive of social order." See Carlson, *Policing the Second Amendment: Guns, Law Enforcement, and the Politics of Race* (Princeton, NJ: Princeton University Press, 2020), 41.

25. "Private Firearms—Cornerstone of Freedom," *Armed Eagle*, no. 19 (April 1969).

26. "National Assn. to Keep and Bear Arms: What and Why?"

27. *F&VIAL*, 12.

28. "Arthur James Hollowell," *Carbon County (MT) News*, January 16, 2020, https://www .carboncountynews.com/content/arthur-james-hollowell; "Miscellaneous Douglas County, Oregon Obituaries," Genealogy Buff, https://www.genealogybuff.com/or/or-douglas -obits15.htm; Richard Lee Worley, "The Eagle's Talon's [*sic*]," *Armed Citizen*, no. 28 (February 1970), HH, box 46-2, folder 435.

29. Jennifer Carlson, *Citizen-Protectors: The Everyday Politics of Guns in an Age of Decline* (New York: Oxford University Press, 2015); see also Kevin Lewis O'Neill, "Armed Citizens and the Stories They Tell: The National Rifle Association's Achievement of Terror and Masculinity," *Men and Masculinities* 9 (April 2007), 457–75.

30. "What Do You Tell Your Children?" *Armed Eagle*, no. 14 (October 1968), HH, box 46-2, folder 435/1/1.

31. "What Do You Tell Your Children?"

32. AKBA flyer, "Handguns Are a Girl's Best Friend," undated [1972–73], HH, box N-13, folder 621.

33. "Official Slogan," *Armed Eagle*, no. 18 (March 1969), HH, box 46-2, folder 435/1/1.

34. Quoted in Frank Smyth, *The NRA: The Unauthorized History* (New York: Flatiron, 2020), 76–77.

35. Davidson, *Under Fire*, 29.

36. "Shinn, Major Reginald (USAF) Ret.," *SB*, February 8, 2012.

37. See J. M. Berger, "Patriot Games," *Foreign Policy*, April 18, 2012.

38. Reginald Shinn, "1979 NRA Convention," *APRA News*, vol. 1979, no. 4, HH, box 43-1, folder 1043. On the creation of the Law Enforcement Assistance Administration,

see Elizabeth Hinton, *From the War on Poverty to the War on Crime: The Making of Mass Incarceration in America* (Cambridge, MA: Harvard University Press, 2016).

39. Shinn, "1979 NRA Convention."

40. Horwitz and Anderson, *Guns, Democracy, and the Insurrectionist Idea*, 49; Tom Diaz, *Making a Killing: The Business of Guns in America* (New York: New Press, 1999), 65.

41. Michael Waldman, "How the NRA Rewrote the Second Amendment," *Politico*, May 19, 2014.

42. Cornell, *A Well-Regulated Militia*, 2.

43. *American Challenge*, October 15, 1969, HH, box 43-1, folder 1776. Several issues of *American Challenge*, which covered a range of right-wing concerns, including gun rights, can be found in the George Washington Robnett Papers, Kenneth Spencer Research Library, University of Kansas, box 1, folder 24.

44. "Association Organizational Objectives," *Armed Eagle*, September 1968, HH, box 46-2, folder HH435/1/1.

45. *Armed Eagle*, May 1968, HH, box A-92, folder HH35A:55; emphasis in original.

46. "New Organizattion [*sic*] Plans to Oppose Gun Controls," *Roseburg (OR) News-Review*, February 6, 1968, clipping in *Armed Eagle*, March–April 1968, HH, box A-92, folder HH66A:25.

47. Hollowell likely meant the "Pistol Packing Posse" in Orlando, a program sponsored by the *Orlando Sentinel* and Orlando Police Department that hosted several classes a week to familiarize women with handguns. See, for example, "Does It Really Kick?," *Orlando Sentinel*, October 31, 1966.

48. Willis Hobart, "Local Right to Bear Arms Drive Organized at Fairgrounds Meeting," *Daily Courier* (Grants Pass, OR), March 29, 1968, clipping in *Armed Eagle*, March–April 1968, HH, box A-92, folder HH66A:25.

49. Oral history transcript, Milton S. Eisenhower, interview 1 (I), undated [1969?], by Joe B. Frantz, LBJ Library Oral Histories. Milton Eisenhower was occasionally the focus of Bircher conspiracy theories about a communist takeover of the US government. See D. J. Mulloy, *The World of the John Birch Society: Conspiracy, Conservatism, and the Cold War* (Nashville: Vanderbilt University Press, 2014), 1.

50. Smyth, *The NRA*, 47.

51. AKBA flyer, "Don't Let Them Take Your Guns Away!!," 1969, HH, box A-92, folder 35A:55.

52. Donald Janson, "Communist 'Rules' for Revolt Viewed as a Durable Fraud," *NYT*, July 10, 1970.

53. "Castro Used Gun Control Law," clipping from *CR*, in *Armed Eagle*, March 1969, HH, box 46-2, folder 435/1/1; "Private Firearms—Cornerstone of Freedom," *Armed Eagle*, April 1969, HH, box 46-2, folder 435/1/1.

54. See *The Gun Owners*, June 1983, 18, HH, box 46-4, folder 3393.

55. APRA flyer, "Should Americans Give Up Their Guns?," undated [1975–76], HH, box 43-1, folder 1043/1/1.

56. See Luis Manrara, "Freedom: Read about a Man Who Lost His," *Armed Citizen News*, no. 41 (June 1971), HH, box N-13, folder 381A; "Batista's Gun Laws Aided Fidel Castro, Says Refugee," *Armed Eagle*, December 1968; and "Castro Used Gun Control Law."

57. "Gun Laws Prevent Irish Citizens from Defending Their Homes," *G&A*, December 1971, reprinted in *Armed Citizen News*, January 1972; and Rev. Robert W. Parr, letter to the editor, *Armed Citizen News*, January 1972, both in HH, box N-13, folder 621.

58. Worley, "The Eagle's Talon's [*sic*]"; and W. M. Peters, "Guns?," *Armed Eagle*, no. 23 (September 1969), both in HH, box 46-2, folder 435.

59. *American Challenge* 11, no. 2 (October 15, 1969), HH, box 43-1, folder 1776.

60. Laurie Roese, "Bill Richardson—The Gun-Money Dealer," *California Journal*, July 1976, copy in CHCR, box 2, folder 26.

61. NCCH press release, November 2, 1978, CHCR, box 3, folder 31.

62. Jim Halpin and Paul de Armond, "The Merchant of Fear," *Eastsideweek*, October 26, 1994.

63. Halpin and de Armond, "The Merchant of Fear."

64. "U-T Group Fights Back with Buttons," *Johnson City (TN) Press*, January 25, 1970.

65. Halpin and de Armond, "The Merchant of Fear."

66. Halpin and de Armond, "The Merchant of Fear."

67. J. S. Bainbridge, "Inching toward a Single Gun Law for the Entire Nation," *Baltimore Sun*, April 27, 1975.

68. Halpin and de Armond, "The Merchant of Fear"; Rick Anderson, "Barack & Load," *Seattle Weekly*, November 10, 2009.

69. Second Amendment Foundation, "National Opinion Survey on Crime Control," undated [1976], CHCR, box 2, folder 24; Ron Arnold and Alan Gottlieb, *Trashing the Economy: How Runaway Environmentalism Is Wrecking America* (Bellevue, WA: Free Enterprise Press, 1993), 75; italics in original.

70. Second Amendment Foundation, "National Opinion Survey on Crime Control," undated [1976], CHCR, box 2, folder 24.

71. Halpin and de Armond, "The Merchant of Fear."

72. *The 2nd Amendment Annual Reporter*, Second Amendment Foundation 1979 Annual Report, HH, box S-11, folder 2548:99.

CHAPTER 9

1. Alan M. Gottlieb, fundraising letter, Second Amendment Foundation, May 1993, RWHC, box 3, folder 39.

2. On US-Japan relations during this era, see Andrew C. McKevitt, *Consuming Japan: Popular Culture and the Globalizing of 1980s America* (Chapel Hill: University of North Carolina Press, 2017).

3. John Katz, "Guns, Guns, Guns: The War in the United States," *Globe and Mail*, July 2, 1993.

4. Quoted in T. R. Reid, "Shooting Draws National Attention in Japan," *Advocate*, October 20, 1992 (reprinted from *WP*).

5. T. R. Reid, "Angry Japan Lays to Rest Student Shot Dead in U.S.," *WP*, October 27, 1992; David Schimke, "Each Other's Arms," *Carleton College Voice*, Spring 2020.

6. "Defense Depicts Japanese Boy as 'Scary,'" *NYT*, May 21, 1993.

7. Rogers Worthington, "Cease Fire," *CT*, September 9, 1994; Yoshi quotes from Keisuke Nishikawa, "Letter to America," *Tell*, Fall 1993, 58–59, copy in RWHC, box 2, folder 101.

8. Reid, "Angry Japan."

9. T. R. Reid, "Guns: Topic A for U.S. Students in Japan," *WP*, April 1, 1994.

10. "Japan Tries to Understand Why U.S. Tolerates Crime," *Asahi Evening News*, April 1, 1994; Thomas Easton, "U.S. Violence Again at Center Stage," *Japan Times*, March 31, 1994.

11. "Head of College in Japan Is Murdered in Boston," *Chronicle of Higher Education*, February 26, 1992; Brian Ford, "Thai Woman Denied Parole," *Tulsa World*, September 22, 1995; "Japanese Student Dies after California Shooting," *NYT*, August 23, 1993; "Father Outraged over Son's Slaying in N.Y.," *RS*, August 17, 1994; Kevin Moll email to Richard Haymaker, January 10, 1994, RWHC, box 2, folder 102; "Number of Victims Rise," *DY*, March 28, 1994; T. R. Reid, "Ruling Softens Japan's Image of Violent U.S.," *WP*, September 18, 1994.

12. Reid, "Guns"; "Japan Tries to Understand Why U.S. Tolerates Crimes," *Asahi Evening News*, April 1, 1994; Ambassador Walter F. Mondale, press conference transcript, March 28, 1994, RWHC, box 2, folder 106.

13. Editorial, "Gun Crazy," *NYT*, May 25, 1993.

14. Frank Smyth, *The NRA: The Unauthorized History* (New York: Flatiron, 2020), 54–55.

15. See James William Gibson, *Warrior Dreams: Violence and Manhood in Post-Vietnam America* (New York: Hill and Wang, 1994), 170–92.

16. Edward Pratt, "Central Neighbors Say Peairs Just an Average Working Guy," *Advocate*, October 20, 1992.

17. Gibson, *Warrior Dreams*, 82–83.

18. Worthington, "Cease Fire."

19. *Defensive gun use* is a contentious social science term most closely identified with the work of criminologist Gary Kleck and economist John R. Lott. For an overview of the debate, see "The Challenge of Defining and Measuring Defensive Gun Use," Gun Policy in America, RAND, March 2, 2018, https://www.rand.org/research/gun-policy/analysis/essays/defensive-gun-use.html. Economist John Donohue, among many others, argues that the numbers are wildly inflated, citing a recent study, for instance, that found only 48,000 "defensive gun uses" across a five-year span. See John Donohue, "How U.S. Gun Control Compares to the Rest of the World," *The Conversation*, June 19, 2017. On Lott, see Mike Spies, "The Shoddy Conclusions of the Man Shaping the Gun Rights Debate," *New Yorker*, November 3, 2022.

20. Editorial, "Slaying of High School Student Bares Dark Side of U.S. Gun Culture," *NW*, November 16, 1992.

21. "Acquittal in Doorstep Killing of Japanese Student," *NYT*, May 24, 1993.

22. Andy Crawford and Edward Pratt, "Hattoris Urge Review of U.S. Gun Laws," *Advocate*, October 21, 1992; "300 Mourn Hattori's Death," *DY*, October 27, 1992; Itsuki Iwata, "AFS Student Hattori's Slayer Indicted," *DY*, November 6, 1992; Hattoris to Michael Armacost, December 15, 1992, RWHC, box 2, folder 9.

23. Karen Blakeman, "Japanese Couple Joins Anti-gun Fight in U.S.," *Honolulu Advertiser*, July 9, 2000.

24. See the profile of the Hattoris in Analisa Nazareno, "The Passion of a Father and Mother," *RS*, December 29, 1993.

25. David E. Sanger, "After Gunman's Acquittal, Japan Struggles to Understand America," *NYT*, May 25, 1993; Kiran Chawla, "Gun Violence Conference to Remember 20 Years since Yoshi Died," WAFB (Baton Rouge, LA), October 19, 2012; "Slain Exchange Student's Mom: Stop Gun Violence," *Advocate*, October 22, 2012; Mieko Hattori quoted in T. R. Reid, "Parents of Slain Japanese Student Mulling Civil Suit," *WP*, May 26, 1993; Holley G.

Haymaker and Richard Haymaker, "Another Magnum, Another Victim," *NYT*, October 31, 1992.

26. Holley Galland Haymaker to Anne Barley, October 12, 1993, RWHC, box 2, folder 13.

27. "Hattori's Parents to Ask Peairs for Gun Rather than $650,000," *DY*, November 2, 1994; Reid, "Ruling Softens Japan's Image of Violent U.S."; Steve Crump to the Haymakers, May 22, 1993, RWHC, box 2, folder 98.

28. Peairs explained his rejection of various offers in Rodney Peairs interview with Kazuki Ohno, "Why I Shot Yoshi Hattori," *Weekly Bunshin*, translated by unknown, June 1993?, RWHC, box 2, folder 26. As far as I can tell this article appeared only in Japanese and was translated for the Haymakers, perhaps by Yoshinori Kamo.

29. Isabel Reynolds, "Shot in the Dark: Exchange Student's Parents Keep the Memory Alive," *DY*, April 15, 2000; "Two Anti-gun Groups Receive 'Yoshi's Gift,'" *RS*, September 25, 1996.

30. Haymaker and Haymaker, "Another Magnum, Another Victim."

31. "Jottings," *DY*, May 24, 1993.

32. Richard Haymaker to Kevin Moll, July 13, 1993, RWHC, box 2, folder 103.

33. Kristin Goss, *Disarmed: The Missing Movement for Gun Control in America* (Princeton, NJ: Princeton University Press, 2006), 47, observes twenty-six new state and local groups founded at the peak of gun control organizing in 1993–95 but notes that most were "little more than letterhead organizations."

34. Richard Haymaker, "Yoshi's Death Changed So Many Lives Forever," *MDN*, October 17, 1993; Richard Haymaker to Michael Armacost, December 4, 1992, RWHC, box 2, folder 9; Richard Haymaker to Bernard Friedlander, July 27, 1993, RWHC, box 2, folder 55.

35. Richard Haymaker to Kevin Moll, July 13, 1993, RWHC, box 2, folder 103.

36. Richard Haymaker to Kevin Moll, July 9, 1993, RWHC, box 2, folder 103; Richard Haymaker to Michael Armacost, December 4, 1992, RWHC, box 2, folder 9.

37. "Transcript—President Bill Clinton's Phone Call to the Hattori Family," July 6, 1993; and Richard Haymaker to Kevin Moll, undated [July 1993], RWHC, box 2, folder 103.

38. Haymaker, "Yoshi's Death"; Richard Haymaker, Newsletter 2, January 1994, RWHC, box 2, folder 16; Richard Haymaker to Josh Horwitz, June 18, 1993, RWHC, box 2, folder 108.

39. Richard Haymaker, "Open Letter to President Clinton," unpublished, November 8, 1993, RWHC, box 2, folder 139.

40. Shigekatsu Matsunaga, "Hattori Parents Talk to Clinton," *DY*, November 18, 1993; Worthington, "Cease Fire."

41. Alexander DeConde, *Guns in America: The Struggle for Control* (Boston: Northeastern University Press, 2001), 249–50.

42. Jens Ludwig and Philip J. Cook, "Homicide and Suicide Rates Associated with Implementation of the Brady Handgun Violence Prevention Act," *Journal of the American Medical Association* 284, no. 5 (2000): 585–91.

43. Christopher S. Koper, *Updated Assessment of the Federal Assault Weapons Ban: Impacts on Gun Markets and Gun Violence, 1994–2003* (Washington, DC: National Institute of Justice, US Department of Justice, 2004), 1–4.

44. Kevin Moll to Richard Haymaker, August 21, 1993, and Richard Haymaker to Kevin Moll, undated letter [August 1993], RWHC, box 2, folder 103.

45. Katrina E. Kerndole, "Not a Problem of Guns but of Fear," *Mainichi Weekly*, December 11, 1993.

46. On crime trends in the 1980s and early 1990s, see Barry Latzer, *The Rise and Fall of Violent Crime in America* (New York: Encounter, 2017), 171–220.

47. Holley Galland Haymaker to Judith Gingerich, June 10, 1993, RWHC, box 2, folder 144.

48. See the many letters in RWHC, box 3, folder 39 ("NRA/Hate Mail"); quotes from anonymous annotated copy of Haymaker petition, undated; and M. J. Green to Richard Haymaker, undated, both in RWHC, box 3, folder 39.

49. "Gun Controls: What Other Countries Do," *NYP*, June 21, 1968; "Gun Curbs Are Stricter in Many Nations than in U.S.," *WP*, June 23, 1968; "Minutes of Cabinet Meeting, June 12, 1968," LBJC, box 14, folder Cabinet Meeting, June 12, 1968, 1 of 3; Ramsey Clark letter to members of the Senate, September 10, 1968, LBF, Gun Control, box 2, folder Firearms Act (1968) (2); Emergency Committee for Gun Control, "Fact Sheet on the Need for Stronger Gun Control," 1968, JHGA, box 53, folder 24; Robert Sherrill, "High Noon on Capitol Hill," *NYT*, June 23, 1968.

50. Laura Fermi to Superintendent General, Metropolitan Police Board, Tokyo, Japan, March 29, 1972, CDCR, box 1, folder Corres. 1971–1972; Tokyo Metropolitan Police Board, "Weapons Used in Crimes in Tokyo in 1970," [1972?], CDCR, box 3, folder Int'l Corres., Stats., Publicity, 1968–1972.

51. See CHCR, box 21, folders 213 and 214.

52. Richard Halloran, "Crime in Tokyo a Minor Problem," *NYT*, October 3, 1971.

53. Steven Brill, *Firearms Abuse: A Research and Policy Report* (Washington, DC: Police Foundation, 1977), 78.

54. For example, see Hunter's Lodge advertisement, *AR*, November 1962, n.p., discussed in chapter 1.

55. Analisa Nazareno, "Tourists Attracted to Loaded Weapons," *RS*, December 29, 1993; Tom Diaz, *Making a Killing: The Business of Guns in America* (New York: New Press, 1999), 32.

56. John Dower, *Embracing Defeat: Japan in the Wake of World War II* (New York: W. W. Norton, 1999), 550. On the discourse of race and maturity in US-Japan relations, see Naoko Shibusawa, *America's Geisha Ally: Reimagining the Japanese Enemy* (Cambridge, MA: Harvard University Press, 2006).

57. Letters to the Editor, "What the Japanese Are Saying: No Sympathy Shown for the Shooting Victim," *DY*, June 2, 1993.

58. Hiroyuki Nishimura, "Baton Rouge Judgment Draws Fire from Japan," *NW*, May 31, 1993; Clayton Jones, "Cultural Differences Thrown into Relief by Louisiana Case," *CSM*, May 27, 1993.

59. Letters to the Editor, "Louisiana Justice," *DY*, May 30, 1993.

60. Letter to the Editor, "A Japanese View of the Incident," *Advocate*, October 31, 1992.

61. Kevin Rafferty, "Japanese Learn to Duck and Freeze in the Land of the Gun," *Guardian*, June 12, 1993.

62. Letter to the Editor, "Man's Acquittal in Student's Death Prompts Outrage," *St. Petersburg Times*, May 29, 1993.

63. Letters to the Editor, "Shame and Outrage," *DY*, May 27, 1993; Letters to the Editor, "Louisiana Justice," *DY*, May 30, 1993; Letters to the Editor, "Three 'Don'ts,'" *DY*, May 31, 1993; Letters to the Editor, "Cowboy Mentality," *DY*, June 6, 1993; Letter to the Editor, "Gunman's Acquittal Sends World a Message," *NYT*, June 7, 1993.

64. "Civil Rights Groups Call for Further Investigation in Hattori Shooting," *RS*, May 25, 1993.

65. Japanese automobile companies, for instance, built many facilities across the South in the 1990s and 2000s, none of them in Louisiana.

66. David E. Sanger, "'Freeze!' and Other Helpful Phrases," *NYT*, June 17, 1993; Ned Zeman, "Buzzwords," *Newsweek*, November 9, 1992; "Japan to Issue American Phrase Book," *St. Petersburg Times*, June 18, 1993; Rafferty, "Japanese Learn to Duck and Freeze"; Shigeru Wada, "Safety Specialists Joining Major Corporations," *NW*, November 9, 1992.

67. David E. Sanger, "Off to U.S., Japanese Pack Words Like 'Police!,'" *NYT*, January 10, 1993.

68. Keisuke Nishikawa to Richard Haymaker, November 7, 1992, RWHC, box 2, folder 105.

69. Keisuke Nishikawa to Richard Haymaker, May 20, 1993, RWHC, box 2, folder 105.

70. Keisuke Nishikawa to Richard Haymaker, May 1993; and Satoe Takahashi to the Haymakers, December 6, 1992, RWHC, box 2, folder 105.

71. Nishikawa, "Letter to America."

72. "An Interview with Richard and Holley Haymaker Concerning Mr. Peairs' Statements in the Japanese Press," unpublished transcript, June 14, 1993, RWHC, box 2, folder 26.

73. Yoshinori Kamo to Rodney Peairs, undated [June 1993], RWHC, box 2, folder 26.

74. Steve Crump, "Opening Words," delivered at Yoshi Hattori memorial, Baton Rouge, October 20, 1992, RWHC, box 2, folder 98; emphasis in original.

75. "Making a Difference," *Advocate*, October 31, 1993; Curt Eysink, "Mayor's Committee Plans Yoshi Hattori Memorials," *Advocate*, May 27, 1993.

76. See Latzer, *The Rise and Fall of Violent Crime*, 171–220.

77. Steve Wheeler and Curt Eysink, "'It's Everyone's Problem,'" *Advocate*, October 31, 1993.

78. Peter Shinkle, "'We Are Worshipping Guns,'" *Advocate*, October 31, 1993.

79. Eysink, "Mayor's Committee"; "Panel Recommends Plaque to Hattori," *Advocate*, December 2, 1994.

80. Letter to the editor, "Opposition to Hattori Plaque," *Advocate*, December 20, 1994.

81. Letter to the editor, "Another View of Hattori Plaque," *Advocate*, January 28, 1995.

82. Richard Haymaker, "Yoshi's Death Changed So Many Lives Forever," *MDN*, October 17, 1993.

CHAPTER 10

1. Katharine Q. Seelye, "National Rifle Association Is Turning to World Stage to Fight Gun Control," *NYT*, April 2, 1997.

2. Ronald Bailey, "Global Gun Grabbers," *Weekly Standard*, February 23, 1998.

3. John Lewis Gaddis, *The Long Peace: Inquiries into the History of the Cold War* (New York: Oxford University Press, 1989).

4. See, for example, Paul Thomas Chamberlin, *The Cold War's Killing Fields: Rethinking the Long Peace* (New York: Harper, 2018); and Odd Arne Westad, *The Global Cold War: Third World Interventions and the Making of Our Times* (New York: Cambridge University Press, 2011).

5. The classic work on these conflicts in the 1990s is Samantha Power, *"A Problem from Hell": America and the Age of Genocide* (New York: Basic Books, 2002).

6. Michael T. Klare, "Stemming the Lethal Trade in Small Arms and Light Weapons," *Issues in Science and Technology* 12, no. 1 (Fall 1995): 52–58; Aaron Karp, "The Arms Trade Revolution: The Major Impact of Small Arms," *Washington Quarterly*, Autumn 1994, 67; Jeffrey Boutwell and Michael T. Klare, "A Scourge of Small Arms," *Scientific American*, June 2000, 48; Andrew Latham, "Taking the Lead? Light Weapons and International Security," *International Journal* 52 (Spring 1997): 319.

7. See the home pages for IANSA and the Small Arms Survey, iansa.org and smallarms.org.

8. Wendy Cukier and Victor W. Sidel, *The Global Gun Epidemic: From Saturday Night Specials to AK-47s* (Westport, CT: Praeger Security International, 2006), 3; Swadesh Rana, *Small Arms and Intra-state Conflict*, UN Institute for Disarmament Research Paper NE 34 (New York: United Nations, 1995), 1.

9. Boutwell and Klare, "A Scourge of Small Arms," 49–51.

10. United Nations, General Assembly Security Council, "Supplement to an Agenda for Peace: Position Paper of the Secretary-General on the Occasion of the Fiftieth Anniversary of the United Nations," January 25, 1995, UN Digital Library, A/50/60, S/1995/1.

11. Wayne LaPierre, *The Global War on Your Guns: Inside the UN Plan to Destroy the Bill of Rights* (Nashville, TN: Nelson Current, 2006), quote from dust jacket.

12. James E. Goodby, "The US Arms Control and Disarmament Agency in 1961–63: A Study in Governance," Hoover Institution, 2017, https://www.hoover.org/sites/default/files/research/docs/goodby_the_us_arms_control.pdf.

13. US Department of State, *Freedom from War: The United States Program for General and Complete Disarmament in a Peaceful World*, Department of State Publication 7277 (Washington, DC: US Government Printing Office, 1961).

14. "Statement by President Kennedy," in United States Arms Control and Disarmament Agency, *Blueprint for the Peace Race: Outline of Basic Provisions of a Treaty on General and Complete Disarmament in a Peaceful World* (US Government Printing Office, 1962), no page number.

15. See US Department of State, *Freedom from War*, 5–10, for a sketch of the disarmament stages; United States Arms Control and Disarmament Agency, *Blueprint for the Peace Race* expands on this proposal at length.

16. Lawrence S. Wittner, *Confronting the Bomb: A Short History of the Nuclear Disarmament Movement* (Stanford: Stanford University Press, 2009), 107.

17. See Kathryn S. Olmstead, *Real Enemies: Conspiracy Theories and American Democracy, World War I to 9/11* (New York: Oxford University Press, 2009), 11; on investigations in the 1970s, see Katherine A. Scott, *Reining in the State: Civil Society and Congress in the Vietnam and Watergate Eras* (Lawrence: University of Kansas Press, 2013).

18. Michelle M. Nickerson, *Mothers of Conservatism: Women and the Postwar Right* (Princeton, NJ: Princeton University Press, 2012), 90–95; Elizabeth Gillespie McRae,

Mothers of Massive Resistance: White Women and the Politics of White Supremacy (New York: Oxford University Press, 2018), 138–64; Donald T. Critchlow, *Phyllis Schlafly and Grassroots Conservatism: A Woman's Crusade* (Princeton, NJ: Princeton University Press, 2005), 85.

19. For example, see "A Strange 'Conspiracy' Indeed," *Minneapolis Tribune*, January 17, 1965; Michael Barkun, *A Culture of Conspiracy: Apocalyptic Visions in Contemporary America*, 2nd ed. (Berkeley: University of California Press, 2013), 7.

20. Pete Brown, "Blueprint for Peace—A Threat to Gun Ownership?," *Sports Afield*, August 1963.

21. *American Challenge* 11, no. 2 (October 15, 1969), HH, box 43-1, folder 1776; Seattle Arm Member, "Legislation by Assassination—A New American Phenomenon," *Armed Eagle*, March 1969, box 46-2, folder 435/1/1.

22. Brown, "Blueprint for Peace."

23. Another example worth noting is Phoebe Courtney, *Gun Control Means People Control* (Littleton, CO: Independent American Newspaper, 1974), which connects proposals for handgun bans to a conspiracy by the Council of Foreign Relations, in collusion with Henry Kissinger, to impose a world government.

24. Second Amendment Committee flyer, "Unless You Know This . . . Your Guns Are Gone," undated [c. 1991], HH, box S-11, folder 193B:38; "U.S. Convicts G.I. Who Refused to Serve under UN in Balkans," *NYT*, January 25, 1996.

25. John Kifner, "Oklahoma Bombing Suspect: Unraveling of a Frayed Mind," *NYT*, December 31, 1995.

26. Kathleen Belew, *Bring the War Home: The White Power Movement and Paramilitary America* (Cambridge, MA: Harvard University Press, 2018), 210; Joshua Horwitz and Casey Anderson, *Guns, Democracy, and the Insurrectionist Idea* (Ann Arbor: University of Michigan Press, 2009), 53. On right-wing internationalist organizing in the 1970s and 1980s, see Kyle Burke, *Revolutionaries for the Right: Anticommunist Internationalism and Paramilitary Warfare in the Cold War* (Chapel Hill: University of North Carolina Press, 2018).

27. Alan Gottlieb, "Repeal Gun-Control Laws," reprinted in *Gun News Digest* 1, no. 2 (Summer 1995), copy in HH, box 46-3, folder 2085. Gottlieb noted that most of the articles had been written just before the Oklahoma City bombing even though the issue was published in its aftermath.

28. Karen L. MacNutt, "Militias: Training for Doomsday . . . or Feeding Anti-gun Strategists?," *Gun News Digest* 1, no. 2 (Summer 1995), copy in HH, box 46-3, folder 2085.

29. United Nations, Department for Disarmament Affairs, *The United Nations Disarmament Yearbook*, vol. 25, *2000* (New York: United Nations, 2001), 96–103; for a chronology of events, see Graduate Institute of International Studies, Geneva, *Small Arms Survey 2002: Counting the Human Cost* (New York: Oxford University Press, 2002), 204.

30. Charlton Heston, "The President's Column," *AR*, April 2001.

31. Mark Strauss, "Global Shootout," *Slate*, July 20, 2001; on McVeigh and guns, see Horwitz and Anderson, *Guns, Democracy, and the Insurrectionist Idea*, 27, 53.

32. See "Taking Aim," *CBS Sunday Morning*, CBS News Transcripts, May 21, 1995; "Members Resign from NRA as Organization Is Linked to Oklahoma City Bombing," *CBS Evening News*, CBS News Transcripts, May 12, 1995; Smyth, *The NRA*, 127–28, 142–43.

33. Emails to DDA, various dates (2001), UN Archives and Records Management, Item S-1092-0085-05-00015—Disarmament 2001—DDA, January–August, https://search .archives.un.org/disarmament-2001-dda-jan-aug-7.

34. DDA memo, June 25, 2001, UN Archives and Records Management, Item S-1092-0085-05-00015—Disarmament 2001—DDA, January–August, https://search.archives .un.org/disarmament-2001-dda-jan-aug-7.

35. Thalif Deen, "Disarmament: UN Meeting No Threat to Gun Owners, Says Official," *Inter Press Service*, July 5, 2001.

36. Jayantha Dhanapala to Shashi Tharoor, "A United Nations Response to the Campaign against the UN Conference on the Illicit Trade in Small Arms and Light Weapons in All Its Aspects," June 20, 2001, UN Archives and Records Management, Item S-1092 -0085-05-00015—Disarmament 2001—DDA—January–August, https://search.archives .un.org/disarmament-2001-dda-jan-aug-7.

37. John D. Holum, "Holum on Illicit Trafficking in Small Arms, Light Weapons," US Department of State, Washington File, February 4, 2000, https://usinfo.org/usia/usinfo .state.gov/topical/pol/arms/stories/00020202.htm.

38. Graduate Institute of International Studies, Geneva, *Small Arms Survey 2002*, 219.

39. Holum, "Holum on Illicit Trafficking."

40. John R. Bolton, "Plenary Address to the UN Conference on the Illicit Trade in Small Arms and Light Weapons," July 9, 2001, US Department of State Archive, https://2001 -2009.state.gov/t/us/rm/janjuly/4038.htm.

41. "Mr. Ashcroft and the NRA," *WP*, August 1, 2001.

42. Bolton, "Plenary Address."

43. Bolton, "Plenary Address."

44. Bolton, "Plenary Address."

45. Bolton, "Plenary Address."

46. Rachel Stohl, "United States Weakens Outcome of UN Small Arms and Light Weapons," *Arms Control Today*, September 2001, https://www.armscontrol.org/act/2001-09 /features/united-states-weakens-outcome-un-small-arms-light-weapons.

47. "An American Retreat on Small Arms," *NYT*, July 11, 2001.

48. Barbara Crossette, "Effort by UN to Cut Traffic in Arms Meets a U.S. Rebuff," *NYT*, July 10, 2001.

49. "U.S.-EU Statement of Common Principles on Small Arms and Light Weapons," US Mission to the European Union, December 17, 1999, US Department of State Archive, https://2001-2009.state.gov/p/eur/rls/or/3750.htm.

50. United Nations, *Report of the United Nations Conference on the Illicit Trade in Small Arms and Light Weapons in All Its Aspects* (New York: United Nations, 2001), 7, 9.

51. Graduate Institute of International Studies, Geneva, *Small Arms Survey 2002*, 220.

52. Human Rights Watch, "UN: 'Program of Inaction' on Small Arms," July 18, 2001, https://www.hrw.org/news/2001/07/18/un-program-inaction-small-arms; Aaron Karp, "Small Arms: Back to the Future," *Brown Journal of World Affairs*, Spring 2002, 179; Cukier and Sidel, *The Global Gun Epidemic*, 232.

53. David Morton, "Gunning for the World," *Foreign Policy*, October 19, 2009.

54. Missy Ryan and John Hudson, "During NRA Speech, Trump Drops Out of Another Global Arms Treaty," *WP*, April 26, 2019.

55. Natalie J. Goldring, "The NRA Goes Global," *Bulletin of Atomic Scientists* 55, no. 1 (January–February 1999): 61–65.

56. John Howard, "I Went After Guns. Obama Can, Too," *NYT*, January 26, 2013; Alexander DeConde, *Gun Violence in America: The Struggle for Control* (Boston: Northeastern University Press, 2001), 263.

57. Jason Vest, "The NRA Goes Global," *Salon*, April 3, 2000.

58. John Darnton, "Scottish Inquiry's Focus: Why Strict Gun Law Failed," *NYT*, March 18, 1996; Sarah Lyall, "Britain May Forbid Private Ownership of Most Handguns," *NYT*, October 17, 1996; Peter Squires, "Dunblane 25 Years On: How a Mass School Shooting Changed British Gun Laws," *The Conversation*, March 11, 2021.

59. "United Kingdom—Gun Facts, Figures and the Law," Gun Policy, https://www.gunpolicy.org/firearms/region/united-kingdom.

60. Squires, "Dunblane 25 Years On"; Alan Travis, "Who's Who in the Shooting Lobby," *Guardian*, March 19, 1996; Jay Rayner, "Gospel of a Gun Man," *Guardian*, February 23, 1991.

61. Ben Dobbin, "Hungerford Massacre Forces Review of British Gun Laws," Associated Press, September 3, 1987; John Craig and James Cusick, "Gun Lobby Wages 'Dirty' War over Firearms Curbs," *Sunday Times* (London), November 1, 1987; Andrew Neil, "Quick-Fire Action Needed to Disarm the Gun Lobby," *Sunday Times* (London), March 24, 1996; British minister quoted in Cukier and Sidel, *The Global Gun Epidemic*, 127; *Daily Record* quoted in Seelye, "National Rifle Association Is Turning to World Stage."

62. Wendy Cukier, "The NRA's Hemispheric Reach," *Americas Quarterly*, April 22, 2013.

63. Thomas McKenna, "Crime Control Not Gun Control in Brazil," American Society for the Defense of Tradition, Family and Property, August 13, 2003, https://www.tfp.org/crime-control-not-gun-control-in-brazil/; David Morton, "Gunning for the World"; quoted in Cukier, "The NRA's Hemispheric Reach."

64. Wayne LaPierre, "Canada's Reversing the 'Irreversible Ratchet' of Gun Control," *AR*, March 2010, 12.

65. Goldring, "The NRA Goes Global," 63; Seelye, "National Rifle Association Is Turning to World Stage."

66. Karp, "Small Arms," 184.

67. "Iraqi Civilians," Costs of War, Watson Institute for International and Public Affairs, Brown University, https://watson.brown.edu/costsofwar/costs/human/civilians/iraqi.

68. Wolf Blitzer, "Search for the 'Smoking Gun,'" *CNN*, January 10, 2003.

69. Graduate Institute of International Studies, Geneva, *Small Arms Survey 2004: Rights at Risk* (New York: Oxford University Press, 2004), 49.

70. Edward G. Salo and F. Patricia Stallings, *"There Is More Ammunition in Iraq than Any Place I've Ever Been in My Life, and It Is Not All Securable": The U.S. Army Engineering and Support Center, Huntsville Captured Enemy Ammunition and Coalition Munitions Clearance Mission, 2003–2008* (Huntsville, AL: US Army Engineering and Support Center, 2013), 1–2.

71. Joel D. Rayburn and Frank K. Sobchak, eds., *The U.S. Army in the Iraq War*, vol. 1, *Invasion, Insurgency, Civil War, 2003–2006* (Carlisle, PA: US Army War College Press, 2019), 115.

72. Graduate Institute of International Studies, Geneva, *Small Arms Survey 2004*, 46.

73. Salo and Stallings, *"There Is More Ammunition,"* 19; Dan Murphy, "Iraq Awash in Military Weapons," *CSM*, October 20, 2003; Laura King, "Surrounded by Chaos in Iraq, Middle Class Takes Up Arms," *LAT*, May 12, 2003.

74. Graduate Institute of International Studies, Geneva, *Small Arms Survey 2004*, 44–50.

75. John R. Lott, "Armed, and Safer, Iraqis," *NYP*, June 26, 2003.

76. P. Mitchell Prothero, "Coalition Losing War for Iraqi Arms," United Press International, September 29, 2003; Murphy, "Iraq Awash in Military Weapons."

77. Prothero, "Coalition Losing War for Iraqi Arms"; Murphy, "Iraq Awash in Military Weapons."

78. King, "Surrounded by Chaos in Iraq."

79. For example, see Christopher S. Koper, *Updated Assessment of the Federal Assault Weapons Ban: Impacts on Gun Markets and Gun Violence, 1994–2003* (Washington, DC: National Institute of Justice, US Department of Justice, 2004).

80. Adam Winkler, *Gunfight: The Battle over the Right to Bear Arms in America* (New York: W. W. Norton, 2011), 39.

81. See Timothy D. Lytton, ed., *Suing the Gun Industry: A Battle at the Crossroads of Gun Control and Mass Torts* (Ann Arbor: University of Michigan Press, 2006).

82. "Gun Policy Center Recommends Alternatives to Expired Weapons Ban," Johns Hopkins Bloomberg School of Public Health, September 23, 2004, https://publichealth .jhu.edu/2004/webster-assault-weapons.

83. Heath Druzin, "From Banned to Beloved: The Rise of the AR-15," WAMU, February 28, 2019.

84. Ryan Busse, *Gunfight: My Battle against the Industry That Radicalized America* (New York: PublicAffairs, 2021), 222; Evan Osnos, *Wildland: The Making of America's Fury* (New York: Farrar, Straus and Giroux, 2021), 263.

85. Vedran Radić, "The Highest-Selling Call of Duty Games, Ranked (& How Much They Sold)," *GameRant*, August 17, 2021, https://gamerant.com/highest-selling-call-of -duty-games-ranked-by-amount-sold-world-at-war-modern-warfare-black-ops/.

86. Andrew C. McKevitt, "'Watching War Made Us Immune': The Popular Culture of the Wars," in Beth Bailey and Richard H. Immerman, *Understanding the U.S. Wars in Iraq and Afghanistan* (New York: New York University Press, 2015), 253.

87. On the militarization of social life in the twenty-first century, see Seth Ackerman, *Reign of Terror: How the 9/11 Era Destabilized America and Produced Trump* (New York: Penguin, 2021).

88. Jill Lepore, "Battleground America," *New Yorker*, April 16, 2012.

89. Violence Policy Center, *The Militarization of the U.S. Civilian Firearms Market*, June 2011, 9, https://www.vpc.org/studies/militarization.pdf; Tom Diaz, *Making a Killing: The Business of Guns in America* (New York: New Press, 1999), 92–93.

90. Quoted in Diaz, *Making a Killing*, 91.

91. Violence Policy Center, *Militarization*, 11, 32; Michael S. Sherry, *The Punitive Turn in American Life: How the United States Learned to Fight Crime Like a War* (Chapel Hill: University of North Carolina Press, 2020), 1.

92. Urban Dictionary, "Tacticool," https://www.urbandictionary.com/define.php ?term=tacticool.

93. Chad Kautzer, "America as a Tactical Gun Culture," *Boston Review*, December 17, 2021.

EPILOGUE

1. "President Trump's Inaugural Address, Annotated," NPR, January 20, 2017.

2. Michelle Ye Hee Lee, "Fact-Checking Trump's Rhetoric on Crime and the 'American Carnage,'" *WP*, January 30, 2017.

3. Philip J. Cook, "The Great American Gun War: Notes from Four Decades in the Trenches," *Crime and Justice* 42, no. 1 (August 2013): 19–73.

4. Colleen Long, "Once U.S. Murder Capital, NYC Close to Record Low in Homicides," Associated Press, December 21, 2017.

5. Franklin E. Zimring, *The Great American Crime Decline* (New York: Oxford University Press, 2007), 22–23; Kevin Drum, "A Very Brief History of Super-predators," *Mother Jones*, March 3, 2016; see also Patrick Sharkey, *Uneasy Peace: The Great Crime Decline, the Renewal of City Life, and the Next War on Crime* (New York: W. W. Norton 2018).

6. Ryan Busse, *Gunfight: My Battle against the Industry That Radicalized America* (New York: PublicAffairs, 2021), 209, 179, 252, 272–73. One way of counting gun sales is through the National Instant Criminal Background Check System (NICS). It is monitored by the FBI, which anonymizes and archives the data. Every time a gun buyer purchases a firearm from a federal firearms licensee (anyone doing legal business in firearms must be one), the buyer's eligibility is run through NICS. As scholars have noted, it's not a perfect one-to-one estimate of gun purchases, though Busse (*Gunfight*, 10) says that the industry generally accepts one NICS check to equal one gun sold. NICS data are available at https://www.fbi.gov/file-repository/nics_firearm_checks_-_month_year.pdf/view.

7. Zusha Elision and Cameron McWhirter, "The 'Trump Slump': With a Friend in the White House, Gun Sales Slag," *Wall Street Journal*, August 30, 2018.

8. Brad Tuttle, "You Can Tell It's an Election Year Because Gun Sales Are Hitting Record Highs," *Money*, November 8, 2016.

9. Peter Holley, "The NRA Recruitment Video That Is Even Upsetting Gun Owners," *WP*, June 29, 2017.

10. It's important to note "by a single gunman" because several nineteenth-century massacres of Indian peoples by the US government surpassed these death tolls. See Dana Hedgpeth, "This Was the Worst Slaughter of Native Americans in U.S. History. Few Remember It," *WP*, September 29, 2021.

11. Eric Westervelt, "After a Vow to End 'This American Carnage,' a Year of Deadly Violence," NPR, December 27, 2017; see Gun Violence Archive, gunviolencearchive.org.

12. "Grief. Horror. Inaction. Texas Mass Shootings Follow a Numbing Script," *Texas Tribune*, May 24, 2022.

13. Westervelt, "After a Vow to End 'This American Carnage.'"

14. Lois Beckett, "Trump Vowed to End 'This American Carnage'—but the Attacks Keep Happening," *Guardian*, February 17, 2018.

15. On the Parkland students' movement, see Dave Cullen, *Parkland: Birth of a Movement* (New York: Harper, 2019).

16. Kathryn Watson and Melissa Quinn, "Biden Hails Passage of New Bipartisan Gun Law," CBS News, July 11, 2022; Sheryl Gay Stolberg and Astead W. Herndon, "'Lock the S.O.B.s Up': Joe Biden and the Era of Mass Incarceration," *NYT*, June 25, 2019.

17. Dave Cullen, "Republicans Are Breaking with the N.R.A., and It's Because of Us," *NYT*, December 13, 2022.

18. This critique comes from prominent conservative jurist Richard Posner. See Adam Winkler, *Gunfight: The Battle over the Right to Bear Arms in America* (New York: W. W. Norton, 2011), 283.

INDEX